HUYTON'S TITANS

By: Mark Campbell

THE FOREWORD

Foreword by Alan Bleasdale

I Didn't Know That!

Mark Campbell is the author of this truly remarkable book, 'Huyton's Titans'. It is a stunning achievement.

However, it is my firm belief that in another life, many many lifetimes ago, when woolybacks were fearsome beasts lurking in the hills beyond Knowsley Safari Park, Mark was the greatest hunter-gatherer known to man in the noble and glorious history of Huyton.

I can see him now, mighty in heart and stature, vaulting clear of the raging torrents of the River Alt, beating a track that others would follow religiously through the centuries, towards where Longview shops now stand, and where, even in those long, near forgotten days of old, there would still be a queue to get into Longview Labour Club. And then, lightly refreshed, Mark would march onwards, upwards towards the sun-lit paradise of Prescot, following his dream and answering the call of the wild.

And both legend and truth would have it, Mark would always find his prey and always, before the sun fell out of the sky just beyond Page Moss, and the moon rose above the Bluebell Inn, he would bring back a feast to feed not only his family but the whole of his tribe - the Huyton tribe.

I am a member of the tribe and would not have wanted to have been born and brought up anywhere else in the world. Not even Halewood or Kirkby.

And what of today's hunter gatherers? Where are the bravest of the brave? What do they do now? Well, now they are called "researchers" and they no longer have to fight tooth and nail to gather and provide. They collect facts. And the weapon of their choice is a computer screen.

I have worked with numerous researchers in film and television. They know what books to look for on the exact shelf in any library; they can dig up the particular field in Northern France that the Battle of the Somme was fought on; they will tell you the exact scientific differences between the compounds of Marmite and Oxo even if you don't want to know. But, frankly, none of those learned men and women are in the same class or the same division as Mark Campbell when it comes to this book. With 'Huyton's Titans' he is top of the Premier League.

For a start, 'Huyton's Titans' isn't a job for Mark. It isn't an occupation. It's a passion. A wonderful obsession.

Just open this book at any page. You will find someone and something to surprise you. For example, you might think you have a good idea how many professional footballers came from this community. I thought so too. I know nothing. But I know who does, to the exact number. He's written this book! And, finally, I can promise you, while you're discovering all these footballers you never even imagined came from just down the road from you, or lived on the corner where you used to kick a ball about when you were a kid, you will forever be saying to yourself, "I DIDN'T KNOW THAT!"

And.........and Mark Campbell has a day job too!

CONTENTS

THE WARM UP

I decided to write this book following a typical Monday morning discussion with a group of friends. It was our usual informal analysis of the weekend's football during which we would become pundits and mull over the performances of the various teams and players. Similar conversations take place up and down the country every week of the season but on this occasion our discussion was slightly different and, I believe, unique.

Our 'expert' appraisals included comments such as "Gerrard was magnificent again", "Tony Hibbert didn't put a foot wrong " and "I see David Nugent grabbed another goal". We continued with "That Lee Trundle's got a few tricks up his sleeve" and "Ronnie Moore has got Tranmere playing really well". The chat probably went on to extol the virtues of the 'flat back four', 'zonal marking' and to highlight the failings of the 'rotation system'. However, by this stage I wasn't contributing or even listening – the realisation that every player we had just talked about had grown up within a couple of miles of where we stood had captured my attention and my mind started to work overtime.

I have always been aware of the conveyor belt of footballing talent in my home village of Huyton and for as long as I can remember I have been obsessed with football. I have vivid childhood memories of the local Huyton & District Schools representative side playing at Huntley and Palmers, Plessey's Sports Club and even Anfield and Goodison Park. I have closely monitored the progress of players graduating from the Schoolboys to join the ranks of the professionals and taken great pleasure and a strange sense of pride in following their career paths. However, until that conversation I had taken it for granted and not appreciated the magnitude of each individual's achievement of playing football for a living. To hear the names of so many local people in that context made me realise just how special this discussion was. As I broke away from the group I began thinking of other players from the area and as I wrote down one name another two jumped into my head. If I included players from the small adjoining villages of Prescot and Whiston, the lengthening list became even more impressive. Further research unearthed many more players. Some were household names with hundreds of top-flight games under their belts whilst others had made just a handful of appearances in the less-glamorous lower divisions. All of them though were able to boast that they had succeeded where hundreds of thousands of others had tried and failed - they had played in the English Football League.

This book is a celebration of all things good about my area's involvement in football. Huyton, Prescot and Whiston have produced a wealth of talent which I am sure would compare favourably with any other area of the country of a similar size and population. In addition, an atmosphere exists which makes all aspects of football a way of life. The radio and satellite dish are essential items in most homes in order to keep abreast of the latest football scores and news. It is virtually impossible for a passing driver to ignore an amateur or junior football match - an irresistible magnetism takes over and the driver must pull the car over to the roadside and spend five minutes watching the blood, sweat and tears before resuming their journey, the thirst for football temporarily quenched. From that conversation with my mates I set off on my own journey and discovered many like-minded football obsessives who contribute towards making Huyton, Prescot and Whiston the ideal environment for young and old to enjoy the beautiful game at all levels.

THE PITCH

On the outskirts of Liverpool, the conjoined towns of Huyton, Prescot and Whiston are located less than ten miles away from the city centre. The areas rural landscape changed dramatically in the 1930s when Lord Derby sold large swathes of his Estate to the local authority. The resultant public and private sector house building programme involved the construction of estates including Longview, Fincham House, Huyton Farm, Woolfall Heath, Thingwall Farm, Page Moss, Sunnyside, St Johns and Bowring Park. Huyton's population quickly quadrupled and by the end of the decade the area boasted 20,000 residents. This number continued to swell and it became apparent that the provision of a suitable community infrastructure, including recreation facilities, was required.

By the end of the Thirties this had begun to be addressed by Huyton and Prescot District Councils in partnership with the National Playing Fields Association and notable generous local beneficiaries. Much-needed football pitches were provided at Page Moss and Jubilee Parks with the latter also offering cricket, bowls and tennis facilities. However, the most ambitious and extensive provision at this time, and probably since, was the King George V Playing Fields which were officially opened on Saturday 28 October 1939. The following week the Prescot Reporter captured the events of the day superbly-;

"High tribute to the generosity of the Misses Constance and Christine Pilkington, of The Hazels, Prescot, in donating about forty acres of grassland adjoining their estate for a multiple recreation ground as a memorial to the late King George V, was paid when the ground was opened by Lord Derby on Saturday afternoon. The King George's Playing Fields, as the ground is to be called, is situated in Longview Lane and is bounded by Liverpool Road and Huyton Lane. It has been laid out to accommodate seven football matches at once, with additional provision for hockey, tennis, bowls and children's playground. A handsome brick built pavilion, with hot and cold showers, dressing room accommodation for both sexes and a caretaker's flat are also provided.

The playing fields have been developed so far at considerable expense, towards which a sum of £3,500 has been donated by the King George V Playing Fields Foundation. A distinguished gathering of people interested in the playing fields movement were present, as well as the Mayor of Liverpool (Ald Sir Sydney Jones), Coun J Speakman (Chairman of Huyton Council), Mr H E H Lawton (Clerk), Coun Ernest Taylor (Chairman of Prescot Council), and Mr W Cross (Clerk), the Rev W H Lewis (Vicar of Huyton), the Rev J G Millward (Prescot Congregational Church) and the Rev Edgar F Thomas (Prescot Wesley Church). The Rev O Lunn Martin (Vicar of Prescot) was unable to be present. The inauguration of play on the fields began with the ceremonial opening of the memorial gates by Lord Derby. Memorial plaques, commemorating the late King George, ornament the main pillars of the gates and after the key had been turned, Lord Derby, the trustees and the guests proceeded up the main drive between lines of youths in football kit and girls in hockey kit.

The key of the memorial gates was handed to Lord Derby by the architect (Lieut-Col J M Gornall). Mr R A Pilkington (Chairman of the Trustees) expressed on behalf of the other trustees their appreciation at being asked by the Misses Pilkington to accept the trust to keep and maintain the fields with the help of the endowment which they had given. For a long time, the Misses Pilkington had been interested in work for young people and had felt very strongly the importance of voluntary work for such purposes. "We congratulate them on the completion of this great enterprise and we believe that the future will show that their gift is as valuable to this growing neighbourhood as it has been generous on their part" continued Mr Pilkington.

Lord Derby was president of the National Playing Fields movement said Mr Pilkington, and he did not think any function could cause him greater pleasure. It was largely through his persistent advocacy in connection with the movement that it had become so extensive throughout the country. Lord Derby, who said he had come over "as a neighbour" said Mr Pilkington had referred to the generosity of the two ladies who had presented the memorial. "Those two ladies are your sisters and although you would not mention that, I am not going to allow it to pass without asking all here today to realise the generosity of the gift and to thank the donors with all sincerity" he went on. "Those of us who live in this part of the world know well the generosity of the Pilkington family. They have always been to the fore in all good works and now they have added to the large debt of gratitude that we owe them by the gift of the playing fields - a gift that I hope for many, many days to come will be of value to the inhabitants of this neighbourhood."

The article continued by outlining that the playing fields would be of tremendous value not only to the people of Huyton but also many Prescotians. It highlighted that Prescot was so congested that it lacked recreation grounds. Four Prescot clubs had already rented pitches on the ground to enable them to play in the recently established Prescot and District Amateur League. The article concluded with a letter from the Pilkingtons received by the newspaper's Editor which stated, "My sister and I were grateful for the appreciation on Saturday of our gift of the King George's Field, Longview, but we should like to emphasise how much the project owes to the trustee and management committees. But for their experience and indefatigable work, often given at the end of a busy day, the scheme would never have come to fruition, and it is a great satisfaction that it's future development is in safe hands."

Just as the Pilkingtons had intended, the KGV Fields became a thriving facility and home to many amateur and junior football teams. Over the years it has undergone many changes, not least of all between 1943 and 1948 when it was utilised as a prisoner of war camp and was 'home' to future Manchester City German goalkeeper Bert Trautmann.

Whilst Huyton could boast new, first class facilities, the same could not be said of Prescot. Although there were a number of pitches in the area, it wasn't until the early Sixties that Prescot teams were afforded the same luxury as their Huyton counterparts. On 10 July 1963 the Liverpool Echo, referring to what is locally known as 'Brown's Field,* reported "The sporting youth of Prescot - who have so often complained of a lack of facilities in the town - will soon be able to play football, tennis and other games on their own £10,000 playing fields. Work on the scheme is now underway and it is expected that the sports ground, off Huyton Lane, will be open sometime next year. Preliminary site work has been going on for a couple of months and the fields will be seeded this autumn. Two full size football pitches, a number of tennis courts and a modern pavilion are among the provisions made at the playing fields which will be dedicated to the trustees of the KGV Playing Fields Association. This society has donated £3,000 to the total cost of the scheme. Prescot Council's deputy clerk Mr G Peet said, "Work is progressing satisfactorily on the site. Before now it was more or less an open field although some of the local football teams did play their matches on it. When work has finished there will be organised soccer with showers and spacious changing accommodation at the pavilion."

Huyton's KGV pitches were the focal point of our teams' participation in the Prescot and District and later the Huyton Sunday League but there were numerous others being fully utilised. Nowadays, in addition to KGV, there are pitches which are in regular use at Jubilee Park, Brown's Field, Lord Derby Academy, Windy Arbor Road, Prescot Soccer Centre and the magnificent new jewel in the area's crown on Knowsley Lane which is home to AFC Knowsley.

The old pavilion the day before it's demolition

*Brown's Field was named after Prescot butcher Mr Brown who utilised the space for his livestock to graze on until such time as the animals just became 'stock' for his Market Place shop.

THE KICK OFF

Founded on 17 April 1888, The English Football League was the first league in the world and consisted of 12 clubs - Accrington, Aston Villa, Blackburn Rovers, Bolton Wanderers, Burnley, Derby County, Everton, Notts County, Preston North End, Stoke, West Bromwich Albion and Wolverhampton Wanderers. Preston were the inaugural champions and repeated the feat the following season pipping Everton to the title by a two-point margin. The positions reversed in the 1890/91 season with Everton accumulating a couple of points more than The Lilywhites. The League was gaining in popularity and in the 1891/92 season, 28 teams competed in two divisions with Sunderland topping the 16 teams in Division One and Small Heath heading the dozen clubs in the newly formed Division Two.

At this stage, no local players were involved. However, this would change forevermore when on 26 March 1898 **John Barlow**, who had signed from his hometown club Prescot, pulled on an Everton shirt to play the first of four games for the club. The match, at Burnden Park, ended in a 1-0 victory for the hosts Bolton Wanderers but Barlow did not have to wait too long to taste success. With 10,000 in attendance seven days later, the Blues accounted for Nottingham Forest 2-0 with goals from Bell and Divers. In 1899, he signed for non-league Reading before joining Western League side Tottenham Hotspur for whom he made 20 appearances.

After briefly returning to Reading, he re-joined Football League action with Leicester Fosse who became Leicester City when, in 1919, King George V recognised Leicester as a city. His debut for the Second Division outfit resulted in a 1-1 draw versus Barnsley on 5 September 1903 and the last of his 27 appearances took place on 26 March 1904 when Bristol City provided the opposition. Shortly after, he returned home and turned out for St Helens Recs. Having gained the distinction of becoming the first local man to play in the Football League, Barlow led the way for many others.

Remarkably, since 1898 at least one player (and often many more) from Huyton, Prescot or Whiston has appeared in every season of the Football League's existence. It is reasonable to assume that similar to today, in the League's formative years local players aspired to play for Liverpool or Everton. Everton enjoyed early success and after finishing eighth in the League's debut season, they did not finish outside of the top six in the following decade and established themselves as one of the leading sides in the country.

John Barlow

Harry Singleton

Liverpool joined Division 2 from the Lancashire League to compete in the 1893/94 season. They won the division that year conceding just 18 goals from 28 games played and did not lose a single match. They 'yo-yoed' between Divisions 1 and 2 for a couple of seasons before becoming established competitors in the top flight. In 1902, Prescot-born winger **Harry Singleton** played three times for the Blues in 1901 after spells at Stockport County and Bury. He also played 18 games for Grimsby Town and, in Leeds City's debut League season, he scored seven goals from 45 appearances.

Tom Rogers

Striker **Thomas Jones** left Bootle FC to play 15 games for the Toffees between 1905 and 1910 before leaving to join Birmingham and forging a prolific partnership with Jack Hall.

On the Liverpool side of the coin, **Tom Rogers** made his debut for the club at Anfield in a 2-2 draw with Sheffield United on 27 April 1907 shortly after signing from Rossendale. The Prescotian left fullback struggled to hold down a regular place in the team but during a 5-seasons spell at the club, he did play forty times for Liverpool. Following his retirement, he was actively involved with Prescot Cables and was a Committee member for nearly thirty years. Known by the nickname 'Tim', speedy winger **James Speakman** from Huyton Quarry became a Liverpool player on 5 February 1909. His journey to Anfield included spells with local sides St Agnes, Garston North End and Prescot Wire Works. Tim made his debut for the Reds on 9 October of the same year when they accounted for Manchester United by a score line of 3-2 before a 30,000-strong crowd. As understudy to virtual ever-present Arthur Goddard, he was restricted to just eight first team appearances and a single goal – the opener in a 2-0 victory over Bradford City on 8 April 1912. His Liverpool career was topped and tailed by opposing Man United when on 29 March 1913, he faced them in a 2-0 reversal, which proved to be his final game before joining South Liverpool FC.

Unusually, as one member of the Speakman family packed his kitbag and departed Anfield, another joined the club and was about to embark upon his own first team career. On 27 January 1909, the Lancashire Evening Post reported, "**Sam Speakman**, who played right fullback for Colne last Saturday, hails from Prescot where he was associated with the Wire Works team. He is young and sturdily built and given a continuance of his form against Accrington Stanley he should prove of material to the Colne defence." More specifically, James' brother Sam was 25 years of age, lived in Elm Street, Huyton Quarry and "proved material to the Colne defence" for four seasons before joining Liverpool on 4 September 1912. He figured in 15 games in his debut campaign and made the first of these appearances on 20 September 1913. Manager Tom Watson threw him in at the deep-end in a Goodison Park Merseyside derby in front of 40,000 Scousers. Sam and his new teammates coped admirably and accounted for the Blues 2-1 with Bill Lacey bagging a decisive brace. All but one of Sam's 26 officially recorded Liverpool appearances came in League affairs, the exception being an FA Cup round 2 victory over Gillingham.

He played no further part in the competition as they progressed to the last FA Cup Final played at Crystal Palace where they were defeated 1-0 by Burnley. Between 1915 and 1919, World War One put paid to formally recognised Association Football League fixtures but Sam continued to play in regional leagues and was still with Liverpool when normal service resumed in August 1919. He played in the opening four games of the 1919/20 campaign but a 1-0 defeat at the hands of Arsenal at Highbury on 8 September 1919 was the last occasion on which he would turn out for the Reds. Following his brother's footsteps, he also joined South Liverpool. Sadly, Sam passed away in 1934 aged just 50 and James died in 1962 at the age of 74.

Whilst Everton and Liverpool tapped into the talent that was available locally, a less obvious but undeniable link existed between Prescotians and Hull City. The early lynchpin in the relationship was **William Robinson**. The former Prescot, Skelmersdale, St Helens Recs and Manchester City centre half, joined Hull City in 1905. On 2 September of the same year he proudly played in the club's first ever Football League fixture, a 4-1 trouncing of Barnsley. He did not miss a single game during his four years with the Tigers, making 119 appearances before leaving to join Bolton Wanderers in 1908. After two seasons with the Trotters, he spent a short spell at Accrington Stanley before bringing his playing days to a close. He rekindled his relationship with Hull by acting as a scout and it was in this capacity that he recommended a number of Prescotians to the East Yorkshire club. Goalkeeper **Ed Roughley** who had previously turned out for Prescot, Skelmersdale and St Helens Recs, gained legendary status at Hull for whom he played 166 times between 1906 and 1914. He signed for the Tigers at the same time as fellow Prescotians **Ned Neve** and **Sam Lyon**. Neve made his Football League debut in a 2-0 victory over Clapton Orient on 8 September 1906. He struggled to claim a regular place in the team's line-up yet made 13 appearances in each of his first three seasons. Then, during the 1909/10 campaign, he featured in more than half of their fixtures as Hull finished third in Division Two and narrowly missed promotion.

James Speakman

The tricky outside left signed for top flight Derby County in the summer of 1912 and registered a single goal from 49 Rams appearances. Prior to the enforced suspension of League football, Ned spent the 1914/15 season as a Nottingham Forest player. During the War, he guested for Chesterfield Town and, after receiving his call up papers in 1916, fought as a bombardier with the Royal Garrison Artillery. Tragically, he passed away four years later due to valvular heart disease, which some people attributed to him being gassed during his service in the Army of Occupation in Germany. Inside forward **Walter Dagnall** enjoyed three spells with his hometown club Prescot. Sandwiched between these, he pulled on a Hull City shirt and scored two goals from his eight appearances in the 1906/07 campaign. He also turned out for St Helens Recs, Skelmersdale United and Rossendale United.

W S Robinson

Sam Lyon's six games for the Tigers came during four seasons between 1910 and 1914 prior to him joining Barnsley. When Roughley left Hull to ply his trade in non-league football with Chesterfield Town, Rugby Town and Great Heath, Prescotian **Billy Mercer** took up the position between the sticks. Having earlier played for local youth team Grosvenor, he joined the Tigers from Prescot Athletic on the same day as teammates **James Middlehurst** and **Tommy Burns**. He managed a single appearance before the outbreak of World War One, a 3-0 victory over Clapton Orient on 23 January 1915.

When he returned to the club post-war, he missed just five games between 1920 and 1924, making 203 appearances. In November 1924 League champions Huddersfield Town's Manager Herbert Chapman recruited Mercer who appeared 28 times in his debut season as the Terriers retained the title. A couple of seasons later on 21 April 1928, Town were favourites to lift the FA Cup at Wembley in front of a 92,041 expectant, mainly flat-capped crowd. However, a first minute Blackburn Rovers goal upset the applecart and gave the underdogs the perfect start.

Mercer and co were defeated 3-1 in what proved to be his penultimate game for the club. He put in 19 Blackpool appearances before retiring in 1929.

Another local lad who gained his Football League spurs before the War was **John 'Jack' Birchall**. The former Whiston Ramblers, St Helens Recs and Liverpool left half made his mark at Blackpool for whom he made 86 appearances before signing for Blackburn Rovers in February 1903.

Billy Mercer

AFTER THE WAR

John Houghton

When the Football League reformed in 1919, it did so with gusto. The 1920/21 season welcomed the introduction of 'Division Three South' and the following season 'Division Three North'. The Football League now consisted of 86 clubs, which increased the playing opportunities for our local men who were quick to seize their chance. Some had continued to play during the war years in the regional leagues and guested for teams but there are no formal records of these appearances. Others waited until they completed their National Service before resuming their Football League careers. However, one of the early new recruits to the post-war ranks of the League would also become one of the first locals to display his footballing talents internationally. Fullback **John Houghton** had played locally for Prescot and St Helens and outside of the Football League for Norwich City and Glasgow Rangers before Fulham handed him a League chance in 1919. Two games for the Cottagers were followed by a move to Third Division (North) outfit Wigan Borough for whom he played 29 times. When Houghton left England to start a new life in America it did not curtail his involvement with football – based initially in Chicago, he became a regular for the local Mistletoe Lodge team and then the Canadian Club in the American Soccer League. John Houghton, who had also worked in a chocolate factory and for an engineering firm in Niagara Falls, passed away in 1991 in Lamesca, California, shortly after his 100th birthday.

After the war, the Hull City connection with our local players was still in evidence with Sam and **Jack Lyon**, **George Davies** and **Tom 'Ghandi' Gardner**. George Davies was a Prescotian wing half who spent a couple of seasons at Hull where he made 11 appearances before going on to play for Merthyr Town, Grimsby Town, Whiston, Llandudno, Caernarvon Athletic, Ashton National and Northwich Victoria. Born on 3 November 1893, Jack Lyon had followed his brother Sam from Prescot to Hull and played in 26 games prior to WW1. The inside left added a further 13 post-war appearances before joining Leeds United for £300 in July 1920. He debuted in a 2-0 defeat of Port Vale in United's first ever Football League fixture on 28 August. The League had expelled Leeds City a year earlier and United rose out of the club's ashes. In their second match, Jack provided the cross from which Len Armitage registered their first League goal. With 16,958 in attendance at Elland Road, the game finished 2-1 to the visitors, South Shields. He featured in 33 games in Leeds colours before returning to Prescot. Jack then crossed the River Mersey where he put pen to paper to sign for New Brighton at the commencement of the 1921/22 campaign, which was also their first season in the Football League. He found the back of the net five times from his 28 appearances for the Rakers before moving to Mold and picking up a Welsh League winners medal at the end of the 1924/25 season. Jack Lyon ended his playing days back in his native Prescot to bring his career full circle.

Scouts from Football League clubs were regularly present at matches in our area hoping to unearth players who were capable of making the transition to a higher level. Their efforts would frequently prove worthwhile. In addition to securing the services of Jack Lyon, New Brighton also signed **Jack Leadbetter, George Gutteridge** and goalkeeper **Jim Foulkes** whose son Bill became a Manchester United legend. Their Wirral neighbours Tranmere Rovers were also successful in bagging Prescot players **Billy Rainford** (22 games played), **Tommy Naylor** (81 Rovers games), **Dick Platt** (173 appearances) and **Jack Almond** (22 games) – although Almond arrived at Prenton Park via Stoke City.

As WW2 and another enforced Football League break approached, a number of local players started careers that would resume at the end of the hostilities. **Reginald Butcher** was one such man. He first played outside of the League for Shrewsbury Town but signed for Liverpool in 1937. After failing to break into the first team, Reg joined Chester of the Third Division (North) on 11 January 1938. He made 23 appearances before war broke out. When football formally resumed in 1946, Reg was still only thirty years of age and featured in 132 additional games over the following four seasons. Another player whose career straddled the war was **Harry Topping** who, after cutting his teeth with non-league Rossendale United, played three times for Stockport County between 1938 and 1945. He was another who joined New Brighton and during his two seasons there, played 67 games before finishing his career with Prescot Cables.

TOMMY "GHANDI" GARDNER

Born on 28 May 1910 in Huyton, Tommy Gardner played his early football for Orrell FC before joining Liverpool in 1928. He signed his first pro contract in April of the following year but due to the quality and consistency of Tom Morrison, his rival to the halfback berth, his opportunities were limited. However, with 28,592 fans present at Anfield on 25 January 1930, Tommy made his Football League debut as the Reds accounted for Manchester United 1-0 courtesy of a Henry Race goal. This was the first of five consecutive matches in which Tommy featured but when Morrison recovered from the injury which had side-lined him, he was reinstated to the team by Manager George Patterson and it was time for Gandhi to find pastures new.

He joined Grimsby Town on 1 June 1931 making 13 appearances in a season that concluded with relegation to Division Two and Tommy's departure. Two great seasons with Hull City followed during which the club became Third Division (North) champions. His stock was so high due to his performances for the Tigers that on 1 February 1934 Aston Villa stumped up £4,500 to take Tommy to Villa Park. At the end of the 1933/34 campaign, he was included in the England squad and made his international debut on 16 May 1934 at the Letna Stadium in Prague where England lost 2-1 to Czechoslovakia. Although Tommy was a squad member for four additional matches, he had to wait a full year before donning his second and final cap. Holland provided the opposition in Amsterdam on 18 May 1935 when a 46th minute strike from Portsmouth outside right Fred Worrall proved the difference between the two nations.

Domestically, Tommy's form dipped and he managed just a handful of appearances in the 1935/36 season, at the conclusion of which Villa lost their First Division status. On 1 April 1938, he signed for Burnley but after 42 games and 3 goals, World War Two signalled an end to his relationship with the club from Turf Moor. However, the hostilities did not stop Tommy from playing football. On 9 March 1940, he returned to Anfield to take part in a charity match between a British Army XI and a Football League XI. Twelve thousand fans turned up to watch an array of players who were, or would become, legends of the game including Joe Mercer, Ted Sagar, Bill Shankly and Stanley Mathews. Tommy represented the Army team which ran out 5-2 winners. He also guested during the war years for Blackburn Rovers, Preston, Manchester United, Southport and Blackpool with whom in 1943 he won the Football League War Cup defeating Arsenal by a 4-2 scoreline.

When the War was over, Tommy made 39 appearances in the Third Division (North) for Wrexham before turning his attention to playing, coaching and managing in non-league football. He represented Wellington Town, Saltney and Oswestry Town before becoming assistant trainer at Chester City in 1954. After 14 years of loyal service to the Seals, he and his wife took over the stewardship of the club's Sports and Social club. Football ability was and still is in the Gardner family genes. Tommy's son Keith was on Liverpool's books in the early 1950s and his great granddaughter Hannah Keryakoplis became a Welsh international and played for a host of teams including Liverpool, Stoke and Derby. It is unclear however, if either of them could match Tommy's achievement of winning a Daily Mail long throw-in competition with an impressive distance of 32 yards and 2 inches.

As the referee puts the whistle to his lips, brings the first half to a close and the players disappear down the tunnel for their half-time oranges, let us concentrate upon other aspects of our area's rich footballing heritage before an impressive new team emerges for the post-war second half of our story of the players.

PRESCOT FOOTBALL

Prescot has hosted organised football since the early 1880s. The first recorded game took place on Saturday, 29 November 1884 at Prescot cricket club near an area known as 'Slacky Brow'. The cricket club was located on land nowadays bordered by Warrington Road, Bridge Road, Kingsway and Ash Grove. A young St Helens team, St Thomas, whose superior quality enabled them to run out 3-0 victors, provided the opposition on the day. Despite the disappointing start, Prescot FC was in business and further friendly games followed against St Saviours, Primrose Olympic, St Marks and Liverpool Gymnasium. The club, (initially nicknamed 'The Watchmakers' due to the town's reputation as a leading timepiece manufacturer), entered various cup competitions and reached the Liverpool Junior Cup Final in 1888. Although defeated 3-1 by Aintree Church, the club secured its first trophy by winning the same competition two seasons later. They joined the Liverpool & District League for the 1890/91 season, finishing fourth. Whilst the team fared well in the league, they enjoyed greater success in the cups and in 1894/95 season, were defeated in the final of the Liverpool Senior Shield at Goodison Park in front of 3,000 spectators. The following campaign saw the club go one better and win the Shield defeating Tranmere Rovers in a replayed final.

Positive progress continued with the club moving up the League ladder to join the Lancashire Alliance and win its League title in the 1899/1900 season. Two years later, the club took another step up in class to become a member of the Lancashire League but this proved to be a leap too far too soon and Prescot FC struggled to make an impression. In addition, due to a major dispute with the cricket committee the club found itself homeless, unable to fulfil its fixtures and remained dormant for four years. However, the couple of decades the Prescot team spent playing at Slacky Brow had highlighted the demand for a local football team. Supporters turned out in great numbers and at important games (or those featuring local rivals Whiston), it was not unheard of for as many as 4,000 fans to be present. Unsuccessful attempts to establish a new Prescot team followed and it became obvious, particularly to local politician the Hon Arthur Stanley MP, that changes were required if the town was to have a club with a long-term sustainable future. As a result, land at the club's current site in Eaton Street at the foot of Hope Street was secured for Prescotians to participate in a variety of sports, with a football pitch located in the middle of a cycling and athletics track. Prescot Athletic FC was born and played its first game on 29 September 1906. The team finished runners-up in the St Helens and District League in its inaugural season and proved to be formidable opposition, particularly at home. In due course the club joined the Liverpool League and, in turn, the County Combination. The 1927/28 campaign proved important for the club on and off the pitch. Dramatic improvements to the stadium included new turnstiles and the provision of covering over the Hope Street End terracing. In February 1928, such was the standing of the club, Prescot FC (the club reverted to its original name after WW1) was invited to replace Fleetwood in the Lancashire Combination, taking over Fleetwood's record and fulfilling its fixtures. In addition, on Easter Monday the club won the first of three consecutive Liverpool Challenge Cups with a 3-1 victory over Liverpool 'A' at Goodison Park. The club strengthened the team in order to deal with the step up in class and results were impressive.

The 1928/29 season brought about another change of name for the club. In an early example of corporate sponsorship, 'Prescot Cables FC' reflected the support given to the club by the town's main employer B.I.C.C (British Insulted Callender Cables). The company funded further ground improvements including a new grandstand, covered paddock and an impressive new entrance to the ground. In return, leading members of the company occupied seats on the club's committee. The team continued to produce the goods on the pitch and they retained the Liverpool Challenge Cup via a 3-1 trouncing of the old enemy Whiston in front of 6,000 fans at Goodison Park. The Cables were extremely ambitious and with the team playing fantastic football in a superb stadium, the club submitted an application to the Football League to join its Division Three (North). However, although the committee were convinced everything was in place for the granting of the bid, the application was unsuccessful. In October 1931, Prescot Cables applied to the Football League to replace Wigan Borough, who had been forced to resign due to financial issues. Again, the club's application was rejected and no other bid has ever been made to join the Football League.

The average attendance during the early 1930s was approximately 1,800 which was considered disappointing, especially as the club finished as runners-up in the Lancashire Combination three years in a row. One notable exception to the 'poor' crowd figures occurred when a match in the

Prescot Cables, Liverpool Challenge Cup Winners 1928

preliminary round of the FA Cup secured the biggest attendance Hope Street has ever housed. Eight thousand one hundred and twenty two fans of both Prescot and opponents Ashton National (who had laid on four special trains) crammed into the ground to witness a 3-0 Cables victory. The period prior to WW2 was unremarkable. The only real developments at this time were that the club joined the Cheshire League for three seasons before returning to the Lancashire Combination but failed to pull up any trees in either. During this time, a new Supporters Club was formed and Cables became a nursery club for Liverpool FC, resulting in a change from the amber and black colours adopted following the BICC sponsorship to a red kit. The relationship with Liverpool was a two-way affair with Cables players turning out for Liverpool and vice versa. Following the end of WW2, the status of nursery club, which had prevented Prescot Cables from entering the FA Cup, was dropped. A modified arrangement existed between the two clubs with Liverpool paying Prescot for the use of Hope Street as a training facility and venue for 'A' team home fixtures. Cables continued to do well in cup competitions and in April 1948 were the winners of the Lancashire Combination Cup defeating Lancaster City in the Final. The following season they pulled off a magnificent achievement by lifting the Liverpool Challenge Cup at Anfield by inflicting a 2-0 defeat upon an Everton team which contained players who collectively had featured in no fewer than 1,201 Football League games.

*Prescot Cables 1948
Lancashire Combination Cup Winners*

The Supporters Club continued to do a sterling job raising much-needed funds and during the late Forties and Fifties they were providing as many as 50 double-decker buses to transport fans to away games. The 1950s proved to be an unpredictable decade for the club. Fortunes fluctuated between relegation, promotion, Cup victories, the heaviest ever defeat at home (8-0 versus Fleetwood) and the biggest away victory (12-0 versus Stubshaw Cross Rovers). Prescot won the 1956/57 Lancashire Combination Championship - which had narrowly evaded them on numerous occasions. In addition, qualification to the First Round proper of the FA Cup had seemed beyond the club yet the following year the team delivered. They defeated Earlestown, Runcorn, Bangor City, Stork and Morecambe to earn the right to face Hartlepools United. On 6 November 1958, Prescot took to the field in front of 9,424 spectators at the Monkey Hangers' Victoria Ground and although they were trounced 5-0, they had made local footballing history.

If the Fifties were an unsettled period for the football club, the Sixties presented problems from which the club has arguably never fully recovered. Crowds dwindled significantly and a visit to Hope Street was no longer a fortnightly 'must' for many Prescotians. On 24 August 1960, a major fire caused the destruction of the Main Stand putting a tremendous financial strain on the club. In May 1962, a replacement stand cost the club a crippling £25,000 and things got so bad that the club placed its entire squad on the transfer list. Two years later, the club changed its name to Prescot Town and became

Prescot Cables 1950s

a limited company in the hope that the enormous debt incurred by the construction of the new stand could be wiped out. In addition, the club agreed that its future player recruitment policy would place greater emphasis on local amateur players. However, with only 14 points secured from 42 games in the 1964/65 season and the club rooted firmly at the foot of the table, the decision seemed flawed. Whilst the club avoided the drop on a technicality, the writing was on the wall and the following season the club again picked up the wooden spoon and suffered relegation for the first time since 1954. Although they bounced back the following campaign, the cracks were beginning to show. In May 1975, after 39 years of continuous membership, Prescot were found guilty of breaching League rules and were effectively thrown out of the Lancashire Combination. This was a reflection in many ways of a decade or more of steady, sometimes rapid decline. A lesser club than Prescot may well have folded there and then but, showing a grit and determination which had enabled them to survive for nearly 100 years, they secured a place in the First Division of the Mid-Cheshire League

The club then enjoyed a mini-revival when local business tycoon and former Cables player **George Glover** took over at Hope Street and invested some of his personal wealth. The 1976/77 season saw the club romp home with the League Championship scoring 99 goals from 30 games and suffering only two defeats. Victory over Waterloo Dock in the Final of the Liverpool Challenge Cup made it the sixth time Prescot had won the trophy and the first time since 1962. After an absence of 42 years, the club joined the Cheshire County League in 1978. Starting in Division Two, they gained promotion in 1979/80 following an end of season run-in of seven consecutive victories. The 1979/80 season also offered the club's older fans the chance to recall what supporting the club used to be like when it reached the Final of the Liverpool Senior Cup. Safe passage to the Final of the competition brought 2,000 fans flocking to Hope Street hoping to see the mighty Liverpool Reserves put to the sword. Unfortunately, a single goal from Huytonian Brian Kettle handed victory to a Liverpool side that included stars Steve Ogrizovic, Kevin Sheedy and Dave Watson in its ranks. In 1980, perhaps with one eye on the club's 1984 centenary, nostalgia filled the Prescot air. The old 'Cables' name made a welcome return and the reintroduction of the black and amber club colours rekindled thoughts of the 'Tigers' nickname. In addition, after a 21-year absence, the match day programme was revived. It was not, however, an immediate return to the glory days.

Prescot Cables 1980s

A couple of years later, Cables became founder members of the NW Counties League, which was an amalgamation of the Cheshire County League and the Lancashire Combination. Apart from relegation to Division Two in 1986 and an immediate return from whence they came the following season, the twenty years after joining the NWCL were largely uneventful. However, as we entered a new Millenium, Cables fans enjoyed a tremendous upturn in the club's fortunes. Atherton Colleries FC were defeated in the 2001/02 League Cup Final and the club amassed 97 points to finish runners-up in the table behind Kidsgrove Athletic who were promoted to the Northern Premier League Division One. The following campaign, an almost identical playing record returned one less point but proved sufficient to secure a place in the higher standard of competition when 2003/04 season kicked off. In 2004, a restructuring of the National League system coupled with Cables' performance, resulted in the club's promotion to the NPL Premier Division – their highest ever standing in the Football League pyramid. Prescot Cables rose brilliantly to the challenge by reaching the play-offs where Workington put paid to their National League North aspirations.

Prior to the Workington play-off game, members of the Supporters Club, which had been re-formed in 2000 to help finance the club, took over the running of the football side. The Supporters Club formed a limited company and for three seasons rented the ground from the former Chairman before it was sold to a Development Company, which offered to relocate the club to a new site within Knowsley. On the pitch, results were indifferent and the club's NPL status was under threat at the latter stages of numerous campaigns. This was never more evident than on the final day of the 2007/08 season when any one of more than a dozen clubs faced possible relegation. With 15 minutes of their fixture with Lincoln United remaining and trailing by a single goal, Cables appeared doomed. However, two late strikes saved their skin and due to the closeness of their rivals, the points for the victory elevated them to 13th place in the table! The club continued to struggle with limited finances and over the next half a dozen years it was difficult to keep track of who was in charge of team affairs.

During the 2011/12 campaign, there were no fewer than five different occupants of the Manager's office but the appointment of **David Powell** proved inspired. After a dodgy start, Powell's new squad settled down and thrilled the fans with some of the best football seen at Hope Street for a long time. However, the office's revolving door was in action again as Powell, **Neil Prince** then **Andy Paxton** came and went. Paxton had turned the club's League fortunes around and took the team to the Liverpool Senior Cup Final. Everton proved too strong for Cables in the 2015/16 contest and ran out 3-0 victors. When Paxton left, **Brian Richardson** replaced him and picked up where his predecessor had left off. In his debut season, the club again reached the Senior Cup Final where they dispatched Southport by a scoreline of 2-0. The trophy cabinet had been locked for a number of years before this feat but the key was required again at the end of the following season as Prescot refused to relinquish the Cup with a 4-0 Final drubbing of Marine. A fourth consecutive Final appearance in 2018/19 attracted 1,200 supporters to Hope Street. Unfortunately, penalties were required after a deadlocked game and it was the Sandgrounders who came out on top. Brian Richardson had done a sterling job before leaving at the end of the season to join FC United of Manchester. The joint management team of **Steve Pilling** and **Roy Grundy** was installed as his replacement.

Whilst the team had been performing miracles on the pitch, members of the Board of the limited company, which had evolved into a Community Interest Company in 2009, had been working their socks off behind the scenes for a decade. In December 2018, the Development Company, which had been in administration for seven years, brought matters to a head by coming out of administration and putting demands on the club that it could not meet. However, Knowsley MBC were aware of the club's plight and the ground at Hope Street had become the first asset to be listed as a Community Asset under the Localism Act (2011) by Knowsley Council in 2013. To the credit of all involved, Knowsley Council purchased the asset from the Development Company and granted a 99-year lease to Prescot Cables at an affordable rent. Council Leader **Graham Morgan** acknowledged the club's dilemma and stated, "Prescot Cables Football Club has been a huge part of this town since 1884 and it would have been a terrible blow if the club had to close its doors."

At the end of the day, the club is a Community Interest Company and is owned by the community. The Board of Directors are frontline supporters of Prescot Cables, elected by other supporters who are, and always have been, the backbone of the club. Prescot Cables FC has witnessed many changes during its lengthy existence and the fans have largely remained loyal to their team. It is not just about the eleven players on the pitch - its most important team is the legion of volunteers without whom the club simply could not operate. With the club's future seemingly safe for another century, the current Prescot Cables 'family' includes **Mick Flaherty, Joe Gibilru, Matt Roberts, Jamie Weston, Robbie Williams, Michael Corless, Peter Kneale, Doug Lace, Phil Blundell, Bob Nicholson, Keith Brown, Ken and Lynda Derbyshire, Paul Goodwin, Richard Tigwell, Norman Parr, Garry Williams, Tony Carroll, Vicky Tigwell, Harry Boydell, Sandra Williams, Alan McNally, David Hill, Paul Watkinson, Billy and Yvonne Maund, John Hendry, John Middleton and Gareth Coates.**

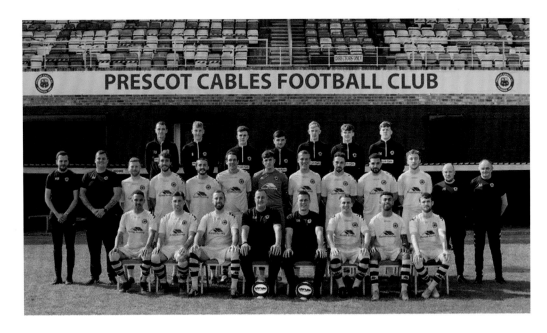

Prescot Cables 2020/21

Footynote:

*One of the joys of going to watch a Cables game is that there is always a chance of seeing a special player. It could be a homegrown lad or an opponent. It may be someone starting out who goes on to enjoy a fantastic career or a 'great' from yesteryear squeezing the last bit of gametime out of a sport they love. Whichever it is, Hope Street continues to provide valuable surroundings for footballers to display their talent and for the spectators to enjoy. Listed below are players who made appearances for Prescot **and** in the English Football League (and the team for whom they made the most appearances)*

Alan A'Court (Liverpool), Roger Aindow (Southport), Gillie Alldis (Tranmere), John Almond (Tranmere), Len Ashurst (Sunderland),Carl Baker (Coventry), Jack Bamber Leicester), John Barlow (Leicester), James Bell (Accrington), Stuart Bimson (Lincoln), Dick Birchall (Bradford), Bill Bradbury (Wrexham), Peter Burke (Norwich), John Butler(Wigan), George Carter (Southport), Karl Connolly (Wrexham), Colin Corbishley (Chester),Tommy Corcoran (Bradford), Harold Cothliff (Torquay), Billy Cotton (Wrexham), Peter Cowper (New Brighton), David Craig (Southport), Nick Culkin (Bristol Rovers), Walter Dagnall (Hull), George Davies (Grimsby), Mark Duffy (Sheffield Utd), John Evans (Barnsley), Ken Fletcher (Chester), Eddie Follan (Aston Villa), Jack Grainger (Southport), George Gutteridge (Hull), Ron Guttridge (Aston Villa), Alan Hampson (Halifax), George Harris (Southport), Tony Hateley (Notts County), Freddie Haycock (Aston Villa), Derek Hennin (Bolton), Jim Holmes (Sheff Utd), John Houghton (Fulham), Peter Houghton (Wigan), Wally Hughes (Sheff Utd), Barry Jones (Wrexham), Griff Jones (Barnsley), Jackie Keeley (Southport), Tony Kelly (Bolton), Steve Kennedy (Southport), Eddie Kilshaw (Bury), Fred Kilshaw(Leicester), Jeff King (Bolton), Josh Klein-Davies (Bristol R), Terry Leath (Southport), Tommy Lindsay (Southport), Eric Littler (Wrexham), Gavin Lynch (Chester), Jack Lyon (Hull), Sam Lyon (Barnsley), Tom Lyon (Chesterfield), Josh Macauley (Tranmere), Arden Maddison (Port Vale), Lance Marshall (Southport), Tommy McHale (Bradford), David McKearney (Crewe), Donald McKinley (Liverpool), Billy Mercer (Hull), David Mercer (Sheff Utd), John Miller (Liverpool), Andy Morris(Wigan), Sam Morris (Sunderland), Peter Murphy (Accrington Stanley), Tommy Naylor (Tranmere), Ed Neve (Hull), Terry Nolan (Southport), George O'Brien (Southport), Jim O'Donnell (Oldham), Elkanah Bollington Onyeali (Tranmere), Jack Ormandy (Bradford), Mark Peers (Fleetwood), Jim Pennington (Grimsby), Jack Pilling (Liverpool), Billy Pye (Chester), John Quinn (Sheff Wed), Tom Reid (Man Utd), Dave Ridler (Wrexham), Neil Robinson (Macclesfield), Jack Roscoe (Rotherham), Frank Ryder (Port Vale), Peter Sanders (Newport), Frank Soo (Stoke), Ged Stenson (Port Vale), Jim Taylor (Southport), Kevin Thomas (Southport), Roy Tickell (Tranmere), Henry Topping (New Brighton), Steve Torpey (Port Vale), Franklin Twist (Halifax), Jimmy Veacock (Southport), Bill Watkinson (Accrington Stanley), Steve Yawson (Morecambe).

THE SCHOOLBOYS

I was a very young schoolteacher and I was an only child. I also had a kind and loving father. I didn't think I needed another father. And if the truth be told, I wasn't sure I wanted any brothers or sisters. Yes, that's right - I was spoilt rotten.

Shortly afterwards, I had 17 unexpected but truly gifted younger brothers and I had acquired a wise and memorable father figure.

Let me explain.

In the summer of 1969 I was appointed team manager of Huyton Boys. I had previously been assistant to Eddie Kilshaw, a former footballer of renown, an excellent coach but with very wonky knees.

So, the 17 younger brothers were the squad of young footballers from Huyton we had largely assembled earlier that year and Eddie Kilshaw was my father figure. I was wildly lucky on both counts, for what followed in the next two years reads more like a fable or a feel good movie that doesn't only have a glorious happy ending, but also had a happy beginning and middle too.

The events of that time are all captured in precise detail in the pages that follow, expertly compiled in depth, as ever, by Mark Campbell. Just the bare facts alone make the most vivid reading. Basically, on previous history Huyton Boys winning the English Schools Trophy - a trophy that 256 town and city teams competed for - was something similar to the possibility that Tranmere Rovers would win the FA Cup at a stroll and North Macedonia would thrash Brazil in the World Cup Final. Seriously. That's how good Huyton Boys were. And no surprise at all that they were described in the Sports Section of the Daily Express at the time as "the greatest schoolboy team in living memory".

So. Here we are now. Over fifty years later.

I am an old man.

And those teenage brothers are following fast behind me, while Eddie Kilshaw is limping at speed along a touch-line somewhere heavenly.

It would be best to let the story of Huyton Boys tell itself. It doesn't need much help. And, personally, I never tell anybody about that time, that team, those happy memories - not even my grandchildren - because I'm not sure anyone would ever quite believe me! I wouldn't believe me if I didn't still recall those glory days; if I didn't have the faded press cuttings gathering dust in the attic. But I don't have to go into the attic anymore to relive those events, to revisit my brothers and my two fathers. All the history of Huyton Boys is in this book and is now about to unfold in the following pages....

Some achievements need to be recognised. When Huyton Boys won the English School FA Cup they were, and are still, the only non-city side to have done it.

Huyton has been a breeding ground for footballers, I along with my brother Shaun have enjoyed playing football at a level where we were fortunate enough to be paid for it. When we used to watch multiple games on St George's playing fields it was clear that our love of the game wasn't an isolated one.

When you consider how many exceptional footballers have come from the area you realise how important the game is to the area. Hope and football make good companions.

This book celebrates, rightly, the contribution that Huyton has made to football in this town, city, country and internationally.

IN THE BEGINNING

On 6 May 1946, a meeting took place at St Aloysius School, Twig Lane in Huyton that resulted in a dramatic change in the way local schools football was organised. The Allies' Headteacher Mr Houlton and a group of like-minded teachers from the area formed the Prescot and District Schools Football Association. Prior to this, schoolboys from Prescot and Whiston represented St Helens Boys whilst those from Huyton turned out for the Liverpool Boys team. The group felt that sufficient talent existed locally to provide a team capable of representing the area and giving a good account of itself. At the meeting, various appointments were made; **Mr Houlton** became Chairman, **A Welsby** was installed as Vice Chairman; **Jack Farrelly** was named as Secretary and **Stan Juneman** assumed the Treasurer's role. On Friday 20 September of the same year, the Prescot and District Reporter informed its readership of the latest developments, "For years past there has existed a popular demand for a Schools Football Association to be formed in Prescot district and now its establishment has been realised.......Prescot and District Schools FA expects to consist of four divisions, two senior and two junior leagues during its initial season. There are to be League and Cup competitions, magnificent trophies having been presented to the Association by British Insulted Callender's Cables Ltd."

Although cup competitions had been in existence for some time, this initiative provided a more structured approach to schools' football. The participants in the debut season of the Senior League were Huyton Modern, Longview Modern, Prescot RC, St Aloysius Modern and Whiston Modern. The Huyton Schools Junior League consisted of Park View, St Aloysius, Longview Council, Sylvester, Huyton CE, St Dominic's, St Columbas, Page Moss Council and Knowsley Maypole schools. The Prescot Junior League contained six schools - St Bartholomew's, Prescot RC, Prescot Council, St Lukes, Rainhill CE and Halsnead Council. In addition to the Association ensuring that the league and cup fixtures were fulfilled, trials for a District representative team were authorised. At this post-war time, funds for such a venture were in short supply but the Association was extremely resourceful. Ration coupons were collected to purchase equipment and the needlework department at Whiston Modern made a kit featuring a badge designed by teacher **Mr Fazakerley.**

The District side played its first ever game in October 1946 and the Reporter's coverage of the event could have been written yesterday. "Amid the present uproar in the sporting world concerning footballer's pay and the transfer of players hither and thither at tremendous cost, it was refreshing to go to Prescot Cables ground at Hope Street on Saturday afternoon and watch twenty-two schoolboys showing us how to play and enjoy soccer for the love of the game. Can anyone find anywhere in these days of big money football, two teams cramming into sixty minutes the enthusiasm and grand sporting spirit of these young lads? I think not." The article continued, "Prescot and District schoolboys team were playing their first match in public and although they went under to five goals to one, they were not too easy game for an experienced and well coached Liverpool side. By half time Liverpool were leading four goals to nil but after the interval the Prescot team not only managed to concede just one more goal but managed to score a goal of their own." The honour of being the scorer of the District's first goal fell to Huyton Modern pupil Rabone who found the net shortly before the final whistle. Perhaps encouraged by their second half performance against Liverpool, the team's next match was a different affair with a vastly different outcome. Rawtenstall provided the opposition in the first round of the English Schools Shield and were swept aside by nine goals to one. Although they were to fall at the next hurdle of the competition at the hands of Southport, there had been sufficient evidence in the District's opening trio of games to provide optimism for the future. The squad for these historic games was **Fenton** (Longview Modern), **Scott, Hepworth, Jones** and **Houghton** (Whiston Modern), **Ryan**-captain (Prescot RC), **Waywell, Robinson, Rabone and Thorne** (Huyton Modern), **Hankin** (Rainford Modern), **Higgins, Crawford** and **Kirkby** (St Aloysius).

Over the next few months, the District team and the inter-school competitions progressed well. The District ended its inaugural season with a resounding 4-1 victory over Bootle, Huyton Modern defeated Whiston Modern 3-2 to lift the J Hanson Challenge Cup and Prescot Council won the Prescot & District Junior Cup.

The Prescot and District Schools Football Association was up and running operating U-14 and U-15 District sides in addition to the Schools League and Cup competitions. For the best part of two decades, the teams failed to pull up any trees but in 1964, when Huyton Hey teacher **Mr Kilshaw** returned to manage the U-15s team after a 10-year absence, their fortunes changed immediately. Former Sheffield Wednesday player Eddie Kilshaw's previous stint in charge was curtailed due to ill health but there were no such problems the second time around. Regular training sessions plus the introduction of an Easter tour paid dividends when the District team not only shared the Dimmer Cup with Liverpool Boys but also lifted the Woodhead and Snowden Cups for the first time. Over the next five years, Mr Kilshaw and U-14s Manager **Ian Robertson** assumed control of the two teams in alternate years and captured silverware every season.

In August 1969, Mr Robertson stepped aside to become the Association's Secretary and served the district superbly in a variety of roles for decades to come. Upon the strong recommendation of Mr Kilshaw, his role was taken by twenty-three-year-old **Alan Bleasdale**. Born in Huyton and brought up on the Mosscroft Estate and Page Moss, at the side of the Farmers Arms, Alan Bleasdale was teaching PE and English in St Columbas School and had recently gained his preliminary FA Coaching Badge. He also played centre-forward for Warrington Town in the mid-Cheshire League and for any Sunday League team that turned up one man short!

His first game in charge was a 6-4 away victory over St Helens on 20 September which highlighted the team's strengths and exposed their defensive frailties. The side included **Keith Saunders, Gerard McGuinness, Mick Rea, Pat Phillips, Ray Murphy** and **Brian Henderson** in its ranks. Messrs Bleasdale and Kilshaw held further trials and Monday after school training sessions in an attempt to unearth additional talent. Alan also assessed the youngsters taking part in the many schools matches he refereed and **Jimmy Shields, Peter Reid** and **Tommy Evans** soon came onboard. Whilst the squad was greatly strengthened by the addition of **Don Tobin** and young powerhouse **Frank Pimblett**, a twice-broken leg sadly put paid to the involvement of **Stephen Jenkinson** who had shown great early promise. Despite a stuttering start to their defence of the Snowden Cup, the team reached the final courtesy of four consecutive victories. After an Easter tour of Lancashire brought the lads closer together, they defeated Kirkby Boys over two legs to retain the trophy.

Eddie and Alan knew they had assembled more than the nucleus of a good team but were desperate to add a couple of centre halves and a striker. When Prescot Grammar school's new Headteacher overturned his predecessor's policy by allowing his pupils to attend the trials prior to the 1970/71 season, the managerial duo had their fingers crossed that their number contained players who could fill the team's weak spots. In **Gerard Thomas** and **Roy Bradford** their defensive dreams were answered and quicksilver **Derek McClatchey** proved the perfect foil for Pat Phillips up front. **Brian Jones** and **Roy Clarke** added to Prescot's contingent whilst **Andy Rogan** and **Brian Scott** put the finishing touches to a squad capable of taking on all and sundry. With an exceptional group of young footballers assembled, Mr Bleasdale's next task was to appoint a team captain. Frank Pimblett was a year younger than the rest of the lads but despite this it was felt that he was most suited to be handed the responsibility of leading the side. Initially, Mr Bleasdale was concerned about how Frank's teammates would take the news. He needn't have worried. There wasn't a single dissenter as the boys were aware of the qualities young Frank possessed as were the scouts from up and down the country who tried to sign him.

1970/71

The 1970/71 campaign really was a season like no other and the people of Huyton and Prescot bought into the experience by turning up in droves to cheer the boys on to victory after victory. The only blip on an otherwise perfect year was a defeat in the two-legged final of the Lancashire Schools Cup.

LANCASHIRE SCHOOLS CUP

After cruising past Chadderton 4-0 in the opening round of the competition, the team took just two minutes to get their noses in front in their next match. Pat Phillips bagged the goal versus much-fancied Wigan with a powerful strike and Don Tobin increased the lead on 17 minutes. Phillips grabbed another to seal a 3-0 result. A mouth-watering tie opposing Liverpool Boys lay in wait for the winners of their next game and our lads set about Prestwich as if their lives depended upon the outcome. Two goals in the opening ten minutes by Phillips and McClatchey set up a resounding victory and safe passage to the semi-final stage for the first time in the District's history. Phillips added a further two goals to complete his hat trick before Pimblett scored from the spot and Ray Murphy added a sixth. James Shields made a number of excellent saves but was denied a clean sheet when, in the last minute, the home side scored a consolation goal.

The semis provided new territory for Huyton but Liverpool had lifted the Lancashire Cup on fifteen occasions. In an evenly balanced contest at Penny Lane it was the home side who took the lead on the stroke of half-time. Our boys showed their mettle after the break and bounced back with an equaliser courtesy of

Roy Bradford before Murphy showed the class which made him an England trialist and grabbed the winner with just six minutes remaining. On 30 March 1971 Huyton took to the Bloomfield Road pitch to face Blackpool brimming with confidence on the back of a 19-game winning streak. However, a Michael Betts hat trick within 21 minutes of the kick-off put the Tangerines well in control of the final. McClatchey pulled a couple of goals back but, against the run of play, Blackpool again found the net twice over to leave Huyton dumbfounded, 5-2 in arrears and with a mountain to climb. On 6 May 1971 torrential rain didn't deter the locals from turning up in their thousands for the return at Huntley and Palmers ground on Wilson Road. Despite a Herculean effort and a 4-2 victory, our boys lost by the smallest of margins. However, before the second leg had taken place, two other trophies had been secured.

THE DIMMER CUP

The Schoolboys began the Dimmer Cup campaign with resounding 7-2 and 6-2 victories over Wirral and Bootle respectively. The resultant semi-final fixture took place at Plessey's sports ground which was located on Roby Road where a housing estate now stands. Chester provided stubborn opposition but overall a 2-1 win didn't flatter the home side. A repeat of the previous season's two-legged final facing Kirkby was the full time conclusion.

On 28 April 1971 a bumper crowd surrounded Plessey's pitch for the first encounter. Roy Bradford rose salmon-like to powerfully head home from a corner to give Huyton the lead. Don Tobin smashed a brilliant 20-yarder past the keeper before Kirkby pulled one back to leave the destination of the Cup on a knife edge. A week later at a packed Kirkby Stadium, the contest continued to be delicately poised until the last five minutes when goals from Clarke and Murphy secured the trophy for Huyton Boys.

The 4-1 aggregate result was magnificent but not wholly unexpected as Huyton had kicked off the final as the newly-crowned Champions of English Schools football.

Huyton Boys take first leg lead

HUYTON BOYS 2,
KIRKBY BOYS 1.

HUYTON BOYS, the English Trophy winners, were confined to a one goal lead in the first leg of the Dimmer Cup final last night.

Kirkby's goal came in the last minute and gave a just ending to a fine game in which Huyton created the most chances without really getting on top.

So the stage is set for an interesting second leg at Kirkby Stadium next Monday evening.

Centre half Bradford moved up for a corner kick after nineteen minutes to put Huyton in front with a brilliant header. The keeper had little chance seven minutes later when Tobin cracked the ball into the corner of the net from 20 yards.

Kirkby's goal was scored through outside right Joe Stanley after Hayes had worried Jones in the Huyton goal into an error.

ENGLISH SCHOOLS FOOTBALL ASSOCIATION TROPHY

This most prestigious of schools football competitions involves almost 300 teams from the length and breadth of the country, all aspiring (some unrealistically) to win the ESFA Trophy. It was first contested in 1905, more than forty years before our District Schools Association was formed. Our representative team had failed to get beyond the Lancashire stage of the competition since 1949 until the team of '71 graduated from also rans to serious contenders. The squad that managers Bleasdale and Kilshaw had meticulously assembled was capable of turning over any opposition. Team talks were brief with the emphasis placed upon the players taking to the pitch to express and enjoy themselves. Throughout the season this trophy had been the one the team and managers had set their sights on but they nearly fell at the first hurdle.

Huyton manager's happy problem

ALAN BLEASDALE, team manager of Huyton Boys, has the kind of problem most soccer managers welcome—who to leave out for Saturday's English Trophy third round match against Pendle at the King George V playing fields, Longview (10.30).

He has named 16 players and his main "worry" appears to be the front four. Here it is any four from six, the six being Lancashire trialists Don Tobin and Ray Murphy, Pat Phillips, who has scored six goals in his last two outings, Roy Clarke, who scored a hat-trick in his last match, and Derek McClatchey and Brian Henderson, who several league club scouts regard as Huyton's best forward prospects.

But whatever line-up Mr Bleasdale decides upon, I expect his side to enter round four with a handsome victory. The 16 named are:

Shields, Scott, Rae, Bradford, Roone, Thomas, Saunders, McClatchey, McClatchey, Phillips, Henderson, Clarke, Tobin, Murphy,

Andy Rogan (St. Edmund Arrowsmith) is a new addition to the Huyton squad, and may play in the back four in

SCHOOLS' SOCCER
by Paul O'Brien

Willows, has signed schoolboy forms for Liverpool.

The Warrington team is:

Farnworth, who created a shock in the Lancashire Cup by defeating Manchester after two replays, visit Bootle in another English match. The match is at Bootle Stadium (10.15).

With Wirral not playing their English third round game against Crewe until November 23 (7.0) under the Crewe Alex lights focus on the

In Welsh Shield games on Saturday morning, Chester entertain Crewe at Overleigh School (10.30), while Flint receive Ellesmere Port at Flint Town United's ground (11.0).

Chester have not yet chosen their side, but Flint have chosen:

[illegible column of names]

Staged at St Dominics, it was largely due to the goalkeeping heroics of James Shields and a last minute Frank Pimblett goal that Huyton overcame Preston 2-1 to progress to round two. This proved to be a much more straightforward affair with the lads accounting for Lancaster and Morecambe by a 6-1 scoreline. Unsurprisingly, Pat Phillips bagged a brace and a hat trick from Roy Clarke highlighted the squad's strength. Despite an impressive goal tally (including some vital strikes), Roy was unable to secure a regular starting place. King George V was the venue for the third round tie with Pendle taking the 'Away' dressing room. Phillips and McClatchey grabbed four goals apiece as Huyton romped home 9-0. Victory in the fourth round would have taken our Boys into the last 32 of the competition for the first time for 22 years but when Blackpool took a 2-0 lead the odds were stacked against them. In an

scot & Huyton Reporter

Page 22—Friday January 15 1971

amazing turnaround, the referee's whistle brought the game to a close with Huyton having gone nap-handed and scored five times to seal a magnificent win.

Before the second phase of the competition was under way, Mr Bleasdale had resigned as manager to take up a teaching post in the Gilbert and Ellice Islands in the Western Pacific. Before doing so, he attended training for his new job in Farnborough. This enabled him to keep tabs on the team's progress and take up his place on the touchline for some of the subsequent matches. His mentor and co-manager Eddie Kilshaw once again stepped up to the plate to lead the Boys to glory.

Derby Boys, captained by England midfielder Steve Powell, were the visitors to Huntleys for round five. Powell was later signed by Brian Clough for Derby County and would go on to play on 420 occasions for The Rams. But, in Reid and Pimblett, he more than met his match as the duo inspired Huyton to a narrow 1-0 win. North East outfit Bishop Auckland brought 1,000 fans to Wilson Road for round six to swell the attendance to a remarkable 2,700. In horrible conditions, the game was only four minutes old when Reid chipped the ball to Phillips who nodded it into Tobin's path and Don made no mistake as he left the keeper stranded to the delight of most of those present. Shortly before halftime they again had reason to celebrate when Pimblett's defence-splitting pass

released Phillips who produced an unstoppable strike to send the home side in 2-0 up at the break. The Bish upped their game in the second half and were rewarded when they reduced the deficit. Passions were high on and off the pitch and the atmosphere was electric but the biggest cheer of the day was reserved for the final whistle which prompted a joyous pitch invasion by the Huyton faithful.

The quarter final brought about the team's only away fixture at Dartford versus North Kent. Mr Bleasdale greeted the lads at the train station brandishing a homemade banner prophetically exclaiming 'Huyton Boys – The English Schools Trophy Winners,1971'. North Kent were recognised as formidable opposition but Huyton put in their best performance of the season (and perhaps of all time) to register a 4-1 win with goals provided by Reid, Murphy and a brace from, of course, Phillips

A semi-final versus Barking was the reward with the added bonus of the match being staged at Anfield - a boyhood dream for many of the participants. Barking's victory over Neath in the quarters meant that a difficult decision for the ESFA had been avoided. Bizarrely, Neath had stated that if they had progressed they would be unhappy about meeting Huyton under Anfield's floodlights. Barking won 2-1 so the problem was averted. Having attended the North Kent game, Barking's manager was full of praise, "I watched this Huyton team against Kent and outside of the League programme they are the sweetest and most organised side you could wish to see". The lads confirmed his findings in a tight contest in which McClatchey was the hero with two goals. The Prescot Reporter stated "It was the speed and opportunism of McClatchey in the penalty area that proved to be the decisive factor which turned the game for the home side." Barking stuck to their task though and with five minutes remaining pulled one back to set up a grandstand finish. If McClatchey was the main man upfront, his defensive equivalent was Keith Saunders. Along with Ged Thomas, he marshalled the backline to ensure that the Barking threat was thwarted. At full time the 7,441 present raised the roof to celebrate Huyton reaching the two-legged final and set up the Association's greatest achievement since its conception 25 years earlier.

THE FINAL

Huyton Boys' big test

by Paul O'Brien

HUYTON BOYS have a full strength line-up available for this evening's English Trophy final, first leg, against Stoke Boys, at Stoke City's ground (7.0).

Team manager, Eddie Kilshaw has named 15 players—the 11 who were successful in the semi-final against Barking, plus goalkeeper Jones, full-back Rea and forwards Clarke and Henderson—in Huyton's bid to win the trophy for the first time.

The second leg will be at Goodison Park next Monday, with a 7.30 kick-off.

Huyton Boys (From):—Shields, Jones; Evans, Saunders, Rea; Reid, Bradford, Pimblett, Murphy, McClatchey, Phillips; Clarke, Thomas, Tobin, Henderson.

A special report on tonight's game will appear in tomorrow's Daily Post.

Huyton's midfield pair, Peter Reid (left) and skipper Frank Pimblett, who could play a vital role in tonight's game.

On Wednesday 14 April 1971 at Stoke City's Victoria Ground, Huyton Boys faced a Stoke-on-Trent team that boasted a fine pedigree in the competition. They had won the trophy on two previous occasions whereas our team were in uncharted territory. The game brought about a reunion for the side's bosses as Eddie Kilshaw and his Stoke counterpart Ralph O'Donnell had both been on the books at Sheffield Wednesday back in the early '50s. McClatchey may have been the king of the semis but Pat Phillips stole his crown in the final. After an assured start by our youngsters, he found the net after just 13 minutes. Stoke enjoyed a great deal of possession at the start of the second half but with 47 minutes on the clock Phillips notched his second. Stoke were no match for the rampant Huytonians and although they did reduce the margin in the 40th minute with a blistering shot from the halfway line, it only inspired our boys to reach new heights. The Victoria Ground had witnessed many exceptional examples of top drawer wing-play from Stoke's most famous son Stanley Matthews. Throughout the game, Ray Murphy delighted the crowd with his Matthew-like performance and he was rewarded for his efforts with Huyton's third goal. Then, when McClatchey's fine strike hit an upright, it was no surprise that Phillips rattled home the rebound to complete his hat trick, prompting the Reporter to describe his contribution in glowing terms, "He lurked around the penalty area like a tiger and pounced on his chances with a hungry determination and cool precision." Stoke were a quality side but the collective drive, determination and superior ability of Huyton Boys meant that they had at least one hand on the ESFA Trophy at the halfway stage of the contest. Five days later, Huyton and Prescot witnessed a mass exodus as the local population beat a path to Goodison Park for the final's second leg.

Huyton get a hand on that trophy

By Paul O'Brien

Huyton Boys don't need to be told how good their 4-1 victory over Stoke Boys in the first leg of the English Trophy Final at Stoke City's ground last night was — the applause of the 8,833 as they left the pitch did that.

From the start Huyton showed that the best form of defence is attack. They settled more quickly than the home side, and it was no surprise when centre forward Pat Phillips put them a goal up after 13 minutes.

Most people thought that the ball would pass way above the cross bar when Phillips hit it towards goal from 12 yards but to the amazement of all and especially Stoke goalkeeper, Stuart Thomas it dropped a yard in front of goal and

hovered into the top of the net.

Stoke's midfield trio Frank Pimblett, Peter Reid and Don Tobin, who had one of his best games, all played a part in the build up to this goal. In fact the only time they lost control of the centre of the field was early in the second half when Stoke threatened to equalise.

As it was 12 minutes after half time Phillips scored his second and although Stoke fought back with a superb 30 yards goal by right back John Lumsden, further goals by outside right Ray Murphy and Phillips gave Huyton a victory margin which did not flatter them.

Murphy, who delighted the crowd with some fine runs, rounded off a Tobin-Phillips move by holding off challenges from two defenders and sliding the ball under Thomas.

Phillips completed his hat-trick with a fine angled shot after inside right Derek McClatchey had hit the inside of an upright after a run which split the home defence.

Huyton were at their best in the final 25 minutes when they drove forward in such a way that Stoke were far too occupied keeping themselves to give any thought to performing the deficit before the second leg at Goodison Park next Monday.

Stoke, with players who left half Pat Johnson, a member of the England squad; Lumsden, a right back who can hammer the ball goalwards; and a dangerous inside right by the name of Matthews — Stuart that is — will obviously give a better account of themselves in the return match but the odds are on Huyton.

LIVERPOOL STADIUM WRESTLING

TO-MORROW (FRIDAY), APRIL 16, AT 7.30.

BIG RETURN CONTEST

TONY RODA v GEOFF PORTZ (Bradford)
(LL/Manager's Champion of USA)

JOHNNY CZESLAW (Poland) v STEVE VIDOR BELL (Lamont)

ALBERT WALL (Doncaster) v PAT BEACH (Birmingham)

ALL ACTION TAG MATCH

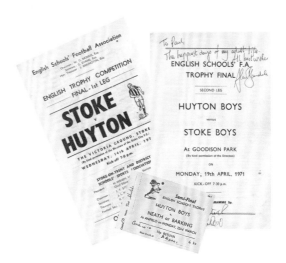

English Schools' Football Association

ENGLISH TROPHY COMPETITION FINAL - 1st LEG

STOKE v HUYTON

THE VICTORIA GROUND, STOKE
WEDNESDAY, 14th APRIL, 197
Kick-off 7-0 p.m.

STOKE-ON-TRENT AND DISTRICT SCHOOLS' SPORTS ASSOCIATION

To Paul,
The happiest days of my adult life. All best wishes

ENGLISH SCHOOLS' F.A.
TROPHY FINAL

SECOND LEG

HUYTON BOYS

versus

STOKE BOYS

At Goodison Park
(By kind permission of the Directors)

ON

MONDAY, 19th APRIL, 1971
KICK-OFF 7-30 p.m.

Semi-Final
ENGLISH SCHOOL'S TROPHY
HUYTON BOYS
v
NEATH or BARKING
At Anfield on Monday, 22nd March

The match programme summed up the size of the task facing Stoke if they were to overcome the 4-1 deficit, "Skipper Frank Pimblett, who was only 14 last month, and his midfield partner Peter Reid have been the engine room of a team that has grown in stature with every game. They are the perfect foils for one another, and as a partnership they have no equals. Behind them is a powerful defence, strengthened with the addition of Lancashire player Roy Bradford and his Grammar School colleague Gerard Thomas. Right back Tommy Evans has also been a member of the Lancashire squad, while left back Keith Saunders must at present be the finest player in his position in the country. Goalkeeper Jimmy Shields, in spite of tremendous competition in the squad, has finally made the custodian's job his own. Yet it is up front where the strength of Huyton really lies, with six County class players, competing for four places. Most of the goals come from lethal header Pat Phillips, at centre forward, and from the quick-silver Lancashire striker, Derek McClatchey; yet Brian Henderson and Roy Clarke have scored over 20 goals between them and cannot establish a regular place. Ray Murphy is a Lancashire player and England Trialist, while left winger Don Tobin is considered by many shrewd judges to be the finest attacking player in Lancashire. These lads are supported admirably by Brian Jones, Mick Rea, Brian Scott, Gerard McGuinness and Andy Rogan, who have filled the breaches admirably when called upon. We salute all these boys for their magnificent achievement!" Not wishing to jump the gun, the "achievement" only referred to them reaching the final. Whilst the game was not as eventful as the first leg, in the 15th minute Pat Phillips picked up where he'd left off in the Potteries and latched onto a 60-yard pass from Saunders to register his 25th goal of an amazing season and the only goal of the game. The referee's full time whistle signalled an aggregate victory of 5-1 and was greeted with delight by the crowd of 7,130 who saluted a team able to boast that they had become the first side from an urban area to ever win the English Schools Trophy.

The Huyton Boys team of 1971 shared a tremendous team spirit fostered by Messrs Bleasdale and Kilshaw and benefitted

from the hard work done behind the scenes by Chairman **Bob Hurst,** Vice-Chairman **Terry Sweeney,** Secretary Ian Robertson and Coach and Treasurer **Steve Bradford**. Shortly after the game, the team received a congratulatory telegram from Huyton MP Harold Wilson and a few weeks later Huyton Council held a civic reception for the team at which each member of the history-making squad received a special commemorative plaque to acknowledge their amazing achievement. Huyton Boys – The English Schools Trophy Winners,1971!

Footynote:

In 1975, Bleasdale changed career completely and became, in the years that followed, a renowned playwright, both on stage and screen, writing most notably 'THE BOYS FROM THE BLACKSTUFF', 'GBH', 'SCULLY' and 'ARE YOU LONESOME TONIGHT?' However, he has often been quoted as saying that his best achievement by far in public life was being team manager of Huyton Boys.

THE STORY OF THE SEASON

HUYTON BOYS 1970/71 ESFA TROPHY

3/10/70
Round One   Huyton   2 (Henderson, Pimblett)
             Preston   1

24/10/70
Round Two   Huyton   6 (Clarke 3, Phillips 2, Bradford)
             Lancs & Morcambe 1

14/11/70
Round Three Huyton   9 (Phillips 4, McClatchey 4, Murphy)
             Pendle   0

5/12/70
Round Four   Huyton   5 (Phillips 3, McClatchey, Murphy)
             Blackpool 2

16/1/71
Round Five   Huyton   1 (Phillips)
             Derby   0

13/2/71
Round Six   Huyton   2 (Tobin, Phillips)
             Bishop Auckland 1

27/2/71
¼ Final   Huyton 4 (Reid, Phillips 2, Murphy)
             North Kent 1

22/3/71
Semi Final   Huyton 2 (McClatchey 2)
             Barking 0

14/4/71
Final   Stoke 1
(1st Leg)   Huyton 4 (Phillips 3, Murphy)

19/4/71
Final   Huyton 1 (Phillips)
(2nd Leg)   Stoke   0

             (Huyton won 5-1 on aggregate)

HUYTON BOYS 1970/71 DIMMER CUP

6/10/70
Round One   Huyton   7 (Henderson 3, Clarke 2, McClatchey 2)
             Wirral   2

4/1/70
Round Two   Huyton   6 (Tobin 2, Phillips 2, Thomas, McClatchey)
             Bootle   1

15/3/71
Semi Final   Huyton 2 (Tobin, Phillips)
             Chester 1

28/4/71
Final   Huyton 2 (Bradford, Tobin)
(1st Leg)   Kirkby   1

3/5/71
Final   Kirkby   0
(2nd Leg)   Huyton 2 (Murphy, Clarke)

HUYTON BOYS 1970/71 LANCASHIRE CUP

10/10/70
Round One   Huyton   4 (Phillips 3, Clarke)
             Chadderton 2

21/11/70
Round Two   Huyton   3 (Phillips 2, Tobin)
             Wigan   0

9/1/71
Round Three Huyton   6 (Phillips 3, McClatchey, Murphy, Pimblett)
             Prestwich 1

11/3/71
Semi Final   Liverpool 1
             Huyton   2 (Murphy, Bradford)

29/3/71
Final   Blackpool 5 (McClatchey 2)
(1st Leg)   Huyton   2

6/5/71
Final   Huyton   4 (Phillips 3, Clarke)
(2nd Leg)
             Blackpool 2

             (Blackpool won 7-6 on aggregate)

Season Summary

Games Played 21, - Wins 20, Draws 0, Losses 1

Scorers - Phillips 31, McClatchey 13, Clarke 8, Murphy 7, Tobin 6, Henderson 4, Bradford 3, Pimblett 2, Thomas 1, Reid 1

76 Goals scored, 21 Conceded

Although future Huyton Boys teams have not been able to scale such dizzy heights as the Team of 71, they have enjoyed a great deal of continued success. The formation of Knowsley Borough Council in 1974 brought about changes to the way in which schools football operated. Players from primary schools continued to represent Huyton whilst senior school pupils played for Knowsley. A hugely influential figure around this time and for decades to come was **Bob Downing** whose contribution to local schoolboy football was recognised in September 2019 when, at a celebration evening in his honour, a long line of notable players paid tribute to him. Others who are worthy of our gratitude for their contribution and for bringing success to the area include **Brian Summerskill, Matt Aslanian, Paul O'Brien, Julie King, Colm Whelan, Andy Corcoran, P Gallagher, W Hall, Kerstine Hogg, David McDiarmid** and **Dave Sweeney.** In recent years their boots have been filled by **Dave Harvey, Barry Grant, Danny Embleton, Dan Evans, Karl Bell, Tom Killen** and **Tony James.**

60's

80's

70's

90's

The youngsters chosen to represent the District were whittled down to a manageable squad size following extensive trials. Schools would put forward players for consideration based upon their performances for the school team in league and cup games. From top to bottom Halsnead Primary, Sylvester (1937), Malvern (1972), St Columbas (1954 & 1967)

THE DALLAS CUP

In 1991, Knowsley Borough Council agreed to send a squad of under-19s to the USA to participate for the first time in the Dallas Cup. This was a huge decision by the local authority, reflecting its commitment to local football. It also confirmed the Council's acknowledgment of the cultural impact involvement in the tournament could have upon the youngsters fortunate enough to participate. The initiative signalled the beginning of a fantastic 30-year relationship shared by the competition organisers and those responsible for arranging Knowsley's involvement. Established in 1980 by the Texas Longhorn Soccer Club, the Dallas Cup has developed into one of the most competitive tournaments in the world. Top clubs from around the globe take part including Real Madrid, Barcelona, PSG and AC Milan as well as English Premier League outfits. The competitions' alumni read like a 'Who's Who' with the likes of Michael Owen, Wayne Rooney, Andrea Pirlo, Raul, Chicarito and David Beckham amongst its ranks. Entry to the tournament is by invitation only, with the young players staying at the homes of host families for the duration of the three-week trip. Many long-term friendships have been forged in this way and the Knowsley squad members' families have often reciprocated the hospitality by welcoming their American hosts to Liverpool.

Knowsley's involvement in the tournament can be traced back to when Council Officer **John Scott** (who sadly passed away in 2002) saw first hand the impact the competition had upon its participants. In addition to putting the wheels in motion to create our own very successful 'Liverpool - Knowsley International Youth Soccer Tournament', John set about unraveling the red tape to send our young lads across the pond.

From the outset, it was agreed that if our lads were to be involved, it was going to be done properly. They would not just go along to make up the numbers – Knowsley would do their utmost to win the prestigious Boot and Ball trophy. Annually, a few months before the Dallas Cup kicked off, local coaches would be drafted in to identify the best players and to mould an 18-man squad capable of not only performing on the pitch but to also act as ambassadors for the Borough. It is to the credit of all those who attended the hugely successful Dallas trips, that the invitation was extended year after year. In addition to the team attempting to progress as far as possible in the competition, scouts from US colleges and universities would monitor each game with a view to offering scholarships to the players who displayed the greatest potential. Consequently, the lives of dozens of promising Knowsley youngsters were changed for the better.

Whilst the first decade of Knowsley's Dallas Cup exploits was deemed a success on a number of fronts, reaching the semi-finals in 2000 proved to be a landmark achievement. After coming so close to walking away with the trophy, all concerned were determined to go the extra mile and bring it home to Huyton. In 2006, Tranmere Rovers coach **Kevin Hodgson**, who had previously been a Knowsley player in 1996 and '97, took the team to the Final only for them to be defeated 3-1 by locals Texas Black Heat FC. However, Knowsley were now regularly reaching the latter stages of the competition and in 2011 the boys finally got their hands on the coveted Bat and Ball trophy. The team's only defeat came in a 2-1 reversal versus DC United but they qualified for the Final by defeating Andromeda SC (3-1), Davis Legacy (5-2), Santos FC (8-3) and C2-Elite (2-1).

On Sunday 24 April at FC Dallas Park Stadium, they faced Canadian side Ajax Gunners. Adam Black, Paul Mooney and Steven Tames added to an own goal to run out 4-2 victors and add Knowsley's name to the list of winners. The successful squad of 2011 consisted of **Luke Edwards, Adam Black, Todd Blaney, Michael Brown, Phillip Davies, Alex Ellis, Shaun Holden, Nathan Hopkins-Brabin, John Humphreys, Michael Jordan, Paul Ledsham, Adam McCarthy, Josh Molloy, Paul Mooney, Jordan Nield, Chris Piercy, Steven Tames and Adam Wilson.** Knowsley's triumph was due in no small part to the efforts of a team of dedicated individuals who, for decades, worked tirelessly behind the scenes. Administrators, coaches and team managers included **Dave Mercer, Alan Tyrell, Eddie Jennings, Andy Gray, Barry Lloyd, Sharon Doyle, Leslie Pilkington, Lisa Corkhill** and **Gordon Dickson.** Although Knowsley Youth U-19s could not repeat this feat, they came close in 2017 when they again reached the Final before tasting defeat to Liverpool Foundation by a 2-1 scoreline. However, every cloud has a silver lining and it was reported that every member of Knowsley's 2017 squad received the offer of a university scholarship – a remarkable achievement. Unfortunately, three years later Knowsley Borough Council made the extremely difficult decision to cease funding the Dallas trip. The powers that be reported that the cost to Knowsley council tax payers had been £37,000 in 2019 which, due to government cuts, was difficult to justify. Ironically, a few months later the Covid-19 pandemic, which caused worldwide disruption and affected millions of people, caused the cancellation of the Dallas Cup. Only time will tell if the funds can be found in the future to rekindle Knowsley's involvement in a tournament which for three decades enhanced so many local people's lives.

THE AMATEUR GAME

The desire to play football locally has existed for many years but hasn't always been encouraged.

On 22 June 1889, the Prescot Reporter informed its readers that "On Tuesday at the Petty Sessions held at Prescot, Peter Casslin, Peter Maloney, Patrick Cavanagh, James Moran, Richard Thomas, James Brogan, Edward Cavanagh and James Thomas were summonsed for playing football in a public place - PS Walker stated that at quarter past one o'clock on Saturday, the 9th instant, he saw the defendants playing football in Moss Place, Prescot. He watched them for ten minutes. They were divided into two sides and they played like a regular football team and shouted "Off-side" and other football phrases. Superintendent Barker said this playing of football was a perfect nuisance in the town and property owners complained of their windows being broken and property damaged. The Chairman said that this kind of thing could not be allowed to go on and they must understand if any of them were brought up again they would be heavily punished." The culprits were each fined two shillings and six pence and court costs or faced seven day's imprisonment. It's not clear if such a hard-line approach worked but the men of the area were soon participating in organised football even though they had to travel in order to do so.

Early teams included Whiston Ramblers, Huyton Quarry Recs, Prescot Rovers, Whiston North End, Huyton AFC and Tushingham Brickworks and they found competitive football by joining competitions such as the Stanley League, the Church of England League, the South Liverpool League and the Liverpool and District Combination.

However, by the late 1930s dozens of local teams had found a home following the formation of the Prescot and District Football League.

THE PRESCOT & DISTRICT FOOTBALL LEAGUE

In early 1939, with the prospect of new pitches and improved facilities on the horizon, meetings were held to explore the possibility of forming a football league for Prescot, Huyton and adjacent areas. It soon became apparent that a host of teams existed, all keen to become involved. One of the first tasks was to appoint the league officials and by June the committee was in place. **Tom Stone** was named as Patron with **Mr J Lucas** installed as President. There were four Vice-presidents (**Messrs Pilkington, MacDermott, Tushingham** and **Seddon**) with another 13 interested parties completing the line-up. Secretary Mr Winn was inundated with requests from local teams desperate to be involved and on 2 September 1939 the first fixtures took place. St Theresa's were pitched against St Aloysius whilst the other debut First Division games were Huyton Labour versus Holt, Dovecot v Prescot Albion, Whiston v Prescot Blues, Tushingham v Prescot Ceteanco and Longview Athletic opposed Prescot Imps. The Second Division was exclusively for under-19s and had Dovecot versus Prescot North End, Prescot Rovers v Roby, Longview Tenants v Prescot Utd and Prescot Rangers taking on Prescot Wanderers. These matches had been eagerly awaited but the timing could not have been worse as it coincided with the outbreak of WW2. Although the league was temporarily suspended, it was going to take more than Hitler's invasion of Poland to stop our teams attempting to secure the three trophies which had been generously donated. After a stuttering start, the Prescot & District Football League grew in stature and was hugely important to local amateur football for decades to come.

THE HUYTON & DISTRICT SUNDAY LEAGUE

Formed in 1971, the Huyton and District Sunday League existed for twenty years before merging with the Kirkby Newtown Soccer Combination to form the Knowsley Sunday League. In the early days, the Eagle were regularly the cream of the crop although they were given a good run for their money by, amongst others, Boundary FC, Rose & Crown, Dovecot, Farmers Arms, Quiet Man, Huntley & Palmers, Huyton Quarry Recs, Huyton Park, St Columbas, Webbro, Caledonia, Green Dragon, Wardonia, Victoria Athletic, Greyhound, Barley Mow, Winfield Utd, Meccano and St Agnes Labour. The League Committee included such luminaries as **Eddie Edwards, JR McDermott, R Birchall, D Monteith, W Swindells, W Fulham, J Woods** and **K Montgomery**. These were good men and true who often put in serious hours to ensure that amateur football continued to operate, often against the odds. There was a time when the dozens of pubs and clubs in the area operated a football team. For a host of reasons, not only have the teams disappeared, so have the majority of the watering holes.

A shortage of referees was a constant problem season after season and, despite numerous efforts to recruit more men in the middle, the powers that be conceded defeat in this respect and in 1991 reluctantly took the decision to merge the Huyton League with the Kirkby Newtown Soccer Combination to form the Knowsley Sunday League. This continued to serve the wider community before eventually calling it a day.

St Dominics

There have been many exceptional local teams but the best Saturday outfit was undoubtedly the Doms.

Formed in 1935 by the male parishioners of St Dominics Church, located at the time in Yew Tree cemetery, few teams made a bigger sustained impact on Saturday amateur football than St Dominics FC. Prior to the outbreak of WW2, the team engaged in regular friendly matches under player/manager **Jack Quinn**. His early teammates included **Frank McHale, Tom Watson, Jack Douglas, Alex Galvin, Pat Redmond, Larry Redmond, Jim Mountaine, Joe Hopkins, Paddy Fay, George McKinley, Pat McKeown and Joe McGuinness**. Many of these players remained involved with the club in various capacities for decades to come.

The team reconvened after the hostilities had ended and in 1948 joined the Catholic Young Men's Society League. Buoyed by the experience, they entered a team in the Prescot & District League and found immediate success. In their debut 1949/50 season, the first of dozens of trophies was secured when they lifted the Earl of Stanley Cup. Amongst their number was **Terry Ledgerton** who in 1951 would make his Football League entrance with 2nd division Brentford. He was the first of many Doms players to make the step up and scouts would regularly be seen on the touchline. In addition to Ledgerton, **Frank Gamble, Paul Fitzpatrick, Dave Martindale, Lee Trundle, Tony Kelly, Dave Bleasdale, Graeme Worsley, Joe Duncan** and **Dave Higgins** wore the club's colours and also earned their Football League spurs. Others, such as **Victor Martindale, Tex Kirwan, Brian Finnigan** and **Billy Huyton** shunned the chance of pro football when presented to them. In addition, centre half **Keith Garland** enjoyed great times in a Doms kit in the 1970s before upping sticks to New Zealand where, not only did he play international football on 13 occasions for the All Whites, he later took on the role of Assistant Coach of the Kiwi squad.

During St Dominics' lengthy existence, barely a season went by without another piece of silverware finding its way to their bulging trophy cabinet. They achieved numerous successes in the CYMS, Prescot & District, Liverpool League and County Combination. The club also proudly came out on top in a host of cup competitions to break record after record. In 1981/82 season they became the first team to win both the Liverpool Challenge Cup and Lancashire Amateur Cup in the same campaign. Amazingly, they also walked away with the Liverpool County Combination title, achieving a unique treble. The following year the feat was repeated and the Challenge Cup was retained for the next two seasons cementing their dominance as the top Saturday team for miles around.

Throughout the Nineties this continued as the team won the County Combination five times and at the turn of the Millennium they were still picking up silverware. The Doms again lifted the Lancashire Amateur Cup in 2001/02 and retained it the following year. 2005/06 proved to be a particularly poignant campaign when the Brickwork Cup and Peter Coyne Cup were both won in similar dramatic fashion. St Aloysius and Waterloo Dock provided the opposition and both finals finished in 2-2 draws. **Jeff Dodd** and **Bobby Jones** got on the scoresheet in each contest but the real hero was goalkeeper **Robbie O'Connor** whose crucial saves in both penalty shoot-outs handed St Dominics the trophies, the first time this particular double had been achieved since 1956. Sadly, following the 2008/09 campaign, after more than 70 years of unbridled success, the club reluctantly called it a day. Similar to many clubs, the management and committee found it increasingly difficult to operate at the level they had always achieved but there can be little doubt that St Dominics were synonymous with top drawer amateur football.

For decades, not content with cleaning up on a Saturday, many Doms' players also turned out on a Sunday for the legendary Eagle FC.

Eagle FC

The Eagle & Child pub stood on Liverpool Road, on land currently occupied by McDonalds and the Lidl supermarket. There had been a football team associated with the Eagle for many years but, following an amalgamation with the Longview Labour club's successful setup, they soared to local and national success. Throughout the Seventies, the side romped to numerous league and cup titles in the Huyton & District League before taking on a fresh challenge by joining the Liverpool Sunday League for the 1980/81 season. A third place finish in their debut campaign confirmed the belief that the team could compete at this level and it wasn't long before they were staking their claim to being one of the country's best Sunday League sides.

The Eagle always attracted a large and very vocal band of supporters which ensured a great atmosphere at their Jubilee Park or Alt Park home matches and it wasn't unheard of for as many as three double-decker buses to be necessary to transport the fans to away games and finals. Inspired by player/manager **Peter Rowlands**, his assistant **Bunner O'Keeffe** and an extremely active committee with **Eddie Robb** fulfilling secretarial duties, the Eagle reached the pinnacle of their performances during the 1982/83 campaign. At the conclusion of this monumental season, the trophy cabinet in the famous Eagle hostelry contained the Ken Gillies Memorial Trophy, the Liverpool & District Premier League Winners Cup and the most attractive and prestigious of all, the FA Sunday Cup.

Donated to the FA on 15 June 1964 by the Shah of Iran, this quickly became the most sought after trophy for amateur Sunday teams with, at its most popular, in excess of 1,000 clubs involved in the competition. At Runcorn FC's Canal Street ground on 1 May 1983, 3,000 supporters of the Eagle and their opponents Lee Chapel North witnessed what many consider to be one of the finest amateur football matches ever staged. Considering the atrocious weather conditions and the sloping pitch, the level of football on display in a fantastic Sunday Cup Final was remarkable. The Eagle were quicker out of the blocks than their Basildon opposition and the enigmatic Joey Duncan almost put Rowlands' side ahead twice in the opening ten minutes before Brian Blythe volleyed over with the goal at his mercy. However, on 30 minutes, it was Lee Chapel who opened the scoring with a fine header from former Chelsea player Tony Gamma. To make matters worse, Eagle legend Tosh Hendry received his marching orders leaving them to play the majority of the game with ten men.

On the stroke of half-time, Steff Hagan was brought down in the box and the ref pointed to the spot. When Dave Parker's penalty was saved and the official blew his whistle for half-time seconds before the rebound was forced over the line, it looked like it was not going to be the Eagle's day. But this side didn't know when it was beaten and despite Chapel's one man advantage, it was they who had their backs to the wall. The 'home' crowd were also playing their part in driving the lads from the Moss on and their efforts paid off in the 76th minute of a pulsating match. Joey Duncan's pinpoint free kick found Parker who powered a fine header past the keeper to make amends for his earlier faux pas. The game excitingly swung to and fro but no further goals could be added. As the ref signalled the end of extra time, the Lee Chapel contingent celebrated as if to indicate that the replay would be a formality.

The following weekend, supported by the fund-raising efforts of the Eagle faithful, the squad travelled down south and checked into a hotel before going to watch Luton Town versus Everton in what proved to be Steve McMahon's last game for the Blues. The Toffees 5-1 victory over the Hatters set the Eagle up nicely to do their bit for the north/south divide. Urged on by tremendous travelling support, which included a Scottish Pipe Band, the Eagle eased to victory over Lee Chapel 2-1, a score which flattered the Essex outfit. Peter Rowlands squad for their finest hour consisted of **Mick Riley, Dave Higgins, Tosh Hendry, Mick Rea, Tommy Riley, Billy Roberts, John Perry, Pat McCarthy, Brian Blythe, Joey Duncan, David Parker, Tommy Bramwell, Steff Hagan, John Warriner,** and **Dave Elliott.** The Eagle had represented

the Liverpool Sunday League superbly and followed in the footsteps of previous local winners Lobster, Fantail and Dingle Rail. Unfortunately, although they again reached the final, the Eagle side couldn't repeat the feat the following season when Lee Chapel gained revenge with a 4-3 extra time win. Although the Eagle (later known as Salerno Eagle) continued to pick up trophies for many years after their 80s successes, that particular period was undoubtedly when they were most potent and that team is still revered to this day.

In recent years participating in amateur football has, for a host of reasons, become less popular locally and nationally. However, the Sunday Cup is still the trophy every club wants to win and in 2010/11 season Huyton's **Paddock FC** came painfully close to doing so in an historic match played at Prenton Park. The club formed in 2001 and, during the ensuing decade, enjoyed a meteoric rise through the ranks of the Liverpool Sunday League. After entering the Third Division, they gained promotion in two of their first three seasons and followed that by winning every fixture as they stormed to the Premier Division title. Along the way the club also picked up the Liverpool Premier Cup twice before reaching the Sunday Cup Final. Paddock were run by **Billy** and **Darren Owens** who were ably assisted by secretary **Mike Duffy**, coach **David Agga**, physio **Richie Burcher**, sponge man **Jim Scanlon** and additional committee members **Carl Owens, Mark Thomas, Denis Kelly** and **Sheila Holleran**. Their route to Prenton Park involved victories over Ford Motors (6-1), Dawdon Colliery (3-0), Hetton Lyons (3-2), Queens Park (2-1), Knighton Arms (4-1) and Comets SC (4-1).

On Sunday 1 May 2011 at the home of Tranmere Rovers Paddock faced Oyster Martyrs - the first time since the competition's formation in 1964 that two clubs from the same city and league had faced eachother in the Final. In front of 1,105 spectators both sides gave their all and the game could have gone either way. Unfortunately for the Huytonians, with 15 minutes remaining it was Oyster's Leighton McGiverin who broke the deadlock and, despite a couple of strong Paddock penalty claims, it was the team from Croxteth whose name was engraved on the trophy. Although defeated, Paddock came extremely close to joining the illustrious list of winners and the squad who had done themselves proud were **Robbie O'Connor, Anthony Shinks, John Shaw, Steven Maddocks, Kieran Dolan, John Harrison, Paul Langley, Tony Langley, Lee Stacy, Steven Brown, Joseph Duncan, Paul Whelan, Paul Inman, Brodie Kearns, Jamie Henders, Joseph Marsden, Lee Prior, Johnathon Boggan, Stephen Hussey** and **John Reilly.**
Nowadays, with open-age players and teams thin on the ground, chances of a local side lifting the Sunday Cup are limited to just a few candidates. However, Huyton Cons, Mayfair FC, etc. will do their upmost to add their name to the illustrious list of previous winners.

Paddock FC   **Huyton Cons FC**

JUNIOR FOOTBALL

Junior football teams have existed in our area for the best part of a century. The story of the development of local clubs and leagues could alone fill the pages of a sizeable book. However, space is at a premium and dictates that only a short but important section of 'Huyton's Titans' can be dedicated to this aspect of our area's football narrative.

In years gone by, with notable exceptions such as Whiston Juniors, St Anne's Rovers Huyton Labour and the extremely successful Gleneagles, junior football clubs often consisted of just a single team assembled by an individual or small group of people. Teams were frequently ran by parents wanting to give their children and their friends the chance to take their games from the street to the park in an organised fashion. In addition, representatives of organisations such as youth clubs, churches, pubs and workplaces would form teams in order to do their bit for the community. Team names often reflected this or gave a nod to the addresses of the managers and players. This was evident in some of the participant teams in the Prescot and District Junior League. Formed in 1939, the under 18 and 16 divisions contained teams such as Whiston Youth Club, Churchdown, Fairclough YC, Tarbock Athletic, Crawfords, Dovecot & Huyton Juniors and St Edwards. The League presented youngsters with the first opportunity outside of school to locally play against eachother in a regulated format.

Soon after, the Huyton with Roby JFL was established. Competing for the Angus Johnstone Cup and the B P Jordan Shield, this League consisted of two divisions of 14 teams. Local outfits such as Endmoor Utd, Gordon Boys, Haydn Boys and Roby Juniors would compete at under 13 and under 15 level against teams from as far afield as Aintree, Halewood, Norris Green and Maghull.

When, in the mid-Sixties, families moved into the recently built Cantril Farm estate, it wasn't long before a thriving junior football league was formed. The Cantril Farm Junior Football League was set up in 1968 and just a year later, due to the efforts of its 56 volunteers, it boasted three divisions catering for in excess of 500 players aged between 8 and 16 years of age. Every Sunday, Mab Lane pitches would stage dozens of games officiated by a legion of 24 referees who all lived on the estate. This weekly festival of football once prompted a watching Dixie Dean to comment "I've seen football played all over the world but I've never seen anything quite like this !"

At the start of the Seventies, **Harry Atkinson** and **Andy Kearns** set up a new Huyton Junior League. Early documents reveal that their intention was to give youngsters who couldn't secure a place in their school teams an opportunity to get involved. However, such was the success of the league, it soon attracted a host of teams of varying ability which included some of the best players around at the time.

In addition to Harry and Andy, the hard-working committee also included **H Higham, E Sabatina, W Joynson, S Faye, DW Russell, C Ralph, P McGavan, T Harbourne** and **K Avery**. Largely due to their efforts, the League became hugely popular and was crucial to the Huyton football scene for many years.

When, in the 1980s, the local landscape began to change and many of the organisations which ran teams disappeared or became less popular, it could have signaled the end of local junior football. It is to the credit of a huge number of committed individuals and their clubs that, although the way in which youngsters are brought together may have changed, there is still a thriving environment which encourages and develops talent and promotes a healthy lifestyle. Nowadays, whilst there are undoubtedly fewer clubs, the likes of Whiston Juniors, Huyton Juniors, AFC Knowsley, MHS, Prescot Cables and St Annes Girls operate dozens of teams of various ages and abilities resulting in as many, if not more, teams than before. They are highly tuned setups which exist to provide the best footballing opportunities for local boys and girls. Unfortunately, although the Knowsley Junior Football Development League, based at Prescot Soccer Centre since 2013, caters for as many as 60 teams of the younger footballers, it's true that many of our teams do have to travel, often far and wide, to participate in established leagues. This puts further pressure on club administrators but, in typical fashion, they rise to the challenge. Without the amazing efforts of these local heroes, so many young footballers, including the professionals mentioned elsewhere in these pages, simply wouldn't have the opportunity to develop and thrive.

There have been many leading lights in this respect. Names that were repeatedly mentioned during the researching of Huyton's Titans include **Harry 'Skip' Warburton, Eddie Sabatina, Keith Skinley, Tony McDonough, Barney Muldoon, Harry Tyrell** and more recently **Michael Corless, Terri Fitzpatrick, Liam Kennedy, Chris Hunt** and **Mike Gibbons**.

It would be impossible to namecheck everyone who has contributed managerially over the best part of a century, but at the risk of offending anyone who should be included but isn't, other managers and key personnel whose names were put forward for recognition include **Harry Atkinson, Ken Avery, Norman Ball, E Birch, Ian Bleasdale, Terry Bleasdale, H Boardman, H Brown, Mark Burke, Jo Carus, Brian Cashman, Chris Cavanagh, Joey Connolly, Ian Cooper, Andrew Critchley, E Davies, Alan Davis, Pop Delaney, Steven Donnelly, Ged Dowling, Les Dowling, John Doyle, P Duffin, Chris Edwards, Mike Edwards, N Edwards, John Elias, Ron Ely, Brian Evans, Kate Farnell, Tony Foley, Mike Forrest, Andy Foster, Catherine Gilhooley, Arthur Green, Les Green, T Harbourne, Mr Heston, Harry Higham, Steve Hook, J Houghton, P Howard, Mike Howe, Dave Hughes, George Hughes, Jimmy Hughes, K Hughes, Ste Hughes, Mr John, Chris Johnson, Paul Jones, Willie Joynson, Andy Kearns, Jonny Kehoe, Liam Kennedy, John Lawless, Tommy Lawless, Ian Leadbetter, Brian Ledsham, Brian Lee, P Longworth, John Lynskey, Norman McCrudden, Eddie McGovern, P McGowan, Ben McIntrye, Don McKenzie, Eddie McKeown, Chris Marsh, M Marsh, Eddie Marshall, Marty Martindale, Sharon Mather, Steven Milburn, Ken Montgomery, Freddie Morgan, Teddy Moss, Tony Murphy, Howard Nulty, Mark O'Neill, Gary Palethorpe, H Parkes, C Ralph, Mr Redhead, John Rennison, Phil Riozzi, Eddie Robb, John Rotherham, W Russell, Eddie Short, John Simnor, G Simpson, Keith Skinley, Billy Skinner, Alf Taylor, Jack Tattan, Alan Tyrell, Steve Waite, Andrew Wallace, Fred Webster, B Wheaton, John Whitehead, Neil Wigglesworth, W Wilkinson, Jamie Woods, Billy Worthington, Joe Wright.**

Sincere apologies to any people (and there will be many) who deserve to be included here but have been inadvertently omitted.

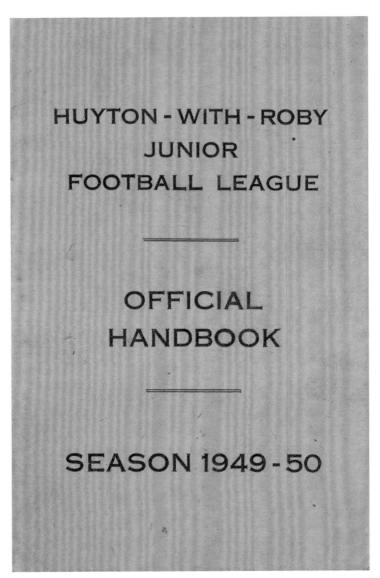

HUYTON - WITH - ROBY
JUNIOR
FOOTBALL LEAGUE

———

OFFICIAL
HANDBOOK

———

SEASON 1949 - 50

St Annes Rovers

Holy Family Social Club

WOMEN'S FOOTBALL
SYLVIA GORE

It is fitting to open the 'Women's Football' section of this book by focussing upon trailblazer Sylvia Gore whose contribution to the development of the women's game should not be underestimated. Born in Prescot on 25 November 1944, Sylvia grew up living in South Avenue with her parents, John and Eileen. Her dad was a regular at Hope Street to watch Cables play and he would often be accompanied by his footy-mad daughter. Sylvia loved the half-time interval when, even before the players had disappeared down the tunnel, she would run onto the pitch to repeatedly slam her ball into the empty net. Cables fans affectionately dubbed her 'the little girl who loved football' but this carried no sway with the Headteacher of Our Lady's School who refused to allow her to join their team despite Sylvia being one of the best players. The decision was in line with the English FA's stance on females playing the game which, introduced on 5 December 1921, effectively banned women from using its pitches. Undaunted and determined, 12-year old Sylvia made the weekly journey with her supportive parents to Manchester to play for Corinthian Ladies. Formed in 1949, Corinthians took part in an ambitious, unsanctioned programme of charity matches at home and abroad. One of Sylvia's proudest memories of this time involved stepping out to play at Milan's San Siro Stadium in front of 80,000 fans.

England's 1966 World Cup success triggered a surge in female interest in the sport. Designed to raise the profile of the game and to encourage young girls to get involved, the Butlins Cup became a popular and prestigious tournament with matches held at holiday camps throughout the United Kingdom. In 1967, Sylvia joined top Cheshire outfit Foden's Ladies and as the Sixties drew to a close they twice won the Butlins Cup defeating Westthorn United in successive seasons.

With Sylvia and Foden's leading the way, attitudes to women's football were changing and in 1971, the FA finally succumbed to public pressure and lifted the ban that had scandalously been in place for 50 years. On 18 November of the following year, a game of huge significance took place at the Ravenscraig Stadium in Greenock, Scotland. With a hardy 500-strong crowd in attendance, England Ladies took to a frozen pitch to face their Scottish counterparts. Trailing 2-0, Sylvia sparked a comeback when she latched onto a pass from teammate Pat Davis, ran half the length of the pitch and coolly slotted the ball past the keeper. England's first ever goal inspired the team to add two further strikes to win the historic encounter.

A couple of years later, Sylvia was a member of the Foden's team that defied the odds to overcome strong favourites Southampton 2-1 in the Mitre Challenge Trophy Final at Bedford Town's ground. Although a midfielder, Sylvia once scored a remarkable 134 goals in one season before, aged 36, she retired from playing due to a troublesome back injury. However, Sylvia continued to be at the forefront of the development of Women's football on a number of fronts in a variety of roles for decades to come. Throughout the Eighties and Nineties, she kept the plates spinning with

©Playing Pasts

managerial and secretarial positions with the Welsh International team, Knowsley Utd and Liverpool Ladies, in addition to taking her place on the FA Women's Committee – an organisation she had lobbied the FA to establish. Sylvia also worked for Knowsley Borough Council as its Women's and Girl's Football Development Officer long before other authorities grasped that particular nettle. Concentrating on the grassroots of the game, she set up leagues and cup competitions and co-ordinated coaching sessions to give young girls opportunities that were never afforded to her. In 1990, Sylvia received the NW Amateur Sports Personality award and she picked up many future accolades in recognition of her contribution as a pioneer of the Women's game. Nine years later, she was presented with a Special Achievement award at the inaugural FA Women's Awards and a year later was honoured by the Queen when she received an MBE. Then, accompanied by her cousin **Carol Parry**, Sylvia travelled to Monte Carlo where she picked up the EUFA Magnificent Seven award.

As women's football became the country's fastest growing sport, Sylvia was in the thick of its evolution and in October 2014 she was delighted to be inducted into the National Football Museum's Hall of Fame. Fittingly, in 2016 to mark International Women's Day, Manchester City named Sylvia as their Club Ambassador but, just six months later on 9 September, the world of football lost a true 'great' when she passed away aged 71.

It is worth pointing out that in 1972, the crowd of 500 who witnessed England's first official game and Sylvia's ground-breaking goal, was considered a decent turnout. On 9 September 2019, three years to the day since Sylvia passed, the attendance to watch England Lionesses take on Germany at Wembley Stadium was an all-time record of 77,768. This was 491 more fans than the men's fixture versus Montenegro attracted six days later at the same venue. Women's football is now unrecognisable from the game 'the little girl who loved football' had played many moons before and Sylvia Gore was hugely instrumental in its transformation.

Sylvia created an environment that encourages girls to take up the sport she loved. Many of the players she coached and managed achieved tremendous success and have proved inspirational to the next generation of women footballers. Fern Whelan is one such player.

FERN WHELAN

Born on 5 December 1988 into a footballing environment (brother Spencer was on Liverpool's books at the time and would go on to enjoy a decade in the game), Fern grew up in the Bowring Park area of Huyton. Her early memories revolve around kickabouts with her friends but after starting at Pascal Baylon Primary School, Fern got her first taste of organised football as she sailed into the mixed boys and girls team. Teacher **Emma Bowley** was one of the first to recognise Fern's ability and took the 8-year old along to turn out for Liverpool Feds. It was whilst playing for the Feds at the Heron Eccles pitches in Allerton that she first came into contact with Sylvia Gore. At the time, Sylvia was in charge of Tranmere's Centre of Excellence and after seeing Fern's ability and potential, she had no hesitation in recruiting her. Fern is extremely grateful for the contribution Sylvia made to her career and states, "I spent a lot of time under her wing through those years and she helped me achieve my first England youth call up at 13." Centre-half Fern would become a regular in England's youth set-up and captained the U-15 and U-17 sides.

Whilst a pupil at St Julie's Senior School in Woolton, she enjoyed a couple of seasons with Liverpool Ladies before signing for Everton in 2005. This heralded the start of a ten-year relationship with the Blues during which time she established herself as a major force in the game. The 2007/08 season was a rollercoaster, bittersweet affair for Fern. Internationally, she scored a 94th minute equaliser versus Poland in England's opening match of the U-19s Euros in Iceland. Subsequent victories over France, Spain and Norway provided a path to the Final where they were defeated 2-0 after extra time by Germany. Fern's outstanding captaincy and performances throughout the tournament were recognised when she received the 'Player of the Tournament' award. Back on home soil, Fern played in every round of Everton's journey to the League Cup Final. However, after picking up a season-ending cruciate injury in January 2008, she missed the showpiece game as the Blues overcame Arsenal to lift their first trophy for nine years. Whilst delighted for her teammates, Fern was gutted to miss the match but was overwhelmed as the campaign still finished on a personal high when she was named the 'FA Young Player of the Year'. Fern battled back to fitness and England Coach Mo Marley had no reservations about installing her as captain in the squad for the 2008 FIFA U-20s World Cup in Chile. The young Lionesses reached the quarter-final stage of the competition before losing 3-0 to eventual winners USA.

On Sunday, 2 May 2010, Fern played her part in a monumental Everton performance as the Blues accounted for Arsenal Ladies to secure the FA Cup against the odds. The Gunners had been hot favourites to win the trophy for the fifth time in succession but Everton ran out 3-2 winners with Natasha Dowie grabbing the decisive goal with seconds of the match remaining. The following season saw Fern feature prominently in the club's Champions League campaign, reaching the quarters where FCR Duisberg of Germany put them to the sword.

On 17 May 2011, Fern completed her collection of England jerseys when she came off the bench to represent the nation's senior team in a 2-0 victory over Sweden at Oxford United's Kassam Stadium. Fern also appeared for the Lionesses versus Slovenia (4-0 win) and in the 2012 Cyprus Cup opposing Switzerland (1-0 win). However, in the Cyprus Cup tournament she aggravated her cruciate injury, which had again been hampering her for some time. Fern made the difficult decision to go under the knife meaning that she missed the 2012 London Olympics and 2013 Euros.

©BHAFC Paul Hazlewood

Whilst this was a bitter pill to swallow, the injury coincided with Fern becoming a qualified physiotherapist. The insider knowledge and experience she had under her belt helped her come to terms with the injury and prepare for her return to action. Sidelined for 20 months, she made her comeback for Everton versus Aston Villa in February 2014. Four months later, she made a substitute appearance in the FA Cup Final at Stadium MK in front of 15,000 fans. Opponents Arsenal avenged their defeat of 2010 to take the shine off Fern's day but she felt great to be back. At the conclusion of the 2014 season, Fern made the difficult decision to leave her beloved Toffees following their Super League relegation and joined Notts County on a two-year deal. In a repeat of her 2007/08 experience, Fern played in every FA Cup round for County as they progressed to the Final for the first time in their history (defeating Everton en-route). An ankle injury picked up a week before the Wembley showdown versus Chelsea cruelly put paid to Fern's involvement in the game, which the Londoners won 1-0 in front of a crowd of 30,710. Fern's 23 Notts County appearances returned a couple of goals including the only strike in a game versus the old enemy Liverpool on 10 May 2015. When, in 2017, a new Chairman was installed at County, he wielded the axe on the Women's team as a money-saving exercise. Consequently, Fern found herself without a club and having to move out of her home which belonged to the club.

She briefly returned to Everton before joining Brighton & Hove Albion where a single goal victory over Aston Villa in her first game provided a sign of things to come. In Fern's debut season in East Sussex, they finished runners-up to Doncaster Rovers Belles in WSL2 and secured promotion to the top flight. Fern combined her role as the club's vice-captain with working as a pundit in the media. In addition, she has acquired an excellent reputation for her multi-sport physiotherapy duties. Since graduating from Salford University, she has worked extensively in private practices and for Whiston and Liverpool hospitals, Everton FC and Nottingham University. Her achievements on and off the pitch over the past couple of decades would undoubtedly have brought a smile to the face of Sylvia Gore.

Footynote:

In October 2020, on medical advice, Fern Whelan made the decision to retire from the game after 15 years as a pro. Shortly after, she joined the PFA to take up a position within its Women's Football and Equalities department.

KELLY MCDOUGALL

Another player who benefitted from the influence of Sylvia Gore was Kelly McDougall. Born in Whiston hospital on 22 January 1984, Kelly grew up living in Cross Lane, Prescot. She was a pupil at Our Lady's RC Primary School and St Edmund Arrowsmith Seniors - the same learning establishments Sylvia had attended decades earlier. It is unquestionable that Sylvia's ground-breaking efforts resulted in Kelly's passion for football enjoying greater support and encouragement from the teaching staff than Sylvia had received. The boys, however, were initially less welcoming and it was only after Kelly had proved herself by winning 'keepy up' or 'one on one' competitions against them that she was allowed to join in their lunchtime matches. Once accepted into the fold, she thrived and would practice anywhere and everywhere with her dad, grandad and brother. Her favourite venues included the local park, the school field and best of all, Prescot Leisure Centre. Kelly spent hour after hour playing in the hockey goals with friends **John Stott** and **Wesley** and **Jamie Richardson** before being moved on by the caretaker - until the next time. Once perfected, Kelly would put her tricks and skills to good use whilst playing for Rainhill United. Hugely respected manager **Albert Fellows** was only interested in football ability - boy or girl, if you were good enough you were in his team. Kelly was, however, the only girl considered good enough at the time. She more than held her own and loved it until, at the age of eleven, league rules outlawed mixed-sex teams.

Although she is extremely grateful to her family, friends and Albert for the role they played in her early development as a player, Sylvia was her greatest influence. In addition to conducting school training sessions, she included Kelly in the Knowsley girls team for the Merseyside Youth Games. Kelly and teammate **Nicola Harding** were singled out for praise in the local press when, in 1993, Knowsley won the competition despite the team being assembled just three weeks earlier. It was becoming increasingly obvious that Kelly possessed all the attributes to go a long way in the game. Sylvia wanted her to join Liverpool Ladies but lifelong Evertonian Kelly spotted an advert in a matchday programme inviting players to try out for the club's newly formed ladies team. Aged just 12, Kelly's dad took her along for trials and so began a marvellous career. She turned out for the U-14s side for two years and in 1997 picked up the 'Player of the Year' award as the team secured the Lancashire League title. It wasn't long before coach **Judith Hughes** recommended Kelly's promotion to the first team squad. After participating in a few training sessions, husband and wife management team **Mo** and **Keith Marley** had seen enough to convince them that Judith was right and to Kelly's delight she signed for the Toffees.

In 12 hugely enjoyable years with the Blues, Kelly established herself as one of the best players in the country. She represented England at U-16, U-18 and U-19 levels and won nine full caps for the Lionesses. She made a goal-scoring debut for the U-16s versus Scotland in a home international tournament in Ireland. However, young Kelly's next appearance versus the Scots (her Wembley debut) was a bittersweet affair. A 5-0 victory was overshadowed when, in the 50th minute of the game she fell and painfully fractured her wrist. In 2002, Kelly was a member of the U-19s squad which took part in the FIFA World Championships in Canada. This was a thoroughly enjoyable experience for Kelly although on the pitch the team underachieved. Despite only winning one group match, they reached the quarter-final stage where the host nation thrashed our girls 6-2 in front of 23,596 patriotic Canadians at the Commonwealth Stadium in Edmonton.

By this stage, Kelly was an established member of the Everton team. She had made her debut on 8 February 1998 when coming off the bench to join the action in a 1-0 home victory over Millwall. Only 14 years of age, the senior players took Kelly under their wing and helped her settle into the team which won the Premier League title. To the Everton hierarchy's satisfaction, she was progressing nicely but a goal against Arsenal on 12 March 2000 made the wider football community sit up and take notice of her. Over the next couple of seasons Kelly consolidated her place in the side before joining the National Player Development Agency at Loughborough University in 2001. Whilst she loved her time there, she missed her family and returned to Cross Lane every weekend. She paid for her journeys by working in the Prescot Guild Hall before taking the Monday morning train back to Leicestershire. Kelly believes that her experience at Loughborough played a massive part in her development as a player. Her theory was borne out when, on 24 February 2003 at the Stadio dei Pini, she was rewarded for her performances with the first of her England caps in a 1-0 defeat by Italy.

Domestically, she proudly took charge of the captain's armband and came close to lifting trophies with Everton. In the 2004/05 season, Kelly rattled home ten league goals to help the club to a third place Premier League finish - their best position since winning the title seven years before. She also chipped in with a couple of goals as they reached the FA Cup Final where, on 2 May 2005 at West Ham's Boleyn ground, Charlton Athletic pipped them to the trophy courtesy of a Eniola Aluko goal. The following campaign the team came close to glory again but agonisingly had to settle for the League runners-up spot behind Arsenal whose superior goal difference proved crucial. This was the first of three consecutive seasons when the Blues occupied second place at the season's end. With Kelly driving the team on, they were playing fantastic football and rarely lost a game. Silverware continued to evade them until 28 February 2008 when a seventh minute Amy Kane strike accounted for Arsenal and secured the Premier League Cup. Unfortunately for Kelly, she spent much of the season on the treatment table and was an unused substitute in the game. She had, however, played her part in the success during the competition's early rounds, not least of all when she registered a fine hat-trick in a 6-0 demolition of Barnet. The 2007/08 campaign proved to be Kelly's last in an Everton shirt.

In August 2008, after 12 years of valiant service to the club she loves, she made the heart-wrenching decision to leave and join Sunderland. Having graduated from Edge Hill University, Kelly had opted for a career in teaching. Her training post was in Northumbria which would have been a commuting nightmare. She let her head rule her heart and in typical fashion tackled head on the challenges presented by a new club and job. The Lady Black Cats were, at the time, a young team brimming with potential but maybe lacking leadership and experience - qualities Kelly provided in abundance. She hit the ground running with a goal on her debut and didn't look back. Kelly picked up both the Players' and Manager's Player of the Year awards as the club won the FA Women's Premier League North Division. In addition, on 4 May 2009 at Pride Park with 23,291 present, the team appeared in the FA Cup Final for the first time in the club's history. By contrast, Sunderland's opponents Arsenal were in their fourth successive final in the competition and it was the Gunners who won the day by a 2-1 scoreline. Much to the delight of her family who were present, Kelly got her name in the FA Cup record books with her team's consolation goal.

Over the next few seasons and with Kelly pulling the strings from midfield, the club enjoyed unprecedented success without receiving the rewards their achievements deserved. Despite winning five League titles in six seasons, the club were only promoted twice and were repeatedly denied the chance to join the top flight. Whilst this could have been partially due to the restructuring of the Women's Leagues, they were also the victims of unfair non-football decisions. Justice was finally served at the climax of the 2014 campaign and Kelly was in the thick of the action. On 24 October of that year the Lady Cats faced Millwall, knowing that victory would guarantee the Women's Super League 2 title and, more importantly, the elusive automatic promotion to the Women's Super League. Anything less than a win would open the door to the Doncaster Belles, who were opposing bottom of the table London Bees. The Yorkshire side made an explosive start to their game, scoring four goals in the opening 17 minutes to pile the pressure on Sunderland. However, just as their fourth was hitting the net, Kelly struck a wonderful 25-yarder past the flailing keeper to relieve the tension at The Den. An additional trio of second-half Sunderland goals meant that Donny's 9-0 mauling of the Bees was irrelevant and there was nothing they (or the FA) could do to prevent Sunderland's promotion to the Super League.

Throughout her excellent 20-year career, Kelly always gave 100%. When she joined the full-time teaching ranks of an Ashington Primary School, it soon became apparent that the demands of the job could have a detrimental effect upon her performances on the pitch. Disappointed but pragmatic, she decided to hang up her boots and concentrate all her efforts on her new profession. Kelly is extremely grateful for the support she received as a pupil from her own schools' teaching staff (especially from **Mrs Smith, Mrs Walsh, Mr Campbell** and **Mrs Moore**) and would love to replicate this and make a difference to young people's lives. Nevertheless, she loved coaching the Sunderland youth team and is still hopeful that at some stage in the future she may be able to also make a difference to young footballers' lives by putting her vast knowledge, experience and EUFA coaching badge to good use.

KNOWSLEY UNITED WFC

In May 1989, respected England international footballer and coach **Liz Deighan** established a new club, Newton Ladies. Two years later, encouraged by their early success in the North West Regional League, the club applied to join the inaugural season of the National Premier League. In order to meet the FA's affiliation criteria, they had to find a new ground and, in turn, a new name – Knowsley United. In their debut season, the club finished a respectable mid-table fourth and won the Lancashire International Tournament. They repeated this achievement the following campaign and added the Moss Farm 7-a-side trophy. However, this was not good enough for ambitious Liz who persuaded England internationals **Clare Taylor** and **Kerry Davis** to join the fold, which propelled the club to greater heights.

Knowsley finished the 1992/93 season in an improved third place, were runners up in the Reebok International Tournament and secured a Premier League Cup Final appearance at Wembley. In previous seasons, the Final had been held at Barnet's ground so this represented a prestigious step up for the competition's showpiece event. Played on Saturday 29 May 1993 prior to the Football League Third Division play-off decider between York City and Crewe Alexandra, Knowsley's opponents were Arsenal Ladies. Although the Gunners ran out convincing 3-0 winners, the season's achievements were remarkable considering Knowsley were very much a fledgling outfit. Immediately after the game, Liz retired and **Angie Galimore** took over the reins.

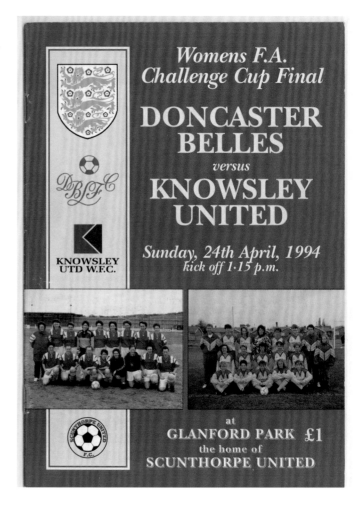

The Women's game was now gaining greater national attention and Knowsley, operating from their Alt Park home in the Woolfall Heath area of Huyton, were doing the locals proud. The game's raised profile was evident on Sunday, 24 April 1994 at Scunthorpe United's Glanford Park ground. The venue played host to the Women's FA Cup Final as Knowsley faced the mighty Doncaster Belles. Whilst the 1,674 paying customers represented a decent attendance, it was the premiere appearance of Sky TV's cameras and the live broadcast of the game which suggested a bright future lay ahead for women's football. Hot favourites Doncaster secured the trophy for the sixth time with a single goal victory but only after a valiant effort by United. Indeed, there could have been a different outcome when, in the 91st minute of the game, a powerful strike by Knowsley's Karen Burke beat the keeper only to rebound off the bar – narrow margins. The Knowsley squad for the biggest game of its short but impressive history was **Jill Thomas, Sammy Hayward, Clare Taylor, Diane Coughlin, Joy McQuiggan, Donna Baker, Kerry Davis, Cathy Gore, Angie Galimore, Karen Burke, Marie Harper, Debbie Holland, Nicki Barnes, Margie Parsons, Debbie Phillips** and **Pam Markey**. This proved to be Knowsley's last hurrah before changing their name to Liverpool Ladies and becoming affiliated to Liverpool Football Club. However, the club still maintained a local connection by playing their home games for a number of seasons at Prescot Cables ground. In addition, Sylvia Gore remained heavily involved as the club joined the national and international Women's Football revolution.

THE RISE AND FALL OF KNOWSLEY UNITED

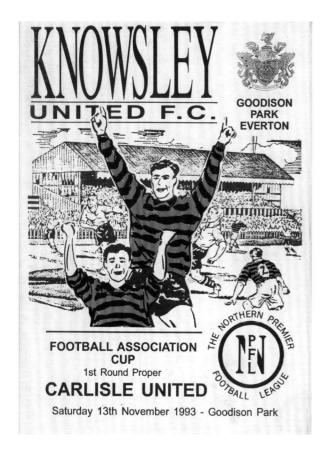

Knowsley United FC was formed in 1988 after appearing to rise phoenix-like out of the ashes of the defunct Kirkby Town FC – in reality, many of the same personnel were involved with both clubs suggesting the only changes involved the club's name and location. In the early 1960s, Kirkby Urban District Council had been extremely supportive when a group of local men, brimming with ambition and enthusiasm, came together to give the people of the new town of Kirkby a football team they could be proud of. In order to gain entry to the Second Division of the Lancashire Combination League, the Council granted the club use of its 12,000-capacity Sporting Club of Kirkby Stadium. Located in Simonswood Lane on land now taken up by the Liverpool FC Academy, the stadium was officially opened during the club's inaugural 1963/64 season by Councillor **Albert Cook** and Everton legend **Dixie Dean**. In just their fourth season, the team were promoted after topping Division Two. Shortly after, on Friday, 7 September 1967, Prime Minister **Harold Wilson** flicked the switch on the club's new floodlights and opened a new grandstand. The ceremony was followed by a Kirkby Town v Prescot Town Lancashire Combination Division One match. During the next 25 years, the team also played in the Northern Premier League, the Cheshire League and the North West Counties League. Whilst they enjoyed a great deal of success with four additional promotions, they also suffered a couple of disappointing relegations.

As the end of the 1980s approached, in order to keep afloat the club relocated and changed its name. Knowsley United FC was born and took up residence at Alt Park, which had recently been vacated by Huyton Rugby League FC. Not only did the new set-up continue to emulate Kirkby's achievements, they also took the club to previously uncharted territory. They finished runners-up in the North West Counties First Division in each of their initial two seasons and the Raab Karcher Cup and Champions Cup were safely stored in the Alt Park trophy cabinet during the same period. The 1990/91 season saw the club progress to the fifth round of the FA Vase – an indication of future cup competition intentions. In the same season, fifty goals from future Accrington Stanley Assistant Manager **Jimmy Bell** helped the club secure the Bass NWCFL Division One Champions title and promotion to the Northern Premier League First Division. Manager **Paul Orr** also picked up the Manager of the Year award in recognition of his fine efforts.

Twenty years earlier, their predecessors Kirkby Town had joined the same arena but were unable to meet the challenge, suffering relegation straight back whence they came. However, this team were made of sterner stuff and took the step up in class firmly in its stride by finishing a respectable eighth at the conclusion of the 1991/92 season. Former Liverpool and Swansea defender **Max Thompson** assumed managerial duties in April 1992. Orr moved upstairs to become the club's General Manager working alongside his uncle Paul Snr who had been the club's Chairman since the Kirkby Town days. The gamble paid off when Max delivered a runners-up spot and promotion to the League's Premier Division. When Thompson left the club for personal reasons, Paul Junior nipped back downstairs to resume control and oversee the club's finest hour.

Life in a league two rungs on the football ladder below the English Football League proved difficult and the club finished the 1993/94 season in a lowly 18th place. However, this campaign was all about the FA Cup and results that stirred the passion of local people reminiscent of the support afforded to the successful Huyton Schoolboys team in 1971.

Knowsley's exploits in the competition began away from home and a 1-1 drawn match with Salford City. The replay was a one-sided affair with Knowsley brushing aside the team now owned by a group of former Manchester United players, by six goals to nil. The second and third qualifying rounds were safely negotiated at the first time of asking with 2-1 and 3-0 victories over St Helens Town and Colwyn Bay respectively. The prize of a place in the 1st Round Proper beckoned for the victors of the resultant Knowsley versus Stafford Rangers clash and neither side would go down without giving their all. Home and away matches could not separate the sides, setting up a third contest at Alt Park. The lack of local support for the team from Woolfall Heath would be a major factor in the club's demise a few short years later but the cup run had captured the imagination and the Mike Marsh stand (funded by the £40,000 sale of the club's most famous ex-player to Liverpool FC) and the rest of the stadium were packed to the rafters. When a single Mick Jones strike hit the back of the net to account for the GM Vauxhall Conference side, the fans' celebrations could be heard for miles around.

Orr's men had made history for the club by reaching this stage of the competition and they were rewarded with a tie facing Carlisle United of the Football League Third Division. However, due to the delayed conclusion of the Stafford tie, the club had insufficient time to meet crowd segregation conditions, throwing the biggest match in their history into doubt. A fantastic solution was found when Everton FC offered Knowsley the use of Goodison Park and TV's Match of the Day decided to cover the game. On 13 November 1993, they faced the Cumbrians on the back of an 11-game unbeaten run. Within their ranks, Orr had accumulated a side rich in character, talent and with no little experience. Well-travelled **John McMahon** was Liverpool midfielder Steve's brother and a future Liverpool and Tranmere Coach. In **Dave O'Brien**, the team boasted a defender who captained both Everton and England youth teams whilst **Andy Green** had played internationally for Belgian club Lokeren. Goalkeeper **Andy Johnston** was no stranger to the big stage having played at Wembley when St Helens won the FA Vase in 1986. Converted from a forward to midfield general, **Joe Barton** inspired his teammates and his son who, following his early days as Knowsley's ball boy and mascot, would enjoy a very successful career in the game. The other squad members for the tie were **Lee Duffy, Peter Daley, Archie Lloyd, Stuart Gelling, Chris Stanton, Keith Vincent, Brian Kilshaw, Nick O'Malley, Tommy King, Chris Waring, Ray Birch, Dave Siddell, Ronnie Kilshaw, Peter Orr, Steve Jackson, Peter Edwards, Mick Jones, Andy Diggle, Andy Taylor and Paul Mullen.**

With most of the 5,015 present having made the short journey from Huyton, the scene was set for an upset. However, the game was just eight minutes old when Carlisle's Ian Arnold scored to dent the home side's hopes. Two additional first half goals put the game beyond Knowsley but sandwiched between them a Joe Joyce own-goal had given Knowsley hope and prompted the biggest roar of the day. The match finished 4-1 but Orr was rightly proud of his side and the massive progress the club had made in such a short space of time. Unfortunately, the team were unable to build on this success and by the end of the 1996/97 campaign following three disappointing seasons, those in charge of the club decided to call it a day signifying the rise and fall of Knowsley United.

THE SECOND HALF

As they emerge from their dressing room, refreshed and raring to go, let us focus upon the post-war players who have ensured that Huyton, Prescot and Whiston have continued to be in the thick of the English Football League action.

EDDIE KILSHAW

Born on Christmas Day 1919, Edmund Ainsworth Kilshaw made an impressive contribution to local and national football on and off the field of play. After receiving a scholarship, Eddie attended Prescot Grammar School where he not only excelled on the football pitch as a flying right-winger but also in the classroom where his academic brilliance was obvious to those around him. Whilst others got excited about his potential as a footballer, Eddie aspired to further his education and upon leaving school continued his studies at various learning establishments whilst working at Imperial Chemicals Industries. Even though he was a young man, he was mature enough to identify that if he was to pursue a career in football it was important to lay the foundations for life after football – a wise move as it turned out.

Eddie was in great demand as a teenager and played for his ICI works team, BICC Social's junior and senior teams, and even signed for LFC as an amateur. Yet it was with Prescot Cables that he began playing regularly and attracted the interest of scouts from all over the North West of England. Aware of the talent they had in their ranks, the Prescot hierarchy signed Eddie on a pro contract at the earliest opportunity – his 17th birthday. The harsh reality of the business side of football was prevalent even at this time and the club's main sponsors BICC had withdrawn aspects of their support making it difficult to keep the club afloat. The board decided there was only one sensible course of action and on October 2 1937, following a drawn FA Cup tie with South Liverpool, they reluctantly sacrificed Eddie to fund the club's day-to-day operations. Second Division oufit Bury were the club to benefit from Prescot's dilemma and Eddie wasted no time in showing the Gigg Lane fans what the Hope Street faithful had witnessed during his one and only season at his hometown club. A month after signing on 6 November 1937, he gave the 17,221 spectators present a taste of what was to come in a 1-1 draw at home to Aston Villa. It was the first of almost 150 appearances Eddie made for the Shakers during a career that straddled the Second World War.

During the hostilities, Eddie Kilshaw served as a pilot in the RAF Coastal Command based on the west coast of Scotland. On 12 May 1944 he was co-pilot of a nine-strong crew on a night training exercise which ended in tragedy when, in terrible weather conditions, their aircraft crashed on the Island of Vatersay in the Outer Hebrides. Three of those on board lost their lives whilst Eddie and the other five crewmembers survived but sustained injuries of varying severity. A memorial to the dead and survivors, along with the untouched scattered wreckage of the aircraft 'The Catalina,' can be found to this day on the island.

Following the end of WW2, Kilshaw returned to Bury and made an immediate impact by scoring the club's first post-war goal in a 7-2 trouncing of Fulham. He was soon recognised as the best winger in Division Two but in a repeat of his Hope Street experience, the cash-strapped club had to encourage offers for the youngster in order to balance the books. Manchester United, Sunderland and Everton expressed interest but it was Sheffield Wednesday who, in December 1948, won the race to secure his signature. In an attempt to minimise the pressure on Eddie, the fee of £20,000 was deliberately £50 short of the record sum Newcastle United had forked out to Sunderland for Len Shackleton. Unfortunately, after just 19 appearances and one goal for the Owls, Kilshaw's football career came to a cruel, premature end when, on 11 April 1949, he sustained a terrible knee injury in a home fixture versus Leicester City. He initially refused to accept his fate but when an operation and the best efforts of the club's medical team failed to produce a solution, he conceded defeat and hung up his boots.

It was at this stage that his prudent actions as a youngster paid dividends. Whilst playing for Bury, Eddie had continued his studies at the local Technical Institute and trained as an Analytical Chemist. After weighing up his options, he plumped for a career in teaching. He became an extremely popular science teacher at both St Columbas and Seel Road schools in Huyton, the latter being just a short walk from his Tarbock Road home. In 1954, Mr Kilshaw accepted an invitation to become involved with the Huyton Schoolboys team. Many identify this development as being vital to the improved professionalism and success of the Schoolboys and later, in his second spell as manager, he was in charge of the team that won the English Schoolboys Trophy in 1971. Although Mr Kilshaw sadly passed away on 24 July 2006, he is still fondly remembered by the many people he taught, the colleagues he worked alongside and the players he coached.

Footynote:

Alan Bleasdale, former team manager of Huyton Boys and playwright, writes - The very first schoolteacher I ever met in the very first school I ever taught in was Eddie Kilshaw. I could not have had a finer welcome to the teaching profession. It was the late summer of 1967 and Eddie was then in his fifties and, having limped away from footballing glory, trained as a science teacher. He was also the team manager of Huyton Boys. He needed young legs - any legs at all - and took me on initially as his assistant. This most sanguine of men guided me towards so many important principles with regard to educating children. He taught me the value of patience and generosity of spirit, of kindness and trust and, especially, that the child you teach is far more important than you. I was very young and cocky, headstrong and aggressive and more demanding than was helpful to anyone. Eddie calmed me down. In his way, he looked after and encouraged me like he looked after and encouraged the children he taught, who plainly and openly adored him. To have been called "saint-like" would have fiercely embarrassed Eddie Kilshaw at any time in his lifetime, but it was/is absolutely no less than he deserved.

WILLIAM WATKINSON

Born in Prescot on 16 March 1922, William Watkinson attended Whiston Central School. He cut his teeth playing for Prescot Rangers and, in the 1939/40 season, rattled home a staggering 86 goals. He proved this was not a one-off when the following campaign returned 74 goals for Prescot Rovers. Shortly after WW2 broke out, Bill received the call-up to serve as a Marine Commando and took part in the early Normandy landings. He played for his Command team until he signed for Prescot Cables when normal service resumed towards the end of the hostilities. It was as if he had never been away as his goal scoring exploits continued and he found the net 38 times in 22 games for Cables.

This brought him to the attention of a number of Football League clubs and on 22 February 1946, the Prescot Reporter stated, "I was present on Friday afternoon last when Bill Watkinson appended his signature to the papers which meant his transfer from Prescot Cables to Liverpool was complete. It was not without some feelings of regret that Bill left the club to which he had become so greatly attached and to which he had rendered such valuable service. The feelings of regret are shared by the Prescot club officials for Watkinson was a most conscientious team man, the interest of his club were always a prime consideration with him and he was most reliable and could always be depended upon to give of his best. I can now disclose that two other clubs had been seeking the transfer of Watkinson. One of these had been most persistent but the player preferred to remain with Cables and hoped to do so until his services with the Forces terminated. I know that the club were loath to part with him and only a week previously had turned down a tempting offer after consulting the player and ascertaining his desire. Then Liverpool came along in a bit of a hurry. They had previously sought Bill's services so Prescot officials held conference and guided by the fact that Watkinson was soon to be demobbed and had now decided to make football his career, it was considered that in the player's interests the opportunity dictated that the time was right to part company. Watkinson had established himself as a firm favourite with the spectators at Hope Street and there was a general disappointment when it was learned that he was turning out with Liverpool's Central League team instead of Cables on Saturday last. But all wish him well and his progress will be watched with interest."

Watkinson's Liverpool career was probably underwhelming for the Hope Street faithful who, having witnessed his lethal goal scoring, expected more of the same in a red jersey. Although, in front of a crowd of 35,429, Bill scored in the ninth minute of his debut versus Aston Villa on 26 April 1947, he struggled to claim a regular place in his favoured centre forward position, having to make do with occasional appearances in a wide role. He did, however, hold down a place in the team for the last half a dozen games of his first season with the club as Liverpool finished the first post-war campaign as First Division champions. Bill's Liverpool career spanned four seasons. He made the last of his 24 outings for the Reds on 22 April 1950 at Fratton Park in a 2-1 defeat at the hands of Portsmouth. He joined Accrington Stanley for a club record transfer fee of £3,000 and during his three years at the Third Division North club he made 105 League appearances and scored 45 times. A further 60 games for Halifax Town returned 24 goals before being welcomed back to Prescot where his 65 goals helped Cables win the 1955/56 Lancashire Combination Championship. He later joined Skelmersdale United before finishing his career at Prescot BICC Social. Billy Watkinson sadly passed away in February 2001 shortly before his 79th birthday.

TOMMY "THE FLASH" FOWLER

Tommy Fowler was the youngest of five children, with two brothers and two sisters. He entered the world in Prescot on 16 December 1924, and his love of football was evident from a very early age. He would spend hours honing his cultured left foot by volleying a tennis ball against the walls of the Gospel Hall in Evans Street, close to the family's terraced home. His speed of foot later resulted in him being dubbed 'The Flash' and was perhaps first witnessed by the irate caretaker of the Hall as he regularly chased him away. Young Tommy hated school and would frequently bunk off to join in football kickabouts with the bigger boys and adults. Acknowledging Tommy's appetite for the game, his teachers would successfully entice him to attend school with talk of the school team.

A Liverpool fan, Tommy's hero at this time was their outside left Alf Hanson. In the biography 'Quite Simply a Flash of Genius' Tommy admitted "I modelled myself on him…. he was fast, direct and a wonderful crosser of the ball and like myself he was left footed. It's fair to say that when I was running down the wing during those early schooldays football matches I **was** Alf Hanson." His emulation of Hanson for Whiston Modern School earned him a call up to play for the St Helens Schoolboys team. Saints had an excellent side at this time and with Tommy too hot to contain, they won the Lancashire Schools Cup by defeating Blackburn in the Final. When Tommy left school, he continued to excel and develop his left wing play with both Prescot Rangers and Prescot Rovers. Jack Lyon who was already playing junior football for the Toffees, told an Everton Scout about his St Helens teammate and after impressing in twice-weekly training sessions, Tommy signed amateur forms with the Blues.

Football matches played during the war years were outside of Football League jurisdiction and were not formally recognised. However, this did not matter a jot to an elated Tommy when on 24 October 1942 he scored in the 43rd minute of an extremely successful debut for Everton in a 9-2 thrashing of Bury in front of 6,000 Goodison Park fans. The Liverpool Echo described 17-year-old Tommy as "the find of the match….he not only dovetailed perfectly with Stevenson but he had his own direct ideas about shooting." He made a further 16 appearances and netted an additional seven goals before receiving his call up papers which put paid to his brief but impressive Everton career. Whilst on National Service Tommy still managed to play football by turning out for his regimental team against representatives of the other Services. When a bullet wound to the forehead brought the war to a premature end for Tommy, he was shipped back to Southampton and a succession of military hospitals where he was operated on and nursed back to fitness. Whilst in a convalescent home in the Bedfordshire town of Kempston he met two men working there who would have a massive impact upon his future.

Jack Jennings and Harold Shepherdson were former Football League players who enjoyed extremely successful coaching careers – Harold was England Manager Alf Ramsey's Assistant when the World Cup was won a couple of decades later in 1966. As soon as the pair discovered Tommy's Everton connection, they arranged training with nearby Northampton Town followed swiftly by a debut at The Hawthorns against West Bromwich Albion. Tommy continued to play informally for the Cobblers but before the war ended, a full-time professional contract was offered and duly signed on 1 March 1945. This cemented the beginning of a 16-year relationship during which time he appeared in 585 games for Northampton to become the club's record appearance maker. He scored nearly a century of goals in all competitions including a fine hat-trick in a 4-2 defeat of Gillingham on 27 December 1958. When, at the age of 37, The Flash left Northampton Town to join Aldershot on 1 December 1961, Cobblers fans held him in such high esteem that a lounge in his favourite watering hole - The Old White Hart Social Club – was named after him. After two seasons and 14 appearances for Aldershot, Tommy called it a day. Sadly, on 4 May 2009 the world lost a footballing legend when 84-year old Tommy passed away peacefully in his sleep at Cotswold House Nursing Home. However, just as the regulars of the White Hart had immortalised Tommy, the club that played a massive part in his life has done the same. Every year, the Tommy Fowler Merit Award is presented to the individual or organisation who has gone the extra mile for Northampton Town FC – just as Tommy did during his long and illustrious career.

NORMAN CASE

Norman Case was a Prescot lad who was never one to let the grass grow under his feet by staying long at any of the numerous clubs he represented. Born on 1 September 1925, his early football took in local non-league sides Prescot Rovers, Prescot BI and Prescot Town and he gained a reputation as a free-scoring centre forward. Between August 1947 and February 1949, Norman was attached to a number of clubs including Sheffield United, Rochdale, Cheltenham Town and Leyton Orient without featuring in a Football League game. However, when he joined Northern Irish club Ards he took full advantage of the opportunity and became the club's leading goal scorer. After netting five goals in a defeat of Coleraine he got the call to play for the Irish League representative side against their Scottish counterparts at Ibrox Park on 7 September 1949. Much to the delight of the vast majority of the 62,000 fans present, the Irish were humiliated 8-1 with Norman's consolation goal the only highlight for the team from the Emerald Isle.

A month later, Sunderland gave Norman his chance in the English Football League and he hit the ground running. On Boxing Day 1949, he lined up to oppose Stoke City alongside Roker Park legend Len 'The Clown Prince of Soccer' Shackleton who broke the deadlock in the 50th minute of the game. As the Potters pushed forward in a vain attempt to get back on level terms, Case struck twice to give the Rokerites a 3-0 win. Bizarrely by today's standards but commonplace then, the two clubs faced each other the following day and Norman was again included in the starting line-up. Sunderland again took the lead but Stoke struck back twice in the second-half to snatch the points and exact immediate revenge. Norman's next appearance came on 17 April 1950 in the Durham Senior Cup Final when they lost local bragging rights to Darlington who won the game 1-0. The following week, Norman was back in Division One action in a 3-1 defeat at the hands of Huddersfield Town which proved to be his final appearance in a nail-biting finish to the season. Frustratingly for Norman and Sunderland, the team lost three consecutive games in the run-in before winning their last couple of fixtures of the campaign. At the ultimate reckoning, just four points separated the top seven teams and Sunderland finished a disappointing third behind champions Portsmouth and runners-up Wolves.

In the close season, the club embarked upon a tour of Turkey and Norman came off the bench early in the second-half of a 4-3 victory over Galatasaray in the Al Sami Yen stadium in Istanbul. In the fourth game of the 1950/51 campaign played on 30 August 1950, he pulled on the famous red and white striped jersey for the last time in a 3-3 home draw with Aston Villa.

Next stop for Case was Division Three (South) side Watford and he debuted in a 5-1 drubbing dished out by Southend United on 19 August 1951. He played 10 times for the Blues (they were nicknamed the Hornets following a 1959 change in kit colour to their current gold and black) and registered four goals. After Watford endured a poor season and finished 23rd of 24 teams, Case was again on the move and scored 23 Southern League goals during a season-long loan at Yeovil Town. In February 1952, Rochdale paid a modest fee to sign him but he managed just a couple of appearances before finishing his career with a return to Cheltenham Town followed by a spell at Canterbury City. Tragically, Norman Case passed away in 1973 in Watford aged just 48.

NEVILLE "TIM" COLEMAN

Former Huyton Secondary Modern School pupil Neville 'Tim' Coleman was no stranger to being involved in football matches when records were made. On no fewer than three occasions he was in the thick of the action in such games. Born in Prescot on 29 January 1930, as a young man he joined the RAF. Stationed at the Air Sea Rescue base in Gorleston-on-Sea in Norfolk, he was playing for Gorleston FC when spotted by a Stoke City Scout who was keen to secure his services for the Potters. Tim wanted to join the club but before this could be realised the Force would have to agree to his early release from the Service. Following extensive negotiations, this was sorted and in January 1954 Tim became a footballer with the Second Division club although a condition of the agreement was that he would remain an amateur player for a 12-month period.

Whilst playing for Gorleston, Tim had been a free-scoring centre forward but Stoke Manager Frank Taylor wanted to convert him to play on the right wing. In order to get him acquainted with his new position Tim played for the club's reserves although he did make four first team appearances in the 1954/55 season and notched two goals. A couple of months into the following season an injury to regular outside right John Malkin, which ultimately ended his playing days, presented Tim with the opportunity to establish himself in the first team and he took full advantage. He netted six goals from 25 games setting him up nicely to kick on the following season and to contribute twice to his club's history.

On 10 October 1956, local neighbours Port Vale were the visitors to Stoke's Victoria ground to take part in a friendly match to mark the official turning on of the ground's new floodlight system. This was a big deal at the time as permanent floodlights were a recent addition to football grounds around the country. Just two minutes after kicking off, Tim slotted the ball past the Vale keeper to write his name in the club's record books as the first player to score under the new floodlights.

On 23 February 1957, Tim was again making history but this time the achievement was somewhat more remarkable than his 'floodlights' record. With a bitterly cold afternoon contributing to an attendance of 10,790 - considerably smaller than the season's average crowd of 22,146 - Stoke welcomed Lincoln City to the Victoria ground. Wearing the number 7 shirt, previously donned by the Potters' greatest-ever player Stanley Matthews, Tim took to the snow-covered pitch and in an 8-0 trouncing of the Imps he scored an amazing seven times - still a record for a Stoke player. This took his tally for the season to 27 goals from just 33 appearances although, bizarrely, he failed to find the net in any of the 10 remaining games of the 56/57 campaign. Tim added a further 14 goals from 37 games the following season before signing for Fourth Division Crewe Alexandra for a £1,000 fee in February, 1959.

It was whilst playing for the Railwaymen that Tim was involved in the third record-breaker of his career - but by far the least prestigious. On 3 February 1960 at White Hart Lane, Tim scored the first of Crewe's two goals in an FA Cup Fourth round replay versus Tottenham Hotspur following a hard fought draw a week earlier. Unfortunately, in front of 64,365 spectators, Spurs humiliated Tim's side by registering 13 goals, a result that still represents Spurs' biggest-ever win. Although he was not as prolific for Crewe as he had been for Stoke, Tim's return of 18 goals from 84 games was achieved as a right-winger and not as an out-and-out striker, making his career record of 210 games played and 70 goals scored very respectable. After retiring in 1961, he worked for Rolls Royce but passed away aged just 50 shortly after moving to Australia.

"TIM" COLEMAN
Stoke City

ALAN HAMPSON

Alan Hampson was born on 31 December 1927 as the world prepared to welcome in the New Year. As a young man, he found employment as an Estimating Clerk and played for the Air Training Corps team. An inside forward, his big break came when his Station Officer spotted him playing in a kickabout and recommended him to Everton. Impressive performances in three trial games for the Blues A team earned him a place in their Central League reserve side and, in 1950, a pro contract. The Goodison hierarchy had high hopes for their new recruit but in just his third game for the club's second string Alan sustained a serious knee injury. This sidelined him for a year and restricted him to just one first team game in the royal blue kit. This came on 14 October 1950 with 53,421 present at Goodison Park where Bolton Wanderers provided the opposition in a 1-1 draw.

In November 1952, he signed for Third Division North outfit Halifax Town and his four years at the Shay returned 32 goals from 121 League games. He rattled home four goals in just six games for Bradford City in 1956/57 season before leaving League football to briefly join Buxton.

In November 1957, Alan signed as a player for Prescot Cables. After displaying leadership qualities as captain of his hometown side, he rose admirably to the challenge of coaching when Harry Topping quit as player-coach. At this time, League results were poor which had a negative impact on attendances. However, the FA Cup was a different matter and when they put Flint Town United, Earlestown and Bangor City to the sword the locals returned in droves. Altrincham were Cables' 4th qualifying round visitors to Hope Street. With in excess of 3,000 in attendance, they raised the roof when Eddie Forshaw sent a header past the Alty keeper to ensure they were in the hat for the draw of the 1st round proper. Whilst a 4-0 defeat at the hands of Fourth Division Darlington was disappointing, the Cup run had provided some much-needed joy in an otherwise disappointing campaign. It had also whet Alan's appetite for progressing into the world of non-league management and he did so with aplomb.

South Liverpool offered him a player-coach position, which he duly accepted. A month later, the manager's hotseat became available and Alan was the logical choice to fill it. In his second season at Holly Park, he helped the club to promotion out of the Lancashire Combination Second Division. Then, in 1966 just a couple of years after Alan hung up his boots, they secured the Division One title. Alan Hampson's contribution to South's cause on and off the field of play was immense. He persuaded the club's board to invest in new floodlights and switch their home matches to Friday evenings. As a result, they avoided clashing with Liverpool and Everton fixtures which increased their attendance and revenue. On Sunday 14 April 1971, a host of North West giants of the game descended upon Holly Park to turn out in Alan's Testimonial match to pay tribute to his services to local football. Bill Foulkes, Harry Gregg and Dennis Viollet made the journey down the East Lancashire Road to provide support from Manchester United whilst Tommy Lawrence, Roy Vernon, Alan A'Court, Jim Tansey, Tommy Jones and Gordon Milne represented Liverpool and Everton. Local legends Alan Ball and Stevie Heighway added to the celebration by officiating as linesmen.

When Alan eventually retired from the game which had dominated his adult life, he threw himself into running the family draper's business and working as a rep for a motor accessory firm. In August 1989 aged just 61, Alan Hampson sadly passed away.

TOMMY E JONES

Thomas Edwin Jones was born on 11 April 1930 and, after shining in local schoolboy football and impressing as an England youth international, he signed for Everton on New Year's Day 1948. After just one appearance for the A team and a single game for the reserves, he made his debut for Everton's first team on 6 September 1950 in a 2-1 defeat to Arsenal at Highbury in front of 36,576 spectators. Tommy's first season in the team was a bittersweet experience for the young player. Whilst he was delighted to have made the breakthrough to play alongside such Goodison legends as Peter Farrell, Tommy Eglington, Wally Fielding and Harry Catterick, and to feature in thirty games, the team really struggled and suffered relegation to the Second Division.

However, an excellent FA Cup run the following season took the team through to a semi-final confrontation with Bolton Wanderers. Although Everton were to lose the game and Bolton would go onto Wembley (where they lost to Blackpool in the legendary 'Matthews Cup Final'), it highlighted the fact that Manager Cliff Britton had a good side at his disposal with Tommy at the heart of a miserly defence. It came as no surprise the following season when the team clinched a return to the First Division by finishing runners-up. The club consolidated its position in the top flight as Tommy's influence on the team grew and after seven seasons in the team, when he missed just a handful of games, he was handed the club captaincy.

Playing the best football of his career resulted in Tom's inclusion in an English FA squad on a tour of Nigeria and Ghana in 1958. The team was a combination of amateur and professional players and they were victorious in six of the seven games played. Unusually, the seventh game against Northern Nigeria resulted in a draw after its abandonment due to strong winds and heavy rain. In 1962, Tommy shattered a kneecap in a reserve team fixture at Burnley, prematurely bringing to an end the 31-year old's career which had spanned eleven seasons and four managers and involved 411 games making him tenth in the list of all time appearance-makers for Everton.

A few years earlier, Toffees' Chairman John Moores had offered Tommy a job in his Littlewoods Pools Empire upon his retirement from the game, "I wrote to him when I retired from playing and within a week I got a reply offering to give me an appointment with one of the Littlewoods people. I joined the company and was there for thirty years and finished up as the Senior Purchasing Officer."

Tommy remained a keen Evertonian and was an active member of the Everton Former Players Association. In April 2010, aged 80, he took to the Goodison Park pitch for the last time and received a very warm reception. Just a couple of months later on 5 June Tommy sadly passed away and his funeral was held a short pass away from his spiritual home at St Luke's church on Goodison Road with his doting family and many former players and fans in attendance.

TERRY LEDGERTON

Terry Ledgerton was born on 7 October 1930. He attended St Edwards Orphanage and St Dominics School, which was located just around the corner from the family's Lordens Road home in the Page Moss area of Huyton. The speedy left-winger played for the Liverpool County FA side and represented England Schoolboys. As a member of the St Dominics team which won the Stanley Cup in the 1949/50 season, his reputation attracted the attention of a host of clubs. In May 1950, he became the first of many Doms players to join the professional ranks when he signed for Second Division Brentford, however it was not until he was officially demobbed that he got his first taste of Football League action.

Terry made his debut in a 0-0 home draw versus QPR on 9 February 1952 in front of 25,645 supporters in a team that also included future West Ham Utd and England Manager Ron Greenwood in its ranks. Between 1952 and 1953, Ledge played on 47 occasions scoring nine goals. After bowing out following a 5-2 FA Cup defeat by Hull City on 18 January 1954, Terry left Griffin Park to join Millwall in an exchange deal involving George Stobbart.

He made six appearances for the Lions before leaving the Football League and joined Clacton Town where he became something of a legend. He scored in excess of sixty goals in his first two seasons for the Seasiders and was an integral part of the side which lifted the Southern League First Division trophy in 1959/60 - the club's finest achievement. Terry enjoyed a fantastic relationship with Clacton Town and its fans and the family connection continued when his grandson Matt Waters joined the club in 2007. Also a fast, tricky winger with an eye for goal, he found the net 107 times from 228 games during a seven-year spell at their Rush Green Bowl stadium.

DEREK HENNIN

Derek Hennin's ability was spotted at a very early age. On 26 April 1946, The Reporter covered a match between Derek's Whiston Modern School and Birkdale School and stated, "The outstanding player of the day was Derek Hennin who dominated the game from start to finish . . . Whiston Modern has turned out some good footballers in the past such as Jack Lyon, William Watkinson, Tom Fowler and Norman Case while this season the outstanding player has been Derek Hennin whose football control and ability for a lad of fourteen are exceptionally good. He has captained the school team and the St Helens town team in both the Lancashire Cup and the ESFA competitions. It is unfortunate that this season no inter-county or international schoolboys have taken place for Hennin I am sure would have qualified for both." The man from The Reporter obviously recognised a footballer when he saw one because Derek did indeed go on to secure England international youth team recognition when, on 14 May 1949, he was a member of the side which overcame Ireland 4-2 at Hull City's Boothferry Park.

Derek's father Harry played for Prescot Cables and managed local junior side Prescot Celtic. It was whilst playing for his dad's team that he was spotted by a Bolton Wanderer's Scout and, a month after his England youth appearance, he signed for the Trotters. Patience was required as he had to wait until 3 March 1954 before making his debut against Tottenham Hotspur, a game Spurs won 3-2 in front of 16,720 speccies at White Hart Lane. The scoreline and outcome of the game were the same when Derek scored his first goal for the club as Blackpool knocked them out of the FA Cup at the third round stage on 5 January 1957. The following season, the world's oldest association football competition presented no such problems when Derek and his teammates accounted for Preston (3-0), York City (3-0), Stoke City (3-1), Wolves (2-1) and Blackburn Rovers (2-1) to reach the 77th FA Cup Final. Their opponents, on 3 May 1958, were Manchester United who three months earlier had tragically lost eight of their players in the Munich air disaster. Against such a backdrop, the majority of the nation were understandably supporting the Red Devils but their depleted side were unable to prevent Wanderers from picking up the FA Cup for the fourth time. England legend Nat Lofthouse scored both goals of the 2-0 victory and his second was so controversial it resulted in an official rule change. Lofthouse shoulder-charged the United keeper with such force that both the goalie and the ball ended up in the back of the net. The subsequent public and professional outcry following the game saw goalkeepers receiving greater protection and such challenges, which had been legal up to this point, were outlawed.

Hennin's 164-League game, eight-goal career with the Trotters lasted more than a decade. In early 1961 he joined Fourth Division Chester City and, on 18 February, made his debut in a 2-1 victory over local rivals Wrexham. His pro career ended a season and 53 games later when he moved to Springfield Park to join Wigan Athletic of the Cheshire League. In 1962/63 season he made 38 appearances and helped the Latics win the Liverpool Non-League Senior Cup before enjoying a return to Hope Street to become player-manager of Prescot Cables. Derek sadly passed away in January 1989 aged just 57.

BILL FOULKES

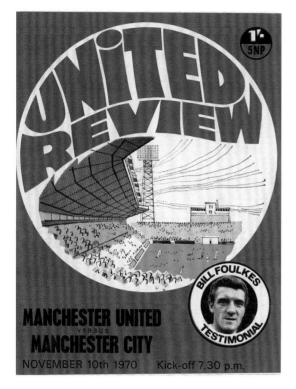

Bill Foulkes was born on 5 January 1932. He spent his early years living in Thatto Heath in a varied sporting environment; his dad was a goalkeeper and played for New Brighton in the old Third Division (North) and his grandfather was a rugby league legend for St Helens and England. Bill's early sporting interests revolved around rugby and crown green bowling but in his autobiography 'Manchester United and Beyond' he acknowledges his teacher's contribution to whetting his appetite for football which justifies his inclusion in these pages "My school was Whiston Secondary Modern where a wonderful man Mr Churchward had a huge effect on my development as a player. Nobody organised football for the local lads until he came along but after his arrival we seemed to spend most of our time playing the game."

Bill left school aged 14 and worked as an apprentice joiner, a brass foundry worker in Rainhill and a painter and decorator. His first opportunity to pursue his football dream ended acrimoniously when he and Prescot Celtic teammate Derek Hennin received an invitation to attend trials with Bolton Wanderers. Derek's father was Prescot Celtic's Manager and whilst he allowed his son to go along to the trials he refused to release Bill from a cup-tie taking place on the same day. This signified the first steps of Derek's excellent Wanderers career but resulted in Bill's relationship with the Prescot team coming to an abrupt end. Celtic's loss was Whiston Youth Club's gain. Bill joined them and played centre forward for the open-aged team and centre half for the under-18s. In 1949, local Manchester United Scout George Davies spotted Bill playing for Whiston and invited him for a trial with the newly-crowned FA Cup winners. An impressive performance resulted in the offer of an amateur contract, which he duly signed. Bill performed well for the A and reserve teams and his efforts paid off when on 13 December 1952 he was included in the first team. His debut was a baptism of fire - versus Liverpool! At Anfield! Marking Billy Liddell! A crowd of 34,450 witnessed Bill's first taste of the big time and, although the Liverpool legend scored, United came from behind and, thanks to goals from Aston and Pearson, left Anfield with the points. Foulkes acquitted himself so well that Boss Matt Busby named him in the side for the next game.

The following season, Bill made 33 appearances and established himself as a regular in the starting line-up. Bizarrely by today's standards, although he was playing in United's first team he was still only a part-time employee of the club. He lived in the Bakers Green area of Huyton and worked at the Lea Green colliery, picking up a greater wage (£15 per week) than United were paying him. It was only when he was called up for an England international match versus Northern Ireland on 2 October 1954 that Bill correctly surmised that he had a long-term future in the game. To Busby's delight, he put pen to paper on a full-time contract and stayed for 18 seasons. Bill Foulkes played 688 games for United, only Ryan Giggs, Paul Scholes and Sir Bobby Charlton have made more appearances for the Red Devils. He won four championships, played in three FA Cup finals (winning one) and in 1968 played a significant role as the club lifted that most coveted of trophies, the European Cup. Ten years earlier, on 6 February 1958, Bill had miraculously survived physically unscathed from the wreckage of a twin-engine Elizabethan aircraft after crashing on the runway at Munich-Riem airport in West Germany. The disaster resulted in the deaths of 23 passengers including eight of Bill's teammates.

On 16 August 1969, Bill brought the curtain down on an exceptional playing career but passed on his knowledge and knowhow by coaching United's reserve side for a further five years. In 1974, after 25 years loyal service, he left Manchester to embark upon a successful managerial career. For the next 17 years, his travels took him all over the world. First stop was the North American Soccer League where he managed Chicago Sting, Tulsa Roughnecks and San Jose Earthquakes. Six years later, he moved on to enjoy "seven fantastic years" in Norway taking charge of Byrnne, Steinkyer, Lillestrom and Viking Stravanger. In 1988, Bill's passport was required again - Japan was his destination, Mazda Hiroshima the club. Three successful seasons qualified the club for the recently-established J League but although he was excited at the prospect of involvement in the Japanese football revolution, Bill and his wife decided to return home to England to be nearer to their family.

On 25 November 2013, aged 81, Bill Foulkes passed away. His funeral took place at St Vincent's church in Altrincham and many fans and former teammates turned up to pay their respects to a true legend of the game.

GEORGE KIRBY

George Kirby was an 'old-fashioned' centre forward. Big, brave, direct, good in the air and with an eye for goal - adjectives often used to describe him but not too prevalent in the modern game.

Born on 20 December 1933, he initially received his education at St Aloysius Juniors before attending senior school in St Helens. He lived in the Longview area of Huyton and played in the Huyton & District League for Longview Rovers, managed by local man and scout for various clubs, Mr Fitzsimmons. George joined Everton as a junior and signed his first professional contract on 6 January 1952. He was one of a dozen players at this time who were part-time professionals whilst also serving in the Armed Services. He made the breakthrough to the first team in the 1955/56 season and on 2 April 1956 pulled on a first team shirt to make his debut in a 1-1 draw versus Sheffield United at Bramall Lane. He squeezed another appearance in, his home debut in a 1-0 victory over Blackpool, before the season's end. The following campaign, he notched eight goals from his 23 appearances – a respectable return for a young player in his first full season in the top-flight. However, George struggled with fitness and form in the 1957/58 season and, in just his second appearance, he picked up a serious ankle injury. Requiring surgery, this put him out of action for months and when he returned to fitness George struggled to reclaim a place in the first team. When Sheffield Wednesday Manager, former Everton player and future Boss Harry Catterick, offered the Toffees £8,000 in exchange for George's services, the Everton board felt the deal made sound business sense and accepted.

He joined the Owls on 3 March 1959 but made just three starts before he was on his way again. He dropped down a division to join Plymouth Argyle and his career really took off. Middlesborough provided the opposition on 16 January 1960 as George made his Pilgrims debut in a 2-2 draw. He remained in the side until the end of the season and although his return of two goals was disappointing, Manager Ellis Studdart kept faith in him. His decision was justified the following campaign when George found the back of the net 19 times. His Pilgrims career included 104 appearances and 39 goals and the Home Park fans loved the big target man's contribution in the green number nine jersey. When he left to join Southampton for a fee of £17,000 on 9 January 1962, they were sorry to see him go. On 19 September 1962, a goal-scoring debut in a 2-1 defeat of Chelsea got him off to a flying start and he continued with four goals in his first five Saints appearances. George played on 72 occasions for the Hampshire club and scored 32 goals. This tally included three FA Cup goals in his first season which helped the club reach the semi-finals where they faced

Manchester United - a Denis Law goal scuppering their FA Cup dream. Between 1963 and 1966, George scored nearly 50 additional goals at a rate of almost one goal every two games for Coventry City, Swansea Town and Walsall.

When he joined New York Generals in the NASL (23 goals, 47 games) many thought that signalled the end of George's involvement in English football but this was far from the truth. He eventually hung his boots up in 1968 after short spells with Brentford and non-league Worcester City. His playing career had involved eight clubs, 350 games and 129 goals.

The knowledge and experience George had gathered from his 16 years as a pro, equipped him to make the transition into management and enable him to continue his passionate involvement in the game. He joined Halifax Town working under Alan Ball Snr and replaced him in 1970 when Ball left to manage Preston. He promised the fans "progressive and entertaining football with a greater emphasis on attack" and he did not disappoint. His first season in charge proved to be the club's most successful ever with 74 goals, 21 wins and 12 draws as the club missed promotion into the old Second Division by just four points. The following campaign also started well but a week after his team defeated Manchester United 2-1 in the now defunct Watney Cup, he shocked the Halifax faithful when he took over the reins at Watford. However, a combination of injuries, boardroom unrest and a lack of luck and investment in the team resulted in disappointing results and his departure from Vicarage Road in May 1973.

He took over Icelandic club IA Akaranes, where he enjoyed five successful seasons before returning to Halifax Town. It has often been said that players and managers should not return to clubs where they have enjoyed earlier success and George's experience at Halifax second time around would probably endorse this argument. Apart from another Manchester giant-killing (a 1-0 victory over Malcolm Allison's City in the FA Cup third round on 5 January 1980), the team was unable to repeat the performances of the early Seventies.

George left The Shay in June 1981, after his side finished second from bottom of the Fourth Division. He later enjoyed stints in the hot seat in Saudi Arabia and back in Iceland. George was a football fanatic who enjoyed an excellent, lengthy career and continued working as a QPR Scout until shortly before tragically losing his battle with cancer on 24 March 2000, aged just 66.

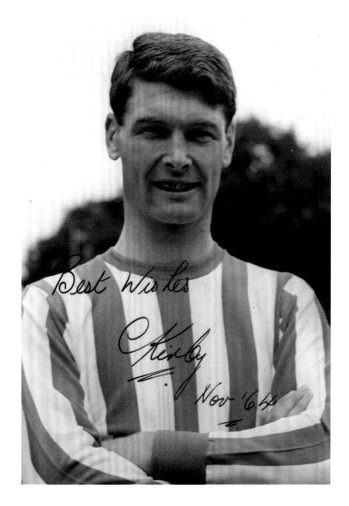

JOE DICKSON

Born on 31 January 1934, Joe Dickson was an England youth international inside forward. After impressing for England and Liverpool on youth team tours of Spain and Italy respectively, he signed for Liverpool as an amateur in November 1951 before turning pro in June of the following year. He graduated through the ranks at Anfield and, in the 1955/56 season, scored 15 goals from just 23 reserve team appearances. Manager Don Welsh wanted to have a closer look at Joe in a first team, Second Division environment so on 29 February 1956, he handed him his debut in front of a crowd of 21,068 in a 1-0 victory over Leeds United. Three days later, he scored his first goal for the Reds in a 4-2 home win over Bury. The highlight of Joe's brief Liverpool career was scoring two goals a fortnight later in front of 48,217 spectators at Anfield in a 4-1 defeat of Swansea Town. This proved to be the last time Joe hit the back of the net for Liverpool and on 7 April 1956, a 3-1 defeat at the hands of Fulham at Craven Cottage was to be his last game for the club.

Twelve months later when his contract expired, he signed for Southern League outfit Headington United. The club were ambitious and determined to qualify to join the Football League. They attempted to attract players by offering higher wages than many of the salary-capped League's top flight players were receiving. In Joe's debut 1958/59 season with Headington, he was the club's top scorer registering 27 goals as the team finished a disappointing tenth in the table. The following campaign resulted in a runners-up spot and ex-Birmingham City Manager Arthur Turner's efforts were beginning to reap rewards. Whilst Joe retired at this time, he did so in the knowledge that he had played no small part in laying the foundations for Headington to achieve their aims. It all came together the following season, when the club changed their name to Oxford United, won the League, won it again the following year and were elected into the Football League to replace Accrington Stanley who had resigned.

JOE MALONEY

Joe Maloney was born on 26 January 1934 and grew up in the Finch Lane area of Dovecot. He joined Liverpool FC as a junior, turned professional in January 1951 and made his first team debut on 4 March 1953 as a replacement for Bob Paisley in a 0-0 stalemate at home to Bolton Wanderers with 24,999 in attendance. Joe made five additional appearances towards the tail end of the 1952/53 campaign. Two months later, he toured the United States and Canada with the club to take part in a very successful close-season tour. The Reds played ten games, won nine and drew one, scored 49 goals and conceded just 12. The only encounter they failed to win took place at New York's Yankee Stadium on 14 June 1953. It was the final game of the tour with the opposition provided by Young Boys of Berne. Trailing 1-0, a 58th minute Billy Liddell equaliser pegged the Swiss Champions back and preserved Liverpool's unbeaten record. Unfortunately, the same could not be said of the Reds upon their return to League action. Joe put in an additional six appearances as they ended the season rooted to the foot of the table and relegated to the Second Division for the first time in 50 years.

In July 1954, after 12 appearances in a Liverpool shirt (which yielded just one victory), he opted to join Shrewsbury Town in an attempt to gain regular first team football. The decision proved to be a wise one as he quickly established himself in the Division Three (South) team. Between 1954 and 1961, Joe made 249 Shrews appearances and was a member of the team that, at the end of the 1958/59 season, gained promotion out of the recently established Fourth Division into Division Three. The campaign was also the 'Benefit Season' for three of the players – Joe, Russell Crossley and

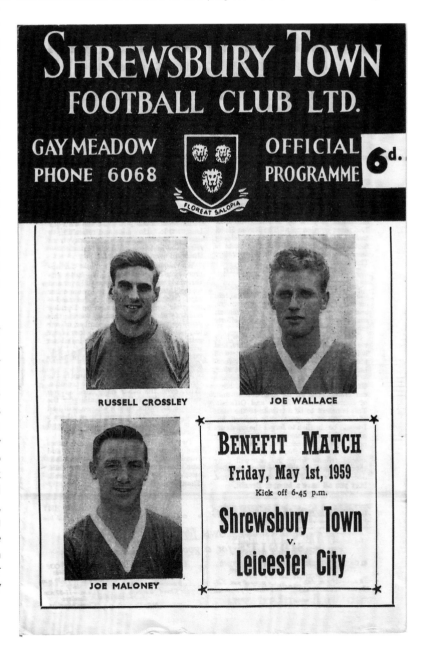

Joe Wallace. On Friday, 1 May, 1959 a bumper crowd turned up at Gay Meadow to watch their team take on Leicester City and to thank these players for their contribution to the Salopian side. Joe was held in high esteem by everyone at the club and the author of the match day programme wrote "This unassuming lad came in as a wing half from Liverpool with Russell Crossley and did not have too happy a time, but astute switching by Walter Rowley and keen application by Joe saw him become one of the leading lights of the Third South and Fourth Divisions. One finds it hard to write of Joe, he is that unobtrusive character who never seeks the limelight, although he deserves plenty of it. A Liverpool lad and great friend of Ken Dodd, one can say he has a quiet sense of humour and is respected by all from Chairman to youngest ground staff boy."

Joe signed for Port Vale on 1 July 1961, but only stayed for a couple of months before leaving to join Crewe Alexandra. Ironically, his only appearance in a Vale shirt was on the opening game of the 1961/62 season, when they were defeated 4-2 by Joe's former employers Shrewsbury. Two days later, he teamed up with the Alex and in his second season at Gresty Road, the Railwaymen enjoyed promotion into the Third Division. Before the commencement of the 1963/64 campaign, Joe left the club and became a non-leaguer with Winsford United, and enjoyed a couple of seasons before ending his playing days in 1965. He returned to Crewe in the early Seventies to become First Team Coach working under fellow Scouser, Manager Jimmy Melia. On 17 October 2006, Joe sadly passed away, aged 72.

DEREK TEMPLE

Derek Temple is officially an 'Everton Giant'. In May 2013, he received the honour of becoming a member of the Everton Hall of Fame and became only the 24th player to receive such an accolade. At the awards ceremony, the 75-year-old joked, "I wish I was getting this for Young Player of the Year!" Possessing blistering pace, great ability with both feet and an eye for goal, Derek would be well suited to the modern game. Born on 13 November 1938 in Mill Road hospital, Derek lived in Stonefield Road, Dovecot and attended the junior school at the end of the street. He did not play organised football until he went to Grant Road Secondary Modern and, like most youngsters his age, he honed his skills practising for hours on end with a baldy tennis ball. Unlike many youngsters, his efforts resulted in a place in the Liverpool Boys, Lancashire Boys and England Boys teams. He used to rely on playing in borrowed boots until, when he was 14 years of age, his older brother bought him his first pair. He put them to good use and in the 1953/54 season, he scored 44 goals from 18 Liverpool Schoolboys games. He received offers to join Liverpool, Manchester United and Wolverhampton Wanderers but Derek opted to join Everton. As a member of the Goodison Park ground staff, his duties included brushing the terraces and stands. Training on a Tuesday and Thursday evenings often took place on the terraces when the boys would run and jump and head balls which were hanging from the girders above the Gladwys Street. Derek longed to get onto the Goodison pitch in front of a roaring crowd and on 30 March 1957, Manager Ian Buchan granted his wish by handing him his first team debut. The Toffees defeated Newcastle United 2-1 and, after the game, his boss predicted that Derek would one-day play for England.

However, before he could make a sustained impact upon the team, Derek received his National Service call-up papers and was shipped off to Kenya. On his return to the Everton set-up nearly three years later, Derek struggled to regain his form and fitness and could not break into the first team. He attributed his lack of fitness to his time spent 7,000 feet above sea level in the Kenyan Aberdare Mountains. Slowly but surely, Derek rebuilt his standing in the club and when new Manager Harry Catterick offered him the chance to prove himself on the left wing, he did just that – scoring 10 goals from 17 games. Derek continued to establish himself as a first team regular until frustratingly a cartilage injury forced him to sit out all but five games of the 1962/63 Championship winning season. Once again, he forced his way back into the team when he returned to full fitness and on 12 May 1965, Ian Buchan's prediction came true when Derek took to the field in Nuremberg to make his international debut in a 1-0 victory over West Germany. Unfortunately, although he was included in Alf Ramsay's initial 40-man squad for the 1966 World Cup, he did not make the final 22-man squad or ever add to his one England cap.

Missing involvement in England's World Cup success was a huge disappointment for Derek. However, 1966 did provide him with his finest footballing moment and ultimately, 'Everton Giant' status. On 14 May of that year, with 100,000 fans inside Wembley Stadium, Everton had clawed their way back from being 2-0 down in the FA Cup Final versus Sheffield Wednesday to be level at 2-2. In the 74th minute of the game, Derek seized upon a mistake by Wednesday defender Gerry Young and ran half the length of the pitch to crack the winning goal past England international goalkeeper Ron Springett. A year later, after 277 games and 84 goals for Everton, Derek left to join Preston North End. Catterick had

told him he did not want him to leave but Derek felt his time at Goodison was coming to an end and made the decision to leave before, he believed, the decision would be made for him. Although his heart was still at Everton, he was a professional footballer and he gave his all for Preston for two years, during which time he played 76 League games and scored 14 goals. Derek spent an enjoyable season with non-league Wigan Athletic before retiring from the game in 1971. He kept himself busy as a double glazing sales representative, shopkeeper and postmaster but always found time to make frequent returns to Goodison Park, where he was always extended a GIANT welcome.

JIM TANSEY

Jim Tansey joined Everton FC as a youth team wing-half in 1948 aged nineteen. Toffees' Manager Cliff Britton converted and developed him into a quality left back and gave him his debut on 5 March 1953 in a 2-2 draw away to Notts County. He played two additional games in his debut season but did not figure at all the following season when the club secured promotion back to the First Division after a three-year absence. Jim played a handful of games in the Blues' first season back in the top flight but really stepped up to establish himself in the following trio of campaigns when he made 121 appearances. However, in the 1958/59 season, Jim picked up a series of niggling injuries which restricted him to just five games in that and the following campaign. Jim Tansey's 139th and final game in a Blues shirt came in a 2-1 defeat away to Bolton Wanderers in August 1959.

The following season he joined Crewe Alexandra of the Fourth Division but, after just nine games, he left Gresty Road and professional football, opting instead to play for South Liverpool FC and become a fitter at British Leyland. Jim passed away on 7 July 2012 after a lengthy illness.

Footynote:

Jim loved regaling his football stories to his family and was immensely proud when his grandson Greg followed in his footballing footsteps. (see page 217)

ALAN A'COURT

Left winger Alan A'Court's signature was much sought after by the troop of scouts who followed his progress with Prescot Grammar School, the County and National Grammar Schools teams and Prescot Celtic. He rebuffed offers from Everton, Wolves and Bolton Wanderers before packing in his job as a trainee supervisor at Littlewoods Mail Order company to sign for Liverpool in September 1952. He made his debut for the first team just a few months later on 7 February 1953, in a 3-2 victory over Middlesborough at Ayresome Park. Alan's big break came when Billy Liddell made the transition from playing wide on the left to become a prolific centre forward. Alan occupied the wing role vacated by Liddell and provided much of the supply line which enabled the Anfield great to find the net with stunning regularity. Alan's career got off to a rocky start when Liverpool were relegated in 1953 and suffered the indignation of a club record 9-1 defeat at the hands of Birmingham City during the following campaign. However, playing in the Second Division did not hinder Alan's personal progress. His performances received rave reviews and England Manager Walter Winterbottom handed him his first international cap on 6 November 1957 versus Northern Ireland at Wembley. He scored, and impressed sufficiently to secure a starting place in all three of England's World Cup games in Sweden '58.

©Tranmere Rovers FC

Domestically, Alan played every game of the 1961/62 season for the team which won the Second Division title at a canter to return to the top rung of the League ladder. Alan also reached an impressive personal milestone when, aged just twenty-four years and eighty-nine days, he became the youngest player in Liverpool's history to play 200 games. However, much to his disappointment, when Shankly's Reds won the First Division title in just their second season back amongst the big boys, Alan did not play a single game due to injury. On 14 September 1964, he played his 381st and final Liverpool game in the club's first European game at Anfield, a 6-1 thrashing of Icelandic side KR Reykjavik in front of 32,597 fans.

Shortly after, for a £4,500 transfer fee, he made the short journey across the River Mersey to join Tranmere Rovers, where he chalked up 50 games and scored 11 goals. On 26 February 1966, Rovers faced Bradford City and in one of his last competitive games, Alan signed out with his first ever hat trick in a 4-2 victory. Aged 32, aware that he would not be offered a new Rovers contract and not wanting to drop down the divisions, Alan embarked upon the second stage of his career. In preparation, he had already obtained his FA coaching certificates and accepted an offer to join Norwich City's backroom staff. Whilst he knew that the world of coaching was not as glamorous as being a player, Alan found it equally as rewarding. After three years at Carrow Road, where he learnt the nuts and bolts of the job, he moved to Crewe Alexandra to become Assistant Manager to Ernie Tagg. However, his stay at Gresty Road only lasted a few months as he found an offer to join Tony Waddington's Stoke City revolution too tempting to turn down. Waddington's "larger than life" personality reminded Alan of Bill Shankly. He had done a fantastic job of turning the Potter's fortunes around combining a blend of youth and experience. With the team languishing at the foot of Division Two when he took control, he pulled a masterstroke by persuading Stoke legend Stanley Matthews to re-join the club. Although Matthews was in his late 40s, his signing captured the imagination of the Stoke fans. Attendances had dwindled in recent seasons but they returned to the Victoria Ground in droves. The move also proved attractive to a host of players who were also in the twilight of their careers but still had something to offer. In 1963, in true Roy of the Rovers fashion, 49-year-old Matthews scored the goal that secured promotion to take the club back to the First Division.

When Alan joined proceedings in 1969, Stoke City were a match for anyone and enjoyed unprecedented success during his seven years in their dugout. Flanked by two FA Cup semi-finals, the club lifted its first major trophy. On 4 March 1972, with 97,582 inside Wembley Stadium, 35-year-old George Eastham scored the decisive goal as they defeated Chelsea 2-1 to win the League Cup. Stoke's time in the top division ended at the conclusion of the 1976/77 campaign after financial difficulties had forced the club to sell its best players. After 17 magnificent years in charge, Waddington vacated the Manager's office and Eastham took control with Alan installed as his number two. Less than a year later, after results failed to improve, the veteran League Cup hero was shown the door. Alan became Caretaker Manager for a couple of games before Alan Durban assumed control of first team affairs. Alan left the Potters soon after and concluded his 28-year career in the game by taking on a variety of football-related positions. These included a return to Crewe Alexandra, joining the sports staff at North Staffordshire Polytechnic and promoting the game he loved in the South Islands of New Zealand. On his return to England, he briefly became a milkman then opened a newsagents' shop before, aged 75, passing away in December 2009.

WILLIE ANDERSON

Former winger Willie Anderson possesses a unique claim to fame in the long and illustrious histories of Manchester United and English football. On 14 August 1965 with 48,502 fans in attendance at Old Trafford, First Division champions Manchester United faced FA Cup winners Liverpool in the Charity Shield curtain-raiser to the 1965/66 season. Having been involved in three first team games in his fledgling career, Willie was United's substitute for the game. This was the first time a match had taken place when teams belonging to the English Football League could select a 'twelfth man'. In the future, substitutions would be allowed for tactical reasons but at this time a substitute could only replace an injured player. In the 18th minute of the match, Denis Law, who had been an injury doubt prior to kick off, was deemed unable to continue participating and left the field of play. Eighteen-year-old Willie joined the action to replace the Scot and take a place in football's record books. The match finished 2-2 with Best and Herd scoring for the Red Devils whilst Stevenson and Yeats registered for Shankly's troops, resulting in each club taking custody of the Shield for six months.

Willie was born on 24 January 1947, and lived in Reeds Road on Huyton's Bakers Green estate. He has clear memories of playing football in the street with a tennis ball but "when an American kid came to live by us and he had a real ball we called on him a lot and went over to the local fields to play on grass." He recalls Everton star Jim Tansey lived a few doors away from his house and future teammate Bill Foulkes' mother-in-law was the Anderson family's next-door neighbour. Willie attended Longview School, his obvious footballing talent earned him a place in the Huyton and Prescot Schoolboys team, and he was "delighted to finally have nets on the goals." Top class performances on the wing made graduation to represent the Lancashire Boys team a formality. This offered him the ideal opportunity to shine and his first appearance in a stadium at Barrow FC's ground was followed by an impressive display at Old Trafford which "for a teenager from Huyton was incredible." The day after the game at the Theatre of Dreams, Manchester United Scouts Joe Armstrong and John Aston tracked Willie down to Reeds Road and convinced the 15-year old to sign as a trainee. "When I got back to school my football coach was not too happy as he had me set to go to Liverpool, which I knew nothing about but I think clubs tend to look after you better if you are living away from home so I was happy with my decision."

On 28 December 1963, apprentice Willie impressed Manager Matt Busby on his first team debut, which was a dramatic affair on and off the pitch. "I found out I was playing on the morning of the game so I had no time to let my family know. Fortunately, they heard it on the radio and my dad, brother-in-law and very pregnant sister drove from Liverpool for the game. My sister never made it as she started in labour on the way and they got a police escort to Manchester Hospital. She had a little girl - born on my debut! By contrast, the game ran smoothly. A brace apiece for David Herd and Graham Moore and a single strike from George Best put Burnley to the sword although the Clarets did manage one goal in reply. "I remember Bobby Charlton saying before the game, don't worry every time you get the ball I will be right there if you need me, and he was. I remember going back to Huyton that night on the train and getting up to watch the pub teams on King George's Fields. I remember having people stare and point me out which was, I guess, the first time I felt kinda famous." On 30 January 1964, Willie signed a professional contract and went on to make 13 appearances for United, which included playing in the 1966 European Cup 1-0 semi-final second leg victory over Partizan Belgrade. Unfortunately, a week earlier the Yugoslavs had won the first leg 2-0 to carry them through to the final where Real Madrid came out on top 2-1.

Almost three years to the day after signing for United, Aston Villa forked out £20,000 to take Willie to Villa Park offering him the regular first team football he craved. Over the following seven years, he was virtually an ever-present in the side and started 264 games and made a further three appearances from the bench. Villa's fortunes fluctuated during Willie's time at the club but he loved it there and quickly became a fans' favourite. The biggest game he was involved in was the 1970/71 League Cup Final at Wembley on 27 February

1971. Much to his satisfaction, they accounted for his former club in the semis and with a capacity crowd of 100,000 in the world's most famous stadium, the Villans took on Tottenham Hotspur. Whilst Villa were languishing in the Third Division, Spurs were flying high in the top flight so were huge favourites to lift the cup and so it proved - but only after a stern test. The underdogs maintained parity until the closing 12 minutes of the match when Martin Chivers grabbed a couple of goals to take the trophy the short distance to White Hart Lane. However, many of the Villa faithful consider this cup run to be the turning point in the club's fortunes. The following campaign they accumulated a record 70 points to win the Third Division Championship. Willie made a massive contribution by scoring 15 league and cup goals, with the spot-kick specialist coolly converting eight penalties.

Although nine years later Willie had long since departed, Villa completed their revival when they won the Division One title in the 1981/82 season, followed by the European Cup a year later. In fact, Willie's career was approaching an end in 1982 and it was pleasing for him to witness their success - even if he was 5,000 miles away! After leaving the Midlands to join Cardiff City for a £60,000 fee in 1973, he terrorised opposition fullbacks with his classic wing play. He helped the Bluebirds win the Welsh Cup in consecutive seasons and in 1975/76 season they finished runners-up in the Third Division to win promotion back to the second tier of English football after being relegated the previous campaign. Willie enjoyed five successful seasons at Ninian Park but, in the summer of 1975, he made a decision that would hugely change his life.

Following an approach from his former Aston Villa Manager Vic Crowe, who was in charge of North American Soccer League outfit Portland Timbers, Willie agreed to play for him during the English League's close season. He made 17 appearances during his summer loan and was instrumental in the club winning the Western Division Championship title. This resulted in qualification for the play-offs and they eventually came out on top in an epic 2-1 game with Seattle Sounders with Willie providing the assist for the winning sudden-death goal. They overcame St Louis All Stars in the semis before being on the wrong end of a 2-0 scoreline in the Soccer Bowl versus Tampa Bay Rowdies. With his tricks, flicks, goals and assists, the Timbers' fans loved Willie's style of play and he regularly had them out of their seats applauding. He loved the football and lifestyle and having dipped his toe in the transatlantic experience, he decided to immerse himself totally by emigrating to the States. However, Cardiff would not release him from his contract so Willie had to bide his time until the Timbers' owners bought him out of his deal. Between 1977 and 1982, he added a further 160 appearances to his career total before finally calling it a day.

Since hanging up his boots in 1982, Willie has worked in radio media advertising and on TV as a football pundit and anchorman. It is more than 50 years since Willie used to play on King George V Playing Fields with the young American boy with the real football, but in view of his fantastic journey, it is fitting that he recalls that story with great fondness.

DOUG LIVERMORE

As a young teenager growing up on the St Johns estate in Huyton, Doug Livermore looked destined for a working life as an electrician or sheet metal worker. Of course, similar to many of his Seel Road School peers, he harboured dreams of becoming a professional footballer and striding out onto the hallowed turf at Anfield in front of a packed house. Much to his delight and surprise, football has dominated Doug Livermore's professional career and he has surpassed many of his schoolboy dreams. He played in 314 Football League games and was involved in hundreds, if not thousands, more in a variety of coaching and managerial roles.

Following a brief spell with Bolton Wanderers, young Doug joined Liverpool in 1963 and turned professional on 1 November 1965 aged 18. After impressing in the reserves, he was often an unused substitute for the first team. He continued to give his all and his efforts were rewarded on 20 April 1968 when he made his first team debut. In the 72nd minute of a 1-0 away defeat to West Ham United in front of a 33,060 crowd, he joined the action from the bench as a replacement for Tony Hateley. A month later, he was a member of the reserves side that lifted the Liverpool Senior Cup by overcoming Southport 4-1 in an Anfield final. He was included

in the club's 1968 tours of the Canary Islands, Portugal and Ireland as part of the first team squad. The following campaign the reserves bagged the Central League title with Doug an integral member of the team. However, he craved first team action but had to wait until 10 January 1970 before he got his chance with another sub's appearance in a 2-0 defeat of Stoke City. A few weeks later on 28 February, he made his first start in the team. A 2-0 reversal at the hands of Derby County did little to dampen his enthusiasm and signalled the first of thirteen consecutive starts as the Reds finished the season in 5th place. When the 1970/71 campaign added just a single appearance to Doug's tally, he regrettably but sensibly acknowledged that his future lay elsewhere.

Initially, 'elsewhere' was Carrow Road the home of Norwich City who Doug joined on 26 November 1970 for a fee of £20,000. He was a vital member of the Canaries' 1971/72 Second Division Championship-winning side and the following season Doug played in the biggest game of his career. Unfortunately, on 3 March 1973 with Wembley Stadium packed to the rafters, Bill Nicholson's Spurs defeated Ron Saunders' Norwich by the narrowest of margins courtesy of a fine Ralph Coates strike. Whilst playing in the same competition versus Southampton a year later, Doug picked up a terrible knee injury, which required two operations. He was restricted to just three additional Canaries appearances and his knee troubled him for the rest of his playing days. Doug loved his time at the Norfolk club but, after 139 games and a short loan spell at Bournemouth, he moved on.

He joined Third Division Cardiff City on a permanent £18,000 transfer and made the first of 88 Bluebirds appearances in a 1-1 draw with Bury on 23 August 1975. Doug left Ninian Park to join Chester City where he added 71 games to his career total before having to hang up his size 9s. In 1978, in what was to be a recurring theme, Doug returned to one of his former clubs, Cardiff City, to take up his first coaching position. It is to Doug's credit that he was welcomed back to no fewer than three of his former clubs when he turned to coaching. He had obviously made a positive impression on his employers during his playing days and in 1980, he became Norwich City's reserve team Manager. Next, he took up a similar position at Swansea City working under his former Liverpool playing partner John Toshack. In an extremely busy period for Doug, he combined his day-to-day responsibilities with simultaneously being part of the Welsh national team's coaching staff. Doug's next stop on his 'coach trip' was White Hart Lane and Tottenham Hotspur. During a rollercoaster period at the club, he filled the role of Manager of the reserves, first team Coach, first team Caretaker Manager and in 1992/93, first team Co-Manager alongside Ray Clemence. Finishing 9th in the inaugural season of the Premier League and reaching the FA Cup semi-finals may have been good enough for some football club owners, but not Alan Sugar. Chief Executive Terry Venables, Clemence and Doug were all harshly axed with Ossie Ardilles installed as the new Manager.

On 28 January 1994, Livermore was back in a tracksuit. This time it was red in colour with a Liver bird on its chest. He became Assistant Manager at Anfield at the invitation of his old mate Roy Evans and together they helped Liverpool lift the Coca Cola Cup in 1995. They also took the Reds to the FA Cup Final the following season, where they were defeated by a solitary Manchester United goal. Evans and Doug left the club by mutual consent when a joint management partnership with Gerard Houllier failed to bear fruit. Livermore was not out of work for long though and was employed as either coach or in a managerial capacity at Nottingham Forest, Norwich (again!) and Leicester City before utilising his knowledge and experience to work as an international football consultant.

RAY MATHIAS

Traditionally, a footballer received a Testimonial game after being at one club for a decade. It was reward for the loyalty shown to the club by the player and in recognition of their unbroken service. Gate receipts from a Testimonial game would provide the player with an often much-needed nest egg for their retirement. Nowadays, it is rare for a player to stay at one club long enough to receive such an accolade. Whilst the awarding of a Testimonial was more prevalent in the Seventies and Eighties, it was still a very prestigious achievement. Therefore, the fact that Ray Mathias received TWO Testimonial games from the same club is simply remarkable. A real one-club man, Ray made 637 appearances for Tranmere Rovers over a 21-year period from 1964-1985.

Born in Huyton on 13 December 1946, Ray attended Park View Primary & Huyton Secondary Modern Schools. He honed his football skills playing with mates on Jubilee Park, which was just a stone's throw from his house in Lincolme Road. He played in the same Huyton Boys team as Willie Anderson and, like Willie, Ray was linked with interest from Manchester United. Willie signed for the Red Devils but Ray heard nothing and joined Cheshire League side Ellesmere Port Town at the tender age of 15. Whilst playing for Port, Tranmere Scout Walter Skinner spotted Ray and was keen to take him to Rovers but every time he called at the family home, Ray was out - probably with a ball glued to his foot on Jubilee Park. Nevertheless, Walter was determined to get his man and used his ingenuity to do so. On 2 May,1964 - FA Cup Final day - Walter had rightly assumed that, like every other football-mad youngster, Ray would be at home sat in front of the television watching the game between West Ham United and Preston North End. Having successfully tracked Ray down, Walter made a good job of convincing the youngster to sign for Rovers.

In December of the same year, Ray formally joined the club which would become a second home to him for decades to come. He made his debut four years later on 22 March 1968 in a 1-1 Third Division draw away from home to Scunthorpe United. None of the 3,986 fans present could have predicted that the young debutant would still be pulling on a Tranmere jersey seventeen years later when he made his final appearance for the club on 14 September 1984 in a 2-0 defeat to Swindon Town.

Between his first and last games, it is true to state that there was not a great deal of glory. There was a legendary 1-0 League Cup victory over Arsenal at Highbury in October 1973 and promotion from the Fourth Division to the Third in the 1975/76 season to crow about but even that was sandwiched between two relegation seasons for the club. However, that should not take anything away from Ray's incredible loyalty, performances and commitment to Tranmere's cause. This received recognition when, on 21 April 1976, Liverpool Manager Bob Paisley sent a strong side over the water to Prenton Park to face Tranmere for Ray's first Testimonial match. Eight thousand two hundred and fifty appreciative fans thoroughly enjoyed the spectacle of seeing their side defeat the Reds 6 goals to 5 (including a hat trick from Liverpool goalkeeper Ray Clemence!) By the time Ray was awarded his second Testimonial game, he was the club's Assistant Manager. The opposition in this match was quite rightly provided by Merseyside's other footballing giants Everton on 23 May 1984.

Having played under five managers during his playing career, it was no surprise when Ray became one himself. He graduated from his coaching duties to take charge of the Wigan Athletic first team in June 1986. Less than a year into the job, his pie-eating Division Three side brilliantly reached the quarter-final of the FA Cup by knocking out Lincoln, Darlington, Gillingham and Norwich City. Although defeated by Leeds Utd 2-0, it had been a great journey for the Springfield Park faithful. Shortly after this, he returned to the Prenton Park coaching staff for the best part of a decade before going back to Wigan at the start of the 1999/2000 season. There was no repeat of their earlier FA Cup heroics but on 18 April 1999 with 53,349 spectators at Wembley Stadium, his team secured the Auto Windscreens Shield by overturning Millwall 1-0. They also reached the play-offs with a sixth place finish but despite this, he parted company with Wigan at the end of the campaign. Over the next ten years, Ray occupied various managerial positions at Tranmere, Chester City, Bury and Stockport County. But it was his spell as assistant to Paul Ince which took him to the highest level of his career. When, on 23 October 2006, Macclesfield Town handed the former England captain the keys to his first managers office, they wisely installed Ray as his number two. Their combination of Ray's experience and Ince's hunger to succeed, worked like a dream. They quickly turned a seemingly hopeless situation around in miraculous fashion to stave off the threat of relegation. Such was their achievement, ambitious MK Dons lured the duo to Buckinghamshire where they delivered the League Two title and promotion at the first time of asking. Once again, success resulted in the offer of a fresh challenge. This time it was Premier League Blackburn Rovers who came knocking and Ray accompanied the top-flight's first black English manager to Ewood Park. However, things failed to work out and, after just 177 days, Ince was shown the door. A brief spell at the helm of Stockport County proved to be Ray Mathias' last formal appointment in a marvellous career which spanned six decades and involved in excess of 1,000 games as a player, manager and coach.

GARY JONES

Winger Gary Jones was born in Prescot on 5 January 1951. He joined Everton as a schoolboy and signed professional forms in October 1968. At this time, Manager Harry Catterick had assembled an excellent squad of players making it extremely difficult for Gary to break into the side. When, in the 1969/70 season the Toffees lifted the League Division One title for the seventh time, Gary could have been excused for thinking that he might never get his chance. However, on 12 April 1971 towards the end of the next season and following a home defeat to Wolves, Catterick rang the changes and granted Gary his debut in front of 24,371 spectators at Goodison Park. Two Joe Royle goals with another added by Alan Ball gave the Blues a comfortable 3-0 victory over Coventry City to ensure that Gary's career got off to a winning start. Although he had made the breakthrough, holding down a regular place in the side proved difficult and during the further two seasons of Catterick's reign, he played on just 19 occasions.

Even when Catterick was sacked and his permanent successor Billy Bingham was appointed at the beginning of the 1973/74 season, he had to bide his time before getting a chance to prove himself. This eventually came along on 5 January 1974 when he replaced Mike Bernard from the bench in a 3-0 win against Blackburn Rovers in the 3rd round of the FA Cup. He impressed sufficiently to be included in the starting eleven in each of the next nine games and only missed being involved in four of the team's last 19 games of the season. However, due to injury Gary frustratingly missed the first couple of months of the 1974/75 season but when he returned to play he came back with a bang. On 19 October 1974, Gary scored his first goal in a blue shirt in a 1-1 share of the spoils with Chelsea at Goodison Park. He stayed in the side and scored in three successive games to cement his place in the side until the end of the season. He grabbed six goals from 29 appearances but Gary's game was not just about goals. He was a flair player who got the fans through the turnstiles and out of their seats. He was also a goal creator and laid on numerous chances for Everton goal machine Bob Latchford. The following season he figured in 25 Division One matches, again scored half a dozen League goals and appeared in the FA, League and Eufa Cup competitions grabbing a couple more goals in the process. The last of his 97 appearances for Everton was on 20 March 1976 in a 3-1 home defeat at the hands of Leeds United.

Before the 1976/77 season had kicked off, Gary had put pen to paper on a deal with Birmingham City whose squad contained a host of Scousers and a few of his old Goodison teammates enabling him to quickly settle into life at St Andrew's. His only goal for the club came in a 2-0 home victory over Sunderland on 11 December 1976 in front of 24,597 fans but, just as he had done at Everton, he provided much of the ammunition for prolific strikers Trevor Francis and Kenny Burns. After just 38 appearances for City, he left the club to take up an exciting offer to play in the North American Soccer League for Fort Lauderdale Strikers. Gary was well suited to the football and lifestyle in the States and loved his time there. He spent two seasons at the Floridian club playing at the Lockhart Stadium alongside legends of the game such as George Best, Ian Callaghan, Gordon Banks and German goal getter Gerd Mueller.

On his return to the UK, Gary became landlord of The Albert pub in Lark Lane near Sefton Park which became a regular haunt of his old playing colleagues and adversaries. He is still highly thought of by the Goodison faithful and regularly attends events organised by the Everton Former Players Foundation.

©George Herringshaw

GEOFF NULTY

Geoff Nulty was born in Whiston Hospital on 13 February 1949 and lived at 5 Duke Street, Prescot. He practised his early football skills on the nearby Prescot Grammar School field and by using the gable end of 1 Duke Street as a goal - much to the annoyance of the occupant, Mrs Larkin. He attended Maryville Road School before passing the 11+ exam and securing a place at Prescot Grammar, a school with a tradition of producing sportsmen and in particular footballers.

As a young teenager, Geoff combined playing for the school team with turning out for Rainford North End FC. Saturday morning's school match would be followed by a frantic dash to catch the direct bus from the Hope & Anchor pub in Prescot to the RNE team meeting place. Failure to catch this bus would mean Geoff's journey would involve three buses, he would probably miss the kick-off and would, therefore, spend a miserable afternoon on the touchline - Geoff hated watching a game when he knew he should be playing! Geoff loved turning out for Rainford, and the challenge of competing with grown men when he was just 15 years of age certainly toughened him up and prepared him for what lay ahead. However, the biggest single influence on Geoff's early football life and the man about whom he states, "if it hadn't been for him I wouldn't have become a professional footballer" was Prescot Grammar's metalwork teacher Jimmy Dewsnip.

When he arrived at the school, Mr Dewsnip took charge of football training and the team. For the first time in Geoff's life, he received proper coaching and consequently made great progress. His performances for the school secured him a place in both the Merseyside and Lancashire Grammar Schools teams. Away from school, Mr Dewsnip played for St Helens Town and he invited Geoff to play for the team, which also included ex-Bolton Wanderers player Derek Hennin amongst its ranks. Whistonian Derek was also a huge influence on Geoff and "offered me a few words of advice I carried with me throughout my career. He told me that if anybody clattered me, I should note their number, bide my time and then effin hit him - then apologise to the ref! "

It was whilst playing for St Helens versus Marine that watching Stoke City Manager Alan Ball Snr was so impressed by Geoff that a couple of days later he turned up at Duke Street and invited the elated youngster to sign schoolboy forms with the Potters. He duly obliged and, even though he was still attending Prescot Grammar School, Geoff turned out on four occasions in the Central League. Geoff's impressive displays earned him a full pro contract but 12 months later he was devastated when a contract extension was not forthcoming and he was shown the Victoria Ground door.

Jimmy Dewsnip once again played no small part in getting Geoff's career back on track when he sent three Prescot lads along to Burnley for trials. He arranged for Geoff to drive the boys to the training ground and told him to take his boots along with him and he would have a word with his contact at the club, Dick Dinnis. Although Geoff only got on the pitch for the last ten minutes of the trials, he made a big enough impression to arouse the interest of Manager Jimmy Adamson. Geoff, at his father's insistence, had secured a job at Pilkingtons Glass factory in St Helens. Just two days after starting work, his boss told him there was somebody at the factory gates who wanted to speak to him. Geoff went outside and found Burnley's Dave Blakey sitting in his car - he asked Geoff to sign on the dotted line and, that was that, he was a Burnley player!

This was the start of a whirlwind couple of days - the Burnley youth team (which had recently won the Youth Cup) was travelling to Germany two days later and Geoff was included in the squad but he did not have a passport. A frantic dash to Liverpool Passport Office resulted in Geoff getting his passport with just five minutes to spare. He then had to travel to Burnley for an overnight hotel stay in preparation of an early start the following morning. Geoff has clear recollections of that hotel stay. The date was 29 May 1968, and he settled down on the eve of his Burnley adventure to watch Manchester United defeat Benfica to win the European Cup. Little did Geoff know that he would soon be sharing a pitch with the European champions.

Geoff made rapid progress through the youth and reserve team ranks to graduate to the first team. His first senior appearance for the Clarets came on 16 August 1969 when he came off the bench to replace Dave Thomas in a 3-0 away victory over Sunderland. A fortnight later, he made his first start in the team and scored in a 2-0 League Cup home win against Rotherham United. On 29 November 1969, Geoff was in the starting line-up for the first time in a Football League match. With a bumper crowd packed into Turf Moor, the team that Geoff had watched lift the European Cup 18 months earlier provided the opposition. Football legend Bobby Charlton showed his class by mouthing "Good Luck" to a nervous Geoff moments before kick-off. He was probably less charitable 42 minutes later when Geoff popped up to score, nullifying an earlier George Best goal, to earn Burnley a creditable draw.

Geoff was an extremely versatile footballer who was comfortable playing in a variety of positions. He was a free-scoring centre forward in his Prescot Grammar, Rainford FC and St Helens Town days whilst he played at fullback for Stoke City and in some early Burnley games. In his second season at the Lancashire club, he played 34 games in six different positions. This was often due to necessity brought about by a combination of injuries and a thin squad.

In 1970/71 season, although Geoff did a sterling job, the club suffered relegation for the first time in a quarter of a century. Two seasons later, with Geoff at the heart of the team, Burnley landed promotion back to the top division. He played 35 out of a possible 42 games that campaign and, in the club's first season back in Division One, he was their only ever-present player. By this time, Geoff had established himself as a box-to-box midfielder, combining his disciplined defensive qualities with an eye for goal. On 30 March 1974, he put in a man of the match performance in an FA Cup semi-final defeat at the hands of Newcastle United - a display that was not lost on the Magpies' Manager Joe Harvey who, in December of the following year, tabled a £130,000 bid for him. Geoff signed, and made his debut on Boxing Day in a 2-1 victory over Carlisle United.

When Harvey left Tyneside shortly after Geoff arrived at St James Park, new Manager Gordon Lee installed him as captain, dispelling any doubts about his place in the team. Geoff loved his time in the North East and claims the fans were magnificent. This was never more evident than in the 1975/76 League Cup semi-final when Geoff scored the winner versus Spurs, "The crowd were amazing that day. Once I had scored they roared us on and pulled us over the finishing line." Unfortunately, Geoff sustained a broken jaw in an FA Cup tie with Bolton, forcing him to miss the League Cup Final defeat to Manchester City.

Newcastle were relegated at the end of the 1977/78 season, but before their Second Division campaign had commenced, Geoff's 101-game stay at the club had ended. He signed for Everton, where he was reunited with former boss Gordon Lee who had taken over the Goodison Park hot seat. However, this was not a fairy tale ending to his career. In just his 28th game for the Toffees, a controversial Jimmy Case tackle in a fiercely competitive Derby match left Geoff with shredded cruciate ligaments. The timing of this career-ending episode was particularly cruel as the day before the game Geoff had been sounded out for the player/managers job at Carlisle United which, at the age of 31, would have been difficult to turn down.

In typical fashion, once Geoff had come to terms with the magnitude of what had happened, he turned his attention to utilising his other talents. With one eye on his future, Geoff had already secured coaching and Open University qualifications, so he was perfectly equipped to accept the offer of Assistant to the Manager, presented to him by the Everton board. When Lee became Manager of Preston North End, he took Geoff with him but, with a number of business interests outside of football, he later decided to focus upon them. Geoff Nulty may no longer be formally involved in football but he is still an avid supporter of Burnley, goes to watch them whenever he can and claims, "It's a fantastic club - best in the country without a doubt."

JOHN MCALLE

Formed in 1877, Wolverhampton Wanderers Football Club was a founder member of the English Football League and in excess of one thousand players have pulled on the famous old gold and black shirt. However, there can be few players (if any) who have displayed more passion or commitment to Wolves' cause than central defender John 'Scouse' McAlle.

Born on 31 January 1950 in Broadgreen Hospital, John spent his early years living in Finch Lane, Dovecot before the family moved to 4 Belton Road on Huyton's Woolfall Heath estate. When he wasn't riding his bike around the local streets John spent every spare minute with a football glued to his foot. Playing on a tarmac pitch with dozens of other eager youngsters, matches lasted from early morning to late at night until somebody would shout "next goal's the winner!"

Although John's uncle Joe Maloney played for Liverpool, John was and still is a staunch Evertonian whose childhood heroes included Alex Young, Roy Vernon, Dave Hickson and Bobby Collins. However, his uncle's career did make a huge impression upon young John who was fascinated by Joe's collection of footballing memorabilia and in particular, an array of souvenirs he brought back from Liverpool's 1953 USA tour. John attended St Dominics School and recalls Mr Corkhill the PE teacher who picked him for the school team and sent him to the Huyton Boys trials, which he successfully negotiated. In 1965, John played a big part in the District representative side reaching the Woodhead Cup Final (defeating Stretford) and the Dimmer Cup Final (losing to Liverpool). His performances at both left half and fullback secured him a place in the Lancashire Boys squad and it was whilst playing for the County that he was spotted by renowned Wolves Scout Jim Moffatt.

Aware that both Manchester United and Leeds United had their sights set on the young Huytonian, Jim wasted no time in inviting him to Molineux. With Uncle Joe's advice of "move away from home" ringing in his ears and working on his own gut instinct, John signed as an Apprentice for the club following a brief meeting with Chairman John Ireland. "It was the very first time I had left home and naturally I was extremely apprehensive about how I would settle.......... I used to go back to my digs worrying about whether I would make it. I was determined to do well but the thought of being sent home and having to face my mother and three sisters preyed on my mind." John's concerns were unfounded but must have been heightened following his first game in a Wolves jersey. It was a Worcestershire Combination match on August 25 1965 and Wolves were on the wrong end of a 7-2 drubbing at the hands of Evesham United! Showing typical tenacity, John got his head down, worked hard and by 14 January 1967, he had graduated to make his Central League debut in a 3-1 win at Blackburn Rovers. He observed the way senior pros Derek Dougan and Mike Bailey conducted themselves and modelled himself on their attitude and application. This paid off the following year when on 29 April he made his first team debut at Chelsea's Stamford Bridge with a Peter Osgood goal proving to be the difference between the two sides. It was the first of 509 games John played for Wolves in a marvellous career which spanned 16 years and included many highs and lows.

In 1972, the team reached the Eufa Cup Final defeating Academica Coimbra, ADO Den Haag, Carl Zeiss Jena, Juventus and Ferencvaros along the way. However, in John's own words, after the excitement of travelling so far and wide, to face Tottenham Hotspur in the final was "an anti-climax". The two English teams faced each other home and away in May 1972 with Spurs winning 3-2 on aggregate. Whilst the club had enjoyed its European adventure, the following season provided the success it and John craved. On 2 March 1974, at Wembley Stadium in front of 97,886 spectators, Wolverhampton Wanderers took on and defeated Manchester City by two goals to one and secured the League Cup. Goals from Kenny Hibbert and John Richards gave the club from the Black Country its first major silverware since lifting the FA Cup in 1960.

John's performances were not going unnoticed and he received a call up to the England U-23 squad. However, the match clashed with a League Cup tie versus Blackpool and the club asked John to withdraw - putting the Wolves' cause before his own personal ambitions, he reluctantly but typically obliged without making a fuss. In the mid-Seventies, the club enjoyed mixed fortunes with relegation from the First Division in 1976 followed immediately by promotion back to the top flight with Scouse at the heart of a resolute defence. On 8 October 1978, Wolverhampton Wanderers acknowledged John's service to the club with a testimonial fixture. Fans flocked to Molineux to show their gratitude to him and not only did Spurs send a strong team along to recreate the Eufa Cup Final of '72 but actors, comedians and even members of supergroups Led Zeppelin and ELO took part in a celebrity match to recognise John's magnificent contribution to football.

However, all good things come to an end and the departure of Manager Bill McGarry, a broken leg and the arrival of Liverpool and England legend Emlyn Hughes contributed to John playing fewer games. In August 1981, he parted company with the club that had dominated his adult life. Perhaps fittingly, his last appearance for Wolves came on 4 May 1981 against his beloved Everton. He found a fresh challenge at Fourth Division Sheffield United and in his only season at the Blades, he made 18 appearances and helped the club win promotion. In 1984, after a short spell with Second Division Derby County, John hung his boots up in a professional sense but enjoyed a successful extension to his career by playing and managing Harrison FC in the West Midlands League.

On 6 May 2015 at the Telford International Centre, John's contribution to Wolves' history received official recognition when the club inducted him into its Hall of Fame to join legends such as Billy Wright, Derek Wagstaffe, Stan Cullis and Steve Bull.

John had always enjoyed gardening and, following his retirement from football, he initially worked at the local Boningdale Nurseries before setting up his own thriving landscaping business.

TOMMY TYNAN

This book highlights the paths that our local players have taken to becoming professional footballers. Whilst no two routes are identical, there are often similarities in many cases. However, Tommy Tynan's journey to the pro ranks was undoubtedly unique. The Tynan family moved to Grant Road, Dovecot from the Scotland Road area of Liverpool in the late 1950s when Tommy was just a toddler. He attended St Margaret Mary's School in Pilch Lane and received his first pair of football boots from a teacher who had appealed to the local community to donate their old boots to the schoolchildren. Scouts from various clubs were aware of Tommy's goal scoring exploits for the school and Liverpool Catholic Schools teams but his big break came courtesy of the Liverpool Echo. In conjunction with LFC, the local newspaper had launched a 'Search for a Soccer Star' competition with the winner securing an apprenticeship with the Reds. Fifteen-year-old Tommy was amongst the 10,000 applicants and successfully navigated his way through to the final trial game at Melwood. With Bill Shankly and his backroom staff watching from the touchline, Tommy rattled home five goals to put the destination of the apprenticeship beyond doubt. This marked the beginning of a successful career which saw him dubbed one of the best strikers never to play in the top flight.

He consistently found the net for Liverpool's reserves (46 goals in 86 games) yet could not break into either Shankly's or Bob Paisley's all-conquering teams. Tommy was sent on a monthlong loan to Swansea City and on 18 October 1975 he made a goal scoring Football League debut in a 2-1 defeat at Doncaster Rovers. A close season loan to NASL side Dallas Tornadoes

followed and proved to be a real eye-opener for Tommy. He thoroughly enjoyed the 19 games he featured in which gave him the chance to share the pitch with a host of international footballing legends including Pele, Bobby Moore, Geoff Hurst and Georgie Best. Tommy returned from his transatlantic adventure to play in Liverpool's Central League games and, having proved to himself and others that he could play at a higher level, he made the tough decision to leave Anfield. Sheffield Wednesday Manager Len Ashurst paid £10,000 to secure Tommy's services and he was rewarded with a goal on Tommy's debut followed by a further 14 goals in his first season for the Owls. The following campaign ('77/78), Tommy continued to do what he had done from the moment he had accepted those boots from his teacher - he found the back of the net. Twenty-one goals in all competitions secured him the first of many Player of the Year awards. However, new boss Jack Charlton's preference of playing with a lone striker did not suit Tommy's style of play and he consequently submitted a transfer request. Lincoln City met Wednesday's asking price of £33,000 and Tommy was on his way to Sixsmiths. The move proved to be a disaster and lasted just nine games and one goal. Tommy's former manager Ashurst was now in charge of Newport County and offered his former striker an escape route, which Tommy did not need to think twice about before accepting.

The £25,000 transfer fee was a record for the little club from South Wales but it would prove to be money well spent. The following seasons were the most successful in the club's history and Tommy was in the thick of the action. Often alongside strike partner John Aldridge, they won both promotion and the Welsh Cup for the first time. This earned Newport a place in the European Cup Winners Cup and they did not disappoint their fans. Brushing aside Irish side

Crusaders (4-0) and the Norwegians of Haugerhsugesund (6-0), they stormed through to the quarter-finals where they faced crack East German outfit Carl Zeiss Jena. Tommy scored two goals to help secure a fantastic 2-2 away draw in the first leg and although they lost the second leg 1-0 to end their involvement in the competition, Newport had made the rest of Europe sit up and take notice of them. In total, Tommy scored 20 goals that season and added another Player of the Year award to his collection. Newport would never scale to such giddy heights again but, despite the club only narrowly fending off relegation, Tommy still managed to score a respectable 13 goals in the 1981/82 season. The following campaign he was on fire and scored a phenomenal 44 League and Cup goals with Aldridge also finding the net on 20 occasions. However, off the pitch the club was in a dire financial position. When they blew their promotion challenge at the business end of the season, the club was on the verge of going to the wall. Consequently, before the start of the next season, Tommy had left the club.

In August 1983, Plymouth Argyle took advantage of Newport's precarious financial plight and paid just £55,000 to take Tommy to Home Park - a snip for a proven goal scorer. It did not take him long to confirm that the Pilgrims had bagged a bargain. He regularly scored in the League and FA Cup victories over Southend United, Barking, WBA and Derby County took the club to its biggest ever game. At Villa Park on Saturday, 14 April 1984 Argyle faced Watford in the FA Cup semi-final. Three goals from Tommy in the earlier rounds had played a massive part in putting the team just 90 minutes away from Wembley's Twin Towers and the biggest game in world club football. Sadly, it was not to be and Watford progressed to the Final where they were defeated by Everton. Tommy was idolised by the Plymouth faithful and his bond with them increased the following season when he won the Third Division Golden Boot with a staggering 31 goals from 45 appearances. Tommy believed that he should have received an improved contract offer as reward for his efforts but when talks broke down he left the club and joined Rotherham United. Typically, he rattled home 17 goals from 39 games but a well-publicised bust up with Manager Norman Hunter resulted in a swift return to Home Park for Tommy - and it was as if he had never been away!

Argyle had nine games of the 1985/86 season remaining when Tommy re-joined them albeit on loan. Well placed to mount a promotion push, Tommy's ten goals helped them to achieve it which resulted in all parties formally agreeing a permanent move in September 1986. Tommy enjoyed four additional Pilgrims seasons and continued to do what he had done since he was a young boy - score goals. His 173 additional appearances returned a further 69 goals. He brought the curtain down on his excellent goal-laden career with spells at Torquay United and Doncaster Rovers followed by a brief flirtation with non-league and a player/manager role at Goole Town. Tommy Tynan, the boy discovered by the Liverpool Echo, made 752 career appearances and scored an extremely impressive 285 goals. His post-football career has included working in the licensing trade, writing a weekly football column for a local newspaper and driving a taxicab around the streets of Plymouth, all of which has kept him in touch with the fans who idolised him.

KEVIN THOMAS

A team's poor run of results is often followed by a change of formation, tactics or personnel. In 1974, when Kevin Thomas was the Southport goalkeeper, the club responded to ten consecutive defeats by allowing half a dozen of their players to be hypnotised!

Born on 13 August 1944, Kevin always had his heart set on becoming a goalkeeper and spent hours working on his game under the street lamps near the family's Dragon Lane home. His efforts paid off when he was selected for his Whiston Secondary Modern and the Prescot and District Schoolboys sides. Football was always at the forefront of Kev's daily activity and, in addition to schoolboy matches, he turned out for Prescot Cables and the Hillside pub teams. After playing in a Sunday league representative match, Blackpool Scout Verdi Godwin invited him to try out for the Seasiders. Verdi had been a prolific goalscorer for a host of clubs including Blackburn Rovers and Manchester City and recognised a good keeper when he saw one. The following weekend, instead of joining two teams of trialists as he had expected, Kevin was plunged into an official reserve team fixture and coped admirably. Shortly after the final whistle, he signed his first club contract heralding the beginning of a relationship with the Tangerines that exists to this day.

Initially, he was understudy to Tony Waiters but when the former England international announced his intention to retire at the end of the 1966/67 season, Manager Stan Mortensen pitched him into action in the final six games of the campaign. The club were heading for the drop to Division Two but the run-in provided Kevin with some poignant memories. On 8 April 1967, as 100-1 outsider Foinavon won the 121st Grand National at Aintree, Kevin debuted in a 1-0 defeat to Sheffield Utd in front of 6,619 spectators. A fortnight later, lifelong Toffees fan Kevin faced the Blues at Bloomfield Road and again Blackpool were on the wrong end of a 1-0 scoreline. Although they won only one of the games in which Kevin featured that season, the victory would prove to be the highlight of his 20-year career. A crowd of 28,773 were present at Anfield on Saturday 13 May 1967 expecting Liverpool to sweep relegated Blackpool aside to bring the season to a close. Prior to kick-off, the Reds had suffered just a single defeat in their previous 20 home games, whilst Blackpool had tasted victory on only five occasions. However, at half-time the score was 3-1 in the underdogs favour and with no goals added in the second 45 minutes, Blackpool (and a delighted Kevin) ended a very poor season with a very good and memorable result. Kevin enjoyed two further seasons at Bloomfield Road but this was in the days before 'player power', lengthy contracts and huge wages - if a proposed transfer deal suited the clubs involved, players had little say in the matter.

When Tranmere Boss Dave Russell identified Kevin as the man to replace Jim Cumbes who had joined West Brom, a £4,000 transfer fee was agreed and Kevin was on his way to Prenton Park. He knew that the move was a mistake and his two-year stay at the club got off to a terrible start. On 13 September 1969, just 30 minutes into his Rovers debut at Doncaster's Belle Vue stadium, a collision with the home side's centre forward left Kevin concussed and stretchered off the field of play. Scottish striker George Yardley, who had started his career as a goalkeeper, deputised until Kevin astounded everyone by emerging from the tunnel to take part in the last 20 minutes of a 2-1 defeat. This was the first of 18 Tranmere appearances Kev made before leaving in July 1971 to join Oxford Utd. His three "thoroughly enjoyable" seasons at The Manor included a short loan spell with Kettering Town who were managed by future Man Utd, West Brom and Aston Villa Boss Ron Atkinson in his first managerial position. Following the birth of Kevin and wife Judy's first child, the couple decided to move back up North to be closer to family. Verdi Godwin stepped back into the picture and, before the commencement of the 1974/75 season, helped to facilitate a move to Fourth Division Southport.

Kevin made his Sandgrounders debut on 21 August 1974 in a 2-0 League Cup defeat to his old club Tranmere but tasted success three days later when overcoming Brentford in a 3-0 home win. Kevin was an ever-present and helped the club to a solid 11th place in the League but the following campaign was a nightmare. Ten consecutive defeats resulted in the team turning to the supernatural when Granada TV's 'Kick Off' programme drafted in well- known hypnotist Romark. In an attempt to reverse their fortunes, Kevin and five teammates were put under his spell before their next match. Unfortunately, shortly before kick-off Kevin inexplicably walked into an iron girder and cut his head open! Opponents Watford left Haigh Avenue with a win and Romark skulked off with his reputation in tatters. Shortly after, Kevin was involved in an innocuous training ground accident which brought the curtain down on his professional career. A Harley Street doctor examined his damaged cartilage and refused to sanction his PFA registration rendering him uninsurable. Down but not out, Kevin correctly believed that at 28 years of age he still had a great deal to offer. Non-league Barrow FC agreed and snapped him up before other clubs got wind of his availability.

Having only lost their Football League status a couple of years earlier, Barrow were a quality outfit geared for success. Wearing his trademark tracksuit bottoms, Kev gained legendary status at the club from Cumbria, making 317 appearances and picking up four Player of the Year awards along the way. His fantastic contribution to the Bluebirds cause was recognised on 8 May 1984 when Ron Atkinson reacquainted himself with his old Kettering keeper. Big Ron sent a strong Manchester United team to Hother Street to face a Barrow side in a well-deserved testimonial match in honour of Kevin and fellow Barrow stalwart Dave Large. Following his retirement, Kevin occupies much of his time playing tennis and is an active member of the Blackpool Former Players Association.

JOHN COYNE

The majority of footballers contained in these pages were spotted by scouts whilst playing for their district or county schoolboy representative teams and joined a League club's youth set up at a young age. A few of the players however, slipped under the scouts' radar and found an alternative route to a professional club. One such player was John Coyne who proved the Liverpool Boys selectors and club scouts wrong by not only joining Tranmere Rovers but also playing hundreds of games around the world alongside some of the best players to have ever kicked a football.

John was born on 18 July 1951 and lived in Penrose Avenue in the Swanside area of Huyton. He attended St Margaret Mary's School and, although he enjoyed playing for the school team, he recalls that they "always got beaten" which may explain why he escaped the attention of the Liverpool Boys Manager when he tried out for the team but wasn't selected. Undaunted, John continued to enjoy his footy - playing in the street from early in the morning until his mum would call him in when it was going dark. He honed his goal scoring skills playing 5-a-side in West Derby Youth Club and turned out for the St Aloysius junior team as well as playing the odd game for the Roby pub which was a stone's throw away from the family home. Young John's favourite player was Everton's 'Golden Vision' Alex Young and he was lucky enough to see him play in one of the Toffees'

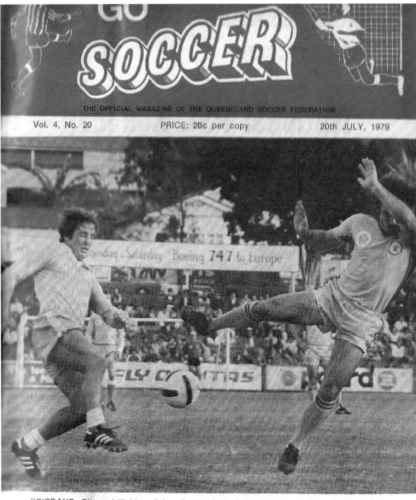

BRISBANE City midfielder John Coyne forced Newcastle United fullback Col Curran to take swift evasive action as he crossed during last week's exciting 1-1 draw at Perry Park.

GO SOCCER MAGAZINE
TRAVELS STATE WIDE
COURTESY OF TAA

most famous games. In May 1966 a couple of months before John's 16th birthday, Everton's Derek Temple gave his father tickets for the Everton versus Sheffield Wednesday FA Cup Final at Wembley. Temple became the eventual match winner when he ran half the length of the pitch to score Everton's third goal to overturn a 2-0 deficit. In the same year, his dad took him to Goodison Park to watch the World Cup group games featuring some of the best players on the planet including Portugal's Eusebio and Brazil's Pele. Taking him to these games was Mr Coyne's way of encouraging his son's love of football and he also played a significant role in John taking his first steps to becoming a professional footballer.

Tranmere Rovers Manager Dave Russell, in addition to turning the club's fortunes around on the pitch, had great foresight and introduced a variety of initiatives that laid the foundations to aid the club's long-term future, including an excellent youth system. John's dad took him to trials with Rovers after seeing an advert in the local paper stating they were seeking fresh talent. Russell obviously recognised something in John which the Liverpool Boys Manager had missed and the young Huytonian's amazing footballing journey was underway. John signed professional forms in August 1971 with the Manager's office now occupied by former Coach Jackie Wright and Russell becoming General Manager. As a member of the squad for the 1971/72 season, John was in familiar company with Ronnie Moore, Dick Johnson and Ray Mathias joining him to form an impressive Huyton quartet. However, Tranmere had a disappointing campaign and when they only just avoided relegation, Wright suffered the consequences. Ex-Liverpool colossus Ron Yeats, who in mid-season had joined as a player from across the Mersey, became the team's new Boss.

Despite showing promise with three goals from 15 appearances, John and Yeats did not see eye to eye and his appointment proved to be the beginning of the end for John at Prenton Park. He joined Len Ashurst's Hartlepool before the start of the following season and got off to a flying start. On 12 August 1972 with 5,789 present at Sincil Bank, John scored on his debut to give the club an opening game of the season 2-1 victory over Lincoln City. However, victories were hard to come by for the Monkey Hangers who scored only 34 goals all season and finished just five places from bottom of the League. On a personal level, John netted nine times to be the team's top scorer. On 12 November the following year, he made his 60th and final Hartlepool appearance in a 1-0 home defeat at the hands of Newport County. He was transferred to Irish outfit Dundalk and a week later made his debut in a 2-0 win against Drogheda in the Leinster Cup, which the club went on to win. In the remaining 20 games of the season, John registered ten goals to become the team's second top scorer.

In the close season (the summer of 1974), John was sounded out by an agent about playing in the North American Soccer League and he jumped at the chance. He joined Dallas Tornadoes for whom he played four games before turning out on 16 occasions for Boston Minutemen returning seven goals. On his return to Dundalk, he improved on his debut season for the Lilywhites by taking the top scorer title with 11 goals from 22 appearances. Brief spells at Cork Hibernian and non-league Wigan Athletic preceded another trip across the pond where he bagged seven goals for Toronto Metros-Croatia before taking part in a series of games that would put him in the record books and see his career scale dizzy heights.

In 1975, the New York Cosmos team pulled off 'the coup of the century', as the world's media dubbed it, when they secured the playing services of Edson Arantes do Nascimento (or Pele, to you and me!). Understandably, with the world's greatest ever player in its ranks, the team were in demand for exhibition matches around the globe. Occasionally, invited guest players joined them on their travels - Gordon Banks, Johan Cruyff and Rivelino would later fill the role but John Coyne became their first recorded 'guest' player when, between 31 August and 28 September 1975, he lined up in the team alongside the player he had marvelled at nearly a decade earlier at Goodison Park. In a whirlwind month, the Cosmos' tour took in games in Sweden, Italy, Norway, Haiti, Jamaica and Puerto Rica and John was in the thick of the action.

A couple of months later in November '75, John added another of the world's best players to his list of playing partners when he signed for Stockport County at the same time as George Best. In a blaze of publicity, the crowds flocked in their thousands to Edgeley Park to watch the Hatters and they were in for a treat. George and John played in four games and the team, who were at the foot of the table, lost one game, drew one and defeated Southport and Swansea City - not bad for a team which won only 13 games all season. John returned to the NASL with Hartford Bicentennials and was amongst the goals again - nine from 24 games - before an agent found him a club in Hong Kong which led to another amazing development in his career.

John's new teammates included a few Australian players who put him in touch with their agent. He was recruiting players for the newly-formed National Soccer League of Australia and in 1977 John joined Brisbane City where he teamed up with fellow Huytonian Frank Pimblett. John spent three seasons and 68 games with

The Azzurri as they were known, and despite some early poor League form, they won the NSL Cup in '77 & '78 and the following campaign reached the Grand Final where they were defeated 2-1 by Sidney City. Whilst playing for Brisbane, John became an international player when he made his full debut for the Socceroos in a friendly 2-0 defeat of Taiwan on 27 November 1979. He made three further appearances for his newly adopted home in two games against Czechoslovakia (a 4-0 loss and a 2-2 draw) and a 2-2 draw with Mexico. John concluded his fantastically varied playing career with spells at Apia Leichhardt FC and Forestfield United.

Having witnessed a host of playing styles and tactics and a variety of managerial and coaching techniques, John was excellently placed to pass on his knowledge and experience to some of the game's youngsters. Just as his father had played a part in helping his son, John encouraged his own kids Jamie and Chris to follow in his footsteps - and they did not disappoint! Jamie enjoyed a successful, trophy-laden, 15-year playing career with Perth Glory, Sydney FC and Melbourne Heart in Australia. He also played in the Dutch Eredevisie for ADO Den Haag and the Indonesian Super League for Sriwijaya. Chris played in excess of 300 career games, mostly for Luton Town but also for West Ham United, Brentford, Southend United, Dundee, Colchester United, Perth SC, Perth Glory and Liaoning Whowin of the Chinese Super League. He also won international honours for Australia's U-17s, U-23s and was a member of the full national side that qualified for the 2010 FIFA World Cup finals in South Africa. John Coyne can rightly look back on his own playing career and those of his sons with pride and joy. Not bad for the lad who was deemed not good enough for Liverpool Boys!

JOHN RELISH

A footballer's career is relatively short. The majority of players end their on-field involvement in the game when they are still young men and most go on to pursue a career outside of football. A relatively small number continue to participate in the sport in a different capacity. John Relish most definitely belongs in the second category. All of his adult life has been spent involved in football - initially as a player, then as a coach, manager and latterly an FA Administrator.

Born on 5 October 1953 at his grandparents' house in Mardale Road, Huyton, John moved to Chester at a tender age but recalls with fondness frequent return visits to the area throughout his childhood. Aged 15, Liverpool's Chief Scout Geoff Twentyman spotted John playing for Chester Schoolboys and invited him to train at Melwood. However, after participating in numerous trials and training sessions, Bill Shankly informed John the club would not be offering him an apprenticeship. Before the disappointment had a chance to sink in, Shanks had made a call to Chester City Manager Ken Roberts who signed John the following day.

John made 14 appearances for the Sealand Road club before, in a magnificent piece of business, Newport County Manager Brian Harris signed him on 20 May 1974. Not only did the club get a player who turned out on almost 400 occasions over a 13-year period, but also a future Assistant Manager and Manager. John's debut took place on 17 August 1974 in an away game at Hartlepool. Newport were struggling at the foot of Division Four for much of the 1970's but John was pragmatic - he had accepted that he was never going to play at the very top level but figured that if he gave his all he could avoid the lower divisions transfer trail and have a satisfactory career. It is fair to say that John's longevity in the game is a reflection of his dedication and professionalism and has surpassed his early aspirations.

The 1979/80 season was arguably Newport's most successful ever but for John it was a bittersweet experience. An injury picked up in a home game versus Hartlepool resulted in him missing the end of season run-in. Consequently, although he was as elated as every other player when promotion and the Welsh Cup were both secured, his absence from the team was a bitter pill to swallow. The following season presented him with the opportunity to put things right and John typically rose to the challenge. John was in the starting line-up on 16 August 1980 when Newport took on Burnley to play in the club's first Third Division game for 18 years. He also played in Newport's first European match when they defeated Irish side Crusaders but picked up another injury to sideline him again for a while. He was, however, back in the thick of the action of their fantastic European Cup Winners Cup run which took them to the quarter-final stage of the competition. This proved to be the pinnacle of John's playing career and of Newport's existence.

On Friday 3 August 1984, the club acknowledged John's dedication to Newport's cause by granting him a Testimonial game. Newport Manager Colin Addison had strong links with First Division club West Bromwich Albion following his time there as Assistant to Manager Ron Atkinson and arranged for them to provide the opposition at Somerton Park. The Newport faithful turned out in great numbers to show their gratitude for the 10 years of loyal service John had given to the club - and there was more to come.

Footynote:

In 1986 John was installed as Newport Manager. The club were in financial turmoil but he battled on before leaving to play for Forest Green Rovers for a couple of seasons. After Newport's troubles forced them into extinction, the club's loyal following reformed the club and, in 1989, John returned to steady the ship and lead them to promotion. John would later take up further managerial positions with Weston-super-Mare, Merthyr Tydfil and Bath City before becoming an administrator with the Football Association. On 18 September 2009 he was inducted into the Newport County Hall of Fame.

RONNIE MOORE

Ronnie Moore spent the first four years of his life living at his grandma's house in the shadows of Everton's Goodison Park. When the family moved to Shelley Close on Huyton's St Johns estate, the garage doors at the end of the Close were just the right size to be used as goals by Ronnie and his mates. They spent hours playing there and unknowingly laid the foundations for Ronnie's future career. Ronnie's house backed onto Sylvester School's playing fields and his mum, who was a cleaner at the school, would pop over to cheer her son on as he played for the school team whilst his dad was working at the Kraft factory in Kirkby. Ronnie also turned out for the St Johns Youth team and both sides enjoyed plenty of success with Ronnie spearheading their attacks and regularly finding the net. When he moved to Seel Road Seniors, Ronnie was immensely proud to be selected for the Huyton Boys side.

At the age of 14, Everton's Chief Scout Harry Cooke invited him to train with and play for the club's youth team with a view to signing as an apprentice on his 16th birthday. However, when his mum passed away it hit young Ronnie hard and, by his own admission, he went off the rails. Rather than help him through this difficult period, Everton lost interest in Ronnie and harshly showed him the door. He continued to play for St Johns Youth and joined local pub side Huyton Park. He was much younger than the men he was playing with and against but was physically equipped to deal with the demands of Sunday League football. He has fond memories of battles with, amongst others, the Eagle & Child at Huntley and Palmers' pitch. After one game for The Park, a Tranmere Rovers Scout asked him to attend training with the club. The Wirral seemed like a million miles away to the 16-year old and he had another problem. Ronnie had recently taken up a job at local firm Weston's Cash & Carry and didn't finish until 5.30pm, which would prevent him from getting to Bebington Oval in time for training. Weston's workers Gwen Elliot and Emily Ellis came to his rescue by clocking him off, allowing him to sneak out of work early. Twice a week, he would jump the bus to the Pier Head, board the Mersey Ferry before taking the number 64 bus to The Oval. He would give his all in training, negotiate the return journey and slump into bed at 11 pm. Ronnie had been given a second chance to become a footballer and showed the determination and commitment which had understandably been lacking towards the end of his time with Everton. His efforts did not go unnoticed and he quickly made his way through the Rovers' ranks.

First team Manager Jackie Wright included him in his squad for a few games but it was not until Liverpool legend Ron Yeats became player-manager that he got his first start for the club. Yeats believed Ronnie had all the attributes to be a top defender but it was not as a defender OR a forward that he made his debut. On 25 August 1973 with 4,749 present at the Recreation ground, Ronnie played his part in a 0-0 draw with Aldershot - occupying a central midfield position! Interestingly, future FA Chief Executive and owner of Tranmere Rovers Mark Palios also made his debut in this match. Ronnie was up and running and Yeats installed him as his defensive partner soon after. The two Ronnies were a solid unit and this was never more evident than in one of the club's greatest achievements when, on 2 October 1973, Tranmere Rovers accounted for the mighty Arsenal 1-0 in a League Cup 2nd round tie at Highbury in front of a crowd of 20,337. In Ronnie's first two seasons they finished 10th and 16th but, following relegation at the end of the 1974/75 campaign, Yeats got the bullet and the new boss wasted no time in putting his own stamp on the team. Former Everton player Johnny King believed the side needed to score more goals and placed his faith in Ronnie to deliver - he did not disappoint. His 34 League goals played a massive part in Rovers bouncing straight back to Division Three and remarkably this tally included three games in which he found the net four times. Towards the end of the 76/77 season and with a mid-table finish already secured, Kingy allowed Ronnie to take up an exciting opportunity to broaden his horizons.

Responding to a request from Chicago Sting's Manager Bill Foulkes, Ronnie and teammate Bobby Tynan went on loan to play in the NASL for the former Manchester United player. He made 22 appearances for The Sting and his eight goals included a bullet header to win the game against the New York Cosmos whose number 10 shirt was filled by Brazilian superstar Pele. When Ronnie returned from the States, he spent another season and a half at Tranmere until Cardiff City tabled a successful £120k bid to take him to Ninian Park. Although he enjoyed a purple patch when he scored three times in five games shortly after joining, goals were hard to come by and he scored just seven from his 56 games. Despite this, he shared a good relationship with the Cardiff faithful who acknowledged his work rate. Ronnie even saw the funny side when some of them started wearing badges stating, "I saw Ronnie Moore score!" Although things did not go as Ronnie had hoped at Cardiff, he still had great self-belief and in Rotherham's Ian Porterfield, he found a manager who shared his faith in his ability. The Millmoor Boss stumped up £100k for Ronnie and it would prove to be the best investment the club would ever make.

He scored 25 goals in his debut season, the last of them ensuring victory over Plymouth Argyle which preserved their seasonlong unbeaten home record and secured promotion as Division Two Champions. The following season saw them finish 7th and Ronnie topped the divisional scoring chart with 22 goals. When Porterfield left to join Sheffield United, it signalled a change in the club's fortunes and ultimately Ronnie's departure. Emlyn Hughes struggled as Porterfield's replacement and when he left, George Kerr took over. Ronnie and Kerr failed to see eye to eye and after 125 games and 52 goals he left Rotherham and joined Charlton Athletic. The Addicks had negotiated a bargain fee of £30,000 for Ronnie but due to their dire financial position, they reneged on the agreement. It was only when the Charlton Supporters Action Committee raised £8,000 to pay Rotherham that the club avoided having points deducted by the FA. Unfortunately, the Inland Revenue were not so accommodating and declared Charlton insolvent. On the pitch, the team managed to ignore the financial turmoil and finished the 1983/84 season in 13th place. Manager Lennie Lawrence utilised Ronnie in both defensive and attacking roles during his two seasons at The Valley making his games to goals ratio of 62:13 more than respectable. However, when Johnny King invited Ronnie to join him at Rochdale where he had recently become Assistant to Manager Vic Hallom, he jumped at the chance.

He signed for the Dale on 1 July 1985 and loved his time at Spotland where he played alongside fellow Huytonians Shaun Reid and Frank Gamble. After 43 games and nine goals scored, he re-joined Tranmere, now managed by Frank Worthington. Just as Yeats had done more than a decade earlier, it was Ronnie's turn to take on the mantle of defensive lynchpin whilst coaching and nurturing the young talent around him. This was not lost on the Rovers hierarchy who installed him as caretaker player-manager when Worthy received his marching orders on 11 February 1986. Ronnie's first venture into management started well with a five-game unbeaten run. When Johnny King returned to Prenton Park after leaving Dale and performing miracles at Caernarfon Town, he installed Ronnie as his number two, alongside Kenny Jones who had been with him at Caernarfon. Tranmere had looked doomed to relegation when Ronnie had taken charge but Johnny continued the progress he had made. When Gary Williams scored the winner against Exeter City on the last day of the season, they achieved the great escape. At the end of the following season (having finished a solid 14th), the club took part in the Mercantile Football League Centenary Tournament at Wembley Stadium. It was an enjoyable event for the players and fans and the team defeated Wimbledon and Newcastle before losing on penalties to subsequent winners Nottingham Forest. This morale boosting performance carried the team into the 1988/89 campaign when they secured second place and promotion to Division Three.

After 700 games and 200 goals, Ronnie deemed this an appropriate time to bring down the curtain on an excellent playing career. He sat alongside Kingy on the management bench for a further seven seasons, which proved to be the most successful in Rovers' history. During this exciting, eventful period, they were beaten play-off semi-finalists on three occasions, lost in a Wembley play-off Final and secured promotion by winning a Wembley play-off Final. In addition, the club were beaten Wembley finalists in the Leyland Daf Trophy but lifted the same prize when they overcame Bristol Rovers at Wembley in 1990. When King moved upstairs to become the Director of Football at Prenton Park and John Aldridge was installed as his replacement, Ronnie decided to put his knowledge and experience to the test.

His first permanent job in the managerial hot seat was at Southport's Haig Avenue. In a repeat of his Rovers baptism, he went unbeaten in his first five fixtures and got off to a flying start with a 2-0 victory over Halesowen Town in the FA Trophy 1st round. The Sandgrounders 11th place finish was enough to convince the powers that be at Rotherham to install him as their man in charge. His first season secured a 10th place finish, followed in 1998/99 by a place in the play-offs where Leyton Orient defeated them on penalties at the semi-final stage. Fans of The Millers readily identify the next two seasons as the most exciting period since the club's formation in 1925. Ronnie received Manager of the Month and Manager of the Year awards as the team romped to consecutive automatic promotions from Division Three to Division One. The following three seasons were enjoyed in the second tier of English football but in 2004/05 they struggled and, although Ronnie left the club by mutual consent, it was undeniable that under his stewardship they had been on a fantastic journey. Unsurprisingly, Ronnie had been out of work for just two months when he landed the top job at Oldham Athletic. The Latics had previously endured a poor season under Brian Talbot and finished a point above the relegation zone. Ronnie took a struggling side and converted them into a solid mid-table team who finished 10th in his only campaign at Boundary Park.

On 9 June 2006, Ronnie Moore walked through the gates of Prenton Park to take over the managerial reins of a club which had just accumulated 54 points, finished 18th in League One and dodged relegation by a mere four points. Over the next three years, he worked his magic in an attempt to bring the glory days back to the Birkenhead club. In 2006/07 season, they improved massively with a ninth place finish and 67 points. They then consolidated their position when they secured 11th place and 65 points. In Ronnie's third season back at the club he loved and where the vast majority of fans held him in high esteem, Tranmere Rovers registered 74 points and finished 7th just a couple of points outside of the play-offs. On 5 June 2009, Chairman Peter Johnson sacked Ronnie Moore sighting poor attendances as the reason! It could be argued that Mr Johnson was being economical with the truth and the appointment of ex-Liverpool player John Barnes just five days later could add fuel to that particular fire. Barnes lasted less than five months in the job and his successor, club physiotherapist Les Parry, was ill-equipped to make any significant improvements. The club finished the season in 19th place, one place and one point above the relegation zone. To add insult to injury, the average home attendance was 149 spectators down on Ronnie's final season! Although Ronnie thought he had seen almost everything during his time in the game, even he was gobsmacked at his Tranmere departure.

However, three months after his dismissal he was back behind the Manager's desk at Rotherham. A bright start resulted in the November 2009 Manager of the Month award finding a home on Ronnie's desk and after finishing fifth, they safely negotiated their way to the play-off Final. In a thrilling game, the Millers found themselves on the wrong end of a 3-2 scoreline against Dagenham and Redbridge. The fickle nature of football was once again evident during the 2010/11 season when, after a six-game winless streak but with the team still occupying a play-off spot, Ronnie was again relieved of his duties - perhaps he had become a victim of his own success? Following his dismissal, the club won just two of their final nine games and slumped to a mid-table finish. Ronnie had been out of the game for almost a year when Peter Johnson ate a large slice of humble pie and invited him back into the Tranmere fold. The club had experienced a disappointing period since Ronnie's departure and almost constantly found themselves in the lower reaches of the table. Therefore, by finishing 12th, 11th and 12th represented progress in his three seasons back in charge. However, in February 2014 Ronnie was suspended and subsequently had his Tranmere contract terminated when he was naively involved in a family betting syndicate that contravened FA regulations. However, you cannot keep a good man down and on 16 December 2014, Hartlepool turned to Ronnie when they were 10 points adrift of safety and looked destined to lose their Football League status. Twenty-Six games later, with nine wins and six draws under their belt, they achieved what had seemed impossible with four points to spare. Once again, Ronnie had repeated what he had done at virtually every club he played for or managed - delivered results. Less than 12 months later though, Ronnie was again out of a job when somebody with a short memory showed him the door.

During a career spanning five decades, he has been involved in more than 1,600 games and achieved tremendous success, often against the odds. He has bounced back from disappointments with a smile on his face and created memories for fans up and down the country. Hopefully, Ronnie will remain involved in the game in some capacity because the world of football is a far more interesting and entertaining proposition when people like Ronnie Moore are involved.

PHIL DEVANEY

Many of the players contained in these pages have enjoyed magnificent successes of national and, in some cases, international significance; World Cup & European Championship appearances, international caps, appearance records, Player of the Year awards - the list is long and impressive. However, success is relative and for one young Huyton man 9 May 1987 is probably just as memorable as any other date for any other player.

Phil Devaney was born on 12 February 1969 in the family home on Cronton Road opposite the Hare and Hounds pub. When, in the late Seventies, the family moved to Whiston Lane, Phil took full advantage of their new home's close proximity to the King George V Playing Fields, and in particular, the football pitches. "From the age of eight, I must have spent half of my life on the Georgies. We'd get home from school and about four of us would play there rain or shine until it got dark. I remember one day getting home covered in mud and my dad made me stand outside in the garden while he hosed me down." Phil's father was a massive influence on him and they enjoyed many a kickabout together. His mum and dad never missed a game he was involved in and were always offering words of advice and encouragement from the touchline.

Phil combined playing for his St Aidan's School footy team with turning out for Huyton Boys, Rainhill United and St Annes Rovers, under Harry Tyrell. Graduation to St Augustine's Secondary School resulted in him securing a place in the Knowsley and Merseyside Schoolboys sides and Phil recalls foolishly playing for the County side whilst carrying an injury and having a stinker. The decision cost him a place in the team that won the 1983/84 U-16s Northern Counties Schools' FA Final by defeating Lancashire Boys 2-0. However, Burnley Scout Eddie Roberts already had Phil's talent on his radar and consequently arranged for the young striker to attend a successful trial with the Clarets. Despite Liverpool also expressing an interest in Phil, he decided to take up Burnley's offer of a schoolboy contract although he did end up on the Liverpool coach after Burnley hosted the Reds in a pre-season friendly. In an excellent example of morale-boosting management, Burnley Boss Martin Buchan arranged with his opposite number Kenny Dalglish, for Phil to travel home to Huyton with the Liverpool team. Imagine his parents' surprise when he turned up unannounced on their doorstep and told them that he had sat next to Reds' legends Steve Nicol and Ian Rush on the journey home! After a year as an apprentice, Phil signed as a full-time professional on his 17th birthday and was involved in the first team squad for the penultimate game of the 1985/86 season. The opposition on that occasion were Leyton Orient and although Phil did not play a part in the match, it gave him a taste of what to expect and he would be in the thick of the action when the sides crossed swords in the following campaign.

On 21 March 1987, with the team struggling at the wrong end of the Fourth Division table, Buchan's replacement Brian Miller turned to some of the young lads in the squad and handed Phil his first team debut versus Aldershot. With 2,690 present, an inauspicious start ended in a 1-0 Turf Moor defeat and Phil relegated back to the reserves. Three consecutive defeats followed to plunge the Lancashire club deeper into the mire and Phil had to wait until the second half of a relegation scrap with fellow strugglers Torquay United before he got his next opportunity. Losing 2-0, Miller threw Phil into the action and just 18 minutes later, he set up Ian Britton who coolly converted the chance to give the Clarets hope. Then, in the 90th minute and with time running out, Phil won a penalty and the veteran Leighton James made no mistake from 12 yards to secure a valuable point. Four days later, Phil's reward was a place in the starting line-up against Rochdale and, with the game less than a quarter of an hour old, he latched onto a fumble by the Dale keeper to hook the ball into the net to score his first and only goal for the club. Joe Gallagher added another to make it a Huyton double and three crucial points in their battle for survival. Phil kept his place in the starting eleven for the remaining six games of the season as the club attempted to maintain its Football League status. Their fate was determined in a nail-biting last day of the season game with Leyton Orient, the club who had provided the opposition when Phil first sampled involvement with the club's senior squad.

Just as Liverpool and Everton fans of a certain age will never forget the events of Istanbul in 2005 and Rotterdam in 1985 respectively, Clarets players and supporters hold the Burnley v Orient clash on 9 May 1987 in similar esteem. Phil clearly remembers the build-up to the game and the air of excitement around the town. The unusual presence of the television cameras at the ground added to the sense of occasion and the fans flocked to Turf Moor. Referee George Courtney delayed the kick-off by 15 minutes to enable all 15,696 fans to gain entry to the ground and give Burnley their biggest attendance for five years. Anything less than a Burnley win coupled with their rivals slipping up, would have seen the club drop out of the Football League and slide into potential obscurity. On the stroke of half-time, Neil Grewcock opened the scoring and Ian Britton made it 2-0 in the 48th minute. Although Allan Comfort pulled a goal back for the O's, it was too little too late. Other results worked in their favour to secure the great escape. The full-time whistle signalled a pitch invasion and scenes of delirium which many fans still fondly recall. Whilst all of the players performed brilliantly, Phil was singled out for special praise from the Burnley Express newspaper whose reporter wrote ".... after so many disappointments this season, all 11 Burnley players were acclaimed as heroes with the least experienced, 18-year old Devaney, having run himself to a standstill. Hardly known by the Burnley fans six weeks ago, he has been pitched into the deep end and grasped the chance brilliantly."

In the close season, the club made eight new signings and Phil found himself back in the club's second string. Disappointed but determined to prove the manager wrong, Phil bagged 10 goals in the first 14 games of the season yet he still wasn't handed a first team opportunity. His frustration brought about a reluctant confrontation with Brian Miller and the following game he was delighted to be involved with the first team, albeit on the bench. However, his elation was short-lived and swiftly turned to dismay when game after game he took his place on the bench and Phil made just four appearances all season. Understandably, Phil became increasingly frustrated and when he was left out of the 13-man squad for the 1988 Sherpa Van Trophy Final, it proved to be the final straw. Striker Dave Reeves picked up an injury a few days prior to the game with Phil the natural like-for-like replacement. However, despite the fact that Phil had spent the vast majority of the season warming the bench, Miller elected to hand 35-year old winger Leighton James the tracksuit and he knew it was time to move on.

He received offers to join Hartlepool and Rochdale but bravely opted for a change of direction. Phil still hadn't reached the age of 20, yet he made the mature decision to turn his back on a career in professional football to concentrate on adding further qualifications to the eight 'O' levels he secured at St Augustine's. He combined playing semi-pro for Morecambe and then Marine with studying at Knowsley Tertiary College. When he took up the offer of a place at Hull University, he joined local club Goole Town. Phil also played in the World Student Games in the USA and spent the summer months coaching at US soccer camps. However, a niggling knee injury, which he had suffered with from his Burnley days, finally got the better of him and he was forced to hang up his boots and dedicate his time to securing his Mechanical Engineering degree. Two years later, a chance meeting with renowned North East Scout Peter Whinham resulted in him returning to the game after the couple struck up a deal. Phil had told Peter about his troublesome knee but the canny scout told him that he would pay for a series of physio treatments for Phil which, if successful, would enable him to turn out for his club Northwood FC in the Hull & District Sunday League. After just four sessions of friction therapy, Phil was able to fulfil his side of the bargain. Using his knowledge and contacts, Whinham had put together a fine team of former pros who gelled superbly and won the Premier Division of a League which contained no fewer than 22 divisions. Phil's appetite for the game returned and word of his performances spread. Northern Premier League outfit AFC Emley provided him with the platform to show what he was still capable of and, in his opinion, he "played the best football of my life". Sheffield United obviously agreed with Phil as they invited him to spend six months with the Blades when the season concluded. However, shortly before the end of the campaign, Phil suffered a horrendous leg break and at the age of 26 he experienced first-hand the truth behind the old adage that football can be a cruel game. This time, his footballing days were definitely over and to add insult to Phil's injury, the timing could not have been worse. With just a few months to go until his final exams, his hospitalisation meant he missed a great deal of study and revision time. It is to his great credit that he applied himself and secured a First-Class Hons Degree.

Initially, finding employment was a struggle as Phil literally was not fit for work and potential employers were not prepared to wait for him to recuperate. However, when he attended an interview with BAe SEMA, the interviewer was more interested in talking football than Phil's suitability for the vacant post. The job was in the bag when he explained that although he was unable to play for the company's team, he could help in a coaching capacity. This has been the case on more than one occasion during Phil's post-playing career and it is startling just how many people remember THAT game versus Orient.

After spending seven years working in and around London as a Systems Developer and then in the world of 'Finance & Trading', Phil took a leap of faith when he was offered a position with Suisse Bank and has been there ever since. He lives 30 kms away from Zurich in a small town called Wilen Bei Wollerau but still comes home at least once per year to visit family and friends. In 2017, to celebrate the 30th anniversary of 'The Great Escape', Phil attended a Turf Moor reunion which rekindled some fantastic memories of his brief but poignant time at Burnley.

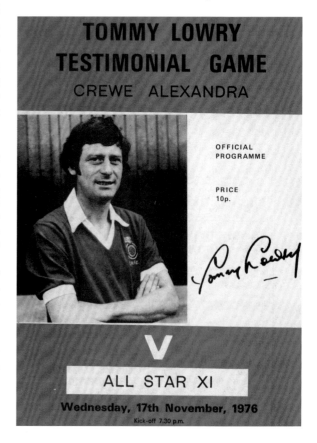

TOMMY LOWRY

Crewe Alexandra FC was founded in 1877 and during its proud history the fans have enjoyed watching a host of players who have graduated to the upper levels of their profession. David Platt, Danny Murphy, Neil Lennon, Stan Bowles, Bruce Grobbelaar, Jimmy Greenhoff and our very own Craig Hignett are just a few who have plied their trade at Gresty Road. However, although he did not scale the same dizzy heights as these Railwaymen, the club's greatest ever servant is, without doubt, Huyton-born Tommy Lowry who rattled up a record number of appearances during an 11-year period.

Born on 26 August 1945, Tommy grew up in the Woolfall Heath area and attended Longview School. Aged 16, he joined Liverpool FC and at the end of the 1962/63 season he was a member of the team that reached the FA Youth Cup Final – the first time the club had achieved this. On Saturday 25 May 1963, a month after signing his first pro contract, Tommy took his place in the side for the 2nd leg of the U-18's showpiece. Leading West Ham 3-1 from the Anfield 1st leg, the scene was set for Tommy and co to lift the trophy. However, teenage striker Martin Britt registered four stunning goals to help the Hammers to a 5-2 victory on the night and 6-5 on aggregate much to the delight of the 13,000-strong crowd at the Boleyn.

Tom's time at Liverpool coincided with Bill Shankly revolutionising the club's fortunes. In 1961/62 season, Shanks' side sealed promotion to the First Division as Division Two Champions and, just two years later, secured their first championship since the 1946/47 campaign. The success and consistency of the team restricted Tommy to a single first eleven appearance and even that was because of a bit of Shanks' ingenuity.

On 1 May 1965, Liverpool lifted their first FA Cup by defeating Leeds United 2-1 at Wembley Stadium. A week earlier, with the Final in mind, the Liverpool Boss protected his first choice players by naming his entire Central League side to play in the club's last League game of the season versus Wolves. In a typically classy move, Shanks rang his Molineux counterpart Andrew Beattie to inform him of his intention to throw his reserves into battle. He followed this by making his decision public knowledge in order to put the fans (who may have expected to see the first-string) in the picture. Tommy was one of four debutants with Hignett, Molyneux and Sealey the others and the 'weakened' side blew their opponents away by a 3-1 scoreline. Tommy had fulfilled a boyhood dream but, unlike his reserve team colleagues Ronnie Moran, Gordon Wallace, Geoff Strong, Bobby Graham and Alf Arrowsmith, the fullback did not figure in Bill Shankly's plans again.

In June 1966, Tommy left Anfield, joined Fourth Division Crewe Alexandra, and stayed for more than a decade. His career with the Railwaymen got off to a stuttering start when the floodlights failed during his debut, forcing the match's abandonment. His third career 'debut' in his third match took place on 22 October 1966 in a 1-0 victory over Southend Utd in front of a crowd of 4,036. Tommy went on to make 481 appearances for Alex – a club record. Early in his career he was given the nickname 'Twiggy' due to his slight build but what he lacked in physical stature he more than made up for in grit, commitment and a determination to give his all. This was never more evident than when he was diagnosed with cancer of the inner ear. Despite having radiotherapy treatment, he carried on playing wearing a massive padded bandage for protection. He missed just one game of the 1967/68 season when, by finishing fourth, they secured promotion to the Third Division - although they went straight back down to the basement division a year later.

Twiggy was a solid, old-fashioned right fullback and unlike the modern day equivalent, his first priority was to defend. Unsurprisingly, he only scored two goals during his lengthy career. The first came in 1971 in a Watney Cup defeat to Carlisle Utd and four years later he notched against Brentford. On Wednesday 17 November 1976, with 10 years' service under his belt, the club handed Twiggy a Testimonial match. The fans flocked to Gresty Road to salute Tommy and to see their team take on a star-studded opposition which included legends Brian Kidd, Jimmy Greenhoff and World Cup winners Gordon Banks and Nobby Stiles. After bowing out of football at the end of the 1977/78 campaign, Tommy joined the workforce at the local Rolls Royce factory and stayed until his retirement in 2003. Tommy Lowry sadly passed away at Leighton Hospital on 22 August 2015 four days before his 70th birthday. The club that had dominated his footballing life held a moving minute's applause at their next home game versus Swindon Town and both sets of supporters showed their appreciation of his contribution to the game with chants of "There's only one Tommy Lowry."

PAUL O'RILEY

Paul O'Riley was born on 17 October 1950 in Whiston Hospital. He grew up living in the prefabricated bungalows in Beldon Crescent, Huyton and attended St Aloysius School. "Football mad" Paul was the captain of both his school and the Huyton Schoolboys teams and, although he initially played centre half, he regularly found the net. He scored a staggering 44 goals in one season -an early indication of the direction his football career would later take. Paul identifies Mr Hurst, his school Science teacher and football manager, as a major early influence. Mr Hurst was the Chairman of the Huyton Schools Football Association and was always on hand to advise and mediate for Paul and others who attracted the attention of club scouts. However, when Hull City's Chief Scout Les Bryan by-passed Mr Hurst and turned up at Beldon Crescent, Paul was impressed by what Les had to say. A trial with the Second Division outfit was successfully negotiated and when Paul left school in 1966 he returned to the Tigers for a monthlong stay with the club. Manager Cliff Britton saw enough to convince him that Paul had a future in the game and secured his signature. When Paul was unable to dislodge the established centre half from his position, he turned out for the junior teams at full back until Mr Hurst informed the coaching staff of his goal-scoring prowess. Given a chance to show what he could do upfront, he scored a hatful and did not look back!

On 24 August 1968, 17-year old Paul O'Riley the striker made his Football League debut versus Oxford United in a 1-1 draw. Over the next couple of seasons, he made the odd appearance but the presence of fearsome double-act Chris Chilton and Ken Wagstaff hindered his chances. Injuries also limited Paul's progress and in 1970 he dropped down a couple of divisions to join Scunthorpe United on loan for the last seven weeks of the season. He grasped the opportunity and made an immediate impact, scoring three goals in three games within seven days of joining the club. He struck up a great partnership with the Iron's other forward whose all-energy performances left Paul in no doubt that the pocket dynamo had a big future ahead of him. He was proved right when, in the close season, Bill Shankly paid Scunthorpe £100,000 for the future European Player of the Year, Kevin Keegan!

Buoyed by the success at Scunthorpe, a confident Paul returned to Boothferry Park with his tail up. He thoroughly enjoyed a pre-season tour of Scandinavia and when Chilton left to sign for Coventry City, he secured an extended run in the team which included a League Cup tie at Anfield when he again shared the pitch with Keegan (Liverpool won 3-0). After six years with Hull, Paul left on a free transfer to sign for Fourth Division Barnsley but his stay was brief - 14 games yielding two goals. Alan Ball Snr offered Paul a place on the Southport FC playing staff, which he accepted. His first game for the Sandgrounders was on 11 March 1975 away to Rochdale. Those present witnessed Paul bang home two goals in a 3-3 draw and the handful of Southport fans amongst the 1,191 crowd must have been rubbing their hands in anticipation. However, after a bright start Paul and Southport really struggled to find their form and over the next three seasons he only found the net twice and the writing was on the wall.

In 1977, Paul was offered a fresh challenge when former Hull City playing colleague Ken Wagstaff invited him to join him in Australia to play for Moorolbank FC whom Waggy had just taken charge of. This was the start of a very successful and enjoyable chapter in Paul's life. He loved the laid-back lifestyle in Oz and also found the football was to his liking. Sandwiched between spells as Moorolbank and Ringwood City FC, Paul also spent three seasons in Hong Kong playing for Eastern FC.

In 1983, Paul O'Riley retired from the game and settled down to continue enjoying life in Australia, however an annual visit home to catch up with family and friends and to enjoy a few pints in St Aloysius Parish club is a 'must' in his calendar of events.

JIMMY WESTON

There are approximately 4,000 professional footballers in the UK. The average length of a player's career is about eight years and the majority of footballers have retired from playing the game by their mid-thirties. Only a very small percentage of players earn sufficient funds during their playing days to offer them the chance of long-term financial stability after hanging their boots up - and many fail to take advantage of that opportunity. Therefore, out of necessity a post-playing career is a must for the vast majority of footballers. Unfortunately, forward planning is often not high on many players' agendas and this can result in problems further down the line. On the other hand, some players have sufficient foresight to wisely acknowledge the reality of their dilemma and do something about it - one such player was Jimmy Weston.

Born on 16 September 1955, Jimmy grew up living in the Woolfall Heath area of Huyton and attended St Columbas Junior School. He played for the school football team and has fond memories of matches against arch-rivals St Josephs and tussles with his midfield opponent, future Everton and England player Peter Reid. When Jim passed the 11+ exam test he qualified to attend SFX Grammar School in Woolton but because the school was located within the Liverpool city boundaries, Jimmy missed the chance to play for Huyton's most successful, all-conquering Schoolboys team. However, he did turn out for the Merseyside Grammar Schools representative side and his school team found glory when winning the Merseyside Grammar Schools Shield. Jimmy's weekends consisted of football, football and more football. He spent Saturday mornings playing for SFX before competing against much older youths for the Bluebell under-18s side. He even played for Huyton Labour's open age team on Sunday mornings until "a scything tackle in a game against the Farmers Arms made me decide to retire from Sunday football at the age of 15!"

Jimmy's performances for his various outfits were not lost on the country's scouting network and in 1972 Division One club Coventry City offered him a contract. He turned this down and opted instead to play for Skelmersdale United of the Northern Premier League. Skem had recently won the FA Amateur Cup and had a reputation for nurturing young talent including Liverpool legend Stevie Heighway. However, on 1 January 1974, Jimmy signed for Blackpool. In May of the same year he was a member of the club's youth team squad that travelled to Northern Italy to take part in the Caligaris International tournament. This prestigious competition was named in honour of Umberto Caligaris who, at the time of his death in 1940, was Italy's most capped player and had been a member of the country's 1934 World Cup winning team. Previously, amongst others Wolves, Stoke City and West Ham had sent teams to compete in the U-21s competition - none had returned victorious but the young Seasiders succeeded where others had failed. They defeated CSKA Sofia and Italian sides Lanerossi and AC Milan before overcoming Napoli 3-1 in the final. In addition to Jimmy, the talented squad contained a number of youngsters who would also go on to carve out successful careers including Paul Hart, Alan Ainscow, Mike Walsh and Billy Ronson. Having served his apprenticeship in the youth and reserve teams, Jimmy took the next step and broke into the first team.

On 29 November 1975 with 5,747 fans watching on, Manager Harry Potts introduced substitute Jimmy into the action against Notts County. The Tangerines defeated the Magpies 1-0 to get Jimmy's career off to a winning start. He made a further 10 League and two FA Cup appearances in his debut season and scored the first of his eight goals in a Blackpool shirt in a 1-1 draw with Fulham. As an Evertonian youngster, Jimmy's hero was former Blue Alan Ball and in just his second season, he faced the flame-haired dynamo in a League Cup third round replay. After two drawn matches, Arsenal defeated Blackpool 2-0 with goals from Frank Stapleton and David O'Leary but Jimmy took great pride in holding his own against the World Cup winner whose own career had also begun in a Tangerines shirt.

In 1977, Jimmy accepted an exciting invitation to play in the States for LA Skyhawks during the English close season. For two years he spent the winters playing in England before flying off to California to compete in the American Soccer League throughout the summer months. The Skyhawks squad consisted of players from nine different countries and in Jim's second season they enjoyed a tremendous campaign. He appeared in 21 games as they got through to the equivalent of our country's play-offs where they were narrowly defeated 1-0 by New York Apollo. Although Jimmy thoroughly enjoyed his transatlantic soccer adventure, he turned down further offers to return as he had one eye on his long-term future and his plans to "get a proper job." However, he continued to ply his trade in the UK with Blackpool and during his five seasons at Bloomfield Road he made 105 appearances under six managers - the last one being Alan Ball! He joined Torquay United in June 1980 and debuted for the Gulls on 16 August in a 1-0 League victory over Crewe Alexandra. After playing in excess of 40 games for the Plainmoor club, he joined Wigan Athletic who were managed by former Liverpool, Nottingham Forest and England centre-half Larry Lloyd. Jimmy's first game for the Tics was on 29 September 1981 in a 0-0 stalemate with Bournemouth. He was an integral part of the team as they gained the first Football League promotion in the club's history. Although Lloyd left him out of the opening fixture of the 1982/83 campaign, Jimmy soon forced his way back into the starting line-up and due to his performances throughout the season, he picked up the club's Player of the Year award.

Jimmy was acutely aware of how short a footballer's career is and how most players need another form of income after retiring from the game. To this end, the latter part of Jimmy's playing career ran in tandem with him laying the foundations for the next phase of his working life. He trained to become an accountant and after a short spell playing non-league football for Morecambe, he threw himself headlong into his new profession. He has worked for the same company in Wigan for more than 30 years and has been a Partner in the successful firm since 1994. Fondly remembered by the fans of his former clubs, Jimmy attends numerous events organised by both the Blackpool and Wigan ex-players and supporters organisations. In 2012, he was reunited with his teammates at a Celebration evening to commemorate 30 years since Wigan's fabulous promotion-winning season.

JOE GALLAGHER

'Big Joe' Gallagher was born on 11 January 1955, lived at 41 Adcote Road, Dovecot and attended St Margaret Mary's School. Playing at centre half, Joe was a regular in the Liverpool Schoolboys side and in 1970 his U-15s team defeated East London in the English Schools Trophy Final at South Liverpool's Holly Park ground. Joe put in a typical, no-nonsense, solid performance and after the final whistle Birmingham City's Chief Scout Don Dorman offered him a trial with the Blues. At the time, Joe had been training with Liverpool and when Bill Shankly got wind of this he hit the roof accusing Dorman of poaching 'his' player. Joe was not registered with any club so, despite the great man's protestations, Don Dorman wasted no time in getting him in. He joined Birmingham as soon as he left school and on his 17th birthday City Manager Freddie Goodwin secured Joe's signature on a full time contract. So began a relationship which is still going strong today.

On 19 September 1973, Joe made his first team debut in a 0-0 Texaco Cup match versus Stoke City with 9,530 present at the Victoria Ground. His first appearance in the Football League followed a couple of weeks later when he took to the field at Highbury to face Arsenal who won the game courtesy of a single Ray Kennedy strike. Joe played 24 games in his first season then hardly missed a game for almost a decade. The only prolonged absence he experienced was due to a non-football related injury. On 7 June 1977, he was driving home from judging a beauty contest when he was involved in a car crash "I woke up in hospital and heard a local radio reporter state that I had broken my leg in several places and may never play again!" Prior to this, Joe's form and consistency had put him in the frame for an England call-up. After the crash Joe was understandably distraught but a get-well message from England Manager Don Revie saying he was still in his plans was a welcome lift. Joe's immediate objective though was to return to fitness and get back in the Birmingham side. He achieved this six month later on 27 December in a goal scoring return against Bristol City. Joe picked up where he had left off and the England call-up duly arrived for a B international match versus Australia played on 17 November 1980. It proved to be his only experience of representing his country but there are many who say he should have received more caps. On 5 May the following year, Joe received a richly deserved Testimonial match versus local rivals Aston Villa. The Birmingham faithful turned out in great numbers to pay tribute to a great servant. During his eleven years with the club, he made 335 appearances, helped them reach two semi-finals and in his last season at St Andrew's played his part in the club getting promoted straight back to Division One after being relegated in 1979/80 season.

The following campaign, Joe reluctantly made the short journey to Molineux to join Wolverhampton Wanderers in a deal which was supposed to involve Wolves striker John Richards joining Birmingham. Richards' move did not happen but Joe joined the club from the Black Country in a £350,000 deal that they could barely afford. This quickly became apparent to Joe when, in an attempt to unsettle him, he was banished to play for the reserves. He was then sacked for failing to attend a photo call - a pedantic move by a club desperate to get Joe's £500 per week wages off the payroll. Joe's suspicions were confirmed in 1982 when Wolves were declared bankrupt. By this time Joe was plying his trade for West Ham United following a shrewd move by Manager John Lyall. However, when Burnley approached Joe to take him to Turf Moor he opted for the security of the four-year contract they were offering him as opposed to the one-month rolling contract he had with the Hammers. Burnley boss John Bond paid £30,000 for Joe's services but unfortunately he spent a great deal of his time at the club on the treatment table. He did however feature in one of Burnley's most important matches ever when on 9 May 1987 they needed to defeat Orient in order to maintain their Football League status. Joe was a rock at the heart of the Clarets defence as they beat the O's in what proved to be his last professional game. Following his retirement from playing, Big Joe managed amateur clubs Colehill Town, Atherstone United and King Heath. In 2012, Joe Gallagher was inducted into the Blues Hall of Fame and on matchdays he began working as a corporate host for the club that he proudly claims "is in my blood. I have been connected with them since 1970 and I always will be."

BIG JOE

JOE GALLAGHER Testimonial BIRMINGHAM CITY V ASTON VILLA Tuesday 5th May 1981 k.o. 7.45 p.m.

TOMMY WHEELDON

The influence of Huytonians on the world of football has spread far and wide. For the best part of two decades, Tommy Wheeldon lived in Canada passing on his wealth of knowledge and experience to nurture the talent of a host of Calgary youngsters. Born in Whiston Hospital on 28 December1956, Tommy spent his formative years in Lancaster Walk and later Stafford Close on Huyton's Mosscroft estate. He has clear, vivid memories of playing with his mates on a pitch in the heart of the estate with team names invented with the surrounding streets in mind (Oxford Road Rovers, Gloucester United, etc). At weekends, the games transferred to nearby King George V Playing Fields.

Tommy attended St Aidan's Primary School before moving a few hundred yards to the newly built St Joseph's at the bottom of Longview Drive. It was here, under the guidance of team manager Mr Yoxall that Tommy started to get recognition for his ability. Although a year younger than the rest of the team, he secured one of the coveted jerseys as the school enjoyed tremendous success. When he passed his 11+ exam, Tommy moved to Croxteth's De La Salle Seniors and whilst he had breezed through the Huyton Boys trials, competition due to the sheer numbers involved was much stiffer when it came to playing for Liverpool Boys. However, Tommy won a place in the team in all age groups. It was after seeing him play for the U-14s side that LFC great Ron Yeats took him to Tranmere Rovers as a non-contract schoolboy. Tommy was thrilled when Everton goalkeeping legend Gordon West would give him a lift to training on Tuesday and Thursday evenings - West had retired from the game at this stage but would later return to League football with the Prenton Park club. Tom was excelling for the various schools representative sides and enjoyed taking part for the county team on tours to Skegness and Cologne. He shone playing for England U-18s in a 1-1 draw with Scotland and again in a 2-1 victory over Wales and soon after spent time with John Lyall and Ron Greenwood at West Ham United. After just three months in East London, Tommy was homesick and returned to Huyton to be around his family and friends.

Aged 19, on the dole, disillusioned and having burned his bridges with Tranmere, Tommy thought his chance of playing League football had gone. He turned out for Prescot pub team New Halls FC and picked up £5 per game playing for St Helens Town. Totally unexpectedly, Everton Manager Billy Bingham (who had monitored Tommy's performances) offered him a two-week trial with the Toffees. A fortnight later and with £1000 deposited in St Helens Town's bank account, Tommy put pen to paper on a two-year pro contract on the same day that Bruce Rioch and Duncan McKenzie joined the club. However, whilst these two players went on to enjoy illustrious careers at Goodison Park and beyond, our man's only first team experiences consisted of a few pre-season friendlies and being 13th man in an away game at Stoke City. The club was very well equipped in the midfield department and, when Bingham got the sack with Gordon Lee installed as his successor, Tommy moved further down the pecking order and was released when his contract expired.

Again, he feared he would never get that elusive Football League game and joined Southport, Marine and Runcorn to ply his trade in the Northern Premier League. Just as Everton's contact and offer had taken him by surprise four years earlier, a call from Bruce Rioch in July 1982 left him equally taken aback. His old club mate had recently taken the managerial reins at Torquay United (the first of many such positions he would occupy) and he wanted Tom to play for him. So the rekindled dream became a reality when, on his 26th birthday, he replaced his gaffer to come on as sub versus Port Vale in front of 4,760 supporters. Although the game ended in a 1-0 defeat with the goal scored by the home team's Ernie Moss, it was still the best birthday present Tommy had ever received. He played a further 15 games for the Gulls in two spells at the club - punctuated by a couple of seasons playing for Falmouth - before a cruciate ligament injury sustained in a tackle with Swindon's Lou Macari brought his career to a premature end.

Aged just thirty, Tommy turned his attention to scouting for, amongst others, Everton. He also became a well-respected coach and worked under Steve McMahon for four years at Swindon Town. When McMahon got the bullet, the entire back room staff also departed and Tommy joined Exeter City as Assistant Manager to Noel Blake. In January 2002, one of the Grecians' Directors offered Tommy an exciting coaching position with the Canadian club Calgary Storm. Tom weighed up his options, decided to take the plunge and has been there ever since. However, he is still a fanatical Evertonian and frequently returns home to see family, friends and of course, his beloved Blues.

DON TOBIN

Every professional footballer will have experienced significant games, goals or events which helped to shape their careers and lives. For Don Tobin, one such occasion followed an innocuous school playground fight. As punishment for his involvement in the scrap, his Huyton Hey schoolteacher, who knew how to hit footy-mad Don where it hurt, banned him from playing for the Huyton Boys team. However, Huyton Boys Manager Alan Bleasdale's intervention, cleverly and compassionately resolved the matter to everybody's satisfaction. Don recalls the future award-winning author and playwright turned up unannounced at the family home in Shelley Close on Huyton's St Johns estate and informed Don's parents what had happened - something Don had conveniently forgotten to do! Mr Tobin gave Don an old-fashioned clip round the ear but Mr Bleasdale stated that, if Don assured him there would be no future problems, he would lift the ban. This simple act of thoughtful ingenuity helped Don follow a path that has resulted in a lifetime involvement in football. He is sincerely grateful for Alan's timely intervention and claims it spurred him on to give his all for him and Huyton Boys.

Don's early football memories revolve around fiercely competitive games for the Park View Junior School team against local rivals St Aloysius in Jubilee Park - he was born and lived in nearby Fairclough Road before the family moved to the Mosscroft and later St Johns estates. His inspired performances for Huyton Boys played a crucial part in the team winning the English Schools Trophy in 1971. The programme notes for the Final versus Stoke Boys described him as "...on his day, the finest attacking player in Lancashire - he can cut a defence to shreds." This ability had already prompted Everton to snap him up on a schoolboy contract and then hand him a full-time apprenticeship. Aged just 16, Don unusually by-passed Everton's B team to be installed straight into the A team. During a pre-season 5-a-side tournament, he displayed real talent and felt at home as a member of the winning team alongside Goodison legends Alan Ball and Brian Labone. Bally was extremely complimentary of Don's performance and even said he was going to speak to Harry Catterick about him joining the first team squad. However, the World Cup winner joined Arsenal shortly afterwards so we will never know if this was a sincere or throwaway comment.

In August 1973, Don followed Ball out of the Goodison Park 'Exit' door when he joined Rochdale to secure the League football he felt he needed. He loved his time at Spotland under Manager Walter Joyce and developed into an accomplished, free-scoring, attacking midfielder. Don made his debut for Dale on 10 November 1973 when he came off the bench in a 3-1 home defeat at the hands of Watford in front of 1,459 supporters. His full debut followed on 26 February 1974 when he took to the field in the home team's starting line-up in a 1-1 draw with Hereford with 1,195 in attendance. Don made a big impact at Rochdale and became a firm favourite with the crowd. However, shortly before Christmas in 1975, a mistimed tackle on a slippery pitch in an FA Cup 2nd round tie versus Gateshead resulted in Don sustaining a serious back injury. Despite three months of intensive treatment, by his own admission Don had 'lost a yard'. He consequently dropped out of the Football League to play for Witton Albion. Still only 21 years of age, he correctly believed that if he worked hard a chance to rebuild his career would present itself. Fortunately, Don's ex-Dale teammate Paul Fielding put his name forward to his Manager Billy Sinclair who acted swiftly to recruit him to his Sligo Rovers squad.

Although Don only played in Ireland for one complete season, he thoroughly enjoyed the experience and played in one particular game that is still fresh in the memory of many fans years later. On Sunday, 30 April 1978, Sligo met old rivals Shamrock Rovers at Dalymount Park in the Irish FA Cup Final. Don produced a fine performance in the semis against Drogheda to help the team reach the Final. However, Shamrock lifted the trophy courtesy of an extremely controversial Ray Treacy penalty that remains disputed to this day.

Shortly after this game, an agent who wanted him to sign for the relatively new United States soccer club California Sunshine approached Don. Initially he rebuffed the offer but when Sunshine put forward an improved package, Don decided to give it a go. This was the beginning of an amazingly successful transatlantic adventure for Tobin. He fell in love with the country and lifestyle and carved out a playing career which lasted 12 years and managerial and coaching positions which he still holds today.

He picked up a host of trophies and personal awards whilst playing in both the indoor and outdoor soccer leagues for Sunshine, Wichita Wings, Carolina Lightnin, LA Lazers, Canton Invaders, Rochester Flash, Tampa Bay Rowdies, Memphis Rogues and Orlando Lions. Regularly selected for various All Star teams, Tobin was often heralded the Most Valuable Player in crucial finals and at the completion of a season. Whilst at Canton Invaders, he got his first taste of management as assistant to fellow Englishman Trevor Dawkins. He held further managerial positions at Memphis Rogues, Tampa Bay Extreme and Tampa Spartans. He is a hugely respected coach and for nearly 20 years he was Director of Coaching at Dunedin Stirling Soccer Club in Florida. He has played a major role in the development of junior boys, girls and women's soccer via his successful Soccer Science Academy. He currently holds a similar position at Pinellas County United and works at the prestigious National Training Centre based in Florida University.

Footynote:

Don Tobin writes:- Alan Bleasdale made us live in the moments of the game. He instilled in all of us, to be fearless and unafraid of being judged and ultimate consequences. By him setting this platform, I never ever thought about losing! To this day, I follow his work ethic, inspiration and leadership, always trying to do the same for my players.

Footynote:

Alan Bleasdale writes :- Donny is extremely generous in his praise of my contribution to his huge success with Huyton Boys. I do love praise - who doesn't? - but it's not the whole story.
There was a background to how and why I suddenly turned up at his home that night in the winter of 1969 in my smart-arse red sports car. I was actually on my way home from having a furious screaming match with two P.E. teachers from two separate schools in Huyton. We were sat in a pub and all three of us were looking for trouble. One of them was Donny's P.E. teacher and the other was the P.E. teacher for another member of the Huyton Boys squad. (I shall tell you now that, by and large, I don't like P.E. teacher. P.S. I was a P.E. teacher).
To put it simply, both teachers wanted to punish both boys for similar offences - a bit of handbags at dawn in the playgrounds of their respective schools. And the punishment that both teachers had come up with was not the cane - yes, they still had the cane in 1969 - or five hundred lines, or even polishing the toilet bowls. No. Don't be silly - or even optimistic - both Donny and the other boy were to be banished, sine die, from ever representing their school in the town football team - representing all that was good about their community.
So,the one great and absolutely outstanding talent that both boys had - their glory - was to be taken away from them - never to be celebrated in their home town in public due to a private misdemeanour in a schoolyard in their own school, supposedly supervised by their own school teachers.
Where was the justice in that ?
I won. In the end. I'm not proud of it. It was getting late. They got hungry. They didn't have pub food in 1969. And I wouldn't go home. I don't think I promised them a chippy dinner, but the punishment was finally reduced to a grovelling apology - neither boy did grovelling, but they tried - and a final warning.
And if you're wondering who the other boy is, I'm no snitch, but he scored goals for fun, played centre forward and bore a strong resemblance to Peter Osgood. And he too, like Donny Tobin, was a pleasure to be with at Huyton Boys. So. Thank you very much for the compliments Donny. I'll take them happily. I'm an old man now and compliments are few and far between. But remember this - if you hadn't happened to have been the finest left winger I ever did see in all of my life, in all of this country, at the age you were at, I would have driven straight past your house that night in 1969. I might have had the mouth, but you had the talent.
And finally, Mr Tobin, Sir, congratulations on the remarkable career you created for yourself in the USA, renowned both as a player and as a coach. You definitely didn't need anyone in a smart-arse red sports car to achieve that !

FRANK PIMBLETT

Frank Pimblett is arguably the best young player Huyton has ever produced. Obviously, this is very subjective, impossible to prove and fans of Steven Gerrard, Peter Reid and co would probably make counter-claims. The 'evidence' that could be provided to support this argument is that Frank was captain of undoubtedly the best Schoolboy side the area has ever assembled.... and he was a school year younger than all of his teammates!

Born on 12 March 1957, the St Dominics pupil had only just turned 14 when he held aloft the English Schools FA Trophy at Goodison Park on Monday 19 April 1971 after defeating Stoke Boys 5-1 on aggregate. His talent was well noted and in addition to playing for the county schoolboys side, he picked up eight England Schoolboys caps. His performances resulted in offers from a number of Football League clubs and in June 1973 he opted to join Aston Villa as an apprentice before signing professional forms on 24 October of the following year. On 4 January 1975, two months shy of his 18th birthday, Frank took to the field in Second Division Villa's claret and blue to make his first team debut. With 14,510 present at Oldham Athletic's Boundary Park he played no small part in helping the Villans overcome the Latics three goals to nil to knock them out of the FA Cup at the 3rd round stage. A week later he made his first Football League appearance as a member of the team which defeated Bristol City 2-0 in front of 21,726 fans at Villa Park with the goals provided by Chico Hamilton and Brian Little. With Ron Saunders at the helm, Villa enjoyed a tremendous campaign and on 1 March 1975 they beat Norwich City 1-0 courtesy of a Ray Graydon strike to lift the League Cup at Wembley. Although Saunders left him out of the Final, Frank wore the number 11 shirt in the first leg of the semis against Chester City to contribute to their success. In addition, the team enjoyed a brilliant second half of the season losing just one of their final 18 League games which secured promotion to the top division, finishing three points behind champions Manchester United. The final game of the campaign attracted a crowd of 35,999 who were in jubilant mood. Frank and his teammates celebrated in style with a 4-1 demolition of Norwich City, although it wasn't all doom and gloom for the Canaries who also achieved promotion.

Pimmo's first taste of the top flight came on 20 September 1975 at Anfield in front of 42,779 spectators and it was a baptism of fire. Goals from Keegan, Toshack and Case accounted for Villa in front of many of Frank's family and friends. This was the first of Frank's seven Division One appearances, the last of which came on 14 February 1976 in a 2-1 defeat at the hands of Sheffield United. A month later he joined Newport County on loan until the end of the season and made a further seven appearances for the Fourth Division side who finished in a lowly 22nd place. They were granted re-election to the Football League for the 1976/77 season but before its commencement, Frank had left Somerton Park to join Stockport County. However, he struggled to make an impact at Edgeley Park and on 11 September 1976 at Bradford City's Valley Parade he came on as sub for Peter Fletcher to make his one and only appearance for the Hatters in a 3-3 draw with the Bantams. It looked like Frank's football career was going to peter out until a relative suggested that he should emigrate and try his hand in Australia - which is exactly what he did!

Apart from a brief three-month, three-games spell with Hartlepool United in 1980, he made a new life for himself in Oz supplementing his income by working in the construction industry. The timing of Frank's move was excellent as it coincided with the formation of the new National Soccer League and over the next three decades he became a footballing legend

in his adopted home. The NSL kicked off on 2 April in 1977 and with 5,214 fans present at Perry Park, Frank's Brisbane City were on the wrong end of a 1-0 scoreline against Marconi Fairfield. Despite a losing start, Frank's new employers enjoyed a great deal of early success winning the Phillips Cup in 1977 and again a year later. Frank went on to become a hugely successful player and coach in Australia and picked up many awards and plaudits during his lengthy career. In 1989, Charlton Athletic played against Brisbane as part of their pre-season tour and Frank ran the show. After the game, Addicks Boss Lennie Lawrence opened the door to Frank for a return to English football but due to his love of the Queensland way of life, he graciously turned the offer down. A few years later, his contribution and dedication to Australian soccer was recognised when he was handed a Testimonial season. This culminated in a match in his honour versus the touring Malaysian national team. Nobody present was surprised when Frank got his name on the scoresheet and was by far the best player on the pitch. Without wishing to understate his achievements, it is probably fair to say that the boy from St Dominics did not fulfil his potential in this country, however nobody could deny that he made a massive impression on the other side of the world.

Footynote:

Alan Bleasdale writes :- I owe Frank Pimblett a huge apology.
I have owed him that apology for nearly 40 years.
Let me explain ....
In the Spring of 1983, The Times newspaper asked me to contribute to a series of articles entitled " WHEN I WAS HAPPY........"
I knew that the editor expected me to write about recent events in my life - the novels, the plays and,sometimes, the plaudits and awards.
I didn't want to do that. Why would I want people to hate me ? Instead, I wrote about a time when I was blissfully happy, and I wasn't anywhere near the centre of attention or glory. So, I wrote about Huyton Boys Under Fifteens football team. English Schools Trophy Winners 1970/71. I was the team manager. I was in the orchestra pit, pretending to be the conductor. The team were in the spotlight, centre stage, the stars of the show.
Which brings me to Frank Pimblett ....
Frank was the captain of that team. He was also a year younger than the rest of the squad - something unheard of at that testosterone and pimples age, at any level in any sport. The simple reason for his captaincy was that he was a man amongst boys. He was thirteen going on thirty. Most boys his age were thirteen going on seven.
And if you need any further convincing - on the day I announced to the rest of the squad that "this little kid" was going to be the captain, I expected some degree of surprise or even half-hidden jealousy. Instead, I got the kind of sideways slightly pitying looks that said "You took your time working that one out, didn't you ? Sir." And you will know now, having read Frank's biography in these pages, the next year, when he was 'the proper age' he went on to captain England Schoolboys. Every top-flight football club in the country wanted to sign him. Desperately. He signed for Aston Villa.
I can only guess that he was in a hurry. He didn't want to serve a five year apprenticeship at one of the true giants such as Liverpool or Manchester United. He wanted to be out there, right now, there and then. After all, he was already a man. And he was out there far quicker than most - making his first team debut when he had only just turned seventeen. Headlines were made. A star was born. Whereupon, Frank, acknowledged to be the greatest schoolboy footballer since the fabled Duncan Edwards, twenty years earlier, seemed to vanish in plain sight. A few more games in Aston Villa's first team, a sudden free transfer to Newport County, and then gone. Gone to Australia.
And this,finally, is where the apology starts.
Some years after Frank had left the country, I was at a social club with my wife and family in the Huyton parish where Frank had lived. Someone approached me and told me that Frank had been a close friend of his, and that he had news. Well, he was no kind of friend, and all he brought me was lies. In essence he said that Frank had hit hard times in Sydney, New South Wales and that he had left the game, or the game had left him. To be honest, I wanted to cry. But, instead, when I came to write "WHEN I WAS HAPPY....." for The Times, I painted a much muted, far less bleak picture of Frank's life in Australia, but it nevertheless wasn't a happy ending. SHAME, SHAME, SHAME. MEA CULPA, MEA MAXIMA CULPA. It was only when Mark Campbell approached me with regard to contributing to "Huyton's Titans" that I discovered, through his brilliant research, that Frank was not down on his luck in Sydney, New South Wales, but a hero and a footballing legend in Brisbane, Queensland. And if you want to know when I was really, really happy, it was when Mark showed me a clip on YouTube and if you don't believe me in these strange and devious days of fake news, look for yourself. (QR below)
It's a happy ending. Everyone loves a happy ending.

DAVID FAIRCLOUGH

Liverpool legend David Fairclough ironically spent his formative years living in the Everton area of the city and attended Major Lester Primary School. When he was 13 years of age the family upped sticks and moved to Cremorne Hey on the newly-constructed Cantril Farm estate, which qualifies David for inclusion in these pages. Having shone for the school team and Fazakerley Colts in the Bootle & Litherland League, he was already the focus of many scouts' attention. The house-move resulted in a change of team and league as Cantril Farm had its own thriving junior competition. David enjoyed tremendous success and his team, Little Moss JFC, won the Intermediate League and the New York Police Cup. Following a particularly impressive goal scoring performance versus rivals Barons Hey, he accepted an offer to attend weekly sessions at Liverpool's Melwood training ground.

On 1 October 1970, his reward for impressing the coaches was an associate schoolboy contract. When David left school three years later, the club gave him a full-time apprenticeship and a professional contract followed a year later in unusual circumstances - popular children's TV programme Magpie filmed the exciting, life-changing developments for a special feature on the show. The cameras captured David running down Anfield's famous tunnel, sprinting onto the hallowed turf and smashing the ball into an empty net at the Kop End. The show also included footage of him signing his contract in the presence of Manager Bill Shankly, the EUFA Cup and the League Championship trophy. For a young, football-mad Scouser it does not get much better than that!

David made rapid progress through the LFC ranks and on 26 January 1974 he made his reserve team debut in a 3-2 victory over Bolton Wanderers. The following season he cemented a regular place in the club's second string with goals aplenty and the local media and Liverpool supporters were speculating about David being called up to the first team squad. Speculation turned into reality on 1 November 1975 when the 18-year old played at Ayresome Park in a 1-0 defeat of Middlesborough. Three days later, he took his place amongst the five substitutes for the second leg of a EUFA Cup second round tie versus Real Sociedad. At half-time David replaced LFC legend Ian Callaghan and just 26 minutes later the seeds of the tag 'Supersub' were perhaps sown in the minds of the watching journalists. David latched onto a misplaced pass and instinctively beat the advancing keeper to score Liverpool's third goal in a 6-0 (9-1 on aggregate) annihilation of the Spaniards.

Over the following eight seasons, he took his place on the first team bench on 138 occasions. Frustratingly, partly due to the amazing success of the team, he was unused in 76 of these games but scored 18 goals in the 62 appearances he did make when coming on as sub. David actually made Liverpool's starting line-up in 92 games and scored a very impressive 37 goals. However, it is for his feats as a replacement player that fans and commentators usually remember him. Davie's pace and directness made him an ideal player to come off the bench to make an impact and change the course of a game. This was never more evident or important than on Wednesday 16 March 1977. With 55,403 packed inside Anfield and thousands locked out, Liverpool faced French outfit St Etienne in the third round, 2nd leg of the European Cup. The Reds trailed 1-0 from the first game but a goal from Kevin Keegan in just the second minute nullified this. The atmosphere was electric but a Dominic Bethenay thunderbolt early in the second half threatened to spoil the party. A Ray Kennedy goal gave them hope but Liverpool still needed another goal to progress in the competition - step up David Fairclough! In the 74th minute, Liverpool Boss Bob Paisley took his last roll of the dice. Ten minutes later a hopeful punt forward by Kennedy was chested down by the lightning-paced sub and expertly dispatched past Curkovic in the French team's goal. Liverpool went on to win the tie and the European Cup and Supersub had cemented his place in Anfield folklore.

Whilst David continued to make significant contributions to Liverpool's successes over the next few seasons, he often felt that he was being unfairly overlooked by Paisley and considered his future on more than one occasion. Even when he played in the European Cup Final victory over Bruges on 10 May 1978, he was so unsure of whether Paisley was going to include him in the starting line-up, he arrived at Wembley Stadium with a transfer request in his suit pocket! David loved playing for Liverpool and enjoyed a great relationship with the fans but he was not getting enough game time and by 1983/84 season he was ready for a fresh challenge and regular first team football. Swiss club Luzern offered him the chance to fulfil an ambition to play in Europe and he accepted. Although the team struggled and only narrowly avoided relegation, David was in impressive form and returned 16 goals. However, after 44 games he and the club parted company after a bust up with the manager - he loved his time at Luzern but was upset it had ended so disappointingly. After a brief, two-game spell at Norwich City was curtailed due to a troublesome foot injury, a word in Oldham manager Joe Royle's ear from the Latics' striker and fellow Cantril Farmer Mick Quinn, resulted in David joining the Boundary Park club on a short-term contract. The highlight of his 20-match stay was undoubtedly a 2nd round, second leg League Cup match versus Liverpool. Although his former employees ran out comfortable winners (8-2 on aggregate), David scored both of Oldham's goals which gave him a great deal of personal satisfaction.

When his contract was up at the end of the season, he joined little known Belgian club Beveren and although they did not secure any silverware, David thoroughly enjoyed his three years at the club. He thrived on feeling wanted by Beveren's Manager which was rarely the case during his Anfield days. In the summer of 1989 David joined Tranmere Rovers and, although his playing days were nearing an end, he had a great time at the Wirral club and would have been happy to finish his career at Prenton Park. However, the club's precarious financial position meant that reluctantly they had to let him go. During his Rovers experience, he helped them achieve promotion out of Division Three, win the Leyland Daf trophy with a 2-1 win over Bristol Rovers at Wembley, and then return to the world famous stadium two weeks later only to lose the play-off Final versus Notts County. If Tranmere had secured promotion they would probably have been able to offer David an extension to his contract but it was not to be.

The last stop of a 17-year playing career that involved 361 games and 107 goals, was Wigan Athletic. David made ten appearances for Wigan before hanging up his boots and turning his attention to the world of football punditry. He is a regular guest on local and national radio stations and LFCTV. However, never a day goes by without somebody mentioning his magnificent achievements as the most famous number 12 English football has ever known and David 'Supersub' Fairclough would not have it any other way!

©Tranmere Rovers FC

PETER REID

Peter Reid is the epitome of a Huyton Titan and was one of the main inspirations behind this book. Not only is he one of the greatest footballers to have emerged from the area (if not THE greatest), he is also fiercely proud of his working class Huyton roots. A committed Socialist, nowadays he is just as likely to be on social media berating Boris Johnson and the Tories as he is discussing his love of football and cricket - which further endears him to the majority of Huyton's Labour-voting population. Born in Sefton General Hospital on 20 June 1956, Peter's first home was in Wimborne Road, Page Moss where his family shared a house with his grandparents. He attended St Dominics School and then, after moving to the Mosscroft estate, time spent at St Aidan's Juniors and St Joseph's Juniors was followed by St Augustine's Seniors. He wasn't a big fan of school, claiming it interfered with his obsessive desire to play football and was much happier when he was on the all-weather pitch, located in the heart of the estate. It acted as a magnet to the local youngsters who were drawn there on a daily basis to represent their respective street footy teams. The Reids lived in Gloucester Road, so that was their team name whilst other kids played for York, Oxford, Warwick and Essex. The shale playing surface was far from ideal but didn't deter Peter and his pals from engaging in hard-fought, must-win games or throwing in tackles which resulted in multiple grazed knees. The pitch he aspired to play on at this time was 'little Wembley' on the nearby King George V Playing Fields. Surrounded by a running track and in pristine condition, Peter would watch the Huyton Boys team play there, not knowing that his own exploits with the District side would take him to far greater stadia or that later he would also grace the real Wembley on numerous memorable occasions.

Influenced and encouraged by his dad and uncle Pat, turning out for the 'Guzzies' and Huyton Boys teams made his schooldays more tolerable and provided the springboard for a brilliant career in the game. The 1971 Huyton Boys squad of players is without doubt the finest ever assembled locally. Managed by future playwright Alan Bleasdale and former pro player Eddie Kilshaw, the team's stunning performances captured the imagination of the local population who shared in their unprecedented success. Thousands attended their matches as they progressed to win the English Schools Trophy. The significance of this stayed with Peter and in a 2011 interview he stated "Huyton Boys were a bloody good side. We beat Stoke in the Final, played at Goodison and the old Victoria Ground and the semi was at Anfield. You've got to remember what an opportunity it was to play at those grounds. As a young boy you're impressionable and it made you want to kick on. Alan and Eddie's philosophy was to go out there and enjoy it. Revel in it. To win a trophy like that for a little town like Huyton was a fantastic achievement."

Peter's performances for the district resulted in national recognition when he was selected for the England Schoolboys U-15s team, further igniting the interest of a host of scouts who had trailed his development. Wolves, Stoke City, Man Utd, Liverpool and Everton all pursued him but, due to their impressive record of nurturing

©Harry McGuire

youngsters through to the first team, it was Bolton Wanderers' Manager Jimmy Armfield and his Assistant Nat Lofthouse who secured his signature. Their replacement, Ian Greaves, proved to be a massive influence on Peter throughout his career and handed him his Football League debut as a substitute in a 2-0 victory over Orient on 5 October 1974 three months after becoming the Trotters Boss. Reidy's first start followed a week later in a 2-0 defeat at the hands of Hull City. It wasn't long before he was an integral part of Greavesy's side as they aimed to return to the top flight for the first time since the mid 60s. Agonisingly, they hit the post on consecutive campaigns (75/76 & 76/77) when missing out on promotion by a single point.

©Harry McGuire

His growing influence on the pitch was rewarded with the first of six unbeaten appearances for England's U-21s in a 1-0 defeat of Scotland on 27 April 1977 at Sheffield Utd's Bramall Lane ground. The recognition represented a brilliant individual achievement but Peter had his sights set on glory for the team and Division One. Coming so close previously had stiffened the team's resolve to succeed and at the conclusion of the 1977/78 campaign their mission was accomplished with promotion as champions of the second tier. Having made it, Peter relished the opportunity to test himself against the big boys but, due to two serious knee injuries, his involvement was minimal. Bolton managed to maintain their Division One status largely without Reidy in their debut campaign but their second season resulted in them dropping back down to Division Two.

Prior to his injuries and relegation, Peter had been hot property with some of the country's top sides linked with luring him away from Burnden Park. Now, although his ability was not in doubt, question marks existed about whether he could be relied upon to stay fit and consequently his stock dropped dramatically. When Sheffield Wednesday tabled a £60,000 bid (a tenth of the amount Arsenal had reportedly offered a couple of years earlier), it looked like Peter was destined for Hillsborough. However, a phone call from Everton Boss Howard Kendall changed his mind, the midfielder's life and the Toffees fortunes. Although he had always been a fervent Liverpool supporter, the opportunity to join the club from the other side of Stanley Park proved too great to turn down and, once pen was put to paper on 22 December 1982, his loyalties changed forever.

Howard Kendall would later describe Peter Reid as Everton's most important post-war signing, an opinion shared by many. But initially, he struggled to hold down a regular place in the side and made just ten appearances as the club finished the 1982/83 Division One season in 7th place. They occupied the same position at the end of the following season but this was a very different campaign to that which preceded it. Everton started poorly, with just two victories from their opening seven fixtures, yet Peter still couldn't command a place in the team. However, when he came off the bench to play no small part in overcoming Coventry City in the third round of the Milk Cup on 9 November 1983, Peter kept his place in the team for the remaining 48 games of the season - and what a season! Prior to this, the Toffees had occupied a lowly 17th place in the table but over the following six months they grew in stature with almost every performance. It would be an insult to the other squad members to claim that Reidy was the sole reason for the transformation but he undoubtedly played a massive part in the turnaround. A 14-game unbeaten run included a 2-0 Milk Cup semi-final victory over Aston Villa, which secured a Wembley encounter with Liverpool on 25 March 1984. With 100,000 fans making the journey down south for the Final and uniting to sing their hearts out professing their Merseyside allegiance, the game was deadlocked at 0-0. There was also little between the sides in the replay three days later until a Graeme Souness strike meant the trophy was destined for Anfield. The Blues were now unrecognisable from the outfit which had looked bereft of confidence a few months earlier. In contrast with the dire first seven games of the season, Everton won five and drew two of their final seven games of a landmark campaign. The last of these matches encapsulated the 'new' Blues. As a youngster, Peter aspired to play on King George V's mini Wembley. On 19 May 1984, he returned to the real McCoy for the second time in a couple of months to face Watford in the FA Cup Final. The Hornets, managed by future England Boss Graham Taylor and owned by a tearful Elton John, put up a brave fight but were no match for a rampant Everton side. Goals from Graeme Sharp and Andy Gray triggered wild celebrations as they lifted their first major silverware for 14 years and provided the launchpad for further glories.

The 1984/85 season is widely acknowledged as Everton's greatest in their long and illustrious history. It began with another Wembley appearance and revenge over Liverpool, when a Bruce Grobbelaar own goal handed the Blues the Charity Shield. During the following ten months and 63 games, Everton proved to be head and shoulders above their domestic opponents and one of the leading sides in Europe. With Reidy irrepressibly driving his teammates on from the heart of the action, they landed the League title on 6 May 1985 with five games of the season remaining. Nine days later, the blue half of the city converged on Rotterdam, where they swept Rapid Vienna aside 3-1 to return to Merseyside with the European Cup Winners Cup. Unfortunately, a fourth Wembley visit in just 14 months failed to see the club retain the FA Cup when Man Utd's Norman Whiteside curled a left foot shot past Neville Southall for the only goal of a tight Final. Peter's remarkable contribution to Everton's cause was acknowledged by his peers when he pipped fellow midfielder Bryan Robson to the 1985 Players Player of the Year award - one of the highest accolades an English footballer can receive in this country.

Although England Manager Bobby Robson handed Peter his first full international cap on 9 June 1985 versus Mexico, and five additional caps over the following year, the records show that his preferred central midfielders were Bryan Robson and Ray Wilkins. For someone who is as consumed by football as Reidy is, to warm the bench in the World Cup Finals in 1986 was hugely frustrating. However, forever the professional, he bided his time in the hope of getting an opportunity to contribute. When, in the second group game, Robson aggravated a shoulder injury and Wilkins was sent off, Peter was called into action. After suffering a 1-0 defeat to Portugal in their opening game and sharing a goalless draw with Morocco in their second, victory over Poland in the final group match was vital if they were to avoid the ignominy of being on an early flight home. With Peter dictating proceedings and Gary Lineker providing a deadly hat-trick, the 3 Lions rose to the challenge with a 3-0 win. When Paraguay were dispatched by the same score in the next match, the scene was set for an England v Argentina quarter-final encounter which became the most controversial football match Reidy was ever involved in.

In searing midday heat on 22 June 1986, with 114,580 in attendance at the Azteca Stadium in Mexico City and a television audience of millions tuned in, the two sides went into battle competing for a place in the World Cup semi-finals. In the 54th minute of the game, Diego Maradona showed why he was considered the best player in the world when he evaded half a dozen attempts to stop him before rounding Peter Shilton in the England goal to register one of the greatest goals ever seen. Sometimes you have to hold your hands up to acknowledge a genius at work and this was one such occasion. Unfortunately, just four minutes earlier, this particular genius had also raised a hand to punch the ball over Shilts flailing arms to give the South American's the lead. The so-called 'Hand of God' goal went unnoticed by the Turkish referee, Ali Bennaceur, meaning a late Lineker strike proved no more than a consolation and England returned home with a bitter taste in the nation's mouth.

Peter had been carrying an injury before and during the World Cup. He had struggled on in domestic fixtures as the Blues finished runners up in both the League and FA Cup and had been determined to participate in Mexico. However, surgery was inevitable and resulted in him missing the first four months of the 1986/87 season. When he returned to action, the team were well placed to mount a title challenge. Kendall had reconstructed the team since they had last won the League and despite not being as naturally gifted as their predecessors, these lads gave their all for the Boss, the badge and the Blues fans. When, on Monday 4 May 1987, fullback Pat Van Den Hauwe scored in the first minute of their match with Norwich City to win the game, the result gave Everton an unassailable lead in the title race with two games of the season remaining.

Whilst many Evertonians were still celebrating the success, Howard took the wind out of their sails by announcing his departure. His decision to take over the reins at Athletico Bilbao presented Peter with an unexpected opportunity when his replacement, Colin Harvey, asked him to take up a position on the club's coaching staff. That was an easy decision, as the move suited all parties. The conversation in January 1989, however, when Harvey informed Peter that his days of playing for Everton were at an end, must have been as difficult for the Boss to say as it was for Reidy to hear. Peter had enjoyed seven marvellous seasons at Goodison but it was time to move on.

He spent an enjoyable nine months at Loftus Road and helped Queens Park Rangers stave off the threat of relegation when they looked certainties for the drop. Peter would have happily seen out his playing days at QPR but, when Howard Kendall returned from Spain to take up the Man City Managers job, he invited Reidy to join him as both a player and his Assistant. Peter jumped at the chance and, not for the first time, a call from Howard shaped Peter's future. City were rooted at the foot of Division One, so the initial challenge was to avoid relegation. This was brilliantly achieved as they suffered just a single defeat from their final 11 games of the campaign.

Howard did so well during his first 11 months at Maine Road that the Everton hierarchy tempted him back to Goodison Park. Howard wanted Peter alongside him but this time he turned his offer down. He felt City were moving in the right direction and was proved right when he was handed the position of player-manager and led the club to 5th place in the table - their highest League standing since 1977. The feat was repeated the following season as he restored the club to their rightful place amongst the upper echelons of League football. Although they slipped to 9th place at the conclusion of the 1992/93 season, many people were understandably shocked when, just 13 days and four games into the following season, controversial Chairman Peter Swales called time on Peter's inaugural managerial position.

Although he hadn't always picked himself for the team in his final full season at City, Peter was still fit enough to pull the boots back on for short spells at Southampton, Notts County and Bury. His final competitive match took place on 13 August 1994, when Bury's opposition on the day was Rochdale and Peter's midfield opponent was none other than his younger brother Shaun. Despite the siblings accumulating nearly one thousand appearances between them, they had never faced each other. That was probably a blessing as, from the first whistle, they were taken back to the games on the Mosscroft all-weather pitch when the tackles flew in and no quarter was given. Although the brothers regale slightly different versions of who came out on top of the blood and thunder clash, it was a fitting way to bring the curtain down on Peter's fantastic playing career.

For the first time in his adult life, Peter now found himself looking in at the world of football from outside of its employ. Although he was itching to get back to work, when the offers didn't come flooding in he took the opportunity to reflect on how he could improve as a manager. He did some soul searching and came to a number of positive conclusions. He got the chance to put them into practice when Sunderland sacked Manager

Mick Buxton and offered Peter the job for the remaining seven games of the season. The Premier League had been launched a couple of years earlier and the Black Cats were in the second tier of English football, now known as the First Division. Having been on a horrendous run of results when they had lost six of their last seven games, the club faced the real prospect of dropping down to the Second Division. Peter replaced Buxton and their fortunes changed immediately. On 1 April 1995, he proved he was nobody's fool by breathing new life into a team that had been down and almost out. A 1-0 victory over Sheffield Utd, with everyone buying into Reidy's philosophy, was a great start but they had six additional 'cup finals' to contend with and they did so miraculously. In view of the results immediately prior to Peter's arrival at Roker Park, to finish the season with one defeat, three wins and three drawn games was nothing short of amazing. The club avoided relegation by six points and Peter landed himself a permanent contract as Manager of Sunderland AFC.

Not prepared to rest on his laurels, Peter made a few key acquisitions to strengthen the team on and off the park. The appointment of Bobby Saxton as his Assistant was inspired as was the recruitment of Paul Bracewell, Tony Coton and then Niall Quinn. His efforts paid off spectacularly when they accumulated 83 points from their 46 games to become Football League Champions and earn a place in the FA Premier League - something they could only have dreamed of 12 months earlier. Unfortunately, their time in the top division only lasted one season, but to survive in that environment so soon after nearly being condemned to the third tier of the football pyramid was always going to be a tall order. It wasn't all doom and gloom though. With home victories over Arsenal, Chelsea and Man Utd, the famous Roker Roar made a few last hurrahs before the club took up residence in their impressive new 'Stadium of Light' home.

Obviously, the aim of the following season was to bounce straight back to the Premier League and, whilst this was not achieved, they could not have come closer. At the completion of their fixtures, Sunderland missed out on automatic promotion by a single point but still had a possible route to the Promised Land via the play-offs. They disposed of Sheffield Utd in the semis to set up a magnificent final. On 26 May 1998, Charlton Athletic stood between Sunderland and the Premier League. Peter and his Charlton counterpart Alan Curbishley were extremely animated on the touchline and who could blame them? The match toed and froed and the Wembley crowd of 77,739 witnessed what many consider to be the best play-off Final since its inception. After 90 minutes the score stood at 3-3. After an additional 30 minutes, you still couldn't put a cigarette paper between the two sides as they were deadlocked at 4-4 and one of the biggest games in British football had to be determined in the cruellest of fashions - penalties. Inevitably in this scenario, there will always be a 'villain'. In this case it was Mickey Gray, who missed his Sunderland penalty - but only after 13 previous penalties had remarkably all been converted!

It may have been understandable if their Wembley experience had cast a shadow over the following season, but Peter and his lads were having none of it. From the opening game of the campaign, a 1-0 defeat of QPR, right through to their final fixture, a 2-1 victory over Birmingham City, they were brilliantly focussed on the job in hand. A record tally of 105 points (18 points ahead of nearest rivals Bradford City) sent them soaring back into the big League.

This was a glorious time to be a Sunderland fan. The club enjoyed consecutive seventh place finishes in the hardest competition in world club football and almost qualified for Europe. Sadly, they failed to kick on from this and in 2001/02, in a reversal of their fortunes, the club finished fourth from bottom. Nobody knows better than Peter Reid that football is a results business and, as a manager, if the results don't go your way you're in trouble. After a poor start to 2002/03, Reidy was relieved of his duties but there were few associated with the club who didn't acknowledge the huge contribution he had made to the positive transformation and expectations of the Black Cats. Overall, it had been an exciting and successful period in the club's history and Peter deserves great credit for his role in that.

He had been out of work for five months when Leeds Utd Chairman Peter Ridsdale came calling. The club had dispatched with the services of Terry Venables and, with eight games of the season remaining, they were in dire straits on and off the pitch. In view of his heroics on arrival at Sunderland, Peter was the logical choice to save the day. Reidy accepted the challenge and although they lost their first game under his stewardship (3-1 to Liverpool), Peter felt he had something to work with. Australian centre forward Mark Viduka was in scintillating form during the run-in and rattled home ten goals from their final seven games as Leeds finished the campaign in a safe 15th place - job done and another well-earned permanent contract offered and accepted. However, the end of season activity had been a fire fighting exercise and the flames had only been temporarily extinguished. The financial turmoil the club had created dictated the transfer comings and goings and Peter was attempting to do his job with one hand tied behind his back. Unsurprisingly, results suffered and in November 2003 Peter was shown the door. His replacement, Eddie Gray, was also unable to stop their demise and it was sad to see one of the great clubs suffer relegation, largely as a result of poor decisions in the boardroom.

Since leaving Elland Road, Peter has occupied a number of managerial hot seats and coaching positions at Coventry City, Plymouth Argyle Stoke City and Wigan Athletic. He has also accepted challenging, eye-opening offers to manage in Thailand and India.

Peter Reid has enjoyed a fantastic career and he is as enthusiastic now as he was when he was a young boy growing up on the streets of Huyton. Whilst the game may have changed immeasurably since his first taste of League football, he has kept apace with developments. Reidy will continue to be involved in the game he loves in whatever capacity he chooses for many years to come and football in this country will be all the better for it.

©George Herringshaw

Footynote:

Alan Bleasdale writes :-
"We all know Peter Reid, don't we ?

Do we ?"

"Of course we do - English legend - loads of trophies and awards - loud and courageous and never say die passion for football and the kind of proper politics that effortlessly presents him as a proper man of the people. After all, he is a man from the people. Real people live on the Mosscroft estate in Huyton, where Peter was brought up.

Oh, and by the way, don't forget his management career. Seen the trophies - seen the clubs he rescued ? Put a load of fires out, did Peter. Should have been a fireman."

"Yes, great bloke. But do we really, really know him ?"

"...Oh stop it. You're giving me a headache."

"Okay, let me take you back to the Easter of 1970 -

"What is this - Doctor Who ?"

"- a hotel on the seafront at Morecambe. Huyton Boys - the whole squad - on a football tour of North Lancashire for the first time in their history, playing local town teams in preparation for major cup games at the end of the season.

They were due to play Morecambe Boys on the following afternoon. After dinner as the sun went down and the lights came on all along the promenade, a couple of the lads approached myself and Eddie Kilshaw, a former footballer and without question the finest football coach who ever stood on a touch line, chain smoking and bandy. There were a couple of nervous coughs and no-one could actually look us in the eye until finally a request was made, asking if those who wanted to, could go for a walk, stretch their legs, perhaps venture onto the beach.

You know, Sir for an hour or so. Or two.

"One hour" we said.

They were very happy.

So they went. Half an hour or so later, Eddie and I followed them out. We looked at the empty promenade and the deserted beach.

And then we heard the easy laughter and high spirits coming from the nearby amusement arcade. And we laughed as much as they did.

It was then that we noticed that there was still a single light on in one of the bedrooms the boys were booked into.

So, we went up and knocked on the door politely, wondering who it could possibly be who was Billy No Mates. And there, sat on his bed, furiously cleaning and polishing his football boots, was Peter Reid, the unlikeliest lad in the whole squad to be "Billy No Mates"

Peter looked me straight in the eye and said "We're playing tomorrow."

And that's the end of the story.

You might think it's a disappointing end. With a whimper and not a bang. No sex. No drugs. No alcohol, no rock and roll. But, to be fair to Peter, he was only just fourteen at the time.

You might even say that it makes Peter out to be a bit of a Goody Two Boots. But you don't know Peter Reid, do you ?

Peter Reid is a natural born leader - a voice to be heard, listened to and reckoned with. Yes, he could be the life and soul of the party, a lad amongst lads when the game was over. But on the night before the game, Peter Reid was sat alone, cleaning his boots until they were shining. And here's a final thought. There were eighteen members of that Huyton Boys squad in that Morecambe hotel that night in 1970. Some of them, quite a few actually had, as Peter would be the first to agree, as much natural talent as he had. Seventeen lads went to an amusement arcade that night in Morecambe. One lad stayed in his room to clean his boots. One lad went on to play for England.
Just a thought. Just a fact."

GEORGE TELFER

©George Herringshaw

When 15-year old George Telfer signed as an apprentice for Everton he was carrying on an existing connection with the Moores family, who at the time were the majority shareholders in the club. In addition to the many Telfers who were employed by the Moores' Littlewoods Pools Empire, George's father worked as a Gamekeeper on the Moores' estate in Scotland which was partly why, despite interest from many topflight clubs, Goodison was always going to be George's footballing destination.

Born on 6 July 1955, he spent much of his childhood living at 18 Reva Road and, whilst attending Malvern school, his obvious talent was encouraged by teacher Mr Gerrard. George graduated to the Huyton Boys team with whom he won a share of the Snowdon Cup spoils when, in June 1969, after trailing 3-0 they drew 5-5 with Kirkby in a thrilling final encounter. Playing at centre forward, George regularly topped the goal scoring charts which helped him secure a place in the Lancashire Boys team. He was often utilised as a winger for the County side, which didn't really play to his strengths - a dilemma which was repeated later and probably hindered his professional career.

With fellow Huytonian Don Tobin for company in the Everton youth team, George's impressive performances resulted in a dream debut for the reserves. On 25 September 1971 and still only 16 years of age, he bagged a brace at Goodison Park in a 3-1 win over Derby County Reserves. He continued to find the net for the ressies and when John Connolly failed a fitness test before the first team's league game with Arsenal, George got the chance he had been working and waiting for. December 22 1973 marked two years to the day since Everton legend Alan Ball had left Goodison Park to join the Gunners and he celebrated by scoring the game's only goal in front of a 19,886 Highbury crowd to put a dampener on George's day. There were no such problems four days later when 36,007 witnessed George's home debut in a 2-0 victory over Manchester City and before the year was over he got another game and two points under his belt with a 2-1 defeat of Derby County. Having made the breakthrough, George made 17 appearances during the 1973/74 season and found the onion bag three times. On 16 February 1974 he scored twice to open his account as West Ham turned the Blues over 4-3. The game was also significant as Bob Latchford made his Toffees debut. Latch went on to become an Everton legend with 106 goals for the club making George's task of filling a forwards role extremely difficult. Although his opportunities were reduced due to a catalogue of injuries, George did continue to be an important member of the squad for seven additional seasons making 116 appearances, returning 22 goals.

In 1977 he picked up a League Cup runners-up medal when Aston Villa defeated Everton in the final. However, a couple of season later he turned down the offer of a renewed contract and on 4 April 1981 he pulled on a royal blue jersey for the last time in a 2-2 draw with Tottenham Hotspur at White Hart Lane. Despite interest from a number of clubs, George decided to take up an exciting offer to cross the pond and play in the NASL for San Diego Soccers. Albeit an enjoyable experience, the transatlantic adventure lasted just a single season as the Telfer family became homesick and returned to Blighty. He joined Scunthorpe United and rose brilliantly to the challenge by becoming the club's top scorer in his debut season for the Iron. George thoroughly enjoyed his time at the Old Show Ground where he struck up a great on and off the field relationship with cricket great Ian 'Beefy' Botham. It could be argued that the larger than life character wasn't fit to lace George's football boots but, when his teammate sustained a painful broken hand, that is exactly what Beefy did for the next few games ! In August 1983, George's injuries finally caught up with him and after a brief spell with PNE he reluctantly brought his professional career to a close. Over the next couple of seasons he turned out for local outfits Prescot, Runcorn and Formby and scored on his debut for each club. In 1984, George's love of the game helped him secure a position as a Football Development Officer and, along with Hugh McAuley, he ran successful coaching courses for young players. In 1986, the duo managed the team which lifted the Lancashire FA Youth Cup by defeating Skem 4-3 in the final. Now retired, George lives in Widnes with his wife Pam and regularly attends events organised by the Everton Former Players Association.

RICHARD JOHNSON

There can't have been many 18-year-old debutants who have upstaged a World Cup winner on his return to the area where he was idolised but that is one of Richard 'Dick' Johnson's claims to fame. On 23 September 1971 when regular Tranmere Rovers goalkeeper Frank Lane informed Manager Jackie Wright that he was unable to play in the following evening's fixture due to an ankle injury, understudy Richard was given less than 24 hours to prepare for the biggest game of his young life. Bolton Wanderers, who included former Liverpool and England legend Roger Hunt in their line-up, provided the opposition underneath the Friday night Prenton Park floodlights. This was the first time he had been back to Merseyside to play in a competitive match since leaving the Reds in 1969. Hunt was a devastating goal scorer with a hugely impressive record of finding the back of the net with stunning regularity but, despite his best efforts, he was unable to beat Richard who made a string of fantastic saves. Prior to kick-off, few of those present would have been able to name Lane's replacement between the sticks but that changed when Dick's Man-of-the-Match performance resulted in a 0-0 draw and him stealing the weekend's headlines from Sir Roger.

Hunt was not the only Merseyside legend that Dick had to contend with in order to progress his career. Shortly after the Bolton game, Lane moved across the River Mersey to join Liverpool whilst Scottish international Tommy 'The Flying Pig' Lawrence moved in the opposite direction and went straight into the Tranmere team. Dick made just nine first team appearances in the 1972/73 season but in the following campaign he became the regular number 1 making Tommy surplus to requirements and signalling an end to his professional career. Richard also saw off a challenge to his position when Gordon West came out of retirement in 1975 to join Rovers' playing and coaching staff. Former Everton and England keeper 'Big Westy' figured in just 17 matches before he also called it a day. Ironically, West had been one of Dick's heroes and, as a child, he had tried to emulate him in the small orchard at the family's Pilch Lane East home where the tree trunks were

the correct distance apart to serve as goalposts. Richard's journey to Prenton Park had involved developing his goalkeeping technique whilst playing for Malvern Primary School, Huyton Hey Secondary Modern and the Huyton & District Schoolboys teams.

His debut got his career off to a flying start and on 2 October 1973 he played no small part in what many people consider Tranmere's greatest ever result. The vast majority of the 20,337 spectators present at Arsenal's famous Highbury Stadium expected the team that had achieved a momentous League & FA Cup double just 18 months earlier to sweep Rovers aside and progress to the third round of the League Cup competition. Indeed, Tranmere's new player-manager Ron Yeats had selected a team and formation with damage limitation in mind. Bizarre by today's standards, Richard recalls that the squad travelled down to the capital on the early morning train on the day of the game and checked into the Russell Hotel. After a mid-afternoon stroll, a short kip and egg on toast (which Dick jokingly says felt like the last meal of a condemned man!), they made their way to the ground like lambs to the slaughter. However, in the 29th minute of the game striker Eddie Loyden gave Rovers an unexpected but thoroughly deserved lead with a close range strike. With 35-year old Yeats winning header after header and marshalling a resolute defence which included Huytonians Ronnie Moore and Ray Mathias, Dick had a quieter than expected evening. Yet, in the closing seconds of the tie he pulled off a fantastic save to deny John Radford an equaliser and to send the Gunners crashing out of the competition. Third Division Tranmere's victory is still recognised as one of the biggest upsets in League Cup history and is a tremendous feather in the cap of each member of that victorious side.

In 1979, the League Cup again provided Dick with happy memories when, on 29 August in a second round, 1st leg home match, he was equal to everything that was thrown at him and kept a clean sheet against mighty Liverpool. At half-time in the 2nd leg a week later, the teams were still deadlocked but in the 46th minute Phil Thompson scored and despite Dick pulling off a host of saves the Reds ran out winners by four goals to nil. Between 1971 and 1982 Richard Johnson made 355 Football League appearances for Tranmere Rovers and kept an impressive 109 clean sheets. He bowed out of the pro game following a 2-2 draw with Mansfield Town on Boxing Day 1981. Tranmere rewarded him for his loyal service with a Testimonial match versus Everton on 10 May 1982. The game ended 1-1 after Dick stepped up to even the score from the penalty spot much to the delight of the 5,500 fans who had turned up to show their appreciation of his commitment to their club.

Richard went on to combine playing non-league football for Altrincham, Burscough, South Liverpool and Prescot Cables with working for Liverpool City Council's Sports & Recreation Department. He also proudly spent 14 years as a part-time goalkeeping coach for LFC and helped, amongst others, Ian Dunbavin from Huyton who, after enjoying a lengthy playing career, became a coach himself at the Liverpool Academy. Dick is now retired and lives in Widnes with his wife Rose. He spends much of his time surrounded by his extended family of two grown up children and five grandchildren but always keeps close tabs on how his beloved Tranmere are performing.

DAVE BAMBER

Born on 1 February 1959, Dave Bamber grew up in St George's Avenue, Windle - just outside of our catchment area. His first football pitch was, like many others, illuminated by a standard street lamp that enabled Dave and his mates to hone their skills until long after the sun had gone down. His first encounter with Huyton football was when his Bleak Hill Junior School football team (which had won its league) took on and defeated its Huyton counterparts - a rare occurrence. When Dave passed the 11+ exam and subsequently attended Prescot Grammar School to secure safe passage to these pages, he recalls being the talk of the school when his team won one game 9-0 and centre forward Dave scored all nine goals!

Prescot teacher and scout Jim Dewsnip had already helped other pupils to get onto the football ladder so when Dave consistently found the net for the school and Huyton Boys, he had no hesitation in recommending him to Liverpool FC. Dave played for the Reds between the ages of 15 and 18. During this time he continued to turn out for Huyton Boys and the Merseyside U-19s team. This enabled him to participate in the prestigious home and away games between the county side and a team from Liverpool's twin city of Cologne. Having attended Everton games as a child (courtesy of tickets provided to Dave's uncle by Toffee's winger Jimmy Husband), Dave took great satisfaction in the home fixture when he scored in a 5-3 victory over the Germans at Goodison Park. Liverpool's Youth Development Officer and school headmaster Tom Saunders constantly drilled into the young players the importance of a good education. This was not lost on Dave who passed his A levels and secured a place at Leicester University to study for a degree in Economics.

He successfully juggled his studies and football and played for Altrincham, St Helens Town and the British Universities team that reached the quarter-finals at the World Student Games in Mexico. Following the tournament, respected Uni team coach Roy Rees recommended Dave to Blackpool FC. However, with interest shown by Millwall and Bradford City and Liverpool tabling a six months contract, Dave had to weigh up his options. Putting his economics studies to good use, he plumped for the relative security of a three-year deal with the Tangerines. Unusually, Dave made his debut whilst still a student when, on 28 September 1979, he came off the bench at Springfield Park to play the last ten minutes of a 2-0 FA Cup 1st round defeat at the hands of Wigan Athletic. His full debut followed on 29 December 1979 versus Chester City - this game also ended in defeat for Blackpool but the disappointing result was tempered by Dave's delight at getting a Football League game under his belt. He opened his goal scoring account in a home match against Carlisle Utd in a 2-1 victory on 7 April 1980 in front of 6,054 ecstatic supporters - the fans roar after a goal would become a familiar sound to Dave.

The club's followers had not had too much to cheer about in recent campaigns and in Dave's first full season the team suffered the ignominy of relegation to the old Fourth Division. With the team struggling and managers coming and going (four in four seasons), it was difficult for a young player to make an impression. However, after a while Dave felt more at home in the side and consequently made a greater impact. In his third season he scored 15 goals and followed with 10 in the next. His impressive tally of 36 goals from 104 appearances caught the eye of a number of clubs and on 6 January 1983 Bobby Gould, newly appointed as First Division Coventry City's Manager, made Dave his first signing when he paid £50,000 to take him to Highfield Road. Unfortunately, his spell in the top flight only lasted 12 months, 19 League games and three goals. This was largely due to a mystery illness which dramatically affected his fitness. Even though his time with the Sky Blues was short-lived, it still contained a memorable 4-0 victory over all-conquering Liverpool and a goal at Highbury on 15 October 1983 that put the Gunners to the sword.

Next, Walsall Manager Alan Buckley successfully tabled a £40,000 bid for Dave and he spent two seasons with the Saddlers, returning seven goals from 20 Third Division games. Former Blackpool Boss Alan Ball then took Dave to Portsmouth but the pair never saw eye to eye (hardly surprising, Dave was 6'3" tall and Ball only 5'6"!) and after just four League games both parties agreed a parting of the ways was inevitable. After a brief loan spell at Swedish club Trelleborgs, Dave joined Swindon Town on loan to begin the most enjoyable spell of his career. Over a trio of seasons, during which time the loan move became permanent for a bargain price of £15,000, Dave played 134 games and registered 47 goals. Under Lou Macari, the club achieved back-to-back promotions and Dave was integral to their success. He loved his time at the County Ground and it was with a heavy heart that he left to join Watford in a deal that was more about the £105,000 fee than football. A solid season with the Hornets resulted in a fourth place Division Two finish but it wasn't long before Dave was again on his travels with Stoke City's Victoria Ground the destination and £200,000 the fee. However, at the end of the 1988/89 season, relegation brought about the sacking of Manager Mick Mills. Alan Ball was installed as his replacement and Dave sought pastures new. Hull City's Boothferry Park provided a disappointing couple of seasons for the target man before he returned to the club where it all began for him.

Dave's spiritual home Bloomfield Road was an ideal fit for the Bamber family. Whilst his five seasons in his second spell at the club (making nine in total) undoubtedly contained heartache, there were sufficient goals and celebrations to justify the return to the town where he had met his wife ten years earlier. The heartache arrived when Dave missed the decisive penalty at Wembley in the 1990/91 Fourth Division play-off Final shoot-out after the Tangerines and Torquay had played out a thrilling 2-2 draw. This was a devastating experience for him at the time but to his eternal credit he used the disappointment to spur himself and the team on to success the following season. The 1991/92 campaign was brilliant for everyone associated with Blackpool. On a personal level, Dave lifted the Golden Boot scoring 36 goals from just 53 games to help the club to return to the Twin Towers. On 23 May 1992 in front of 22,741 supporters, Dave rattled home the last of those 36 goals to give Blackpool the lead but after Tony Daws equalised for Scunthorpe neither team could find the winner so penalties were required. Perhaps understandably, Dave did not take a spot kick but, following much nail biting, Blackpool came out on top and gained promotion to the newly-formed League Two. Dave Bamber continued to play and score for a further two seasons before injuries finally caught up with him to force his retirement. He had enjoyed a fantastic 15-year career that had involved nine different clubs, all four divisions of the Football League, relegations and promotions and many, many goals. His sterling efforts for Blackpool were recognised when, in April 2006, he was inducted to the club's Hall of Fame when it was officially opened by former playing legend Jimmy Armfield.

©phsp@mac.com

BRIAN KETTLE

The great Bill Shankly famously said, "This city has two great teams – Liverpool and Liverpool Reserves." Shanks' tongue may or may not have been firmly in his cheek when he made the provocative comment but there is little doubt that LFC's second string would have given most of the top sides of the day a run for their money. Whilst it was not unusual for recognised 'first teamers' to turn out for the 'ressies' if they were out of favour or returning from injury, the team also contained a number of mainstays who were the backbone of a side which dominated the Central League for many years.

One such player was fullback Brian Kettle. Born on 22 April 1956, Brian grew up living in the Finch Lane area of Dovecot and attended Maidford Road Junior School. Midfield performances for his Yew Tree Comprehensive School and Liverpool Boys teams resulted in him being invited to Tuesday and Thursday evening training at Melwood. Liverpool's Youth Development Officer Tom Saunders converted Brian into a left fullback. He thrived in the position and made his reserve team debut aged just 16 years old. On 1 May 1973 despite interest from Burnley, he became a full-time professional with the Reds just a week after his 17th birthday. He continued to make good progress and on 27 February 1974 Brian proudly took his place in the England U-18s team that defeated Holland 1-0 at The Hague. Brian spent the majority of the Seventies at Anfield and was an integral member of the club's reserve team which picked up seven Central League titles in eight seasons – including three campaigns when he captained the side.

His main objective was to break in to Liverpool's first eleven but apart from four precious games this eluded him due to the quality of his rivals to the left back berth, namely Alec Lindsay, Joey Jones and Alan Kennedy. His debut came in the second leg of the 2nd round of the UEFA Cup on Tuesday 4 November 1975 at Anfield in front of 23,796 supporters. The Reds ran out 6-0 winners to add to the 3-1 victory in the first leg a fortnight earlier. In a dream debut, Brian played a major part in a couple of the goals and prompted Daily Post journalist Horace Yates to report, "The ace in the Liverpool pack was undoubtedly Brian Kettle, the 19-year-old fullback.... Kettle scoffed at the supposed ordeal of a debut and left everybody wondering whether he has outlived life in the reserves." Unfortunately for Brian, Manager Bob Paisley didn't share the scribe's opinion and after taking part in a 2-2 drawn match with the Gunners on 2 December 1975 he returned to the 'stiffs' as the reserves were jokingly dubbed.

Brian made further first team appearances in January 1977 versus WBA and Norwich City but although he was regularly included in the first team squad, it was usually in the capacity of non-playing thirteenth man. In 1978, Brian spent a year in the States on loan at Dallas Tornado and Houston Hurricane before returning home and signing for Wigan Athletic. He put the knowledge and experience he acquired at Anfield to good use when injury ended his full-time professional career after just 14 Wigan games. Brian played non-League football with Burscough, Runcorn and Barrow before trying his hand at management at South Liverpool in 1986. He embarked upon a successful, trophy-laden decade as the boss at South's Holly Park, Southport, Stalybridge Celtic and Rhyl.

Some might say that Brian Kettle should have left Liverpool earlier than he did but he has no regrets. Reflecting on his Liverpool career in 2001, Brian said "The memories I have of the time are absolutely superb. I felt I was brought up by the best. I learnt so much there, I ran out at Anfield and the Kop shouted my name, what a great feeling that was. I would've liked it to happen more often but I did my best and it never quite happened. I'm not ashamed, because there were excellent players in front of me who helped the club to European success. At the end of the day, no one can take what I achieved away from me."

STEVEN WARRINER

In the 1970s and 80s, in view of the fact that Liverpool only granted a small number of apprenticeships to the very best young players, it would have been highly unlikely for two brothers to be taken on by the club. For siblings Steven, John and Mark Warriner to have ALL become apprentices and then professionals at this time is nothing short of remarkable. Mark and John were both fine players who enjoyed successful amateur careers after leaving Melwood but it was the oldest of the trio, Steven, who made an impression on the professional game.

Born on 18 December 1958, the former St Augustine's pupil joined Liverpool at the same time as his Huyton Boys teammate Dave Bamber and secured an apprenticeship in December 1976. The club was thriving with the first team picking up numerous domestic and European trophies and titles whilst the reserve team dominated the Central League. Equally as comfortable occupying a fullback or midfield berth, Stevie picked up a League winners medal after making 13 appearances for the club's second eleven during their 1976/77 campaign. With the first team packed with quality internationals, Woggsy made the decision to move on when Newport County Boss Len Ashurst expressed a desire to take him to Somerton Park.

With pen put to paper on 1 July 1978, he joined the club as they were about to embark upon their most impressive period since their formation in 1912. Liverpudlian Ashurst, who had turned out for Prescot Cables as a youngster before enjoying a fine playing career with Sunderland and Hartlepool, was in his fourth managerial position having previously been in charge of Huddersfield, Gillingham and Sheffield Wednesday. The Scouse heartbeat of the team consisted of John Aldridge and Huytonians Tommy Tynan and John Relish which helped Steven to settle into his new surroundings. They finished eighth in the old Fourth Division in his debut season which included his first Football League goal in a 1-1 draw with Stockport County on 17 November 1978. From that solid platform, Newport County excelled in the following campaign and ventured into previously unchartered waters. They lost only two home games all season which put them in a great position in the table. On 3 May 1980, in front of a home gate of 9,251 they defeated Walsall 4-2 in the season's final fixture to secure third place and promotion. Steven featured in 11 matches and found the net once - in an away game versus Northampton Town. A week later, a good season became a great season. Having overcome Cardiff City, Wrexham and Merthyr Tydfil, they faced Shrewsbury Town in the Welsh Cup Final. Over the two-legged affair, County brushed the Shrews aside by an aggregate score of 5-1 to lift the trophy. Ashurst's men had done him proud and by winning the Welsh Cup and subsequently qualifying for the following season's European Cup Winners Cup competition, they had surpassed their predecessors' achievements.

In Steven's third and final season, Newport's only promotion since 1939 resulted in them competing in the third tier of English football for the first time since 1962. They finished in a very respectable 12th place but it was their performances around the continent that put them on the European map. The 'Class of 81', as they have become known, exceeded even the most optimistic County fan's expectations by taking the Cup Winners Cup by storm and accounting for Northern Ireland side Crusaders (4-0) and crushing SK Haugar of Norway (6-0). With a place in the last eight of the competition secured, they were drawn against impressive East German outfit Carl Zeiss Jena. Having already overcome Roma and Valencia, the Germans were huge favourites to make short shrift of the little team from South Wales. However, when in the 90th minute of the tie's first leg, Tommy Tynan scored his second goal to make it 2-2, it looked like a major upset may be on the cards. On 18 March 1981, 18,000 fans crammed into Somerton Park hoping to witness the continuation of their cup fortunes. The game was on a knife-edge and County created numerous chances including a Tynan effort that rattled the East German's crossbar. A goal from a 25-yard free kick proved to be the difference between the sides and denied Newport a semi-final meeting with Benfica.

Before the commencement of the 1981/82 campaign, Steven had found pastures new at Rochdale's Spotland Stadium. His couple of seasons with Dale involved 12 appearances and a single goal - a barnstorming 20-yard strike versus Northampton Town (again!). Steven finished his career with a brief spell on the Wirral with Tranmere Rovers playing nine games under Bryan Hamilton.

Similar to many ex-pros, Steven worked in the licensing trade as manager of the Greyhound public house in Knotty Ash before transferring his managerial skills to a Sefton supported living scheme. Since Steven's Newport days, the club has endured tremendous turbulence which involved relegation out of the Football League and going out of business. However, the club has an extremely loyal and passionate set of supporters who established a Supporters Trust which now owns the club. After reforming as Newport AFC, the team stormed through five non-League divisions to regain Football League status in 2013. A year later, Newport embraced its history and entertained CZ Jena in a pre-season friendly. Many of the Class of '81, including Steven, attended as guests of honour and received a tremendous reception from the Newport faithful.

DAVID MARTINDALE

The late, legendary Tranmere Rovers Manager Johnny King once described David Martindale in a BBC Radio Merseyside interview as "....my Georgie Best. I didn't know from one week to the next whether he was going to turn up - but when he did he was a diamond, albeit a rough diamond." Dave actually turned up on 166 occasions for Rovers and made a massive contribution to the club's most successful period in its lengthy history.

Born on 9 April 1964, the midfielder grew up living in the Page Moss area of Huyton. He spent a number of years with Liverpool and played in the same youth team as fellow 'Huyton's Titans' Tony Kelly and Dave Bleasdale and future Football League players Ian Rush, Ronnie Whelan, Alan Harper and Paul Jewel. When the club released him he joined South Liverpool and was a member of the successful 1983/84 squad that won the treble of Northern Premier League Cup, Lancashire Junior Cup and the Liverpool Senior Cup. The Holly Park club also lifted the Senior Cup two years later but by this time Dave had moved on to play for Caernarfon Town via short spells with Runcorn and Southport for whom he made 12 appearances. Former Everton player King had recently taken managerial control of the North Wales outfit and in a magical two years he assembled a team recognised as their best ever. This was never more evident than in their participation in the 1986/87 FA Cup competition. Having overcome Marine, Winsford, Eastwood Town and Chester-Le-Street in the qualifying rounds to reach the 1st round proper, they defeated Fourth Division Stockport County by a 1-0 scoreline. York City of Division Three provided stiffer opposition in the second round but following a tough 0-0 draw, the Minstermen were accounted for 2-1 in the replay. For a team such as Caernarfon to reach the third round of the FA Cup was a dream come true and the townsfolk got right behind their club. Three thousand fans were present at the Oval Ground for the resultant visit of Barnsley. The club from the second tier of the English Football League were fortunate to get away from North Wales with a 0-0 draw and only narrowly pipped Caernarfon 1-0 in the return at Oakwell to end their run - but what a run it had been for King and his team with Dave at the heart of the midfield. In addition, the club finished third in the Northern Premier League to round off a fantastic season.

Although hugely disappointing, it came as no surprise to the Caernarfon faithful when on 13 April 1987 Johnny King left the club after being headhunted by Tranmere Rovers - or that he took Dave Higgins and Dave Martindale with him. So began the greatest period in Tranmere's 100-year existence which almost saw them reach the giddy heights of the Premiership. At the end of David's first season as a Tranmere player, the club took part in the Football League Centenary tournament at Wembley Stadium, organised to celebrate the 100th birthday of the Football League. Tranmere had only just avoided dropping out of the League by a couple of points a year earlier, however they rose admirably to the challenge. In their opening game in the tournament, played over an April weekend, Tranmere knocked out a full-strength Wimbledon side with

©Tranmere Rovers FC

Marto bursting into the box to slide the ball in off the post to beat Wimbledon goalkeeper Dave Beasant for the only goal of the game. This was no mean feat as a month later Wimbledon were back at Wembley in the FA Cup Final where they achieved their own giant-killing act with a 1-0 victory over nailed-on favourites Liverpool. The reaction to David's goal prompted Match of the Day commentator Barry Davis to proclaim, "The roof has come off here! You'd have thought that was the winning goal in the Cup Final judging by the reaction of the Tranmere supporters." In the second round, Rovers won 2-0 with goals from Morrissey and Muir against a Newcastle Utd side which contained a young Paul Gascoigne and Mirandinha - the first Brazilian to play in England. The following day in the semi-final, Marto lined up for Tranmere against a Nottingham Forest team with Stuart Pearce and Manager Brian Clough's son Nigel in its ranks. The teams from different ends of the Football League played out a thrilling 2-2 draw in which Rovers twice lead. However, Forest won on penalties and went on to defeat Sheffield Wednesday in the Final.

Their performances against loftier opposition in the tournament and the Johnny King effect inspired the Super Whites the following season as they finished runners-up in the League to secure automatic promotion to Division Three. On a personal level, the 1989/90 season was ultimately disappointing for David. Although he played a big part in Rovers returning to the Twin Towers for the Leyland Daf and Division Three play-off Finals, he missed both games. They lifted the LD trophy by turning Bristol Rovers over 2-1 in front of 48,402 spectators but fell at the final hurdle of their League campaign when Notts County beat the Wirralians 2-0 to grab a Division Two place. Remarkably, 12 months later David had an opportunity to make amends when Rovers again made it to the LD Trophy Final and the crucial Division Three play-off match. He featured in both games and, on 1 June 1991 with 30,217 inside Wembley Stadium, a 98th minute Chris Malkin strike beat the Bolton Wanderers keeper to send Tranmere's fans into raptures and the club into the Second Division. A week earlier, Birmingham City had defeated Rovers 3-2 to lift the Daf Trophy but this almost paled into insignificance when compared with promotion.

The club continued to do well under Kingy. In May 1993 they reached the play-offs again but lost in the semis to Swindon Town who beat Leicester City in the Final to reach the Promised Land of the Premiership. David spent seven hugely enjoyable seasons at Prenton Park during which time the Birkenhead club rose from the brink of Football League obscurity to the verge of the highest level of the English football pyramid. However, all good things come to an end and, before the start of the 93/94 season, Marto joined Doncaster Rovers under former Wolves gaffer Sammy Chung. Short spells at Glentoran, Conwy Utd and Altrincham brought his career to a close - David Martindale, Huyton's very own Georgie Best!

MICK QUINN

Mick Quinn has many strings to his bow. Racehorse owner and trainer, radio presenter, television commentator and pundit, author and even winner of TV's Celebrity Fit Club are just some of his claims to fame. However, it was as a top class striker with the ability to find the net with stunning regularity that he initially came to public prominence.

In 1967, five-year old Michael and his parents moved from their home in the Everton area of Liverpool to 16 Roundhey on the new Cantril Farm estate. In order to help the new community integrate, a local junior football league was established and young Mick impressed playing for the Nevitte Close team. After leaving St Albert's Junior School he attended St Dominics Comprehensive where teachers Mr Mellon and Mr Price spotted his ability as an all-round sportsman. They encouraged him and put his name forward for the Huyton Boys side. In his autobiography 'Who Ate All The Pies?' Quinny recalls "I started playing for the Huyton Boys team …We were a great team but we looked like a bunch of urchins; I don't think Huyton council could afford to buy us a proper kit. We all had different colour strips and odd socks but when we played the Liverpool lads, they all looked like junior Charles Atlases. They were all 6-foot-tall with gleaming new kits that Liverpool had given them. We always gave them a good game though."

Michael occasionally played at centre half for the Schoolboys but it was at the opposite end of the field that he came alive. After scoring five in one game for Nevittes he was invited by a watching scout to train with and play for Tranmere's U-16s. His growing reputation as a prolific scorer turned the head of reputable scout Jim Aspinall who would later discover Robbie Fowler and Steve Macmanaman. Jim arranged a trial for Mick at Derby County who were plying their trade in the top tier of English football. He scored a bagful of goals, secured a Rams apprenticeship and moved into local digs. After just eight months, homesick Mick left the club but soon after received another opportunity, this time at Wigan Athletic. Closer to home and at a smaller club, it wasn't long before the Canny Farmer was blazing a trail to the first team. Manager Ian McNeill handed Quinny his first start on 12 April 1980 in an end of season fixture opposing Halifax Town. He repaid his faith in him by scoring their final goal in a 3-1 victory. This was the first of 231 League goals Mick registered from 512 games over 17 seasons. During the 1980/81 campaign, Mick established himself in the side scoring 14 goals including his first career hat trick in a 3-0 win over Doncaster Rovers. However, following McNeill's sacking, Mick fell out of favour with new boss Larry Lloyd who offloaded him to Stockport County. He found the net 23 times in his debut 1982/83 season for the Hatters which alerted the bigger clubs. His form continued into the following campaign and when Oldham Manager Joe Royle paid £52,000 in January 1984 to take him to Boundary Park, he already had 17 goals in the tank. The step up to the Second Division didn't faze Mick in the slightest and from his 80 Latics appearances, he scored 34 goals.

His reputation as an alert, no-nonsense goal scorer was gaining momentum and on 14 March 1986, Portsmouth Boss and 1966 World Cup winner Alan Ball took advantage of Oldham's dire financial position to snap Quinny up for a bargain transfer fee of £150,000. Mick spent three eventful years at Pompey where he scored 54 goals from 121 appearances, enjoyed promotion, suffered relegation, was voted the PFA Division Two Striker of the Year and was appointed captain. However, when Alan Ball left the club and John Gregory was installed as his successor, Mick felt that the magic had disappeared and that he needed a fresh challenge. There was no shortage of potential suitors and amongst others, he was linked with Everton, Man City and West Ham. On 1 August 1989, Mick joined Newcastle Utd and almost immediately gained legendary status. Initially, many Geordies had reservations about the signing, especially at the hefty sum of £680,000. In addition, Boss Jim Smith handed Quinny the number nine jersey with the instruction to bag 20 goals per season. Previously worn by legends Jackie Milburn, Hughie Gallagher and Malcolm Macdonald, the significance of the Magpies '9' shirt was not lost on Mick. It had often weighed heavy on the shoulders of players who failed to meet the demands of the centre forward job - but Quinny rose to the challenge superbly. He made his debut on 19 August 1989 when Leeds Utd were the visitors to

©George Herringshaw

St James Park. It took him just 18 minutes to start winning over the fans and repaying the transfer fee. A converted penalty and three further strikes helped the Magpies to a 5-2 victory and made the Mighty Quinn the talk of the Toon. He followed this up with goals in each of their next four games - a club record - and continued to find the net throughout a remarkable season which made the fee look like a snip. His 32 League goals were a major factor in the team securing a third place finish and a play-off date with Sunderland. However, with a 2-0 victory, the Rokerites won local bragging rights and ultimately a place in Division One. His 18 goals the following campaign cemented Mick's reputation with the Geordie faithful but overall results were poor. Osvaldo Ardilles replaced Smith presenting Mick with the opportunity to play under another World Cup winner. Despite his undoubted playing pedigree, Ossie was unable to reverse the slide and lasted just 11 months in the job. On 5 February 1992, St James Park Messiah Kevin Keegan took over the managerial reins and during a whirlwind five years he performed miracles and almost landed the Premier League title in 1995/96. Mick's experience under his boyhood hero was bittersweet. Arguments, reconciliations and further disputes resulted in a parting of the ways nine months into Keegan's tenure with Mick finding a new home at Coventry City.

A brace on his debut in a 3-2 reversal to Manchester City endeared him to a new set of followers and he enjoyed a three-year relationship and good-natured banter with the Sky Blues fans. Once again, Mick failed to see eye to eye with Boss Phil Neal and his successor Ron Atkinson who sent him out on loan to Plymouth Argyle and Watford.

After becoming a free agent at the end of his Cov contract, Mick accepted an interesting offer from Greek club PAOK Salonika. Seven turbulent months later, he brought the curtain down on an excellent 17 season, 10-club career. However, as the changing room door closed a stable door opened.

From an early age Mick had been fascinated by horseracing, initially as a punter before later using his knowledge and profile to establish a racehorse owners syndicate and a tipping service. Against the advice of former Pompey teammate and established racehorse trainer Mick Channon, Quinny opted to try his hand at making his own mark in the Sport of Kings. Channon took him under his wing and taught him the ins and outs of the demanding trade. He served a lengthy apprenticeship before his mentor believed he was ready to take the plunge and set up stables of his own. After a number of notable setbacks, Mick is now a respected trainer who is a regular in the Winner's Enclosure.

In recent years he has juggled his equine responsibilities with working as a football pundit and as the host of a national radio show where he put his infectious character to good use. Although the farm he now lives on may have a Newmarket postcode, he still has fond memories of his days living on Cantril Farm. He can probably be best summed up by describing Mick Quinn as a proud Scouser and Huytonian who has remained true to his roots throughout a hugely successful and varied career.

MARK WARD

Mark Ward made a mistake and paid for it with four years of his liberty. The details are documented in his autobiography 'From Right Wing to B Wing' but this book is primarily about football and Mark was one of the finest footballers Huyton has ever produced so that is the focus of our attention.

Born on 10 October 1962 in Belton Road in the Woolfall Heath area of Huyton, Mark constantly had a ball at his feet. He would practise running at speed and dribbling as he dashed to and from Keyo's shop at the top of the street. When the family moved to 23 Walpole Avenue in Whiston, taking his dad's bets to the local turf accountants provided the new destination for the five year old to work on his ball skills. Managed by local men Steve Hughes and Brian Lee, Mark got his first taste of competitive football playing for Whiston Cross. Despite the team getting thrashed 6-0 by an Everton junior team at Bellefield, EFC's youth coach Graham Smith loved Mark's never-say-die approach to the game and invited him to twice-weekly training sessions. Wardy was in his element playing for his Whiston Higherside School team, St Helens Boys, Whiston Cross and now Everton. Blackburn Rovers, Liverpool and Manchester Utd all showed an interest in Mark, prompting the Toffees to act swiftly and offer him schoolboy forms. He was often a ball boy at home games and seeing his idols up close heightened his desire to follow in their footsteps. His first opportunity to play on Goodison's hallowed turf came with Whiston Cross on 12 September 1978 in a 4-1 victory in the Final of a tournament organised by Merseyside Police. Shortly after this, the club rewarded Mark for his progress by handing him an apprenticeship. When he excelled in a U-19s youth tournament in Holland, where he scored the winner in the Final and picked up the 'Player of the Tournament' award, he bagged a full-time professional contract. However, Mark's joy turned to despair just 12 months later when Manager Gordon Lee informed him his contract would not be renewed. Mark later stated, "Leaving the club I loved hurt very badly at the time but it was to be the making of me as a player and a man."

©George Herringshaw

Much to his father's dismay, Mark hastily signed for Alliance Premier League side Northwich Victoria, managed by former Everton player and Tranmere Rovers legend Johnny King. Mark's gamble to play in non-League football paid off when, during his two seasons with the Vics, he shone and grabbed the headlines. Only 20 years of age, Mark was adamant he would still make the grade and Division Two Oldham Athletic Manager Joe Royle shared his belief. He paid £9,500 to take Mark to Boundary Park with the fee rising to £35,000 if he played 25 games. On 25 August 1983, 5,750 fans witnessed Mark's goalscoring, match-winning debut versus Brighton and it wasn't long before Northwich's Chairman received the additional £25,500. Mark played every one of the next two seasons 96 games and his outstanding performances attracted the attention of the big boys.

On 14 August 1985 less than two years after that debut, West Ham Utd Manager John Lyall paid £250,000 for Mark's signature. He soon became a Hammers favourite by working his socks off in the wing back position at Upton Park. In his first season, he only scored three goals but his focus was on providing the ammunition for strike partners Tony Cottee and Frank McAvennie who collectively bagged 46 League goals to help the club secure third place in the First Division. Mark thoroughly enjoyed his four seasons with West Ham but when John Lyall left and Lou Macari was installed as his successor he struggled to get along with his new boss and a move became an inevitability.

Manchester City Manager Howard Kendall offered Wardy the chance to join him at Maine Road and Mark didn't hesitate to accept. City were in a relegation dogfight but a 2-0 victory over Millwall on Mark's 30 December 1989 debut was followed by just one defeat in their final eleven games of the season. Relegation avoided - job done. When the following campaign kicked off the team enjoyed a flying start with only two defeats in their opening 16 games. However, Kendall's success had meant that when the Manager's job at Goodison Park became available, he was Everton's main target. Mark was sad to see Kendall depart down the M62 but delighted that his Assistant, Huyton and Everton legend Peter Reid, stayed to take up his first managerial position. The club finished fifth in the First Division and in a glorious 18-month period Mark missed just two out of a possible 57 games. He was looking forward to the 1991/92 season until Howard Kendall approached City wanting to take him to Goodison Park.

It had been 10 years since Gordon Lee had shown him the door but in the summer of 1991 Mark traded in his sky blue shirt for one of a distinctive royal blue hue in a £1 million deal which took him back to his spiritual home. On 20 August 1991, bursting with pride, Mark took to the pitch to make his home debut - and what a debut it turned out to be! He would later describe it as "My greatest ever game...my biggest and happiest memory in football." Mark scored two goals past England keeper David Seaman as the Toffees defeated reigning League Champions Arsenal 3-1 in front of 31,200 fans. His Goodison dream consisted of 94 games and notably included a goal against arch rivals Liverpool

Having again enjoyed a magnificent relationship with Howard Kendall, Mark was bitterly disappointed when, in December 1993, he left the Blues to try his hand at managing in Greece. When he failed to gel with Howard's replacement Mike Walker and found himself out of the first team picture, he reluctantly accepted that a move away from Goodison was the best course of action. Birmingham City Boss Barry Fry provided a temporary solution when he invited Mark to join him until the end of the season to help them in their battle against relegation. Mark played in the campaign's final nine games for the Midlands outfit but, despite only losing one match, the damage had been done before Wardy's arrival at St Andrews and they went down to Division Two on goal difference. With little prospect of a reconciliation between Mark and Walker, a £200,000 fee was agreed between the two clubs and Mark became City's new player/coach. With such strong personalities as Mark, Fry, owner David Sullivan and MD Karen Brady, it was perhaps inevitable that there would be fireworks in the boardroom. But as far as the football was concerned, it was a successful period for the Blues. On 23 April 1995, Mark put in a m-o-m performance at Wembley, in front of a crowd of 76,663, to help his team overcome Carlisle United 1-0 and lift the Auto Windscreens Shield. A fortnight later, victory over Huddersfield Town handed Birmingham the 2nd Division title and an immediate return to Division One. However, due in no small part to the behind the scenes wrangling, Mark was not offered a new contract signalling his Midlands departure. He enjoyed short spells at Huddersfield Town (8 games), Wigan Athletic (5 games) and Dundee (1 game) before venturing overseas to bring the curtain down on an excellent pro career with stints with Hong Kong club Eastern FC and FC Valur of Iceland. Mark enjoyed a great relationship with the fans of all the clubs he played for but it's fair to say that Everton and West Ham are the two clubs with which he has a special affinity. Nowadays, Mark loves working as a speaker on the after dinner circuit and also as a London Stadium host at Hammers home games.

TONY KELLY

Brazilian Arthur Antures Coimbra, better known as Zico, is one of the finest footballers to have ever graced a football pitch. It was therefore, a huge compliment for Huyton midfielder Tony Kelly to have the nickname 'Zico' bestowed upon him by the Bolton Wanderers fans who also identified him as the 34th best player to have ever played for their club.

Born on 1 October 1964, Tony grew up living in Hillside Avenue and attended St Columba's School. He has many fond memories of playing for the school team and recalls beating St Joseph's by a 4-3 scoreline on the Huntley & Palmers pitch to lift the Hanson Cup. Tony played for Huyton Boys when he was a year younger than the rest of the team and took great pride in helping them turn over Liverpool Boys 2-0 at their Penny Lane ground. The team was so good that they stayed together as Hillsborough JFC and cleaned up in the Norris Green, Kirkdale and Wavertree Leagues.

Tony joined Liverpool as a 14-year-old and stayed with the club for five years becoming an apprentice in 1982. After leaving the Reds a year later, he had a brief dalliance with Derby County before joining Prescot Cables. Whilst playing for the Tigers he was spotted by Wigan Athletic Manager Harry McNally who took him to Springfield Park for the first of three spells with the Latics. Tony made his Football League debut in a 1-0 home defeat to Walsall on 26 November 1983 with 3,485 present. Initially he was employed as a right full-back but when McNally switched him to his more customary central midfield position he flourished and became one of the first names on the team sheet. In his first full season, Tony won the club's Player of the Year award and helped them reach the Freight Rover Trophy Final. At a sun-drenched Wembley Stadium on 1 June 1985 in front of 39,897 spectators, Tony scored Wigan's second of three goals as they accounted for Brentford who could only manage a single goal in reply.

He made 136 appearances and scored 22 goals under McNally and his successor Bryan Hamilton before signing for Mick Mills' Stoke City on 26 April 1986 for a fee of £80,000. He forged a great midfield partnership with ex-England international Brian Talbot whose phenomenal work rate enabled Tony's deft touches and fantastic range of passing to be used to great effect. Their 1986/87 season contained many highlights including 7-2 and 5-1 demolitions of Leeds Utd and Grimsby Town respectively with Tony finding the net in each of these encounters. Stoke finished eighth in Division Two, narrowly missing out on the recently-introduced Football League play-offs, prompting Mills to shake things up. Before the next campaign was under way, Tony was on the move after a single season and 43 appearances. The Stoke faithful were sorry to see him leave and he was always guaranteed a warm reception on his numerous returns to the old Victoria Ground.

On 13 July 1987 West Brom Manager Ron Saunders paid £60,000 to take Tony to the Hawthorns but 51 days later the boss was sacked with Ron Atkinson installed as his replacement. Almost immediately Tony went on a seven-game loan spell to Chester City, followed by three months at Layer Road in Essex where he figured in 20 games for Colchester Utd. Tony's career found much-needed stability when, on 28 January 1989, the Baggies accepted a £30,000 bid from Shrewsbury Town and he was bound for Gay Meadow. During his 120 games for the Shrews, Tony played some great football under Ian McNeil, Asa Hartford and John Bond. He was honing his craft and dictating matches from the heart of the action. His 17 goals for the club included his only career hat-trick in a 5-1 thrashing of Reading in the penultimate game of the 1990/91 season. Tony was in his mid-twenties and carving out a fine reputation as an imposing leader on the pitch.

©The Bolton News

After twice going close but narrowly missing out, Bolton Wanderers Boss Phil Neal identified him as the player to give his team the extra touch of class required to secure promotion. He convinced his Board of Directors to stump up £100,000 to prise Tony away from Shropshire to join the Trotters on 15 August 1991. On a personal level, Tony enjoyed an impressive debut campaign for Neal and was included in the PFA's Division Three Team of the Year. However, a disappointing 13th place finish was not good enough for the board who dispensed with Neal's services and, on 29 May 1992, installed Bruce Rioch in the managerial hotseat.

Neal had assembled a good squad but Rioch added the finishing touches and in his first season he succeeded where his predecessor had failed. They enjoyed a great season finishing in second place, three points behind champions Stoke City and also reached the FA Cup 5th round. On 3 January 1993 with 34,790 fans inside Anfield, Wanderers faced Liverpool in a third round replay in the competition. With Tony pulling the strings, they disposed of the Reds by a 2-0 scoreline. As a Bluenose and former member of the Liverpool playing staff, the result was particularly rewarding for Tony although it stirred mixed emotions amongst his predominantly Liverpudlian family. The following campaign also included stunning FA Cup giant-killing acts with Tony's contribution often singled out for praise. Bolton accounted for Everton, Aston Villa and Arsenal before Oldham Athletic knocked them out in the sixth round. The Gunners were defeated 3-1 on their own turf on 9 February 1994 and England Manager Terry Venables stated that it was the most fantastic performance he had seen from any side at Highbury for many years and applauded Tony by saying he had completely dominated the game. In a majestic couple of seasons, Tony had gone toe-to-toe with some of the best midfielders in the country and come out on top. It was around this time that Bolton's fans christened him 'Zico' in recognition of his ability and massive contribution to their success. However, all good things end and on 23 September 1994 Tony left Burnden Park to join Port Vale - but he would return.

After short spells at Vale, Millwall, Wigan (twice), Peterborough, Altrincham and Sligo Rovers, Tony eventually brought the curtain down on his playing days. Hugely popular and greatly respected in footballing circles, Tony Kelly played in excess of 500 games and scored 52 goals in all competitions. It was almost inevitable that he would stay involved in the game in some capacity and where better than back at Bolton Wanderers? In recent years he has filled a number of roles at the club which means so much to him - 'Fans Liaison Officer', 'Coach of the U-18s & U-23s' and 'Community Ambassador' are job titles which all sit proudly on his CV. He has also worked tirelessly to raise funds for various charities and in 2014 marked his 50th birthday with a 50-miles charity walk. He set off from his parents' home in Huyton, took in Anfield and Goodison before finishing at Wanderers' Macron Stadium.

©The Bolton News

IAN BISHOP

Without a hint of arrogance or conceit, Ian Bishop states that he always knew he would become a professional footballer and didn't consider any other job or prepare for any other walk of life. He chose instead to follow his instincts and philosophy of "it's all about the football", often to his own financial detriment. Born on 29 May 1965, Ian grew up living in Hollowcroft on the Cantril Farm estate and the first team he played for was Woodfarm JFC run by locals Jimmy O'Connor and Bobby Holmes. Aged just seven, Ian was a couple of years younger than his teammates and the opposition but you wouldn't have guessed. One Sunday morning, Woodfarm were playing as usual on one of the local Mab Lane pitches when Everton Scout Les McGreal asked a couple on the touchline if they knew who the lad playing in midfield and wearing the number 7 jersey was. They told him it was Ian and that they were his parents!

That was the beginning of a journey which took him all over the globe in a thrilling career spanning three decades. Les arranged for Bish to attend a trial at Bellefield which, once safely negotiated, resulted in twice-weekly training sessions under the watchful eye of coach Graham Smith. When he signed schoolboy forms and then became an apprentice, there were no complaints from Ian about the daily task of cleaning 13 pairs of boots. This was just something that needed to be done to enable him to play at the weekends for the A team or the reserves and to take him a step closer to his inevitable career. Ian had signed for Everton against the wishes of Jimmy Dewsnip who was his Cantril Farm High School Deputy Headteacher and a Liverpool Scout. He had wanted Bish to join the Reds but Ian figured that he would get more first team opportunities at Goodison Park. However, he found it extremely tough to make the breakthrough into Manager Howard Kendall's first eleven. His 54-man squad contained a host of top class performers including established international midfielders making Ian's task tremendously difficult. His only appearance for the Toffees first string came on 5 May 1984 versus Manchester United with 28,802 present at Goodison Park. The match was drawn 1-1 and Ian came off the bench to replace Rob Wakenshaw who had struck to give Everton the lead before Frank Stapleton chipped Neville Southall to secure a point for his side.

Ian loved his time with Everton but he was eager to play regularly and Kendall was aware of this. Shortly after a four games loan spell with Crewe Alexandra, he informed Ian that Carlisle United Manager Bob Stokoe had tabled a £15,000 bid to take him to Brunton Park and although he did not want him to leave, he would not stand in his way if he chose to do so. Displaying maturity beyond his years, the 19-year old decided that it might be in his best interests to drop down the football pyramid and show what he could do, and so it proved. From the moment he arrived at the Cumbrians on 11 October 1984, 'Uncle Bob', as the young players dubbed him, helped Bish to settle into the club enabling him to concentrate on his game and to flourish. Although Carlisle enjoyed little success during his time there, it was obvious to those around him that Ian was capable of playing at a much higher level than they were able to offer. This was not lost on wily Bournemouth Manager Harry Redknapp who was keen to take Bish to Dean Court but was not prepared to meet Carlisle's £200,000 valuation of him. Deadlock in the negotiations was resolved by a transfer tribunal which placed a £35,000 price tag on Ian's head and, not for the first time, Harry bagged a bargain.

Ian made his debut for the Cherries on 27 August 1988 in a 1-1 draw with Sunderland at Roker Park in front of 17,998 supporters. He missed just two of their 56 games in all competitions that season as the club finished in a respectable mid-table 12th place. He had made an impressively smooth transition from the North Coast Fourth Division to the South Coast Second Division but after just a single season he was on the move again. Perhaps unsurprisingly, when Manchester City Boss Mel Machin made enquiries about the possibility of Ian joining his newly-promoted First Division team, Redknapp's valuation of his man had rocketed and on 2 August 1989 City stumped up £750,000 to take Ian to Maine Road. On the opening day of the 1989/90 season Ian's decision to leave Everton to build a career from the lower echelons of the Football League was vindicated when he took to the field at Anfield in front of a crowd of 35,628. The game was a baptism of fire with the Reds running out 3-1 winners but, during the next four months, he would experience unforgettable glory followed by an unexpected twist of fate. On 23 September 1989 with just a single victory from their opening half a dozen games of the season, City faced United in the Manchester Derby. The Red Devils entered the game as firm favourites on the back of a 5-1 trouncing of Millwall a week earlier. However, in a game that is still fresh in the memories of the 43,246 fans present, United were on the receiving end of the same scoreline. With Ian controlling proceedings from the centre of midfield, he also sent a thunderbolt of a header past keeper Jim Leighton to open his account for the Sky Blues and to permanently endear himself to the City faithful. As a young man, Ian was no stranger to the bright lights of city centre

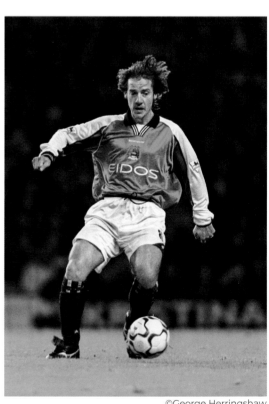

©George Herringshaw

nightlife but, rather than celebrate the events of the day in Manchester's famous Hacienda nightclub, he opted to drive home to Cantril Farm and watch Match of the Day in St Albert's Parish Club over a few pints with his dad!

After a rocky start, the team seemed to have turned a corner and recorded just two defeats from their next seven games. However, club Chairman Peter Swales had a reputation for hiring and firing his managers and after three consecutive defeats in November, Machin found himself out on his ear. Howard Kendall, who had recently been sacked by Athletico Bilbao, replaced him. Even though Ian was only 24 games into his City career and the supporters loved him, one of Kendall's first actions was to sell him and striker Tony Morley to West Ham Utd as part of a deal which saw fellow Huytonian Mark Ward move in the opposite direction. The fans were dumbfounded. Undeterred, Ian knuckled down and the move marked the beginning of a nine-year love affair with the Hammers. Initially, former Celtic and Manchester Utd frontman Lou Macari was in charge of the reins but he resigned following a probe into betting irregularities. Club stalwart Billy 'Bonzo' Bonds replaced him and installed Bish as his captain. In his first full season in charge, they secured promotion to the top flight with a second place finish. The club also enjoyed an excellent FA Cup run which took them as far as the semi-final stage. However, Brian Clough's Nottingham Forest proved too good on the day for the Irons registering a 4-0 victory to deny Ian a trip to Wembley - for now! Unfortunately, this was followed by relegation and then promotion to the newly-formed Premier League. The club's hierarchy was desperate for stability and a sustained period in the highest division and put its trust in Bond's Assistant, Ian's old boss Harry Redknapp. Under his stewardship, the club became a solid, mid-table Premiership side for the remainder of Ian's time at the club.

Bish made 306 appearances for the side from the Boleyn but in the 1997/98 season, he fell out of favour with the boss, made just three starts, and watched 23 games from the dugout. This was of no interest to Ian who just wanted to play football. Despite the club offering him what would have been a very lucrative Testimonial season, this didn't fit in with his ethos of "it's all about the football" and on 14 March 1998 he pulled on the claret and blue jersey for the last time in a 2-1 victory over Chelsea. A fortnight later, he re-joined Manchester City on a free transfer. Ian received other offers but felt he had unfinished business at City and dropped down two divisions in an attempt to help them to get into the Premiership. This was achieved in swift, impressive and dramatic fashion. Following a third place finish in the 1998/99 Second Division table, City defeated Wigan Athletic in the play-off semis to face Gillingham in the Final. The old Wembley Stadium had played host to many great football matches since its opening in 1923 but few could have matched the closing minutes of this game. Played on 30 May 1999 in front of a partisan crowd of 76,935, the teams were deadlocked until the 81st minute when the Gills took the lead. A second goal was added five minutes later to give City a mountain to climb. In the last minute of the ninety, Kevin Horlock registered what most people considered a consolation goal but remarkably, in the seventh minute of added time, Paul Dickov sent the game into extra-time with an equaliser. Ian had been struggling with a hamstring injury in the build up to the game but had convinced Manager Joe Royle to stick him on the bench. He joined the action in the 61st minute of the game and was instrumental in turning the game around. No further goals were added but City came out on top in the penalty shoot-out to gain promotion.

The following season no such drama was required as they finished second to secure automatic promotion to the Premiership and Ian's mission was complete. Although the battle to stay amongst the elite proved too great the following campaign, by the time City's fate was sealed Bish had moved on to his next adventure.

He accepted an exciting offer from across the pond to play in the MLS for Miami Fusion. On his departure, Joe Royle paid him a huge compliment and few disagreed when he stated, "Ian is surely one of the best uncapped players in the last 10 years." The closest he came to international recognition was an appearance for the England B team on 20 May 1991 when they overcame the Swiss 2-1 at Walsall's Bescot Stadium. Ian has spent the past couple of decades in the States where he loves the lifestyle away from football. On the pitch, he was an extremely valuable member of the Fusion team that won the Eastern Division of the MLS. Achieved against a backdrop of financial mismanagement and crisis, the players' wages were often unpaid and Ian assumed the responsibility of fighting their corner. As has already been indicated, money was never a major factor for Ian but he is nobody's fool and as a matter of principle, he and his teammates were not prepared to accept this. Ultimately, Miami Fusion folded due to their problems and, because of the stance he took, Ian found himself effectively blackballed. Whilst half a dozen clubs had previously been interested in signing him, he was now unable to find another club.

He returned home, bought a pub in Birkdale and combined being a licensee with playing for Rochdale, Radcliffe Borough and even made a couple of Champions League appearances for Barry Town. However, the lure of the States proved too great and when in 2004 the opportunity to return and join New Orleans Shellshockers presented itself, he did not need asking twice. After a successful season at the club and at the age of 39, he called time on a playing career during which he played in excess of 700 games - his early, unstinting belief that he would become a professional footballer was obviously well-founded.

Since hanging up his boots, Ian has kept himself extremely busy in a coaching capacity, as an agent for overseas players and as a transatlantic ambassador for West Ham United. Ian Bishop is still loved by the fans of the clubs he proudly represented who appreciate his attitude, his silky skills, his dedication and the fact that it was "always about the football."

SHAUN REID

It has already been stated in these pages that to make a single appearance in the English Football League is a massive achievement. Shaun Reid's tally of 435 games and 82 additional cup appearances is therefore exceptional - if not a little unusual. Most footballers who have played a large number of games in the old Fourth Division (which became the new Third Division following changes to the English Football Pyramid) have done so either en-route to appearing in a higher division or on their 'way down' having previously appeared in a higher tier. The fact that every single one of Shaun's appearances took place in the old Fourth Division or new Third Division is uncommon to say the least but no less impressive.

Born on 13 October 1965, Shaun spent time as a youngster training with Liverpool, Everton and Bolton. In 1982 when Wanderers' player Roy Greaves joined Rochdale as a coach, he recruited Shaun and handed him an apprenticeship as part of the government's Youth Training Scheme. On 20 September the following year, Shaun signed on the dotted line of a full-time pro contract. When the first team suffered the indignation of a 4-1 FA Cup 3rd round hammering courtesy of non-league Telford Utd, Manager Jimmy Greenhoff elected to shake things up by making wholesale changes to the team. A week later on 14 January 1984, in front of a crowd of 2,640 at Crewe Alexandra's Gresty Road Stadium, Shaun took to the field to make his debut in a 1-0 victory over the Railwaymen. In so doing, he gained the distinction of becoming the first product of Rochdale's YTS initiative to grace an English Football League game.

This was an unsettled time for Dale and during Shaun's 159-game, six-season first spell at the club they regularly teetered on the brink of relegation. Consequently, Shaun played under four managers - Greenhoff, Vic Hallom, Eddie Gray and one of the first foreigners to take charge of an English Football League side, Danny Bergara. After working his way into the side, Shaun suffered a broken leg in the 1985/86 campaign. This restricted him to just eight appearances for Dale and an additional three games for Preston North End who he joined as part of his rehabilitation. Back to full fitness at the start of the following season, Shaun hit the ground running and firmly established himself in the Rochdale team alongside fellow Huytonians Ronnie Moore and Frank Gamble. His tenacious central midfield play endeared him to the club's fans and he played some great stuff under former Leeds Utd and Scotland winger Eddie Gray. However, when Gray left to take up the vacant Manager's job at Hull City, it wasn't long before his replacement Bergara was accepting a £32,500 bid from York City to secure Shaun's services. He joined the Minstermen on 23 December 1988 and debuted for them three days later in a goalless draw with Scarborough. Decent 11th and 13th place finishes in the table were followed by a disappointing 21st place, which cost Manager John Bird his job. His replacement John Ward only faired marginally better,

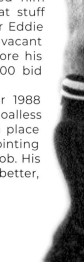

occupying 19th spot at the conclusion of the 1991/92 season. Shaun made 122 York appearances and found the net eight times but when play resumed after the summer Reidy was back at Rochdale. On 16 August 1992 he signed to play for his new boss and former teammate Dave Sutton who had transformed the team's fortunes and style of play. The aim of their attractive, attacking football was to force their way upwardly out of the division they had desperately been trying to stay in when Shaun was previously on their books. They narrowly missed the play-offs on consecutive seasons and Shaun was in the thick of many midfield battles.

Perhaps the most interesting of these took place on 13 August 1994 when Rochdale were the visitors to Bury's Gigg Lane ground for the opening game of the season. The match took on greater significance and interest by the presence of Shaun's brother Peter in the Bury ranks. Following his bizarre dismissal from his first managerial position at Manchester City, Peter had continued his playing career with Southampton, Notts County and this single appearance for Bury. Described by some as "a bruising battle", Peter recalls "the tackles were flying in and I remember smashing Shaun on numerous occasions". Whilst he concurred "we were knocking seven bells out of eachother right from the off", Shaun is adamant that he came out of the tussle on top! The game finished 1-0 to Rochdale and Peter returned to management at Sunderland whilst the following season Shaun donned the Bury shirt his brother had briefly worn.

He signed for the Shakers for a £25,000 fee just before the start of the 1995/96 campaign. A poor start and 5-0 thrashing by Plymouth Argyle resulted in the departure of Boss Mike Walsh with wily Stan Ternent installed as his replacement. For many Bury fans this remains their favourite season. The team went from strength to strength and Reidy's 21 appearances helped the club achieve a third place finish and automatic promotion. They were also promoted the following season but well before the champagne corks were popping Shaun had moved to Chester City. His initial loan became a permanent move when the Seals paid Bury £30,000 to take Shaun to the Deva Stadium on 27 January 1997. This was a precarious period in Chester's long history with uncertainty prevalent on and off the pitch. After defeat to Swansea in the 1996/97 play-off semis, the club deteriorated and a succession of managers were unable to stop the rot. Shaun made 74 appearances in Chester colours, the last of which came on 25 March 2000. In the 88th minute of a home game versus Mansfield Town, Manager Ian Atkins gave Shaun the opportunity to bid farewell to League football and the 1,953 fans present gave him an emotional send off. Despite winning the game 5-0, results elsewhere did not go in their favour and Chester suffered relegation to the Conference. The following season Shaun did make a couple of Conference appearances but for Leigh RMI not the Seals. His made his debut in a 2-1 victory over Lancaster City which landed them the annually contested Peter Swales Shield, named in memory of the former Manchester City Chairman. His brief spell at Leigh proved to be Shaun's swansong as a player and he turned his attention to forging a new career.

Coaching duties at Chester, Swindon and Plymouth Argyle, combined with the experience he had gained from playing under a host of bosses, meant he was well equipped to leap into the world of management. On 24 January 2012 Prescot Cables named him as their replacement for the outgoing Dave Ridler who had left to take up a position with LFC. Unfortunately, due to some of the worst weather the region had experienced for decades, Shaun had to wait almost a month for his managerial debut as fixture after fixture was postponed prompting him to quip "It's the longest unbeaten run of my career!" The action eventually got under way with a 2-2 share of the spoils with Bamber Bridge. Cables made a promising start under his stewardship but when Warrington Town's owners approached Shaun he agreed to take over the reins at Cantilever Park explaining that he had a good feeling about managing the Wire. His decision came as both a surprise and disappointment to Cables supporters but Shaun's "feeling" would be vindicated as the club embarked upon a history-making journey which attracted a level of national attention previously reserved for the town's rugby league side.

The 2014/15 season will stay long in the memory of everyone associated with the club from the eighth tier of English football. Their contribution to the FA Cup put them on the map and secured much-needed finance. After disposing of Barton Town Old Boys in the preliminary qualifying round, they accounted for Trafford, Sheffield, Colwyn Bay and North Ferriby. This earned them the right to play in the FA Cup 1st round proper for the first time in their 64-year history. As the lowest ranked team remaining in the competition, the Northern Premier Division One outfit faced Exeter City of Football League Two. There may have been 100 places separating the two sides but with a packed ground and the game shown live on BBC 2, Shaun's men did him and the town proud. Seven minutes into the game, played on Friday 7 November 2014, part-time defender and full-time plasterer Craig Robinson headed in a David Mannix corner to give the Wire a lead the Grecians were unable to peg back. The resultant second round fixture proved to be a step too far for Reidy's boys as Gateshead accounted for them 2-0 in another televised game. The cup run had made history whilst the revenue generated secured the club's future and enabled them to fund future glory. The following season they romped to promotion to the Northern Premier League's Premier Division, scoring more than 100 goals and gaining 15 points more than their nearest rival. Unfortunately, due to illness Shaun left the club by mutual consent before the campaign's conclusion. A serious brain haemorrhage, suffered in the dugout during a 2-1 away victory at Trafford, forced Shaun to make the decision to put his health and family before football. Shaun remains as passionate as ever about the game which has dominated his life and, having made great strides towards a full recovery, a return to football in some capacity should not be ruled out.

IAN GORE

Born on 10 January 1968, the first seven years of Ian Gore's life were spent living near Whiston's Lickers Lane Playing Fields - ideal for the football-mad youngster. In 1975 the family moved to the Sherdley Park area of rugby league stronghold St Helens and whilst Ian was a decent rugby player who could have had trials for Saints, football was his real passion.

Sherdley Junior School had never tasted football success but with Ian at the heart of their team he remembers winning a local 6-a-side tournament which spurred them on to further honours. Ian's ability was obvious to those around him and a neighbour recommended him to Chris Duffy who was manager of crack local side Penlake Juniors and so impressed was Chris that he had no hesitation in selecting Ian to play with and against players who were older than him. This was also the case when he turned out for Sutton High School, the St Helens Boys side and the county representative squad. Ian shone in central defence for the Merseyside U-14s team and he recalls victorious games played at Anfield and Goodison Park versus Durham and Essex respectively. These games always attracted scouts and Ian was already on the radar of a number of clubs. He made a few appearances for Everton's youth team before joining Bolton Wanderers at the age of 13. When he was 15, he was a member of their U-17s side that lifted the prestigious Lancashire Cup but a year later he opted to leave the Trotters after receiving an offer to join Birmingham City.

Although he was homesick and staying in digs in an unfamiliar city, Ian is extremely grateful to landlady Jan Rogers for providing the perfect environment for him to concentrate on developing his game. He stuck to his task and enjoyed a great FA Youth Cup run which came to a halt when they lost in the semi-final to eventual winners Newcastle United. The following season Ian was in the thick of the action and amongst the goals when they won local bragging rights by defeating Aston Villa 3-2 to secure the Midlands Cup. As captain of the reserve team and on the fringes of the first team squad, Ian was closing in on a full-time professional contract and his future at St Andrew's looked secure. However, in January 1986 first team Manager Ron Saunders, who rated Ian highly, received his marching orders after a poor run of results. John Bond replaced him but Ian was not a fan of his bombastic approach to management and the couple failed to get along. Whilst his career had been on a steady upward curve under Saunders, Ian felt that he stagnated with Bond in charge and in August 1987 he shunned a new contract offer and decided to leave. Not only was this a brave decision by the 19-year old but it also proved to be a wise one.

He briefly returned to Bolton but when Southport Caretaker-Manager Paul Lodge asked him to help them out he obliged and it proved to be beneficial to the club in the short-term and Ian's future prospects. Blackpool centre-half Mike Walsh was present at one of Ian's 10 competitive games for the Sandgrounders and was so impressed by what he saw that he had no hesitation in recommending him to Tangerines' Manager Sam Ellis. His boss shared his admiration of Ian's ability and duly signed him on 21 January 1988. Ironically, prior to the game he had contemplated turning his back on football and had even passed the entry examinations to join the Police Force. The Constabulary's loss was Blackpool's gain as Ian embarked upon a seven-season relationship with the Bloomfield Road club. His 249 games in all competitions understandably included some bitter disappointments but these were outnumbered by many magnificent memories. His early years in the tangerine shirt were difficult times for the club. When Ellis left his post after seven years at the helm, the club's fortunes plummeted and in 1989/90 season they suffered relegation to Division Four. However, when Billy Ayre assumed control in November 1990 the team enjoyed a change of fortune. A run of 13 undefeated home games saw them rocket up the table but defeat in the final game of the season meant that the club missed out on automatic promotion by a single point - hugely disappointing but there was worse to come.

On 31 May 1991 in the shadows of Wembley's Twin Towers, Ian's 49th game of the season resulted in a 2-2 draw with Torquay United after extra-time. Penalties is the cruellest way to lose an important game and so it proved when Dave Bamber missed the decisive penalty to send the Torquay fans into raptures. History repeated itself the following season when they again lost the last fixture of the campaign to fall short of the required points by the narrowest of margins. However, on 23 May 1992 after an extra-time 1-1 draw, the process of determining the outcome of a play-off Final by penalties no longer seemed so harsh to the Blackpool faithful. It was the fans of their opponents Scunthorpe United whose hearts were broken as the Bloomfield Roaders were promoted. Ian was extremely popular in the dressing room and on the terraces and received numerous Player of the Year awards from his teammates and the fans. Therefore, it was a big wrench for him to move on but, in a repeat of his John Bond experience, shortly after Sam Allardyce took over the managerial reigns Ian realised it was time to find pastures new.

He was linked with moves to Millwall, Leicester City and Rochdale but after a short loan spell at Chorley his next destination was Plainmoor, the home of Torquay United. Ian loved playing for and captaining the English Riviera Gulls but after 35 games he joined Doncaster Rovers on 22 March 1996 for a transfer fee of £5,000. With one eye on a post-football future in the licensing trade, a move to Yorkshire suited Ian down to the ground. However, he had unknowingly joined a club in turmoil which ultimately lead to his departure not only from Belle Vue but also the country. In all competitions, Ian made 72 appearances for Donny over three seasons but due to massive financial difficulties the club struggled to pay the players' wages. Consequently, Ian left before the end of a disastrous season which resulted in Doncaster's relegation from the Football League. Ian had more than 350 career games under his belt and former Everton defender Mick Lyons identified him as an ideal acquisition for the Singapore club he was managing. Ian thoroughly enjoyed his time at Marine Castle United - a team formed by a group of Newcastle United fans following a tour to the country by the Magpies. However, the sacking of Lyons ended Ian's Eastern adventure.

Upon returning home he briefly joined Borehamwood of the Rymans League before finishing his career in 2002 after three hugely enjoyable seasons at Gainsborough Trinity. In 2001, a website 'From Both Ends' run by the club's fans described Ian Gore as "utterly reliable and has become a fixture in the team at centre back. Tough and rugged, he gives the impression he would tackle a truck to stop a goal. Every team needs a defender like this, he's ours and he's very good at it." Succinctly put, the compliment could have been written about Ian by the fans of any of the clubs he gave his all for during his excellent career.

KARL CONNOLLY

Born in Whiston Hospital on 9 February 1970, Karl Connolly grew up living in Kingsway, Prescot and attended Prescot C of E School in nearby Gregson Road. As a youngster "football-mad" Karl would play "anywhere and everywhere" and loved to watch his dad (who had trials with Man Utd) playing for the local Victoria pub team. Instead of joining his mates in a game of '3 and in' or '60 Seconds', Karl would stand on the touchline digesting the players' moves and tricks. As soon as the game was over, he would practise relentlessly until he had perfected what he had just observed. His newfound skills would then be put to good use for the school team and junior side All Saints whom he started playing for at the age of nine.

As Karl moved into his teens, football dominated his weekends with a Saturday morning game for All Saints followed by turning out alongside his father in the afternoon for Shaw Lane FC in the Warrington Charity League. Karl was developing his game and gaining a reputation as a prolific goalscorer. He clearly recalls playing in a U-13s Cup Final for All Saints versus Marshalls Cross at St Helens' ground. With his team trailing 1-0 and with time running out Karl demanded the ball from his teammate Barry Jones who duly obliged. From fully 35 yards he blasted the ball past the Cross keeper to take the game into extra-time. He added a second a few minutes later to seal the victory. Prescotian Roy Daley promised Karl that he would buy him a new pair of boots if he scored 40 goals in one season - Karl obliged with 43!

Karl continued to find the net regularly for Prescot Grammar School and All Saints which attracted the attention of Tranmere Rovers. He spent 18 months training with the club at Bebington Oval but when things didn't work out he returned to his Prescot roots and turned out for local sides Rocky's and Napoli. After one game, which Napoli had lost 7-2, Karl was approached by the match referee Keith McKeown who asked him his name. Fearing he was being disciplined, Karl protested his innocence but Keith explained that he was a Wrexham Scout and had been impressed by his two goals contribution and never-say-die attitude despite the thrashing. Karl was unconvinced but gave the ref the telephone number of the Prescot chip shop he was working in at the time. Even when a Wrexham club official rang the chippy on the Monday morning to invite him for a trial Karl believed it was one of his teammates taking the Mickey. However, the caller won him over and a week later he turned up at the Racecourse ground to play for Wrexham reserves versus Carlisle Utd reserves.

Years later, Karl would learn that on first impressions Wrexham Manager Brian Flynn did not believe that the Prescotian looked like a footballer and informed reserves boss Joey Jones to just give him a twenty minutes run-out and then substitute him. Twenty minutes into the game, Karl had scored a hat trick! Jones overruled Flynn and so began Karl's long and illustrious relationship with the Robins. 'King Karl' (as he was dubbed by the Wrexham faithful) enjoyed a 10-year career at the club and has many fond memories of his time there. His debut came on 17 August 1991 in a 1-0 defeat to Hereford Utd in front of 3,225 spectators at the Racecourse. Although Wrexham and Karl enjoyed promotion to the old Second Division in 1992/93, it is fair to say that the club struggled in the League during his time there. However, the team punched well above its weight in the cups. The FA Cup in particular was kind to Karl - he scored a hugely impressive 16 goals from 37 games in the competition and helped the club to secure many memorable victories. On 4 January 1992, mighty Arsenal were the visitors to the Racecourse for a third round tie. The previous season the Gunners had lost just one First Division game on their way to being crowned League Champions whilst Wrexham had finished bottom of the Fourth Division and only avoided dropping into the Conference due to Aldershot being expelled. Even the most optimistic Wrexham fan could have been excused for believing that a defeat was on the cards - especially when Arsenal were leading 1-0 with just eight minutes left in the match. However, this was the FA Cup, a competition famous for its giant-killings and when Mickey Thomas blasted home a thirty-yard free kick to equalise he set up perhaps the greatest giant-killing act of all time. Two minutes later, Steve Watkin's shot found the back of England keeper David Seaman's net to send the majority of the 13,343 crowd delirious and Wrexham through to the fourth round.

During Karl's time at the club, Wrexham also enjoyed victories as the underdog in ties versus Ipswich Town and Middlesbrough whose team at the time was full of international superstars. In addition, Karl tasted success in the Welsh Cup by defeating Cardiff City 2-1 at the National Stadium on 21 May 1995 which qualified the club to participate the following season in the preliminary round of the European Cup Winners Cup. Although Wrexham lost by a single goal over two legs to Romanian outfit Petrolul Ploiesti, the experience proved to be an enjoyable one. On a personal level, Karl was rightly receiving recognition for his performances. Wrexham fans voted him their Player of the Year for three consecutive seasons and his peers selected him for their 1995/96 PFA Division Two team.

However, all good things must end and on 31 May 2000 QPR Director of Football and former England captain Gerry Francis lured Karl to Loftus Road to face a fresh challenge. Francis had long been an admirer of Karl and his Wrexham goal return of 88 from 337 League appearances convinced him to snap him up on a Bosman free transfer. After three years, 72 games and 12 goals Karl left the Hoops to team up again with his old Manager Brian Flynn at Swansea City. However, after just ten games he decided to wind up his professional career. He still enjoyed playing so continued to turn out for Prescot Cables, Cefn Druids and Warrington Town. Karl now lives just a few miles from Prescot and often attends Wrexham's games where he is always extended a warm welcome as acknowledgement of his significant contribution to the club's history.

BRIAN MCGORRY

For many years, young aspiring footballers have been advised to lay the foundations for working life in preparation for when their playing days come to an end. On average, a footballer's career lasts less than a decade and although the rewards can be huge, few players accumulate sufficient wealth during this time to last a lifetime making a second source of income a necessity. Unfortunately, too often the advice is ignored and many former players struggle to maintain the quality of life to which they may have become accustomed. Not only did Brian McGorry heed these warnings but his chosen post-football career path actually provides today's young players with the perfect environment to pursue their footballing dreams whilst simultaneously maximising their long-term employment opportunities.

Born on 16 April 1970, Brian grew up living just a short half-volley away from Jubilee Park in Lincombe Road, Huyton. The park doubled as a huge front garden for the youngster who spent hour after hour there kicking a ball about and perfecting the tricks and skills he had watched his older brother Barry and his mates perform. Local pub the Farmers Arms under-9s side provided Brian with his first taste of organised, competitive football. Managed by fishmonger Martin Cleary, the boys were transported to matches in his work van. The team enjoyed tremendous success, although Brian still wonders whether the lingering smell of kippers and shellfish gave them an unfair advantage due to their opponents being reluctant to mark them too closely! They once won a tournament held on the pub's bowling green and Brian recalls the huge sense of achievement at being presented with his medal by Liverpool winger Stevie Heighway.

The McGorry brothers attended Park View School and Brian remembers the buzz around the classrooms and corridors when Barry's team won the Huyton Schools League - the first time in decades that the school had achieved this. They didn't have to wait as long for their next success because with Brian's captaincy driving the side on they became known as 'The Invincibles' by scooping four trophies in the 1980/81 season. Football was a massive part of Brian's childhood and he loved turning out for the Huyton Boys team and is grateful to manager Mr Lathom for his early support, advice and encouragement. He also played in the Rainhill Junior League for St Annes Rovers and recalls scoring the winning penalty at Everton's Bellefield training ground to hand his side the Cup. After they had joined the highly competitive Walton and Kirkdale League, Brian was headhunted by Allerford JFC who were one of the top sides at the time. Brian won a league and cup double with Allerford and played in the league representative side. He was putting in great performances as an attacking midfielder and occasional striker and an impressive appearance for Knowsley Schools U-14s resulted in him spending the school holidays at LFC's Melwood training ground.

Brian had never lacked self-belief but the recognition he was receiving was inspiring him to reach new heights. Out of the blue a letter from the FA, signed by England Manager Bobby Robson, dropped through the letterbox at Lincombe Road. He had been invited to Lilleshall for an England Schoolboys trial and although he did not make the final squad (he got to the last 25), the experience proved to be a massive confidence boost for him. Brian has fond memories of Tuesday and Thursday nights training at Melwood, going home on the bus and alighting at Page Moss, before buying a bag of chips with his LFC expenses and eating them during his short walk home - bliss! When the club instructed Brian to stop all his other football activities he knew that they were taking him seriously. In 1986 he became a full-time Liverpool apprentice despite receiving attractive offers from Nottingham Forest and Oldham. He was 16 years of age, had just left Prescot Grammar School, where he secured seven 'O' levels, and was living the dream. The highlights included scoring in a 3-3 FA Youth Cup quarter-final match versus Forest at Anfield and playing alongside a host of household names for the reserves. However, two years after becoming an apprentice, his dream was shattered when Kenny Dalglish broke the news to him that the club were letting him go. Down but not out, he had trials with Preston, Wigan, Bolton and Halifax but to no avail.

After playing half a dozen games for Prescot Cables to keep his hand in, he qualified as a lifeguard and boldly took up a job at a holiday camp in Weymouth. Still believing he was good enough to make the grade as a footballer, he began playing for Weymouth reserves. Man of the Match performances and goals aplenty elevated him to the first team for the 1990/91 season and he again started to attract the attention of a number of Football League outfits. After scoring 17 goals from midfield, he travelled across the country at the invitation of Leeds Utd, Nottingham Forest and Manchester City but his venture into the realms of professional football materialised just 30 miles down the road from Weymouth. On 13 August 1991, AFC Bournemouth Manager Harry Redknapp offered Brian a three-year contract and the Terras £30,000. He packed in his HR job at the local MOD base and delightedly made the short journey to Dean Court. So began a pro career in football which would last the best part of 20 years and saw Brian ply his trade at no fewer than 14 clubs.

His Cherries debut came on 5 October 1991 in a 0-0 stalemate with Reading in front of 4,033 spectators at Elm Park. In June 1992, Redknapp left to take up the reins at West Ham Utd and Tony Pulis stepped up from the playing ranks to occupy the first of his many managerial hotseats. A broken shin had denied Brian a great deal of game time but did not stop him becoming the club's top scorer in the 92/93 season. Kenny Dalglish singled him out for a special mention in his programme notes when his Blackburn Rovers side knocked the Cherries out of the FA Cup at the third round stage. The sides met again the following campaign with Rovers once more the victors but considering Kenny's team finished second in the Premiership that year and brilliantly went one better 12 months later, Bournemouth's 1-0 aggregate defeat should be looked back on with a degree of pride. Brian's performances on the south coast were resulting in interest from clubs higher up the football pyramid. Enquiries from Manchester City and Swindon Town were met with a prohibitive price tag being quoted thus stifling Brian's opportunity to progress. However, in February 1994 after three seasons, 83 appearances and 14 goals, he left Bournemouth to join First Division Peterborough Utd for a surprisingly modest fee of £60,000. It was a step up in class but Brian coped admirably.

He made his Posh debut in a 1-0 defeat of Middlesborough on 12 February 1994 and notched his first goal for the club four weeks later in a 2-1 victory over Oxford United. Brian added a further five goals during his 58 games for the London Road club before joining Wycombe Wanders in August 1995. Whilst at Wycombe, an old cruciate ligament injury he had picked up at Weymouth and was initially misdiagnosed, seriously hampered him. After a 12-month rehabilitation process, during which he was advised to retire, Brian lost a yard of his blistering pace and had to reinvent his playing style. He consequently adopted a holding midfield position to great effect, undoubtedly prolonging his playing career.

Off the field, Brian had begun to address his post-playing intentions. Following discussions with surgeons and top physiotherapists during his rehab, he developed aspirations of becoming a physiotherapist. He combined playing for Wycombe with studying at Uxbridge College and when he joined Hereford United he successfully completed his A level Biology course at the local college. Even though the club were relegated to the GM Vauxhall Conference League at the end of the 1996/97 season, Brian stayed for the following campaign. He had assumed coaching responsibilities under Manager Graham Turner and although still only 27 years old he was showing maturity and leadership qualities beyond his years. On 1 July 1998 Brian re-joined Football League action with Torquay United. He was handed the captain's armband, which was the case at most of the club's he subsequently represented. During his yearlong stay at the Devonshire club, Brian made 40 appearances in all competitions before he decided his career needed a shift in emphasis.

Shortly after joining Conference side Telford Utd in July 1999, the club became a full-time operation and although club captain Brian opted to stay, he did so in a part-time capacity. He had recently established a business as a Personal Trainer and was securing a degree in Sports Science and Psychology at Manchester University which was obviously very demanding of his time. However, none of this made him any less competitive or committed when he took to the field of play. He made 72 appearances for Telford before enjoying brief spells at Southport, Woking and Chester City. In August 2002 Brian signed for Tamworth and although he only spent a single season there, he loved it. They were crowned champions of the Dr Martens Premier Division but were denied the double when Huytonian Gary Martindale grabbed a brace at Villa Park to land Burscough the FA Trophy. After almost two decades of involvement in football, Brian brought the curtain down on his playing career with a couple of successful seasons at Nuneaton Borough where he combined playing with his coaching duties.

Since retiring from the game he loves, Brian has not let the grass grow under his feet - far from it. He was re-acquainted with professional football when appointed Head of Performance at Morecambe FC in July 2010 on a six-month contract. When he left the club they were at the summit of League Two. Brian has established a host of successful sport and education-related businesses and in January 2015 proudly opened the Fowler Education and Football Academy (FEFA) with former Liverpool and England striker Robbie Fowler. The college represents the culmination of many years of hard work by Brian, Robbie and their dedicated staff and specialises in providing academic and football opportunities for 16 - 19 year olds. Now recognised as an Ofsted Outstanding Teacher and holding a UEFA A licence, Brian has created the perfect environment for the students to flourish. He is a shining example to any young footballer of what can be achieved on and off the pitch via a combination of talent, dedication and forward planning.

Since opening, FEFA has enjoyed tremendous successes on the pitch and in the classroom. In addition to their teams winning a host of trophies, many players have graduated to the semi-pro and professional ranks. Students have also gained football scholarships in the USA whilst others have found employment within the FEFA organisation. Academically, they boast a tremendous success rate for pupils seeking university places. As the Principal and Academy Director of the college and now qualified as a Corporate Governance Practitioner, Brian plans to start a charity to help the future footballers of Huyton who don't quite make the grade.

GARY MARTINDALE

Football runs through the veins of Gary Martindale's family. His cousin David played 166 games for Tranmere Rovers whilst his father Victor enjoyed a lengthy, trophy-laden amateur career with St Dominics and is regularly cited as a player who "should have made it." Gary was one of those rare players who possessed that precious ability to regularly find the back of the net whether it be in open play, from the penalty spot or as an impact player coming off the bench. However, as a youngster he rarely got the opportunity to show what he could offer as a striker and was usually selected as a defender.

He played right full-back for Colwell Junior School and right wing for West Derby Comprehensive School teams and for local junior side Portlet JFC, run by brothers Brian and Bernie Butchard. Gary longed to score goals and as his frustration mounted he became disillusioned with the game and temporarily stopped playing. Aged 16, he went to watch his brother Colin play for open-aged side Kingsheath who operated out of Dovecot Labour club just 100 yards from the family's Finch Lane home. Their opponents were Waterpark from Cantril Farm and Colin's manager Frank Hughes asked Gary to go sub as they were a player short. With Kingsheath getting thrashed by eight goals to nil, Gary joined the action and scored within minutes of taking to the field. It may only have been a consolation goal but it reignited Gary's interest in the game and he did not look back. In his new, rightful position he closely observed how his hero Bob Latchford and other top centre forwards applied themselves and added elements of their play to his own game. It worked a treat and he banged in goals for Kingsheath, the Boundary and St Dominics.

Gary's reputation was going before him and in 1993 he joined Burscough following an approach from player Bobby Howard. Unfortunately, he was again played out of position and was going to return to the Doms until his dad encouraged him to be patient. Gary was never the sort of player to knock on the manager's door for a showdown but he knew that he had more to contribute to Russ Perkins' side and tactfully told him so. Russ agreed to give him a chance in a game versus Clitheroe - they won 4-2, Gary bagged a brace and Burscough had a new centre forward who scored a further 13 goals in the remaining three months of the season. Perkins had put together a really good side and with Gary spearheading the attack they reached two cup finals. They lost 2-1 to Southport at Goodison Park in the Liverpool Senior Cup but were on the right end of the same scoreline to win the League Challenge Cup. When Gary netted 36 times the following season, Perkins strongly believed he could play at a higher level and vowed to secure him a move to a Football League club. True to his word, on transfer deadline day Bolton Wanderers Boss Bruce Rioch paid the Linnets a massive £10,000 to take Gary to Burnden Park.

He joined a team which in a magical year enjoyed awayday victories over Liverpool, Arsenal and Everton and would visit Wembley twice in a month. This obviously made it very difficult for Gary to break into the side but he applied himself in the reserves and hoped his chance would come along. Yet, despite scoring 20-odd Central League goals he was still well down Rioch's pecking order of strikers. When a hat trick against a Man Utd reserve side full of first teamers didn't improve his prospects he made the difficult decision to move on. There was no shortage of admirers keen to sign him but former Bolton player and fellow Huytonian Tony Kelly convinced Gary to follow him to Peterborough Utd. He joined Posh on 4 July 1995 and a week later made a goal scoring Football League debut in a 3-1 victory over Brighton & Hove Albion in front of 5,394 spectators at the London Road Stadium. The fans were right behind him as he continued to score and on 25 November 1995 he walked away with the match ball after notching a hat trick against Hull City in a 3-2 away victory. Gary was on fire and after scoring 15 goals in just 31 games Notts County tabled an accepted £175,000 bid to take him to Meadow Lane.

On 6 March 1996, Gary joined the oldest association football club in the world and hit the ground running. Ten days after signing, in the 64th minute of his new employer's home game versus Oxford Utd, he got the nod from Manager Colin Murphy to join the action. Trailing 1-0, he scored after being on the pitch for just two minutes to secure a point for the Magpies. The club missed automatic promotion on the last day of the season when they lost and other results worked against them. County faced Crewe Alexandra in the resultant play-off semi-final but in the first leg Gary disappointingly started on the bench. After just 17 minutes they were 2-0 down with a mountain to climb. Future Liverpool star Steve Finnan halved the deficit 10 minutes into the second half to set things up nicely for Gary to come on and contribute - and he did not disappoint. He left the dugout with just a quarter of an hour of the game remaining and with the final whistle imminent, he rose to fire a header past the stranded keeper to level the tie. Three days later Gary was included in the starting line-up and with the second leg delicately poised, struck a brilliant volleyed goal to defeat the

Railwaymen and to make Gary's childhood dream of a Wembley appearance a reality. Unfortunately, on 26 May 1996 with 39,972 fans in the most famous stadium in the world, the dream turned into a nightmare. Bradford City brushed County aside 2-0 to secure promotion to Football League Division One. This was a huge disappointment to Gary who admitted that the occasion got the better of him. He prophetically vowed that if he were ever in a similar situation again he would do everything in his power to ensure that the outcome would be different. On a personal note, Gary's 16 games for County returned six goals and, when added to his tally at Peterborough, his 21 League goals handed him the Second Division Golden Boot.

Whilst the 96/97 season kicked off in great fashion for Marto when he scored an opening day winner versus Preston North End, the season could not have been more different from the previous campaign. Sam Allardyce had been installed as Manager and adopted a direct pattern of play which he presumably felt Gary wasn't suited to as he often left him out of the starting eleven. Though he was County's top scorer with six goals, the club only managed 33 goals and seven wins all season and were relegated. Gary also scored a couple of goals for Mansfield Town during a five-game loan period in February to take his total for the campaign to eight. The following season Big Sam employed Gary in a central midfield role but unlike earlier in his career he had no qualms about playing out of position. It was a joy to play in this team which was head and shoulders above its opposition. County lost only five games all season, scored 82 goals, accumulated 99 points and romped to promotion and the Division Three title 17 points clear of their nearest rival. However, when Gary received the offer of a contract extension by the club he decided to move on for a fresh challenge and a return to the forward line.

He joined Ronnie Moore's Rotherham United but this proved to be a largely frustrating period of Gary's career. Due to a series of injuries, he managed just 28 appearances during his three seasons with the Millers. He had metal pins inserted into a damaged foot which side-lined him for seven months and in his first game back he sustained a broken jaw in a clash with an over-zealous Swansea City centre-half. In addition, in only the second game of the 1999/2000 season Gary was involved in a bizarre incident which ultimately ended his Football League career. On 14 August 1999, Gary opened the scoring from the penalty spot in the 54th minute of a home game versus Chester City. Four minutes later he was bearing down on Chester's goal hoping to add to his tally when the goalkeeper upended him and dislocated Gary's shoulder in the process. This signalled a premature end to the game for him but only after, with his right arm hanging down by his side, he had

©www.karlbrooksphotography.com

converted the resultant penalty kick - a goal is a goal to a striker! Gary was involved in just 13 games in his final season for the club but still made a significant contribution to help them finish League runners-up to gain automatic promotion. However, before the campaign had reached its conclusion Gary had joined Telford Utd on loan. The move became permanent and over the next couple of seasons he found the net 13 times from 53 games.

 When, in August 2002 Burscough player-manager Shaun Teale took him back to where it had begun, Gary had no idea that 10 months later he would experience "the best day of my career." On 18 May 2003, Gary lined up at Villa Park against newly crowned Dr Marten Premier Division champions Tamworth in the FA Trophy Final. Burscough were undoubtedly the underdogs having started the season at 400-1 outsiders to win the competition. Gary was acutely aware of his bitter Wembley experience eight years earlier and the pledge he had made to himself in its aftermath. He used this to spur himself and his teammates on to the performance of a lifetime in front of the live TV cameras. In a 'Man of the Match' display Gary expertly found the net in the 26th and 55th minutes of the game and hardly put a foot wrong before he was withdrawn to a standing ovation in the 79th minute. Mark Cooper pulled a goal back for the Lambs with just over 10 minutes remaining but it was too little too late and the final whistle sent the Linnets fans in the 14,296 crowd into raptures. Gary stayed with the club for a couple more seasons and continued to score regularly - in his final season at Burscough he registered 21 goals from 31 games to finish with a remarkable 102 goals from 180 appearances for a club which will always be close to his heart.

After brief spells at Formby and Runcorn he finally hung his boots up to try his hand at coaching and management. Since 2010, he has been involved in this side of the game with Formby, Vauxhall Motors, Marine, Prescot Cables and the LFC Foundation College with whom in 2014 he took a team to compete in the Dallas Cup. He is currently Assistant Manager at Witton Albion who in 2016/17, were promoted to the Northern Premier League via the play-offs. Gary is as enthusiastic as ever and loves nothing more than passing on his knowledge and experience to the young players – especially the strikers!

BARRY JONES

For any young footballer who has recently been shown the door by a Football League club and believes they have blown their chance of making it in the game, Barry Jones' story should make interesting reading and provide renewed optimism.

As a youngster, Prescot Grammar School pupil Barry from Carlton Street in the town centre earned a reputation as a reliable, cool-headed defender. Scouts from League clubs were often present at school and All Saints junior league matches to cast an eye over not only Barry but also teammate and close friend Karl Connolly. Trials for Bury & Preston did not amount to anything but much to their delight Tranmere Rovers invited the pair to train with and turn out for their youth teams. Barry spent almost two years with Rovers until the club decided he was not going to make the grade - he was seventeen years of age and devastated. He began turning out for Napoli FC, managed by local chip shop owner George Constantinou. It's fair to say that scouts didn't exactly flock to their games - but you never know who's watching and when an opportunity unexpectedly presents itself you must capitalise on it. That is precisely what Barry did when Prescot Cables Manager Dave Shannon turned up at Hope Street one Sunday morning to watch Napoli's meaningless game. Barry did not put a foot wrong throughout the 90 minutes after which Dave invited him to turn out for Cables' reserves a week later. This triggered an amazing sequence of events.

Following his appearance for Prescot's second string, Shannon used his connections at Liverpool to secure Barry a game for the Reds B team. Again, following a flawless performance, he was promoted to the A team. After spending a month at Melwood to enable the club's staff to have a closer look at him, Barry was summoned to the legendary Anfield Boot Room where Manager Kenny Dalglish offered him a full-time professional contract which he signed on 19 January 1989. In less than two months, Barry's life had gone through an amazing transformation which had seen him graduate from playing for Business Houses side Napoli to training daily with his new colleagues Dalglish, Hansen, Barnes et al! Due to the quality of Liverpool's record-breakers, Barry understandably struggled to break into the first team. However, he plugged away in the reserves alongside future stars Fowler, Redknapp and Macmanaman hoping that his chance would come along.

In the 1991 Eufa Cup competition first round, 1st leg tie Liverpool hammered Finnish side Kuusysi Lahti 6-1 making the return leg a formality. However, on 2 October 1991 when David Burrows sustained a 22nd minute ankle injury, this dead rubber became the most important game in Barry's life. Although the Finns won the game 1-0, Barry came off the substitute's bench and gave a good account of himself enabling him to proudly claim he has pulled on one of the world's most famous football jerseys. Nevertheless, Barry was a professional footballer who wanted regular first team football. He found it when, on 10 July 1992, he joined Wrexham and for the majority of the next six years took his place in the side alongside his old mate Karl Connolly. He made 245 appearances for the Racecourse club and in his first season they secured promotion to the old Division Two - a position they consolidated during the remainder of Barry's time with the Robins. Trophies were thin on the ground for the Welsh club but on 21 May 1995 at the National Stadium in front of 11,200 fervent fans, Barry helped Wrexham defeat rivals Cardiff City to lift the Welsh Cup. This guaranteed Barry a brief return to European competition and although the club fell at the first hurdle of the Eufa Cup when they lost 1-0 to Romanian outfit Petrolul Ploiesti, it proved to be an enjoyable experience.

In 1998 an earlier five-game loan spell at York City convinced the club to shell out £40,000 to take Barry to Bootham Crescent. He played 147 games for the Minstermen and twice won the club's prestigious Billy Fenton Memorial Clubman of the Year trophy before dropping out of the Football League to turn out for Southport, Runcorn, Prescot Cables, and Bangor City. Barry finally hung his boots up in 2006 almost 20 years and hundreds of games after he had feared his football career was over before it had begun.

CRAIG HIGNETT

Craig Hignett's professional career lasted 17 seasons during which time he played for 13 clubs in England, Scotland and Cyprus. Born on 12 January 1970 in Whiston Hospital, Craig attended Park View Infants and Juniors and by the time he started at Page Moss Comprehensive, just around the corner from the family's Woodlands Road home, his football potential had shown early signs of being realised.

His father Alan had played for Liverpool and Chester City and "from an early age he had me playing football and he even started up some teams in Liverpool so that I could get a game." Young Craig turned out for local sides The Paddock, Diamonds and Pride & Joy. Everton picked him up aged 11 but, when Liverpool guaranteed him an apprenticeship, the Kopite moved to his beloved Reds. However, when Liverpool dragged their heels over the offer of a pro contract, Craig opted to join Dario Gradi's Crewe Alexandra. He hoped he would join the long list of graduates from Crewe's youth set-up who had achieved success at a higher level - a shrewd decision. He made his first team debut on 8 October 1988 at the Racecourse Ground in a dour 0-0 draw versus Wrexham.

Initially, Craig struggled to set the world alight and was sent out on loan to non-league Stafford Rangers. He got back on track and played 150 games for the Railwaymen, scored 57 goals and, in his first season, the club were promoted to the old Third Division. Craig's energetic, eye-catching performances convinced Middlesbrough Manager Lennie Lawrence to spend £500,000 to take him to Ayresome Park on 27 November 1992. Although they were relegated in Craig's first season, he loved his time at the Teesside club. "I did everything I ever wanted with Boro. I played in the top division, I played in cup finals. I loved it there." There was never a dull moment and his 194 games included 57 goals, promotion twice, relegation twice and League Cup and FA Cup Final appearances (albeit losing ones !) His Middlesbrough experience was followed by a six-months, 15-game spell at Aberdeen until he returned south of the border to join Barnsley in an £800,000 deal.

A brace on his debut in a 7-1 mauling of Huddersfield Town was followed by 12 additional goals as The Tykes finished 13th in Division One. In Craig's second season at Oakwell his 20 goals helped the club reach the playoff final and although Craig found the net they were defeated 4-2 by Ipswich Town.

In July 2000, having played 80 times and registered 37 goals in Barnsley colours, Blackburn Rovers Boss Graeme Souness splashed out £2.2 million to take Craig to Ewood Park. Promotion to the Premiership was achieved in his debut

campaign for the Blue and Whites. Then, in his second season they bagged the League Cup by defeating Tottenham Hotspur 2-1 at the Millennium Stadium on 24 February 2002 in front of a crowd numbering 72,500. Craig's three-year stay at Ewood was punctuated by a short, nine-game loan spell at Coventry City. July 2003 brought about a move to Leicester City and he made 15 Foxes appearances before briefly returning to Crewe, then Leeds Utd, with a 19-game, nine-goal stay at Darlington supposedly bringing the curtain down on a great career in British football. In 2005/06 season Craig took on a new challenge when he joined Cypriot side Apollon Limassol, where he helped the club win the League title. On his return to our shores he reignited his playing career with spells at Hartlepool Utd first as a player and later as manager before carving out a new career in the world of football punditry. Nowadays, Craig is often heard on the radio commentating on matches featuring many of his former clubs.

©George Herringshaw

COLIN TAYLOR

Born on Christmas Day 1971, Colin Taylor spent his early years living at 33 Devon Way on Huyton's Mosscroft estate. He cut his footballing teeth playing in friendly but fiercely competitive matches on King George V Playing Fields versus the lads from the nearby Bakers Green estate. Football dominated his spare time and nothing gave him more pleasure than scoring a goal - it gave him a great feeling which never left him throughout his playing days.

His first school was St Joseph's and he played up front for teacher Mr Rooney's team. Colin also recalls playing for Rainton Rovers in the Rainhill Junior League. Ernie Tickle from Chester Road ran the team and young Colin loved turning out for them throughout his Primary years. When he left St Joey's to move to St Augustine's School at the top of Longview Drive, Colin played for both 'the Gussies' and St Annes Rovers with his good friend and classmate Ged Brannan.

The couple also made the Huyton Boys and later Knowsley Boys teams and it was not unusual for Colin & Ged to play four games in a weekend. Other clubs they played for included Derby Villa and West Moor JFC and they enjoyed a great deal of success with Ged often providing the ammunition for Colin to expertly pull the trigger and find the back of the net. It was around this time that Colin started attracting the attention of scouts from a host of clubs including Chelsea, West Bromwich Albion, Crewe, Shrewsbury Town, Everton and Wolves. Following a game at Barnfield Playing Fields on Eaton Road, West Derby in which Colin rattled home four goals, he received a letter from Everton Scout Alan Kelly inviting him to Bellefield to train on Monday evenings. He gleefully accepted and is grateful to coach Graham Smith for the work he put in to help develop his game. However, he was not formally attached to any Football League club at this stage so played for whoever he could at every opportunity. Colin thrived on the positive comments and advice he received from various influential characters in the game and recalls being buoyed by compliments and encouraging words from Oldham Athletic Manager Joe Royle.

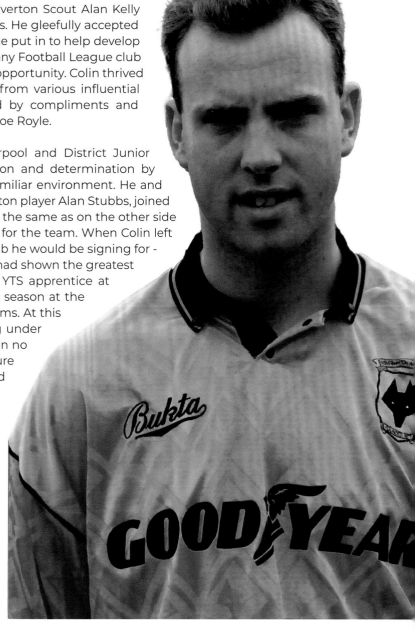

Having played in all-conquering sides in the Liverpool and District Junior League, Colin showed an unusual sense of ambition and determination by deciding he wanted to challenge himself in a less familiar environment. He and Ged, along with fellow Knowsley Boys and future Everton player Alan Stubbs, joined Wirral U-16s team Neston Nomads. The outcome was the same as on the other side of the Mersey - plenty of goals for Colin and trophies for the team. When Colin left school in June 1987 he had already decided which club he would be signing for - Wolverhampton Wanderers. The Black Country club had shown the greatest interest in him which convinced him to become a YTS apprentice at Molineux. He hit the ground running and in his first season at the club he scored 62 goals for the youth and reserve teams. At this time Wolves were in the old Fourth Division playing under the stewardship of Graham Turner. However, thanks in no small measure to local goal scoring legend and future England international Steve Bull, the club secured consecutive promotions to join the second tier of English football. Bull and his strike partner Andy Mutch formed a formidable partnership making Colin's task of breaking into the first team extremely difficult. Preparing himself for his opportunity, he kept working hard in training and for the reserves and found the net with impressive regularity.

He became a full-time pro in March 1990 and made his first team debut six months later. On 25 September 1990, Colin boarded the team coach bound for Hull City for a League Cup tie. A quick head count told him that there were only 13 players travelling. This was in the days of only two substitutes being permitted on the bench and, although nobody had told him, Colin realised he was going to get close to the action. In the second half, in front of a Boothferry Park crowd of 5,283, Colin realised a boyhood dream when Turner introduced him into the action of the 0-0 game. He continued to be involved with the first team squad and three days before his 19th birthday ticked another box. With Andy Mutch sidelined by injury, Colin took a place in the starting line up to face Millwall in a Second Division home match. In the 74th minute with the game delicately poised at 2-1 to Wolves, the Lions centre-half misjudged a through ball which slipped under his foot. Colin seized on his mistake and found himself one-on-one with the keeper. He instinctively slotted it past him to extend his team's lead. Nine minutes later Colin's elation was complete. He intercepted a defensive back-pass leaving him with a tap-in to secure the points in a 4-1 victory and send the 14,504 Molineux crowd home happy.

His brace of goals and performances in December 1990 earned Colin the Barclays Regional Young Player of the Month award - an engraved silver salver. Also in the family trophy cabinet are Colin's three England U-18s international caps. He received these for playing against Czechoslovakia (25/4/90), Poland (15/5/90) and Denmark (6/2/91). The first two of these games took place within a three-week period at Wembley Stadium as curtain-raisers to full international matches. The memory of playing in the shadow of the Twin Towers in front of a massive crowd (which included Wolves fans singing his name) will stay with Colin forever. Back at Molineux, Colin was unable to shift either Bull or Mutch from their first team positions and reflects, "Their partnership held me back. At any other club I might have got more of a chance. A lot of the time I was pushed out left or right but I was a centre forward. I couldn't get a rhythm of playing properly." With this in mind, Colin went on loan to Wigan Athletic.

When he arrived at Springfield Park (after the taxi driver had mistakenly taken him to the rugby league ground first!) he settled in quickly. He scored a respectable two goals from seven games for the Latics and although there was talk of a £200,000 transfer, nothing materialised. The 1992/93 campaign brought about another loan deal. Preston Manager John Beck had opened negotiations with Wolves to take Colin to Deepdale but by the time he arrived to sign Beck had left the club. This left Assistant Manager Sam Allardyce to finalise the deal making Colin future England Boss Big Sam's first ever signing. After four games Colin returned briefly to Molineux before spending a short time with Doncaster Rovers, appearing twice. In July 1993, Colin Taylor's Football League career ended when Wolves released him. He received offers from Shrewsbury Town and Northampton Town but opted instead to join Conference side Telford United. Although this was the end of his participation in the English Football League, it was the start of an illustrious non-League career. Colin played hundreds of games and scored hundreds of goals for Telford, Runcorn, Bangor City, Caernarfon Town, Worcester City, Chorley, Dennington United, Framlington Town and even Knowsley United.

IAIN JENKINS

At the tender age of 14, Iain Jenkins had to make an important decision which would shape the rest of his life - faced with two sporting options, he undoubtedly made the correct choice.

Born on 24 November 1972 in Whiston Hospital, Iain played his early football for Rainhill United. He is extremely grateful to late manager and local legend Albert Fellows for providing him and many youngsters with the opportunity to play the game they loved.

Initially, 'Jenks' played up front and in one season scored a staggering 174 goals. However, it was whilst playing in central midfield for St Helens Schoolboys versus their Kirkby counterparts that a watching Liverpool Scout was so impressed he invited the elated 11-year old to training at his favourite club. Iain spent 12 months at Melwood but disappointedly felt he was not getting enough game time and decided to leave. Manchester City and Tottenham Hotspur were keen to sign him but he was not ready to leave home so chose to take up the offer from Everton's youth set up which enjoyed an excellent reputation. He loved being at the School of Science and learnt a great deal from coaches Ray Hall and, in particular, Graham Smith who was prepared to go the extra mile for those in his charge. However, Iain was again frustrated at being unable to secure a regular place in the youth team until fate showed its hand.

When the regular full back sustained an injury shortly before a game versus Manchester City, Smith asked for a volunteer replacement. Guessing that he was again destined for a place on the bench, Iain leapt at the chance and had the game of his life - scoring one goal and creating four more in a 5-0 thrashing. This performance transformed Jenks' fortunes and in addition to becoming the new regular fullback, by the age of 16 he had become the youth team skipper. It was around the time of the Man City game that Chief Scout Ray Minshull handed Iain an ultimatum which played a massive part in determining his future. Between the ages of six and fourteen Iain was an excellent swimmer who trained up to 12 hours per week at Prescot's Scotchbarn Lane pool and Huyton Leisure Centre. He regularly represented the English Schools squad and was due to attend the National trials which, had they been safely negotiated, could have led to him taking part in the Olympic Games. Minshull was aware of this and concerned that Iain may have been over-exerting himself. He felt that participating in football AND swimming was having a negative effect upon his performances in both activities. He urged Iain to choose between pursuing a future in either football or swimming - a decision that was a no-brainer for footy-mad Jenks.

His subsequent progress through the youth ranks was noticed by Manager Howard Kendall. On 11 May 1991 he showed his faith in the apprentice by naming him in the team for an away game versus QPR. With 12,508 fans in Loftus Road it was clearly the biggest game 18-year old Iain had ever experienced. However, it proved to be anything but a dream debut when a tackle resulted in a broken ankle and time out of the game. The blow was slightly softened a few weeks later when Kendall gave the youngster a full-time professional contract. Iain got his head down and showing grit and determination, which would again be evident later in his career, battled back to fitness. His efforts paid off when, on 20 April the following year, he came off the bench to replace Matt Jackson at Goodison Park in a 2-1 defeat at the hands of Manchester City. Five days later at White Hart Lane he was in the starting line up for a 3-3 thriller versus Spurs in front of 34,630 fans. Before the season ended Iain managed to squeeze in another substitute appearance in a 2-1 home victory over Chelsea on 2 May 1992. Although he featured in two further games the following season (versus Chelsea and QPR), by his own admission Iain failed to reach the standard required for the top division due to the after effects of his broken ankle.

At the start of 1993 Iain joined Bradford City on a monthlong loan and played six games for the Bantams before returning to Goodison Park. However, the writing was on the wall for Jenks and on 28 August 1993 he signed for Chester City. This signalled the start of a five-year spell at the Deva Stadium which contained many ups but also some very serious downs. On a positive note, Iain played in excess of 160 games for the Seals, many as captain. In his first season he played every game and helped the club achieve automatic promotion to Division Two. He also became the first Chester City player for a decade to play international football when, on 30 April 1997 at the Hrazdan Stadium, he was selected to play for Northern Ireland in a World Cup qualifier versus Armenia and proudly picked up the first of six caps. This tremendous achievement was remarkable because just 16 months earlier he had sustained life-threatening injuries in a car crash.

On 11 November 1995, whilst driving home from a 2-1 FA Cup defeat by Blackpool, Iain's car clipped the kerb and ploughed into a tree. He was in intensive care for weeks with a punctured lung, eight smashed ribs, a shattered shoulder and numerous other problems which would later affect and ultimately end his playing career. Doctors told Jenks he would never play again but much to his credit he battled back to re-establish his place in City's team and pick up his caps. On 26 March 1998 Dundee United tabled a £200,000 bid to take him north of the border to Tannadice. Having enjoyed his time at Chester and built up a great rapport with the fans, it was a wrench to leave. Nevertheless, after careful consideration he opted to join the Terrors. Things did not work out as well as he had hoped and, after just 14 games in two injury-ravaged seasons, he was again on the move. However, he enjoyed Scotland, met his future wife whilst at Dundee and was destined to return. Twenty-one Shrewsbury Town appearances preceded a return to Chester.

In 2002, after accumulating in excess of 200 career games, Iain eventually succumbed to his injuries and retired from playing. Whilst still a Chester player he had wisely laid the foundations for the next stage of his football journey by joining the Everton coaching staff on a part-time basis. When he hung up his boots, Jenks jumped at the offer of becoming Chester's Youth Team Manager and thoroughly enjoyed the role.

Two years later, he returned to Scotland where he combined working for his father-in-law's building firm with filling the Manager's position at Broughty Athletic (where he briefly donned his playing boots again).

He also sat behind the Manager's desk at Dundee North End and Tayport FC. He caught the eye of Cowdenbeath Manager Danny Lennon who welcomed him to the club as his Assistant in August 2009.

The duo enjoyed tremendous success securing back-to-back promotions to take the part-time club into the Scottish First Division. When Lennon left the club known affectionately as the Blue Brazil, Jenks turned down their offer to take over the managerial reins. Instead, he opted to follow Lennon and continue their partnership at Premier League side St Mirren. A year later he took up the position of Head Scout at Dundee United which he occupied for a couple of years. In 2014 Iain was a member of the Scotland U-21s coaching staff. Then, with the responsibility of unearthing and nurturing young talent, he joined the Scottish FA's 'Elite National Performance Schools Programme' team. It would appear that having enjoyed decades in the world of professional football and having achieved so much, Iain Jenkins' decision to turn his back on a career in swimming was most definitely the right one!

DAVID RIDLER

When young Dave Ridler was kicking a ball about on the all-weather pitch in York Road near to his Mosscroft home he dreamed of representing his beloved Liverpool Football club. In years to come the dream would become a reality - but not quite in the way he had envisaged! Born on 12 March 1976 in Broadgreen Hospital, Dave's first taste of organised football came when neighbour Terry O'Neill took him along to successfully try-out for top local team Huyton Labour managed by local man Tony McDonough. Rids' dad Phil had been a fine footballer and sportsman and rarely missed a game his son played for the Labour, his Mosscroft and Prescot Comprehensive School sides or the Huyton Boys representative team.

After outgrowing the Labour, Dave joined Whiston Juniors playing under Steve Waite and the legendary Harry 'Skip' Warburton. In addition to picking up a host of league and cup winners medals, Dave tasted success on his first international trip when the Juniors cleaned up at a tournament in Holland. In 1994, Dave was a member of the Knowsley Youth squad that travelled to the USA to take part in the Dallas Cup. He and his teammates gave a great account of themselves and reached the semi-final stage of the prestigious tournament.

With his heart set on becoming a professional footballer, Dave wrote to dozens of clubs asking for a trial but this proved fruitless with few clubs even bothering to reply. Undeterred, he did not lose faith even when the Careers Advisor at Roby College bluntly told him that if a club had not picked him up by the time he had left school he was never going to be picked up. He received a further dent to his ambitions when he was refused a place on the college's Sports course. Although Dave had no interest in becoming a chef, his parents insisted that he needed to do something so he reluctantly enrolled on a catering course and combined his studies with working part-time in Ray's Bakery in Prescot. He graduated but still yearned for a career in football and turned out for local outfit Napoli in the Business Houses League. He also played in the Runcorn League for Prescot team Rocky's, managed by Wrexham striker Karl Connolly. Karl was well aware of Rids' ability and following a particularly brilliant performance he vowed to help him to get the break he craved. True to his word, he spoke to Wrexham Boss Brian Flynn and a trial was arranged.

Having waited so long for his opportunity Dave was not going to blow it and gave his all to secure a contract. Initially, he received a short-term deal which Wrexham extended. Then, in August 1995 the Careers Advisor ate his words when a delighted Dave became a full-time professional footballer. His debut for the Robins came on 28 January 1997 in an away game at Crewe Alexandra's Gresty Road ground. In the 77th minute of the Auto Windscreens Shield tie future Liverpool and England star Danny Murphy found the back of the net with the only goal of the game to hand the Railwaymen safe passage to the third round of the competition. A Football League debut followed on 15 March when, due to an injury to Brian Carey, Rids entered the action from the bench in the 22nd minute of a home stalemate with York City. Three days later he made his first League start as Preston North End put them to the sword by a scoreline of 2-1. Dave appeared in eleven of the team's final 14 fixtures of the 1996/97 season as the club finished eighth in Division Two missing a play-off place by just four points.

During five seasons at the Racecourse ground he made 143 appearances and whilst they usually fell agonisingly short of the promotion places, Dave was involved in some memorable cup exploits. In the 1997/98 season after overcoming Rochdale and Chester City in the early rounds of the FA Cup, they were pitched against Wimbledon's notorious 'Crazy Gang'. It may have been a decade since the Wombles had pulled off one of the biggest-ever FA Cup upsets by overcoming Liverpool in the Final to lift the trophy but with Vinnie Jones et al in the side they were still formidable opposition. On 4 January 1998 with 6,348 present at Selhurst Park, Wrexham matched the Dons in every department to grind out a deserved 0-0 draw. The return the following week proved to be a five-goal thriller but despite Karl Connolly grabbing a brace it was Wimbledon's name in the draw for the next round. However, a couple of seasons later on 11 December 1999 Dave was at the heart of the side which accounted for Middlesborough in the same competition. The Boro eleven contained a host of household names including Gazza, Gary Pallister, Christian Ziege and the little Brazilian wizard Juninho but Dave played his part in the side coming from 1-0 down to run out memorable 2-1 winners.

At the end of the 2000/01 season, much to his surprise and the disappointment of many of the Wrexham faithful, Dave's name was included in the list of players being released by the club. Nevertheless, it wasn't long before word of Rids' availability spread. In July 2001 Macclesfield Town boss Gil Prescott tracked down Dave who was holidaying abroad to try to tempt him to join the Silkmen. When Dave returned, Prescott fought off competition from Carlisle United and convinced him to join Macc's ranks. On the opening game of the 2001/02 season Dave was one of five debutants to face Swansea City and it showed as they were defeated 3-1. Understandably, the team lacked cohesiveness and failed to win any of their first six League fixtures. However, as Dave and his teammates gelled, results improved and after enjoying a purple patch in November and December when they won five on the bounce, they finished in a respectable 13th place in Division Three. Rids was an almost ever-present during his two seasons with the Silkmen before leaving to join Scarborough for the run-in of the 2002/03 campaign. Manager Russell Slade recruited Dave for the season's final six games in an attempt to secure a play-off place and promotion from the Conference to the Football League. Unfortunately, despite Rids' best efforts they only managed to finish 7th ending Scarborough's dreams and Dave's brief stay at the McCain's Stadium.

There was no such disappointment at his next club, Shrewsbury Town. When Dave signed for the Shrews on 4 July 2003 the club had just been relegated from the Football League costing Manager Kevin Ratcliffe his job. His replacement at Gay Meadow was former Northern Ireland international striker Jimmy Quinn whose brief was to take the club back to the Football League at the first time of asking. He made Rids one of his first recruits and added seven more players to his squad before the season kicked-off. Unlike Macclesfield a couple of seasons earlier, Quinn's team experienced no 'gelling' problems and enjoyed a fantastic season. Dave's central defensive partnership with Darren Tinson provided the rock upon which their success was built. An end of season third place finish was followed by victory in the play-off semis to hand them the opportunity to meet their manager's objective. On 16 May 2004, Stoke City's Britannia Stadium was the venue for the Conference play-off Final with Aldershot Town providing the opposition. The match attracted a record attendance for this fixture and the vast majority of the 19,216 present were cheering on the Shrews. However, the Shots' fans were celebrating in the 36th minute when Aaron McLean struck to give their team the lead. Their joy was short-lived as just eight minutes later a Duane Darby goal secured parity at 1-1 which is how the scoreline remained after 120 minutes of play. To determine a game of this magnitude by a penalty shoot-out is heartbreaking for the losers but until an alternative method is devised the current set up will remain and continue to throw up heroes and villains. The hero on this occasion was undoubtedly the Shrewsbury goalkeeper Scott Howie who brilliantly saved three spot kicks to send Shrewsbury Town back into the Football League.

Whilst this was one of the greatest achievements in Dave's career to this point, the club's return to the League resulted in Quinn bolstering his squad with new signings thus reducing Rids' opportunities. He featured in just nine matches the following season and in March 2005 joined Conference outfit Leigh RMI. However, this was supposed to be a fresh start but little did Dave know that his days as a professional footballer were coming to a cruel, life-changing end. Whilst on a night out with friends in Liverpool city centre, he was the

victim of a vicious, unprovoked attack which resulted in Dave sustaining a severe head injury. Although he later appeared for Winsford United, Caernarfon Town and Prescot Cables, it became apparent that he should reluctantly call time on his playing days. This was understandably an extremely difficult time for Rids but, demonstrating the same grit, determination and ability which had proved his Careers Advisor wrong, Dave was able to reinvent himself.

In a bizarre way, his difficulties resulted in him finding a new career path and in turn, fulfilling a dream. With support and encouragement from his wife, Dave embarked upon a fitness regime which reignited his enthusiasm for the game and enabled him to venture into the world of coaching and management. Enjoying a new lease of life, he threw himself headlong into securing his coaching badges and in 2009 started part-time coaching at Liverpool's Youth Academy. Later the same year he became Assistant Manager at Prescot Cables and took over the managerial reins in December 2010 fighting off competition from 20 other applicants. Almost a year to the day since taking the Hope Street job, Dave tendered his resignation to the Prescot hierarchy who accepted his decision, thanked him for his service and wished him well in his new, exciting venture.

For a couple of years Dave's role within the LFC Academy had been developing and he was delighted to take up the club's offer to deliver coaching programmes to young players in Egypt. The operation has enjoyed tremendous success and grown from strength to strength. He is now Head Coach of LFC's International Academy in Egypt and although it may be almost 4,000 miles from Mosscroft to Cairo, the little boy who kicked a ball around on York Road's all-weather pitch has made his dreams come true by representing the club he loves albeit in a different manner!

©www.mjcouzens.co.uk

GED BRANNAN

Wembley Stadium is famous throughout the world. Most players in English football dream of playing there yet relatively few fulfil the dream. Not only did Ged Brannan play at Wembley, he also earned a unique place in the football record books in the process.

Born on 15 January 1972, Ged spent hour after hour with his mates in the caged floodlit pitch behind the Bluebell estate's Salerno Drive shops - just a stone's throw from the family home in Horrocks Close. His performances for the St Aidan's School team paid off when headteacher Mr Cross put him forward for the Huyton Boys U-11s team. The 1982/83 season was a successful (almost perfect) campaign for the Schoolboys. Guided by the management team of Misters Hall & Gallagher, the team completed the entire season undefeated to pip St Helens at the post to win the title. On 28 March 1983, the youngsters (having already overcome Formby, Penketh and Maghull) took on Liverpool Boys at Goodison Park in the Final of the Everton Cup. Liverpool won the match 4-2 with future Liverpool, Manchester City, Real Madrid and England star Steve Macmanaman scoring a hat-trick.

Ged played his early non-school football for Grove Villa & St Annes Rovers who were run by John Lawless and Harry Tyrell respectively. However, when Copperas Villa Managers Joe Murphy and Dave Dixon came knocking at the Brannan's door they convinced Ged to sign for them. The duo had assembled an amazing squad with nine of their youngsters later graduating to the professional ranks. The team took its name from the Copperas Hill postal sorting office in Liverpool city centre where Joe and Dave worked. From the age of 11 to 15, Ged was a member of the Villa side which consistently swept the opposition aside. At this time, he was training with Liverpool but left when he felt he wasn't getting a fair crack of the whip. Ged thoroughly enjoyed playing for Joe & Dave and when he left St Augustine's Senior School they even got him a job with the Post Office. However, when Ged confided to his football-mad mum that he was missing the involvement with a Football League club, she wasted no time in contacting Tranmere Rovers Youth Development Officer Warwick Rimmer who had expressed an interest in her boy. Ged swiftly left his job, his dad chauffeured him to weekly training sessions over the water at Bebington Oval and he was soon rewarded with a YTS trainee contract.

Shortly before a 1st team v reserves game fate dealt Ged a fortunate hand when one of the players

©Kipax Sports Photography

sustained an injury presenting him with a chance to prove his worth. Ninety minutes, two tremendous goals and a solid performance later, Ged had convinced watching first team Manager Johnny King to hand him a place in the club's elite squad and a professional contract which he signed on 3 July 1990. Three months later on 15 October 1990, Ged came off the bench to replace Steve Mungall and make his first team debut in a friendly match versus Leeds Utd - pitching the previous season's Leyland DAF Cup winners against the 1989/90 Second Division champions. Although in general there was little at stake in the match, it was the most important game in the 18-year olds life and he acquitted himself very well. Ged clearly recalls marking future Scotland Manager Gordon Strachan and being hauled down in the penalty box following a rampaging run down the wing to win a spot kick. Ged went on to make 303 League and Cup appearances for Tranmere during the club's most successful period in its lengthy history.

On 1 July 1991 he took his place in the Super Whites side which opposed Bolton Wanderers in the Third Division play-off Final at Wembley. In front of 30,217 spectators a 98th minute goal from Chris Malkin broke Wanderers' hearts but secured Rovers' promotion. It also completed the first part of Ged's record-making achievement, although he would have to wait 16 years to finish the job! Over the next six seasons Ged continued to play a massive part in Tranmere's success which continued under new player-manager John Aldridge following Johnny King's retirement. However, despite Aldo's best efforts and the club offering a vastly improved deal, Manchester City Boss Frank Clarke lured Ged to Maine Road in a £750,000 deal. Even though City were going through a difficult period they were still one of the giants of the game - and there lay a problem. Having come from the intimate Prenton Park 'family' the massive 55-man squad at City including players from all over the globe resulted in what Ged describes as "the dark days".
 Although he played 70 games for City, he wasn't happy there and was delighted when Norwich City Manager Bruce Rioch rescued him from his nightmare to enjoy a couple of months on loan at Carrow Road. The top of the table Canaries wanted to make Ged a permanent signing on a free transfer which he would have loved but City dug their heels in for a fee. When Motherwell tabled a £378,000 bid on 26 October 1998, Ged was on his way north of the border where he was reunited with ex-Tranmere teammate and Motherwell player and Chief Executive Pat Nevin. Ged loved his two and a half years at Fir Park where he also briefly and bizarrely became an international player - for the Cayman Islands! Taking advantage of a loophole in FIFA rules, as the holder of a British passport Ged was entitled to play for this British Overseas Territory. Qualification for the 2000 World Cup was a distinct possibility if victory over Trinidad & Tobago could be secured. Ged and a number of other Brits appeared in warm up games for the Islands but shortly before the crucial match FIFA President Sepp Blatter (a great ally of T&T and later banned amid allegations of financial irregularities) stepped in to change the rules and scupper Ged's World Cup dream.

Domestically, when Ged was approaching the end of his contract he was linked with a move to Miami Fusion but cash-strapped Motherwell were forced to accept Wigan Athletic's £175,000 bid or risk losing him for nothing. Ged struggled for fitness at Wigan but despite being dogged by sciatica he still managed in excess of 50 games for the club. He turned out for Dunfermline and Rochdale on loan before leaving to join Accrington Stanley on 1 November 2003. Two years at Accy were followed by a move to Morecambe and it was during his two seasons with the Shrimps that Ged completed the second part of his unique footballing achievement. On 20 May 2007 at the new Wembley Stadium, Morecambe defeated Exeter City 2-1 in the Conference play-off Final with 40,043 fans in attendance. This sent the club into the Football League for the first time and Ged's teammates insisted he lead the team up the Wembley steps to lift the trophy. His participation in the game meant that he became the only player to gain promotion at both the old and new Wembley Stadiums - giving him a place in the record books which can never be matched.

Ged Brannan loves the game which has dominated his life and although he officially retired straight after that final Wembley appearance, he returned to play for Burscough, Vauxhall Motors and St Aloysius Over-40s. Nowadays, qualified coach Ged gets tremendous satisfaction from passing on the experience he gained from hundreds of competitive games to his football crazy children and other young, enthusiastic players via weekly sessions near his Birkdale home.

Footynote:

Ged is currently the manager of Accrington Stanley's U-23s.

JOHN MURPHY

You could count on the fingers of a pair of hands the number of players who have scored in excess of 100 goals for Blackpool FC during its 130-odd year history. One of those digits would be reserved for Huyton striker John Murphy.

Born on 18 October 1976 in Whiston Hospital, some of John's earliest memories involve kicking a ball around the streets near the family home in Woolfall Heath's Pennard Avenue. The pristine pitches on Lord Derby's Estate in nearby Knowsley Lane were also a favourite haunt of footy-mad John and his pals. He attended St Columba's School and clearly recollects counting the minutes whilst impatiently enduring Mr Lavery's morning Maths and English lessons. The afternoons could not come quick enough for John as they were totally dedicated to PE which usually meant football. He also recalls the school team cramming into Mr Lavery's old army jeep to travel far and wide to take on other school teams. John was extremely tall from a young age and was literally and figuratively head and shoulders above his teammates. When Mr Lavery handed John the team captaincy he demonstrated his faith in him by allowing John to make all the on-field managerial decisions. The team enjoyed numerous successes and LFC fan John has proud memories of leading the team out at Anfield to take part in the Liverpool Echo 7-a-side Cup Final against St Johns. Unfortunately, St Columba's lost the game on penalties which did not sit comfortably with young John who hated losing.

©rickmatthews.zenfolio.com

Away from school, his weekends were filled with football. He played for Manager Mick Duffy's team The Paddock at Springfield Park in the West Derby League on Saturday mornings before dashing down the road to turn out for the Eagle at Barnfield Drive in the afternoon. He would travel over to the Wirral on Sundays where he would finish his weekend with a game for Pride & Joy - another outfit run by Mick Duffy. After helping his teams to numerous cups and titles, regular goal-maker and goal-taker John was recruited by Peter Edwards who was Manager of crack side Pacific. This was a step up in class for John and whilst the team cleaned up in the Walton & Kirkdale Junior League, he has distinct memories of taking part in a tough international tournament on the Isle of Wight when the team got something of a wake-up call. With the preliminary rounds safely negotiated, they reached the Final to oppose Cramlington Juniors. They were a top side whose list of former players included ex-England stars Alan Shearer and Andy Sinton. Graham Fenton, who was to enjoy a future career in the Premiership, captained Cramlington and they proved too good on the day for Pacific. However, revenge was sweet the following year when John's team overcame the same opposition at the semi-final stage before defeating a London side to lift the trophy.

Many of Pacific's players were attached to Football League clubs and it wasn't long before John was attending Liverpool's School of Excellence, although this wasn't as enjoyable as he had anticipated. John had many attributes but was not the most skilful of players and unfortunately for him many of the drills at Melwood focused upon this aspect of the game. Just as he could not wait for Mr Lavery's academic lessons to be over, John wanted the skills sessions to finish so he could show what he had to offer in a game scenario. Around this time, John experienced a setback that threatened to end his career before it had begun. Severe pain and swelling to his knee proved extremely troublesome and although doctors told him he was fine, John knew otherwise and the problem persisted. Eventually he underwent keyhole surgery but when this failed to resolve the issue, the Reds showed John the door sighting his dodgy knee as the reason. It wasn't until he was 22 and had played through the pain barrier for years that an arthritic condition was identified which, when correctly treated, although far from cured became tolerable.

John's experience at Liverpool had a profound effect upon him and, disillusioned, he briefly turned his back on the game until his mates persuaded him to join them playing for Whiston Juniors U-16s. Shortly after, a teacher from his Edmund Arrowsmith Senior School took him for a trial at Chester City and John's all-round play and a stunning goal convinced the club to sign him as a YTS trainee. Cleaning boots, sweeping terraces and gruelling long distance runs were tough going and John considered packing it all in more than once. In addition, the club had a poor youth set up which was evident on match days - the humiliation of a 9-0 defeat at the hands of Liverpool is still fresh in his memory. Despite this, John impressed the Chester hierarchy and on the final day of the 1993/94 season with promotion to Division Two already secured, he travelled with the first team squad for the away fixture versus Northampton Town. When he went on the club's pre-season Isle of Man tour it was obvious that he was getting closer to making his first team debut.

On 30 October 1994, Manager Graham Barrow summoned him from the substitute's bench to play his part in a 1-1 draw against arch-rivals Wrexham in front of 4,974 very vocal fans. John set his sights on a place in the first eleven and it wasn't long before this was also achieved. The home leg of the second round Auto Windscreens Shield on 29 November 1994 handed John his first start in the first team and Crewe Alexandra provided the opposition. Far from being a dream debut, the Railwaymen spanked the Seals 6-0 but the young apprentice was making progress. Prior to the start of the following season, John's efforts resulted in his first professional contract, albeit a rolling one-year deal due to the uncertainty of his persistent knee injury. He bagged his first Chester goal on 15 August 1995 in a 4-1 Coca Cola Cup victory over Wigan Athletic. His debut League goal followed in the 5-1 defeat of Lincoln City a month later. They were the first goals John scored for Chester but he added another 30 to that total during his highly enjoyable 119-game spell at the club.

He loved his time at Sealand Road and wanted to stay but the club was in financial turmoil and in October 1998 went into Administration. They finished 14th in Division Three that season and John was top scorer with 10 goals. This brought him to the attention of a number of clubs and before the following season had kicked off he had left Chester to join Blackpool, managed by Nigel Worthington. Just a couple of days after joining his new employers John came off the bench and in a repeat of his Chester debut Wrexham provided the opposition. This time the outcome was different with Blackpool taking the points with a 2-1 victory. Once again, John was his club's top scorer with 10 goals in a largely disappointing campaign which ended in relegation to Division Three.

One positive from the 1999/2000 season was the forward partnership John struck up with Brett Ormerod which was integral to the team's success the following campaign. With his knee ailment now correctly diagnosed and treated, John enjoyed his most prolific season so far. He played 56 games and the double-pronged Murphy/Ormerod attack returned 50 goals. The Seasiders won their last four League games to finish 7th and secure a play-off place. The momentum of the run-in continued as they reached the Division Three play-off Final by brushing aside Hartlepool 5-1 in the semis. On 26 May 2001 23,600 Blackpool and Orient fans took their places in Cardiff's Millennium Stadium with both groups desperately hoping their club would win the contest to gain promotion. The Tangerines could not have got off to a worse start when the O's took the lead after just 27 seconds. But with John in the thick of the action, they twice pegged their opponents back before going on to win the game 4-2 to bounce back to Division Two at the first time of asking.

Over the next few seasons the club consolidated its position in the third tier and John continued to get amongst the goals to become Blackpool's top scorer in four consecutive campaigns. The Millennium Stadium was again a happy hunting ground for our man as the club were victorious in the 2001/02 and 03/04 Coca Cola Cup Finals. Cambridge United were overcome with ease 4-1 in the first match on 24 March 2002 with John setting up the victory with a goal after just six minutes. Southend United provided a sterner test in the second fixture but once again John opened the scoring (this time after just 74 seconds) before Danny Coid added another to send the Bloomfield Road faithful home happy. There aren't many players who can boast that they made three Millennium Stadium appearances, secured three wins and scored two goals in the process but John Murphy can! His next couple of seasons returned a respectable 18 goals from 70 games but a severe back injury meant that he spent a great deal of time on the treatment table.

On 27 October 2006 John joined Macclesfield Town in a loan deal until the end of the season. It was the first signing by the Silkmen's new Boss Paul Ince who had taken over from Brian Horton with the club in dire straits. The arrangement suited all parties - John needed games and Town needed goals. The transformation in the club's fortunes was staggering. When John came off the bench to join the action in a 3-2 defeat to Mansfield Town, not even the most optimistic spectator at Moss Rose could have predicted the ensuing run of results. Eleven losses and five draws had left them rooted at the foot of the lowest rung of the Football League's ladder and heading for the Conference. However, the following 13 games included just a single defeat, four drawn matches and eight victories. These fixtures also contained the biggest game in the club's history. John's winning goal against Hartlepool in the second round of the FA Cup granted them safe passage to face Chelsea's millionaires in the next round. A crowd of 41,434 attended Stamford Bridge on 6 January 2007 and when Frank Lampard gave Chelsea an early lead, many expected the remainder of the game to be a formality. Although the 6-1 scoreline would suggest that this was the case, it hardly reflects the events of the 90 minutes. The FA Cup has regularly produced magical moments and five minutes before half-time John pounced on a Ricardo Carvalho error to drill the ball past Chelsea keeper Hilario to restore parity and send the travelling Macc fans into raptures. Unfortunately, Lampard grabbed another within a minute - if they had gone into the dressing rooms at half-time level, the outcome may have been different. Just three minutes after the break the referee dismissed the Macclesfield goalkeeper and Lamps converted the resultant penalty to complete his hat-trick. Without a replacement keeper on the bench, defender David Morley became the last line of defence. He kept Jose Murinho's team at bay until late in the game when a flurry of goals provided a flattering scoreline for the team from West London. John's nine goals for the Silkmen played a massive part in changing the club's fortunes and their Football League salvation - job done!

In June 2007, Chester City offered John the financial security of a two-year deal and the opportunity to return to where his professional career had so enjoyably begun. He appeared in 40 games for a struggling Blues side and scored nine goals but was suffering with chronic back pain which hampered his performances. On 3 May 2008 he brought the curtain down on his lengthy career in English football when ironically he played in a 0-0 draw versus Macclesfield Town. However, before he finally called it a day, John spent six months with League of Ireland side St Patrick's Athletic. This finale gave him his first taste of European football in a Europa League match versus Hertha Berlin.

When John retired from football he kept himself busy by working in the building trade. In August 2011 whilst working on a roof in Halewood, he received an unexpected phone call from Blackpool CEO Matt Williams asking him if he would be interested in taking up a coaching position at the club. Although he had no coaching qualifications or experience, they wanted someone with strong links to the club to assist new Manager Ian Holloway. John did not need asking twice and after initially fulfilling coaching duties with the first team he moved on to nurturing Blackpool's young talent as part of their Youth Academy. He loves the job of passing on some of the knowledge and experience he acquired during his excellent 489-game, 142-goal career and was extremely proud when in 2016/17 season the Blackpool youth team won both the Lancashire FA Youth Cup and the North West Youth Alliance League.

STEVEN GERRARD

It's no exaggeration to state that Steven George Gerrard is one of the greatest footballers to have ever played for one of the greatest football clubs in the world. Furthermore, his obvious love of his hometown and its people makes him the ideal 'Huyton Titan'.

Born on 30 May 1980, he grew up living at 10 Ironside Road on the Bluebell estate and the strip of concrete outside his front door provided his first pitch. Predominately playing against older brother Paul and his mates, he may have been physically inferior but that's where the negative comparisons ceased. Metaphorically, he was head and shoulders above his opponents and displayed a drive and determination to be the best that he (and anyone else) could be. These characteristics, along with a host of others, enabled Steven to enjoy a fantastically successful playing career which, although it's early days, he hopes to emulate as a manager.

At the age of eight, the St Michaels pupil joined Liverpool's Centre of Excellence after starring for the school, Denburn JFC and Whiston Juniors. Apprentice and full pro contracts were secured as Stevie moved through the Reds' ranks. On 29 November 1998, Gerard Houllier introduced him to first team football as an 89th minute substitute in a 2-0 victory over Blackburn Rovers before a crowd of 41,753. It was the first of 710 appearances he made for the club in an astonishing Anfield career which spanned 17 seasons. When, a week later, he was turned inside out by Spurs' David Ginola, and substituted after 55 minutes, there may have been some fans who were sceptical about Steven's chances of success. However, his third match in ten days - a Eufa Cup clash with Celta Vigo - produced a Man of the Match performance, giving Houllier's belief in the youngster credence whilst warming the hearts of the Anfield faithful. Steven added another ten appearances to his debut season as the Reds finished 7th in the Premier League. The next season saw him cement his place in the team as he made 31 appearances. He opened his goals account by jinking through a packed defence to beat Sheff Wed keeper Kevin Pressman on 5 December 1999 and, in a goal-laden club career, he found the net on a further 187 occasions.

Such was young Steven's impact on the game that England Boss Kevin Keegan handed him an international debut during the close-season in a 2-0 victory over the Ukraine on 31 May 2000. The game was a warm-up for the European Championships and, in a 17 June clash with Germany, Steven replaced fellow Red Michael Owen as the Three Lions won 1-0 but failed to get through the group stages of the tournament.

From a personal point of view his career was progressing brilliantly but Steven's winning mentality craved silverware and in the 2000/01 season the dreams he'd harboured in those Ironside Road games became reality. On 25 February 2001, at the Millennium

Stadium in Cardiff with 73,500 spectators present, Liverpool faced Birmingham City to contest the League Cup Final. A Robbie Fowler strike looked like it would be sufficient to land Liverpool their first trophy in six years until a 90th minute Darren Purse penalty put the celebrations on hold. No further goals were added during extra-time but in a nail-biting penalty shootout finale Liverpool ran out the victors.

It is often said that success breeds success and this was certainly true as far as this Liverpool team was concerned. In a seven-day period during May 2001, two further trophies were added to the League Cup and a 4-0 defeat of Charlton guaranteed the club qualification to the following season's Champions League competition. A return to the Millennium on 12 May resulted in a Michael Owen brace helping the Reds overcome Arsenal 2-1 to snatch the FA Cup. Then, just four days later, Stevie rattled home Liverpool's second goal in a thrilling 5-4 victory over Spanish outfit Alaves, adding the Eufa Cup to a brilliant season's haul. For his contribution Steven was rewarded with the PFA Young Player of the Year award. Liverpool weren't finished though as, before the following campaign had begun in earnest, the Charity Shield and European Super Cup had also been secured, although an ankle injury deprived the Reds of Stevie's services in the 2-1 Charity Shield win over Man Utd.

No further silverware was added in 2001/02 season but Steven played a huge part in the club finishing runners-up to Arsenal, their highest position for a decade. After a bright start to their Champions League campaign, the club's return to Europe's premier competition after a 15-year absence came to an end when Bayer Leverkusen knocked them out at the quarter-final stage - disappointing, but Steven was far from finished with this particular competition. Unfortunately, a troublesome groin problem forced him to miss the 2002 World Cup although he returned to action for the pre-season Community Shield defeat inflicted upon the Reds by Arsenal.

By the time Rafa Benitez was installed as Gerard Houllier's replacement at the conclusion of a disappointing 2003/04 campaign, Steven was the custodian of the captain's armband. The opposition for the 23-year old's first game as skipper was provided by Olimpija Ljubljana but they offered little resistance and Liverpool cruised to a comfortable Eufa Cup victory. This proved to be the first of 472 occasions that Stevie proudly led the side - a club record. In Rafa's first season in charge, he was unable to improve on Houllier's fourth-place (they finished 5th) and, although the team reached the League Cup Final on 27 February 2005, it ended in disappointment. Despite John Arne Riise giving the Reds the lead over Chelsea after just 45 seconds at the Millennium Stadium, Steven's misguided 79th minute header found the back of his own net to level the tie. The game ended 3-2 in Chelsea's favour to land Jose Mourinho's first piece of silverware since taking charge. However, when the two clubs met again a little over two months later in the Champions League semi-final, goals were in short supply. A single, hotly-disputed Luis Garcia goal proved the difference and sent Liverpool through to one of the greatest occasions in the club's and competition's history and Jose back to London licking his wounds.

On 25 May 2005, 'The Miracle of Istanbul', as the match was later dubbed, pitched six-times winners AC Milan against Liverpool who were chasing their fifth European Cup. A disastrous first 45 minutes left Steven and co 3-0 in arrears and with a mountain of Everest proportions to climb. Step up Rafa, step up the Kop Choir and step up Steven Gerrard. From being a long way second best, Steven inspired his fellow combatants to produce one of the most compelling comebacks in the history of the continent's most prestigious club tournament. The second half was less than ten minutes old when Stevie latched on to a twice-attempted Riise cross to send a looping header past the Milan keeper. Hope springs eternal and, with the Reds smelling fear, before the hour was up, remarkably the score was level thanks to a Vladimir Smicer drive from 25 yards and, after his penalty kick was saved, a Xabi Alonso strike from 25 inches. Milan were understandably shell-shocked. From having one hand on Old Big Ears, Liverpool, urged on by a rampant Gerrard, had wrestled it off them. Steven was all over the shop, occupying, due to necessity, three different positions as the game went to extra-time. Having marshalled the troops superbly and with his second in command Jamie Carragher also playing the game of his life, Steven was not going to allow their hard work to be in vain as he drove the team on. When no further goals were added, penalties loomed. A combination of goalkeeping heroics from Jerzy Dudek and some of the most experienced players to ever pull on a Milan jersey bottling it, Liverpool held their nerve and were able to finish the job, scoring three goals from twelve yards with their opponents registering just two. The boy from the Bluebell had already fulfilled many of his ambitions but this topped them all. Despite this, when the dust settled on his magnificent achievement, there were storm clouds gathering over Anfield.

When, in the close season, the club failed to engage with Steven over a new contract, doubts preyed on his mind about his future. Mourinho had made no secret of his admiration of arguably the world's most influential midfielder and Chelsea tabled a £40 million offer to take him to Stamford Bridge. Steven came within a whisker of leaving Anfield but, after in-depth, heart to heart conversations with his dad Paul, he came to the conclusion that he simply could not leave the club he loved. Having dragged its feet, the club's hierarchy now sprung into action and, much to every Liverpool fan's delight, Steven signed a new four-year deal. The new season couldn't come quick enough for him and he hit the ground running with a stunning hat trick versus Welsh minnows TNS as the club began its defence of the Champions League title in the unusual situation of having to endure the group stages to reach the tournament proper. Disappointingly, Benfica accounted for the Reds in the round of sixteen and overall the season was a combination of highs and lows. The campaign peaked on 13 May 2006 when, with Liverpool trailing 3-2 to West Ham and looking down and out in the 90th minute of the FA Cup Final, Steven pulled another rabbit out of the hat with a stunning 35-yarder to send the game into extra-time and, in turn, penalties. Shot-stopper Pepe Reina saved three West Ham spot kicks and the Reds left Cardiff with the Cup.

At the end of an eventful 12-month period, Steven joined the England squad in Germany for the 2006 World Cup. Surprisingly, he later confessed to feeling homesick but shrugged this off to score in matches versus Paraguay and Sweden to take his season's tally to 26. Ultimately, the Three Lions failed in their mission to capture the biggest prize in World football and, after a disappointing defeat at the hands of Portugal, they returned home empty handed.

The 2006/7 season started well with a 2-1 Community Shield victory over Chelsea but ended in disappointment when AC Milan sought and took revenge on the Reds with a 2-1 victory in the Champions League Final in Athens.

Although Steven continued to perform at the highest level for a further eight seasons and he provided the Liverpool faithful with many memorable moments, this was not Liverpool's most productive of times as far as trophies were concerned. Between 2007 and 2015, the club picked up just one trophy, the League Cup in 2011/12 when they overcame Cardiff City on penalties. For a club of Liverpool's stature this simply wasn't good enough which was reflected in the hiring and firing of a number of managers. Rafa left and Roy Hodgson came and went, Kenny Dalglish took over the reins, delivered the League Cup then left and, in 2012/13 season Brendan Rodgers arrived at Anfield. With the earlier arrival of Luis Suarez at the club, and his excellent on-field relationship with Steven, many people were extremely optimistic that Rodgers would deliver the League title and, in just his second season in charge, he very nearly did. With Steven pulling the strings in midfield, the team played some of the most attractive football seen at Anfield since the glory years. They scored in excess of 100 goals and came within a whisker of snatching the title. An infamous costly mistake by Steven, which resulted in a Chelsea goal and the loss of the match, was a harsh way for the team's hopes to be dashed and a bitter pill for Steven to swallow - so close but yet so far.

The following campaign was Steven's last as a player at the club. After a season playing in the MLS for LA Galaxy he would return to manage Liverpool's Academy youngsters. But on 24 May he took to the field at Stoke City's Bet 365 Stadium to make his final Liverpool appearance. Although Stevie scored in the 70th minute, Liverpool were on the wrong end of a 6-1 drubbing - not how he would have wanted to bow out of the English game. However, there is no denying that despite a disappointing end to his Liverpool career, Steven Gerrard is one of the finest players to have ever pulled on a Liverpool shirt.

Throughout Steven's Liverpool career, he scored and created goals for fun. He was fortunate enough to play with excellent strikers such as Michael Owen, Robbie Fowler, Fernando Torres and Luis Suarez but perhaps they were the fortunate ones ! It's no coincidence that although they enjoyed success after leaving Anfield, these goal scorers were never as prolific without Stevie providing the ammunition for them.

His tally of 710 appearances for the club is staggering. He also won 114 England caps and was showered with numerous awards including the PFA Player of the Year award. He was selected for the PFA Team of the Year a record eight times and, in addition, selected as a member of the UEFA Team of the Year and the FIFA World Eleven on three occasions.

When Steven returned from the States, his appointment as coach of Liverpool's U-18s was no surprise. He was always going to stay involved in the game and there was no better place to start his managerial journey than at his spiritual home. In fellow Huytonian and former teammate Tom Culshaw, Steven found a trusted ally who made the journey across the border with him when Steven left his position at Liverpool's Academy to take up the job as Rangers Manager on 1 July 2018. When Steven arrived at Ibrox he took over a team undoubtedly living in the shadow of their Old Firm rivals Celtic. Steven's brief was to unlock The Bhoys stranglehold on the Premiership title which they had won every year since it's inception in 2013.

Two runners-up finishes in his first couple of seasons laid the foundations for their fantastic achievement in 2020/21 season. Not only did they land the Premiership title, they did so in stunning fashion. When Celtic drew 0-0 away to Dundee Utd with six games of the campaign remaining, it confirmed The Gers had an unassailable lead in the table. This was the earliest the Premiership had ever been won and signalled jubilant scenes in the blue half of Glasgow the like of which some fans had begun to doubt they would experience again. However, there was still a job to do and Steven ensured his team didn't lose focus and continued the campaign with the same enthusiasm they had shown throughout the season. Consequently, Rangers amassed 102 points, 25 ahead of runners-up Celtic, and completed the season unbeaten - a remarkable turnaround in the club's fortunes.

Such was the joy around the club, Steven could probably have been guaranteed a job for life at Ibrox but he is an ambitious man and fully aware that the Scottish Premiership is no match for its English counterpart. When, on 7 November 2021, Dean Smith was relieved of his duties at Villa Park after a run of five consecutive defeats, Steven was installed to the Aston Villa hotseat four days later. He almost immediately showed his influence in the game by drafting in top players, most notably Philipe Coutinho and brought an attractive style of play to the Midlands which resulted in a comfortable mid-table finish in his debut season.

When asked, Steven has made no secret of the fact that one day he would love to manage Liverpool. However, if that appointment is ever to be made, sentiment will play no part in the decision. Steven George Gerrard will have to continue to do what he has done for decades and deliver results on the pitch. For very different reasons, there are many Villa and Liverpool fans monitoring his progress with interest.

IAN DUNBAVIN

Ian Dunbavin's career has turned full circle. At the age of 13 he joined Liverpool and trained at Melwood under fellow Huyton goalkeeper and Liverpool FC coach Dick Johnson. Twenty years later after an excellent playing career, he returned to the fold to work at Liverpool FC's Academy where he now coaches the Reds' youngsters!

©Kipax Sports Photography

Born on 25 May 1980, Ian was a member of the Reds 1996 squad which, for the first time in the club's history, won the FA Youth Cup. Although Bavo wasn't selected to play in the Final (Roy Naylor was preferred), he had made a valuable contribution to the team throughout the season and in earlier rounds of the competition. On 22 January 2000 after seven years at Liverpool, he joined Shrewsbury Town who were managed by former Everton and Wales defender Kevin Ratcliffe. He got a taste of first team action sooner than expected when, on 4 March 2000, regular keeper Paul Edwards sustained a 77th minute injury in a Division Three clash with Cheltenham Town. Ian joined proceedings with the team trailing by a goal to nil. Seconds before the referee brought the game to a close, there was little he could do to prevent the successful conversion of a penalty and Ian's debut ended in a 2-0 defeat. Although a great club, Shrewsbury Town were struggling at the wrong end of the table with their Football League status under threat. Ian appeared in seven of the club's final 14 games of the season including the crucial last match of the campaign. On 6 May 2000, the Salopian faithful made the 200-mile journey from Gay Meadow to Exeter City's St James Park Stadium desperately hoping for a victory and that results elsewhere would work in their favour. Their prayers were answered when defeat for Chester City, coupled with a 2-1 Shrews win, heralded the Seals exit to the Conference and brought Ian's debut campaign to a nail biting but ultimately safe conclusion.

He shared goalkeeping duties with Edwards throughout the following season, making 23 appearances as they finished in 15th place. Matters improved further during 2001/02 when Bavo established himself as the club's regular goalie and the side narrowly missed out on the play-offs with a ninth place finish. However, the optimism evaporated a year later during a dismal season. The team failed to win any of their last 16 games leaving Ratters out of work and the club out of the Football League. Jimmy Quinn was brought in as his replacement and recruited a host of new players. Ian was selected on just three occasions by Quinn and, when the club were winning a play-off Final encounter with Aldershot to return to the League, Bavo was on a three-match loan spell at Morecambe. In the close season he joined Halifax Town and put in 56 Conference appearances before moving on loan to Scarborough on 10 November 2005.

When Accrington Stanley romped away with the Conference title in 2005/06, Manager John Coleman recruited Ian to strengthen his squad and provide competition for Charlton loanee Rob Elliott. With Elliott ruled out of the first League game due to injury, Ian once again got an early chance to stake a claim to a regular place in the starting eleven. He fared extremely well and kept his place in the side until the turn of the year. Coleman was delighted with his acquisition's form but, in a League Cup tie versus Premier Leaguers Watford on 19 September 2006, he made a puzzling decision which left him with egg on his face. Even though Ian had withstood everything Watford had thrown at him for 120 minutes, the Boss bizarrely withdrew him and sent Rob Elliott into the penalty showdown. Elliott did not save a single Watford attempt and the Hornets won 6-5 to progress to the next round. To Coleman's further embarrassment (but simultaneous delight), a couple of days later in their next game, Bavo performed heroics between the sticks and saved TWO penalties! During the following seven seasons Ian Dunbavin managed to see off strong competition from 18 goalkeeping rivals to make 169 appearances for Accy. During this time, with the exception of one season, the club fluctuated between 14th and 18th place in the fourth tier of English football. The exception came in 2010/11 when they finished fifth and reached the play-offs but were defeated in the semis by Stevenage Borough who went on to win promotion.

Ian's final game in not only a Stanley jersey but also in the English Football League, took place on 24 August 2013. The team against whom he got his first taste of Football League action, Cheltenham Town, suitably provided the opposition and, courtesy of a 71st minute Jason Taylor goal, left Accy's Store First Stadium with three points. After a brief loan spell at Chesterfield, Ian brought the curtain down on a career which involved in excess of 350 appearances.

In 2014 Ian returned to where it all began for him when he took up a part-time coaching position at the Liverpool Academy before becoming full-time a couple of years later. He now works closely with the club's young keepers hoping to produce players who will, as he did, enjoy lengthy careers in the game.

©Kipax Sports Photography

CHRIS SHUKER

Standing five feet five inches, Chris Shuker is not the tallest player to have ever graced a football field…. but neither were World Cup winners Nobby Stiles, Alan Ball or Diego Maradona or, for that matter, seven times Ballon d'Or winner Lionel Messi! A lack of inches has never been an issue for Chris, however during his 17-year career his low centre of gravity, ability to turn on a sixpence or to ghost in on a defender's blindside was often problematic to his opponents!

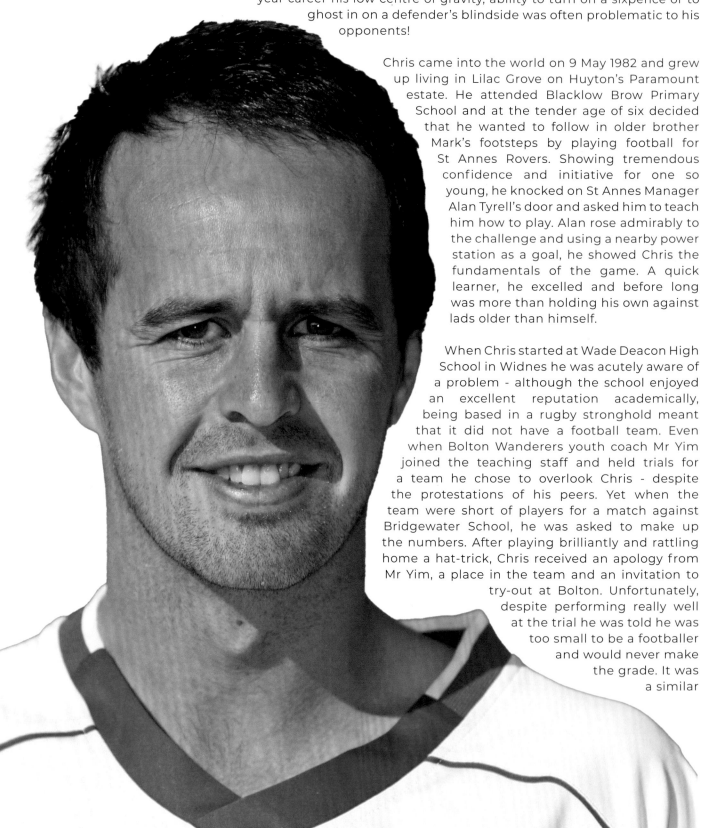

Chris came into the world on 9 May 1982 and grew up living in Lilac Grove on Huyton's Paramount estate. He attended Blacklow Brow Primary School and at the tender age of six decided that he wanted to follow in older brother Mark's footsteps by playing football for St Annes Rovers. Showing tremendous confidence and initiative for one so young, he knocked on St Annes Manager Alan Tyrell's door and asked him to teach him how to play. Alan rose admirably to the challenge and using a nearby power station as a goal, he showed Chris the fundamentals of the game. A quick learner, he excelled and before long was more than holding his own against lads older than himself.

When Chris started at Wade Deacon High School in Widnes he was acutely aware of a problem - although the school enjoyed an excellent reputation academically, being based in a rugby stronghold meant that it did not have a football team. Even when Bolton Wanderers youth coach Mr Yim joined the teaching staff and held trials for a team he chose to overlook Chris - despite the protestations of his peers. Yet when the team were short of players for a match against Bridgewater School, he was asked to make up the numbers. After playing brilliantly and rattling home a hat-trick, Chris received an apology from Mr Yim, a place in the team and an invitation to try-out at Bolton. Unfortunately, despite performing really well at the trial he was told he was too small to be a footballer and would never make the grade. It was a similar outcome at Tranmere Rovers with the Head of their youth setup, Warwick Rimmer, citing Chris' height as a problem - an opinion he would later amend.

Significantly, Chris possessed tremendous faith in his own ability and believed unreservedly that he would become a professional footballer. He used any negative comments to inspire him to prove his doubters wrong. In the meantime, he continued playing for St Annes and enjoyed his other great passion of horse riding. He became such a proficient horseman that he seriously considered a career as a jockey and in recent years he has ridden (although not competitively) for top trainers Donald McCain and Oliver Greenall. After impressing local coach Andy Foster at weekly 5-a-side sessions, he arranged for Chris to join Prescot Cables where he overcame the usual scepticism to impress youth team Managers Tony Murphy and ex-Everton player Mark Ward. When the duo took charge of Runcorn's youth team Chris joined them and quickly caught the eye of a legion of scouts. Two goals in a 3-2 victory over Tranmere prompted Warwick Rimmer to eat his words and offer Chris an apprenticeship. This was firmly rejected by Chris' father who shared his son's belief that other opportunities would be forthcoming. He was proved right when Man City Scout Wally Maudsley spotted 16-year old Chris. Wally had no reservations about his height and preferred to focus on his technical ability, creativity and bags of potential. Liverpool and Everton both showed interest but following a three-week trial at City, Chris signed a three year scholarship.

After making swift progress through the ranks, Chris began the 2000/01 season playing for City's reserves but on 22 March 2001 he joined Macclesfield Town on loan in order to gain first team experience. Two days later in the 79th minute of a 2-1 home victory over Blackpool, Chris came off the bench to replace Richard Tracey and make his English Football League debut. It was the first appearance of a successful nine-game spell with the Silkmen which also included his first League goal - a header in a 1-0 win over Jan Molby's Kidderminster Harriers. He returned to Maine Road in June of the same year hungry to impress Boss Kevin Keegan sufficiently to be given a first team chance.

September 11 2001 will forever be remembered for the horrific terrorist attack on New York's Twin Towers when 2,996 people lost their lives. City had a second round Worthington Cup tie versus Notts County scheduled to take place on that evening and despite Keegan's request that the game be postponed, it went ahead. With 5,972 spectators in County's Meadow Lane ground and the game 56 minutes old, Israeli international Eyal Berkovic made way for Chris to join the action. Five minutes later he had written his name into the record books by breaking the deadlock with a looping header (Two goals. Two headers. Too small?) The match ended 4-2 to City and Shukes had played a significant role in securing a place in the next round of the competition. A fortnight later he again left the bench to make his City League debut in a 3-0 defeat of Walsall which was followed by a sub's appearance in another 3-0 success against Barnsley. The Sky Blues enjoyed an excellent season and romped to the Division One title to return to the Premiership.

In 2002/03 season Chris figured in three games in the top flight including his only start for City in a 2-2 draw versus Blackburn Rovers. This match was sandwiched between two 3-0 defeats at the hands of Leeds Utd and Liverpool. Competition for places was fierce at Maine Road, not least of all in Chris' attacking midfield position. Consequently, he spent a great deal of the season in the reserves which he found incredibly frustrating. In February 2003 Walsall Manager Colin Lee gave Chris the opportunity to play first team football and he thoroughly enjoyed the five games he played for the Saddlers. He returned to City with renewed vigour and optimistically signed a one-year contract extension. His joy was short-lived however when Keegan presented Chris with the fait accompli of joining Rochdale on loan. Shukes was aware there had been approaches from Crystal Palace and Burnley which would have interested him but his Manager dug his heels in and Chris was off to Spotland. Chris Shuker was a fully committed footballer and no stranger to a yellow card (he picked up 25 and 2 reds in his 402-game career). However, the fact that he received a yellow card in each of his first three Rochdale games and a red in his fourth was probably an indication of his frustration at being at Dale under duress. He made 14 appearances in three months at the club and despite Manager Alan Buckley wanting to extend the loan, Chris could not get back to City quick enough.

By contrast, after a brief spell back in City's reserves, he loved his three-month loan period at Hartlepool Utd where he made 15 appearances. His final game for the Monkey Hangers came on 7 February 2004 in an incident-filled 2-2 draw with Barnsley. On the stroke of half-time the Tykes' Chris Lumsden was sent off following a clash with Shukes. Barnsley's fans held Chris responsible and were baying for his blood. The police feared for his safety and deemed it necessary to escort Shukes away from the ground after the full-time whistle. Ironically, watching the game from the stands that day was former Leeds Utd player and Nottingham Forest Manager Paul Hart who, less than a month later, was installed as Barnsley's new Boss and made Chris his first signing. Although initially some fans struggled to forgive the Huytonian, it wasn't long before the Barnsley faithful took him to their hearts due to his outstanding performances. Hart built his team around Chris and they reaped the benefits as he played some of the best football of his career and twice picked up the club's Player of the Year award.

In 2005/06 he played every League game and helped the club to reach the play-offs. However, due to a falling out with the club's Chairman, Chris was left out of the starting eleven in both the semi-final and Final. On 27 May 2006 at Cardiff's Millennium Stadium, Barnsley and Swansea went head to head for a place in the Championship. The game finished 2-2 and six minutes into extra time, Chris came off the bench to join the action. Despite making an impact he was unable to affect the scoreline and the game went to penalties. Chris took Barnsley's second spot kick and calmly stroked it home to help the team overcome the Swans and send the South Yorkshire contingent of the 55,419 crowd into euphoria. Sadly, due to irreconcilable differences with the Chairman, this proved to be Chris' last kick for the club where he had spent two enjoyable and successful seasons. His performances for the Tykes attracted the attention of a number of clubs and Swansea and Blackpool nearly secured his services but on 8 July 2006 Shukes put pen to paper on a two-year deal at Tranmere Rovers.

Manager and fellow Huytonian Ronnie Moore proclaimed, "He is one of the few players I would pay to watch." His debut took place on 5 August at Prenton Park in a 1-0 victory over Oldham Athletic. Chris made 49 further appearances and enjoyed an excellent season. His peers acknowledged his efforts by including him in their PFA Division One Team of the 2006/07 season. However, nine minutes into the following season's Boxing Day fixture disaster struck when a rash tackle by a Carlisle United player resulted in a horrific injury. The damage to his knee was so severe that by his own admission Chris was never quite the same player again. Although he played a further 67 games for Rovers (who narrowly missed a play-off place in 2008/09), he had to adapt his game to compensate for the injury. In August 2010 after four hugely impressive Rovers campaigns, it was time to move on and Chris found a new home at Division Two Morecambe, managed by former Man Utd player Sammy McIlroy. It quickly became apparent to Chris that this was a mistake. He was a player who thrived on the noise generated in a stadium and the fans encouragement but he felt that the average home attendance of 2,256 in the newly-built Globe Arena failed to create a decent atmosphere. Although he made 30 appearances for the Shrimps, he describes his time at the club as "a nightmare" and it was time to find pastures new.

After brief dalliances with Motherwell in Scotland and Wellington Phoenix in New Zealand, on 13 February 2012 Chris signed for League Two side Port Vale. His troublesome knee was affecting his performances but Manager Micky Adams installed Chris in a central midfield role which gave him a new lease of life. Whilst he had to reign in his natural attacking instincts and adopt a more responsible approach, the switch was beneficial to him and the team. In 2012/13 Chris made 34 appearances for the Valiants on their way to promotion - the third time Chris had enjoyed this feat. The following season the injury finally caught up with him and on 3 May 2014 following a 0-0 draw versus Peterborough United Chris was given a guard of honour by the players and a standing ovation from the fans as he bowed out of professional football - albeit prematurely! When Micky Adams left Vale and took over at Tranmere Rovers he had no hesitation in inviting Chris to join him as his Assistant. When results did not go their way, Chris signed as a player and four days later came off the bench to replace Steve Jennings in the 60th minute of a 2-0 defeat at the hands of Burton Albion. Not only was this his second Tranmere Rovers debut but more significantly it was Chris Shuker's 400th career game - a fantastic achievement. After adding two more games to that tally he called time on his playing days - this time for good!

He made a short-lived return to management at Trafford FC and now divides his time between coaching a local college team and working as a personal trainer.

JAMES ROBINSON

Every outfield footballer dreams of scoring the winning goal in a crucial game in a stadium packed to the rafters with their own fans. On 4 February 2007 for James Robinson the dream became a reality. In the 87th minute of the Australian A League Major semi-final clash with Adelaide Utd, James came off the Melbourne Victory's bench with the game locked at 1-1. Just five minutes later he had written his name into the record books by sending a looping header over the Adelaide goalkeeper and into the net. The 47,413 fans went delirious as James' first goal for the club sent them to their first ever Grand Final.

This was a fantastic reward for a player who has not always taken the easy route in a career which began at the shops in Huyton's Woolfall Heath Avenue. "After I scored that goal I thought back to playing headers and volleys in Huyton when I was nine years of age. We'd play against a brick wall with a goal painted on it, using a flyaway. We'd play '60 Seconds to score a goal and you're through to the next round' and that's what the semi-final goal was like."

James came into the world on 18 September 1982 and grew up around the corner from those shops in Mardale Road. He attended St Aloysius and St Michael's Schools and by the age of nine his potential had already been spotted. "A guy called Jimmy G spotted me playing in a summer competition and took me to Crewe Alexandra. He was a fantastic man who opened up a door for me that I will never forget." James has clear recollections of early achievements. At the age of eleven he scored at Anfield to help the school team lift the Liverpool Cup and when he attended Bluecoat Seniors, the Toffees-mad youngster took great delight in scoring for Liverpool Boys at Goodison Park. His performances were noticed by Liverpool and Everton who both offered James the opportunity to join them. However, he was adamant that Crewe was the right club for him and with the unswerving support of his father they made the journey to the Railwaymen's training and matches four times per week. James worked tirelessly, scored goals for the junior, youth and reserve teams and secured a place in the first team squad in 2002.

On 1 March 2003 Manager Dario Gradi called James from the bench to replace Steve Jones and make his first team debut in a 1-0 defeat versus Peterborough in front of 5,704 supporters. It was the first of 15 appearances he made (scoring one goal against Ipswich Town in a thrilling 6-4 defeat) before he left the club by mutual consent. With a year left on his Crewe contract it was a bold move, "I didn't want to spend my time on the bench...so I decided to walk away." He 'walked' to Iceland and spent a wonderful four months playing for IBV Vestmannaeyjar. This proved to be a life-changing experience for 22-year old James - it gave him the appetite and courage to try new things. He returned home briefly and played for Altrincham and Accrington Stanley on a part-time basis. Unfortunately for all concerned, the FA had not received James' international clearance when he played for Altrincham and consequently the club were deducted 18 League points. Only a last-minute reprieve saved the club from relegation.

By this time James had taken another bold move by putting himself in the shop window in Australia. In 2006 he signed for Richmond SC and his 13 goals in 19 appearances helped the club to promotion. The decision to take the plunge in Oz really paid off when Melbourne Victory Manager Ernie Merrick was so impressed with how James played against them in a pre-season friendly he invited him to train with the top-flight A League club. This was another gamble that paid off for the Huytonian because Melbourne already had their full quota of foreign players. This meant that James would be ineligible to play until a foreigner left the club. However, he bided his time and when Belgian defender Geoffrey Claeys retired it offered James the chance he had been waiting for. He seized his opportunity in fine fashion in the club's semi-final clash when his goal sent them to the 2007 Grand Final which Melbourne won at a 6-0 stroll.

James has continued to ply his trade in Australia with Marconi Stallions, Perth Glory, North Queensland Fury, Oakleigh Cannons FC, Bulleen Lions, and Dandenong Thunder SC. On 13 January 2014 he became player-manager of Ballarat Red Devils fulfilling an ambition he had harboured for many years - from the shops at Woolfall Heath Avenue to the Manager's office in Victoria, Australia!

SCOTT TYNAN

When, at the conclusion of the 2014/15 season, Leicester City sat at the top of the Premier League table, many genuine football fans were delighted for them. Totally unexpected, it represented a welcome break from the stranglehold the 'big' clubs had on the title for many years. Former Football League goalkeeper and Huytonian Scott Tynan was one such delighted fan - although there was perhaps an ulterior motive for his celebrations.

After spending time at Wigan Athletic, the Woolfall Heath youngster joined Nottingham Forest and struck up a friendship with centre-half Wes Morgan. When Scott hung up his cap and gloves after a decade in the game, the duo embarked upon a business partnership running a string of tattoo studios - an art form Scott excels in. Following the Foxes' amazing success under Wes' captaincy, the tattooists were inundated with requests from supporters (and even Leicester players) who wanted to immortalise the historic feat by inking various parts of their body and Scott and co were very happy to oblige.

Scott left Forest to join Conference outfit Barnet on 9 September 2004 and three weeks later made his debut in a 3-1 Football League Trophy victory over Stevenage. This was the first of 31 appearances Scott made in a hugely successful campaign as the club romped to the Conference title 12 points ahead of their nearest rival Hereford United. Promotion

©www.paulkylephotography.com

to League Two offered Scott the League football he craved but in Scott and Ross Flitney, Manager Paul Fairclough had two evenly matched keepers at his disposal and he struggled to identify his preferred number one. Scott was between the sticks for the opening League encounters but Ross was handed the job more frequently as the season progressed. On October 26 2005 Ross was selected for the biggest game in the club's history - a League Cup match opposing Manchester United at Old Trafford. Scott was understandably gutted to be on the bench but, in a twist of fate, with less than two minutes on the clock, Flitney was adjudged to have handled the ball when outside his box and the ref gave him his marching orders. Flitney's loss was Scott's gain and although the Red Devils were the victors by a 4-1 scoreline, his Theatre of Dreams nightmare turned into a memorable experience for the 22-year old. After making a single additional appearance for the Bees, Scott left Underhill Stadium in a deal which took him to Rushden and Diamonds on 19 January 2006. Manager Barry Hunter threw him straight into action and he kept a clean sheet in a 3-0 defeat of Oxford - a rare victory in a disappointing campaign. Scott appeared in the final 14 games of the season but was powerless to prevent the Diamonds from finishing bottom of League Two and suffering relegation to the Conference. However, for the first couple of months of 2006/07 Scott remained in League Two after being loaned out to Hereford. Whilst with the Bulls, he helped the club upset the League Cup apple cart by knocking Championship outfit Coventry City out of the competition by a scoreline of 3-1.

Former Spurs keeper Nicky Eyre had been a close-season Rushden recruit but, when Scott was called back to Nene Park from his loan, he reclaimed his position and featured in 24 of the club's remaining fixtures as they finished 12th. It had been a turbulent year on and off the pitch and before the next season was underway, Scott's contract was terminated by mutual consent. It was around this time that Scott picked up the first of two Four Nations Trophy winners medals. In the 2007 tournament he played for England C in consecutive 3-0 victories over Wales and hosts Scotland and the following year helped the nation retain the trophy in Wales.

In July 2007 Scott joined Ebbsfleet before concluding his career with spells at Northwich Victoria, Salford City and Vauxhall Motors. He made in excess of 200 appearances and would surely have added to that tally had he not sustained a serious cruciate injury in 2009. After retiring, he worked as a goalkeeping coach in local grassroots football and in May 2010 opened his first tattoo studio in Liverpool. The business has since expanded and is going from strength to strength. However, if there is ever a slump in trade, it's nothing Leicester City lifting the FA Cup couldn't put right - which they managed to do on the 15 April 2021!!

ANTHONY GERRARD

In the 2012 Carling Cup Final penalty shootout, Anthony Gerrard missed the last spot kick which meant that Liverpool walked away with the trophy. However, it should be pointed out that of the ten penalties taken on the day, only five were converted. In addition, a survey conducted in 2021 showed that of 100,000 penalties taken around the globe during a ten year period, more than 25,000 did not result in a goal. That may be scant consolation to Anthony but it does offer some perspective.

Right, that's addressed the elephant in the room, so let's now concentrate upon the other 500+ appearances Anthony made in an excellent career which spanned 16 seasons.

Born on 6 February 1986, the ex-Thomas Beckett pupil joined Everton's setup aged just eight and in May 2004 he was rewarded for his efforts with a professional contract. David Moyes sent young Ant out on loan to Accrington Stanley for whom he made half a dozen Conference appearances before returning to his parent club. On 12 February 2005, Anthony got the closest he would come to making a first team appearance for the Blues when he took his place on the bench against champions-elect Chelsea.

on 24 March he joined Walsall on loan and made his Football League debut two days later in a 1-0 reversal opposing Oldham Athletic. So impressed was player/manager Paul Merson with the loanee during his 8-game spell at the Bescot Stadium, that he paved the way for Anthony to permanently join the Saddlers on 18 May 2005. In his first full season, Anthony's 41 appearances secured him the Player of the Year award but the 2005/06 campaign was disastrous for the club from the West Midlands as they suffered relegation to League Two. Anthony received another Player of the Year award at the conclusion of the 2007/08 campaign and sandwiched between the two gongs was a return to League One when they pipped Hartlepool to the title by a single point.

Anthony's performances attracted the attention of managers higher up the league ladder and on 2 July 2009 Walsall accepted the inevitable when Cardiff Manager Dave Jones took him to the new Cardiff City Stadium for a reported fee of £200,000. Thrown straight into action, Anthony slotted into his new Championship environment seamlessly as the Bluebirds disposed of Scunthorpe Utd 4-0 on the opening day of the season in front of a crowd of 22,264 - the club's biggest attendance since 1971. His 47 appearances helped the club to their highest ever Championship finish (4th) and a place in the playoffs where, on 22 May 2010, they lost a close-fought Wembley final to Blackpool 3-2.

Anthony was out of favour at the start of the following campaign and moved to Hull City on a season long loan. Unusually, his debut for The Tigers was against Cardiff on 11 September 2010 with the Bluebirds coming out on top 2-0. Once again, Anthony picked up the Player of the Year award after his 42 appearances and five goals helped the club to a mid-table Championship finish. Anthony returned to Cardiff who, in his absence, had again finished fourth and failed in their bid to gain promotion. The 2011/12 campaign proved to be Anthony's last in a Cardiff shirt and the missed penalty in that season's League Cup Final his last kick for them as he struggled to hit it off with new boss Malky MacKay.

On 8 August 2012, he signed for Huddersfield Town and added a further 91 appearances to his tally during a three-season stay. After half a dozen loan games for Oldham, Anthony moved to Shrewsbury Town and put in 15 Salop appearances before returning to Oldham on 25 January 2016. Struggling at the wrong end of the table, Anthony was immediately installed in the starting lineup to shore up a leaky defence. His 18 rocksteady appearances ensured the club accumulated sufficient points to comfortably stave off the threat of relegation. However, although Ant got an additional 51 Athletic games under his belt, a well-publicised spat with the club's owners resulted in Anthony's departure from Boundary Park. On 21 December 2019, Anthony Gerrard called time on an excellent 541-game career following a season at Carlisle Utd and 11 games with Chesterfield of the National League.

NEIL ASHTON

Neil Ashton could be described as one of football's 'nearly men' - he NEARLY won automatic promotion, he NEARLY won two play-off semi-finals, he NEARLY won two play-off Finals and he NEARLY won the Johnstone's Paints Trophy. However, it would be grossly unfair to label Neil or his career as a failure. In order for a team or an individual player to be within touching distance of success, it is often necessary to have already achieved a great deal. Cup Finals and play-off matches are only reached after a long, arduous season or a series of safely negotiated cup-ties. The fact that Neil 'only' possesses one winner's medal (for the FA Trophy) may leave him with a slightly bitter taste in his mouth but his extensive career should be looked back on with a great sense of pride.

Born on 15 January 1985, Neil grew up living in Campbell Drive in the Swanside area of Huyton. He played his early football with mates in nearby Dovecot Park and the Clifford Holroyde Special School playing fields. He recalls strategically positioning a plank of wood across the top of a couple of trees to form a makeshift goal for the football-mad youngsters. Neil attended Malvern County Primary School and under the guidance of teacher Miss Kneale their team twice reached the Merseyside 7-a-side Final. He remembers proudly striding out onto the Anfield turf in a pristine new kit and tracksuit donated to the school by local businessman Ray O'Brien. Although both games ended in defeat for Malvern, it was a fantastic experience for Reds fan Neil. The Knowsley Boys team Manager selected him for the representative side that won the Merseyside Youth Games tournament and so impressed was Liverpool Coach Hughie McAuley that he invited Neil to train at Melwood. Hughie's grandson played for crack junior side Keyways FC, managed by Martin Waldron, future Head of Recruitment at Everton's Academy. Hughie arranged for Neil to turn out for the Kirkby-based team and, playing alongside future Premiership players Leighton Baines and Ryan Taylor, he helped the team sweep aside all before them to win a succession of trophies. Tranmere Rovers Scout Ronnie Taylor subsequently recruited the Keyways trio and fellow teammate Kevin McCormack and Neil loved midweek training and weekend matches. His proud mum, who has travelled the length and breadth of the country to watch him play, often assumed the role of chauffeur to take Neil to training and games.

At the tender of 14, Neil became the youngest ever player to appear for Tranmere's B team and graduated impressively through the ranks of Dave Watson's youth set up. He maintained his involvement in schools' football and in 2001 was a member of the Merseyside team which won the ESFA under-16s County Trophy defeating Oxfordshire in the Final. Two years later, after signing a full-time pro contract, Neil set his sights on a place in the first team. Unfortunately, largely due to regular left back Gareth Roberts avoiding injury and consistently performing to a high standard, this was easier said than done. However, on 10 October 2004 in the 90th minute of an away match at Griffin Park versus Brentford, Manager Brian Little pulled Neil from the bench to replace David Beresford. The game was watched by 4,105 spectators, finished 2-2 and although he only touched the ball once Neil had joined the ranks of footballers who have appeared in an English Football League game. The young Rover was elated and remembers the congratulatory pats on the back he received from his fellow players who understood the significance of the moment. Having made the breakthrough, he was hungry to get more games under his belt but soon realised that in order to do so he may have to leave Prenton Park.

Shrewsbury Town's recently-appointed Boss Gary Peters had been an admirer of Neil's cultured, left footed play since seeing him play for Tranmere against his Preston North End youth side. In a loan deal which suited all parties, Neil joined the Shrews on 9 December 2004 until the end of the season. Two days later with 3,219 present (although Neil recalls the noise generated by the crowd made it feel like there were 20,000 packed into Chester City's Deva stadium) he made his full League debut. With nine yellow cards and three players sent off, the 1-1 draw was a baptism of fire for Neil. He acquitted himself well and went on to make a further 23 appearances before his loan period ended. Neil really enjoyed his spell at Gay Meadow and the feeling was mutual, so much so that before the 2005/06 season had kicked off the move had become permanent. Having finished the previous campaign just above the relegation places, Neil's first full season at the club was a vast improvement. They finished 10th in League Two with Neil making 49 appearances. He scored his first League goal - a sweet 68th minute volley from outside the box - in a 3-1 home victory over Darlington. The 2006/07 season saw the club continue to progress under Peters and by finishing seventh they secured a place in the play-offs. A 2-1 semi-final defeat of MK Dons meant that Neil fulfilled a childhood Wembley dream. On 26 May 2007 a 61,589 record attendance for a game at this level watched on as they faced Bristol Rovers in the Final. Neil got the team off to a flying start when in the third minute he set up a chance for Stuart Drummond which he duly converted. However, the Pirates won the day and a place in the third tier of English football when they scored three goals to break the Shrews' hearts. Neil played 52 games that season so it came as something of a surprise when after just 16 games of the 2007/08 campaign he left the club to join lowly Macclesfield Town on loan.

Shrewsbury's loss was the Silkmen's gain. With new Manager Paul Simpson in charge, poor performances, disappointing results and an 18th place finish in the table displaced Shrewsbury's recent optimism. Whereas, although Macclesfield were a place below Neil's parent club at the end of the season, this represented 'mission accomplished' for Neil because when he joined the Moss Road club they were favourites to be relegated out of the Football League. Sensibly, Simpson recalled Neil to his ranks for the 2008/09 season and a largely successful campaign saw them return to the play-off Final at Wembley. Gillingham provided the opposition on 23 May 2009 and although Shrewsbury had thrashed the Gills 7-0 earlier in the season there was to be no repeat of the scoreline or result. A controversial last-minute goal by Simeon Jackson handed Gillingham a 1-0 victory and promotion. This proved to be a hugely disappointing final game for Neil at a club where he had spent five enjoyable years and it signalled the start of a precarious period in his career.

Neil had been made aware of how cruel football can be when his older brother Stephen's promising Manchester City career was brought to a premature end due to injury. Worryingly, aged just 24 Neil now found himself released by Shrewsbury and without a club. On 1 August 2009 he dropped out of the Football League to join Conference side Chester City which unbeknownst to Neil was a club in financial turmoil. Ultimately, this and other factors resulted in the club's expulsion from the Conference. However, in unusual circumstances these difficulties would lead to Neil embarking upon the most enjoyable spell of his career. Because he spent a great deal of his time at Chester on the treatment table, Neil took on the role of spokesman for the players when they were at loggerheads with the club over unpaid wages. One TV interview was broadcast on BBC Sport and seen by fellow Huytonian and Wrexham striker Andy Mangan. The following morning Neil received a visit from Mangy who, acting on

©rickmatthews.zenfolio.com

behalf of Manager Dean Saunders, offered Neil a footballing lifeline at the Racecourse. So began a five-season, 241-game relationship with a club whose fans took Neil to their hearts as he gave his all for the cause. This would not have been possible had it not been for the support, patience, treatment and rehabilitation Neil received after a hernia operation. He remains extremely grateful to Wrexham teammate Gareth Taylor, physio Ritson Lloyd and fitness coach Mal Purchase who all helped him on his difficult journey back to full fitness.

In his first season the Dragons finished in the play-off places but progress to the Final was denied them by Luton Town. Despite accumulating a massive 98 points the following campaign, they finished second to narrowly miss automatic promotion to the Football League. Luton Town were again their nemesis, winning the two-legged semi-final 3-2. However, on a personal level, Neil picked up the Fans Player of the Year award which slightly softened the disappointment.

It is probably fair to describe Neil's experiences in the 2012/13 season as 'bittersweet' due to a combination of successes and disappointments. He had been installed as the team's regular penalty taker and was deadly from the spot which helped him return his best goals tally of nine. This included two goals in one game against Stockport County - although he received his marching orders from the ref for his over-exuberant celebrations! He was then Man of the Match and scored in the 92nd minute of an FA Trophy semi-final which they won 4-3 on aggregate. However, due to injury he missed the Wembley Final in which the team overcame Grimsby Town (although because he had played in every round of the competition he qualified to receive a winners' medal). Six weeks later on 5 May 2013, the club were back at Wembley and this time Neil was fit enough to play in the Conference play-off Final after scoring in both legs of the semi-final. It was a massive game with a place in the Football League at stake and the opposition provided by Newport County made it an all-Welsh Final. Two late County goals in the 86th and 94th minutes handed them the prize and shattered Neil and Wrexham's promotion dreams again. Neil played exactly 100 games in his remaining two seasons at Wrexham and included a defeat on penalties in the FA Trophy Final at the hands of North Ferriby United.

In July 2015 Neil left the Robins after it became apparent that he did not figure in new Manager Gary Mills' plans - much to the bemusement of the Wrexham faithful. He turned out for Barrow and Southport before joining Welsh outfits Cefn Druids and three years later Llandudno FC. Married to Natalie, Neil still lives in Huyton with their two children Isabella and Franco and will be able to proudly tell them all about his excellent career. To underline Neil's achievement, it is fair to state that since the game of football was invented, many young amateur footballers up and down the country have tried to graduate to the professional ranks but failed to do so - although many will tell you that they NEARLY did!

©rickmatthews.zenfolio.com

170

SPENCER WHELAN

Another St Annes Rovers success, Spencer Whelan was attached to Liverpool as a schoolboy and became an apprentice in 1988 at 17-years of age. Two years later he was devastated to receive the news that the Reds were releasing him. However, Chester City Manager Harry McNally wasted no time in snapping up the 6'2" defender's services on 3 April 1990.

After making his debut from the bench in a 2-0 defeat at the hands of Bolton Wanderers on 3 November 1990, Spencer first appeared in the starting eleven in the third round of the FA Cup. Bournemouth were the visitors to Sealand Road on 5 January 1991 and inflicted a 3-2 defeat upon the Seals. Initially, Spencer was utilised as a fullback with McNally reluctant to disrupt his established central defensive partnership of Graham Abel and Chris Lightfoot. When Abel left the club in 1993 not only did Spencer make the centre-half position his own, he also took ownership of the captain's armband. The 1993/94 season was a particularly good campaign for Chester City and Spencer. The club finished second in the table to secure automatic promotion to Division Two with Spencer cementing his place in the side. By contrast, he sustained a broken leg, was sidelined for the majority of the following season and was helpless to prevent their immediate return to the lower division.

Spencer spent in excess of eight years at Chester before Manager Kevin Ratcliffe accepted a bid of £35,000 from Shrewsbury Town to take him to Gay Meadow. He had been out of action for a considerable time and his injuries restricted him to just 28 Shrews appearances before calling time on his career. At just 29 years of age it was a disappointing, premature end to Spencer Whelan's playing days but he registered 272 games and scored 11 goals during a decade of professional football. Ironically, his last ever game was a 0-0 stalemate on 11 March 2000 with Shrewsbury Town's opposition provided by Chester City!

Footynote:

On 19 June 2021 Spencer Whelan passed away. He was just 49-years of age. RIP Spencer

LEE TRUNDLE

Lee Trundle plays football in the same way he lives life - with a smile on his face. Whether playing as a youngster for Huyton Labour on Jubilee Park, or as a seasoned pro for Swansea City at Cardiff's Millennium Stadium, his attitude towards the game has never changed. It may have taken him until his mid-20s to truly dedicate himself to the game but his journey prior to that was where he honed the skills which led to international manager and former teammate Roberto Martinez describing him as "a Premiership player in a lower league side". Whilst it is true that players of lesser ability than Lee progressed through the ranks to play at a higher level, it is also a distinct possibility that his route to the pro game allowed him to avoid the interference of coaches who may have suppressed his natural flair.

Born on 10 October 1976, Lee played his early football on the streets surrounding the family's Huyton home in Ashbury Road, Page Moss. Forever practicing his tricks and skills, even a trip to the local shops would include a ball stuck to his foot. Eagle Juniors were Lee's first proper team and under Manager Mick Duffy they hardly lost a match - unsurprising, with Lee and future Chester striker John Murphy leading the attack. Aged 16, he took part in Knowsley Council's Dallas trip which, competing against top sides from all over the world, gave him an insight into how professional clubs operate. Although Lee had numerous opportunities to get involved with Football League clubs - Liverpool, Everton, PNE, Charlton and Bolton courted him - he preferred to play with his mates for local sides Quiet Man, Dovecot and the Doms and, in turn, for amateur clubs around the North West. Occasionally, mercurial footballers emerge who are able to bamboozle the opposition with their flicks and tricks but lack an end product. Lee, on the other hand, could mesmerise whilst also scoring a bagful of goals. These qualities enabled him to effortlessly climb the football pyramid via Burscough, Chorley, Stalybridge Celtic, Southport, Bamber Bridge and Rhyl as he rattled home 85 goals from 194 appearances from his time in the North West Counties, Unibond, Conference and Welsh Premier leagues. During his brief spell at Bamber Bridge, Lee's life changed forevermore when he became a father to daughter Brooke. Almost immediately he decided that, in order to meet his parental responsibilities, he would give himself the best possible chance to have a successful career in football.

By the start of the 2000/01 season, he had secured a transfer to Rhyl and, playing under his old Staylbridge boss Brian Kettle, he excelled. Fitter, faster, stronger and with the added motivation of fatherhood, Lee found the back of the net 15 times from 18 appearances before Christmas. When Brian Flynn brought his Wrexham side to Rhyl for a friendly at the start of 2001, Lee rattled home a hat trick within the opening 20 minutes which rubber stamped a £60,000 move to the Racecourse. Although he had never applied himself sufficiently to do so, Lee always harboured dreams of becoming a League footballer. On 17 February 2001, less than nine months after becoming a dad and vowing to give it his best shot, the dream became a reality. He made his debut as an 85th minute sub in a 1-0 home victory over Colchester and followed that up a week later with a dream full debut. Losing 2-0 to Walsall with 60 minutes on the clock, Lee instinctively sprung into action. With his back to goal, he took the ball on his chest before scooping it past the keeper with an audacious bicycle kick. A Kevin Russell equaliser was followed by a last minute winner, set up by Trunds. Not only had his performance convinced those in attendance that he was a special talent, it also reassured Lee that he could compete at this level without having to make dramatic changes to the way he played the game.

To the delight of the Wrexham faithful, he scored in each of his next four appearances, including a hat trick in a 5-3 defeat of Oxford Utd. He finished the campaign with eight goals from 14 appearances as the club finished 10th in League One. Disappointingly, Flynn left the club and the 2001/02 season ended in relegation for the Red Dragons although Lee established himself in the side with ten goals. They bounced straight back to League One the following year but it proved to be Lee's last campaign in a Wrexham shirt. The club had allowed his contract to run down and his record since joining of 33 goals and numerous assists combined with the manner of his play, resulted in a number of clubs seeking his signature.

Port Vale and Tranmere were serious contenders but on 8 July 2003 he put pen to a one-year contract with Swansea City. The swaying factor in his decision to join the Swans was Manager Brian Flynn. Having worked together previously, Flynny knew what made Lee tick and how to get the best out of him. It was a gamble for Lee though - Swansea had narrowly avoided relegation from the Football League the previous campaign - but the move felt right and so it proved. A relationship which is still thriving today kicked off with a 4-2 victory over Bury on the opening day of the 2003/04 season with Lee opening his account with a header. In the next match a stunning Trunds hat trick to drag the team from 3-1 down to a 4-3 defeat of Cheltenham further endeared him to the Jack Army and the relationship continued to blossom as the season progressed. Lee's tally of 22 goals in all competitions not only helped the club to a much-improved 10th place but ensured he was named by his peers in the League Two PFA team of the year.

He also received national recognition from an unlikely but welcome source. Cult television programme Soccer AM included a weekly roundup of the best bits of skill in televised games. It was unusual for a player from League Two to be included but Lee's 'shoulder roll' (which involved chesting the ball, rolling it across the top of his back, over his shoulder and dropping it onto his foot whilst pirouetting to face goal) made a massive impression on the viewing public. Lee's irrepressible character shone when he was repeatedly invited onto the programme and his 'showboating' became a regular feature of the programme.

When Flynny left Swansea before the end of the season, Lee was naturally gutted. He had been one of the main reasons he had joined the club and was concerned that just as Wrexham had struggled after his departure, the Swans may suffer a similar fate. However, former Watford player Kenny Jackett was installed as his replacement and in his first full season and with Lee leading the line superbly with 23 goals, they secured automatic promotion to League One. The 2005/06 campaign was massive for both the club and Lee. Not before time, Swansea had moved to a new ground (the Liberty Stadium) and Lee was determined to do his bit to light up his impressive new stage and prove he could handle the step up in class. He turned to Huyton Boxing Club to try a new fitness regime and it worked a treat.

By the time the new season kicked off he was chomping at the bit and hit the ground running with ten goals from the opening ten games and the team were flying. Trunds' season tally of 21 goals whilst impressive didn't tell the full story. In the second half of the campaign the team began to struggle and Lee's goals dried up. Uncharacteristically, the only time he found the net in his last 15 appearances was in the Football League Trophy Final - although it was arguably his finest ever strike. On 2 April 2006 at the Millennium Stadium, the 42,028 present witnessed a stunning third minute volley from Lee which set the Swans up for a 2-1 defeat of Carlisle to secure the silverware. Whilst this was a great achievement, the club had their sights set on the bigger prize of promotion. After their blistering start, the wheels fell off and they went from certs for automatic promotion to struggling to make the play-offs. However, thanks to four Leon Knight goals on the last day of the season in a 4-0 defeat of Chesterfield, they finished sixth to secure the final play-off place. Brentford were disposed of in the semis to set up a battle with Barnsley for promotion to the Championship. Trunds' dip in form had resulted in him being in and out of the side and for their return to the Millennium on 27 May 2006 he occupied a place on the Swans bench. Barnsley took the lead but Swansea bounced back to turn the game to 2–1 in their favour. However, the Tykes restored parity and the game finished 2-2. Lee had joined the action in the 69th minute but, despite having a couple of half-chances, was unable to make the breakthrough. The outcome was decided by penalties and although Lee dispatched his spot kick, it was the Barnsley fans in the crowd of 55,419 who were ultimately celebrating the victory and looking forward to life in the Championship.

As is often the case in these circumstances, Swansea suffered a hangover from the defeat which lasted for the majority of the following season, cost Jackett his job and resulted in Roberto Martinez beginning his managerial career at the club he had served so well as a player. Lee enjoyed playing under his former teammate and his four goals in the final five games of a difficult campaign took his tally to 20 from 40 appearances but the club fell three points short of a play-off place.

When, in 1995, Lee had signed for Unibond outfit Chorley, manager Dave Sutton had predicted that Lee would one day become a £1 million player. Few believed him but that is exactly what happened on 2 August 2007 when he joined Championship side Bristol City. It was a massive wrench to leave the Liberty but the final game of the 2006/07 season was not his Swans swansong - he would return.

Lee made his Robins debut on 11 August 2007 in a 2-2 draw with QPR but it soon became apparent that he and Bristol were not a good fit. Lee had thrived throughout his career on playing for managers who, on the whole, appreciated and played to his strengths and forgave his weaknesses. However, under Gary Johnson, Lee was asked to contribute in areas of the pitch where he was unable to hurt the opposition and whilst he kept his head down and attempted to fulfil his brief, it was never going to work. Lee made 41 appearances during the 2007/08 campaign but 16 of these were from the bench. However, it wasn't all doom and gloom. He chipped in with six goals including a strike versus Crystal Palace in the play-off semi-final which helped secure a day on the hallowed turf of Wembley with a place in the Premiership the reward to the victorious team. The crowd of 86,703 contained 50 of Lee's mates from Page Moss all proudly wearing their 'Trundle' shirts. Unfortunately, it was their opponents Hull City, courtesy of a Dean Windass goal, whose dream came true whilst Lee was again left with the sinking feeling of disappointment he had experienced versus Barnsley a couple of years earlier.

Trunds was still a City player for the opening few months of the 2008/09 campaign but was desperate to get away from Ashton Gate after his relationship with Johnson broke down beyond repair. A brief ten-game, one-goal period with Leeds Utd was followed by a briefer return to Bristol. He was given just 13 minutes of game time in a relatively meaningless match against Sheffield Wednesday which brought the curtain down on the first disappointing spell of Lee's career. Although the move to Bristol proved to be a financial boon, in some respects leaving Swansea had been a mistake. Trunds was therefore delighted when, on 28 August 2009, he returned to the Liberty and the club which means so much to him.

During a four-month loan period he made two starts, came off the bench on 18 occasions and found the back of the net five times. His bond with the fans was as strong as ever and in 2013 he was thrilled to be appointed as the club's first Ambassador - a position he still holds. However, his playing career after leaving the Swans in June 2010 was far from over. In addition to a brief dalliance with Preston, for whom he made two sub appearances, he played non-league football for Chester City and Marine. But it is in South Wales where he really continued to thrive as he has broken numerous goal scoring records and enjoyed every minute. He returned to the Welsh Premier League when he joined Neath and his record of 26 goals from 59 games was extremely impressive. Following a brief retirement, in 2016 he dug out his shooting boots again to sign for Llanelli Town of Welsh Division Two. He put them to good use with a debut hat trick and, remarkably, added a further eight hat tricks as they did the league and cup double. Back-to-back promotions were secured as Lee's two seasons and 59 appearances returned 86 goals. Due to his ambassadorial commitments with Swansea, he left Llanelli before joining Haverfordwest and scoring four on his debut. Nowadays, Lee continues to fulfil his love of playing by turning out in the lower divisions of Welsh football. He combines this with doing what he has always done best - putting a smile on the faces of Swansea's doting football family - and long may it continue.

©Athena Picture Agency

FRANK GAMBLE

Born on 21 August 1961, Frank Gamble's senior football career began in earnest when he turned out for St Dominics. His exciting wing play and eye for goal attracted the attention of a Burscough Scout who lured him away from Page Moss to join the Linnets of the Cheshire League. Dazzling performances for the side from West Lancashire resulted in Frank going on loan to Derby County in March 1981 to enable Manager Colin Addison to take a close look at him. Obviously impressed, he signed Gamble on a permanent deal a couple of months later. Frank made his Rams debut on 26 September 1981 in a Second Division home fixture versus Queens Park Rangers in front of a crowd of 11,246. A Kevin Hector brace plus a single strike from Alan Ramage secured a 3-1 victory. During a three-year spell at the Baseball Ground opportunities were rare. Frank made just eight appearances finding the net in games against Charlton Athletic and QPR.

After joining Barrow AFC in November 1984, he returned to Football League action with Fourth Division Rochdale, managed by former Sunderland striker and FA Cup winner Vic Hallom. He became a crowd favourite at Spotland playing alongside fellow Huytonians Ronnie Moore and Shaun Reid. Considering he was utilised down the flank, his record of nine goals from 46 appearances was an impressive return. However, Hallom baffled the Dale faithful by signing winger Dave Mossman, effectively showing Frank the door. After turning out for Northern Premier League outfits Barrow and Morecambe, he ended his career with a couple of mid-table seasons at Southport's Haigh Avenue. Frank's 55th and final appearance for the Sandgrounders took place on New Year's Eve 1988 in a 1-0 defeat at the hands of Rhyl in front of a crowd of 414.

Many people believe that with the talent Frank undoubtedly possessed, his career should have involved more games, goals and success but football did occupy a significant chunk of a decade of his life giving him significant memories and hopefully few regrets.

TONY HIBBERT

From an early age similar to many local youngsters, Tony Hibbert was a keen fisherman and would regularly spend hour after hour at Prescot's Carr Lane fishing pond. Nowadays, the man who made 329 appearances for Everton is more likely to be interviewed by a reporter from the Angling Times than someone from Match of the Day.

Born in Mill Road Hospital on 20 February 1981, Tony spent the first year of his life living on Huyton's Mosscroft estate before his mum and dad moved to Cartmel Close in the nearby Woolfall Heath area. He attended St Aloysius School and when his dad Paul was playing for the Allies or Dovecot football teams Tony would be there along with the other players' kids participating in their own little match on the touchline. It wasn't long before St Annes Rovers Manager Kevin Connor was picking young Hibbo for his U-6s team, followed by Barney Muldoon and his U-8s team Town Villa. Tony was initially a forward with a great goal-scoring record and it was around this time that he first caught the eye of an Everton Scout.

After a game in St Helens, Hibbo snr was approached to invite his son to attend a trial with the Blues. After seeking the advice of friends who had been in a similar situation, Paul decided Tony was a little too young and that he should just continue enjoying his footy with his mates. Local manager, scout and radio pundit Ronnie Taylor snapped up Tony for his Denburn Utd U-11s and installed him as captain. With Hibbo spearheading the attack and grabbing a bagful of goals, he led the team to many trophies including the prestigious Keele International Cup. Ronnie felt that Tony was now ready to take the plunge and Paul agreed. He attended a trial with Tranmere Rovers but, although Tony did well, he was not overly impressed with the club's setup and did not pursue it further. However, when Everton's Bob Pendleton encouraged him to reconsider attending Bellefield, he was successful where his Blues scouting colleague had previously failed.

Tony loved training on Tuesday and Thursday evenings and playing for his beloved Toffees at the weekend. When coach Ray Hall dropped him back into central midfield alongside Leon Osman the duo stuck up an excellent partnership which was a match for any opposition. In 1995 the junior Blues entered the Dale Farm Milk Cup - a tournament organised by the Irish FA which attracts clubs from all over the world. Fresh from FA Cup success, Everton Boss Joe Royle officially opened the competition. He wished all of the clubs well but wore his heart on his sleeve by stating that he hoped the young Toffees could emulate the first team and bring home the silverware. It was a big ask but after sweeping aside Walsall and three Irish teams in the early rounds, a semi-final Hibbo goal accounted for Hearts to set up an Everton v Norwich City Final. A few months earlier, Royle's side had thrashed the Canaries 5-0 en-route to lifting the FA Cup and although the outcome was ultimately the same, this contest was a much tighter affair. On 28 July 1995 at the Coleraine Showground following a hard-fought 2-2 draw, Everton eventually overcame Norwich 4-3 on penalties much to Tony and Big Joe's delight.

Hibbo was progressing nicely through the ranks and in 1998 he was a member of Colin Harvey's Youth Cup winning squad. In front of the Sky Sports cameras and a Goodison Park crowd of 15,258, they drew the second leg of the Final 2-2 but having already won the first game 3-1, they overcame Blackburn Rovers to lift the trophy for the first time since 1984. With his sights set on breaking into the first team, Tony did his claims for consideration no harm when in 2000/01 he played a major part in helping the club's second string win the Northern Section of the FA Premier Reserve League. He played in 19 of their 22 fixtures as they became champions – something they had not achieved for more than 30 years. Perhaps significantly, they lost two of the three games that Tony missed but his absence from the reserves was due to his promotion to the first team squad.

On 31 March 2001 Blues Boss Walter Smith had no qualms about drafting Tony into the side for his Football League debut as a replacement for the injured Richard Gough. West Ham United provided the opposition and Hibbo showed his mettle when, in the 45th minute of the game, he threw himself into a full-blooded penalty box challenge with Hammers formidable fullback Stuart Pearce. The veteran hardman recklessly conceded a penalty and received his marching orders for his part in the clash. David Unsworth converted the pen and Niklas Alexandersson added a second goal to get Tony's career off to a winning start and to endear him to the Blues fans. After a few introductions from the bench, Tony made his first start of the following campaign in a 1-0 defeat to Blackburn Rovers. Results were not going well for Everton and Smith paid the price when he was shown the door before the end of the season.

On 16 March 2002 the club installed David Moyes as his replacement and a couple of days later he turned to reserves boss Andy Holden to name the starting line-up for a home fixture versus Fulham. Up to this point in his career, Hibbo had been utilised as a midfielder but Holden boldly selected him as a fullback which, apart from the occasional appearance at centre-half, was the position he occupied for the rest of his playing days. Having seen Tony at close quarters, Holden was confident that Hibbo was ready to slot into Moyes' team and the new man at the top obviously concurred. Tony pulled on the royal blue jersey on 25 occasions during the following campaign as he began to cement his place in the side which finished in a much-improved seventh place in the table. A disappointing 2003/04 was succeeded by their best

©George Herringshaw

season for some years with Tony appearing 36 times. They secured fourth place and qualified for European competition signalling the start of Tony Hibbert's journey into the Goodison Park record books. On 9 August 2005 Spanish outfit Villarreal were the visitors to L4 for the first leg of a UEFA Champions League third qualifying round match. This was Tony's first taste of European competition and during his 16 seasons with the Toffees he featured in a further 23 European games making him the club's record appearance-maker at that time. Goodison legends Colin Harvey and Brian Labone each featured in 19 European games and Tony matched that achievement on 17 September 2009 in a brilliant 4-0 home victory over AEK Athens. He surpassed their total on 17 December of the same year when he was handed the captaincy to face FC Bate Borisov.

In the decade before Moyes' arrival, the club had only enjoyed a top-ten finish once. At the end of his ten full seasons in the Goodison hot seat, they had found themselves in 4th, 5th twice, 6th twice, 7th three times, 8th and 11th. In addition, Moyes took the club to the FA Cup Final in 2009 where, after taking the lead in the 25th second of the match, they lost 2-1 to Chelsea. Tony was at the heart of the team's transformation and he received a resounding endorsement from Moyes in the Liverpool Echo on 31 March 2011 when he said "As long as I'm here, Tony Hibbert and Leon Osman will be here......I know if I put Hibbo in he'll never let me down, he always gives me his best." True to his word, Moyes continued to involve Tony in his squad right up until he departed Goodison to take up the Manchester Utd Manager's job. Tony was the only surviving player from his first game in charge when, in a 2-0 victory over West Ham Utd on 17 May 2013, Moyes brought him off the bench to join the action in the last minute of his last home game before his departure to Old Trafford.

The 2012/13 season had started well for Tony. On 8 August 2012 a decade of loyal service to Everton was acknowledged by the club with a Testimonial game. He proudly strode onto the Goodison Park turf holding daughter Halle's hand under a guard of honour from his teammates and the evening's opponents, AEK Athens - the team against whom he had equalled the Toffees' European appearance record. As part of Everton's pre-season fixtures, this was a seriously competitive match and new signing Steven Naismith enjoyed an excellent debut with a hat-trick. However, Hibbo's dramatic contribution to the game overshadowed that of the Scottish striker. As a trusted member of Moyes' resolute rear-guard, Tony's priority had always been to defend. The fact that he did not score a single first class goal for the Toffees did not matter a jot to him. Contrarily, the media latched on to the fact and the fans turned the situation into good-hearted banter with chants, banners and even a Facebook group 'Hibbert Scores, We Riot.' In the 53rd minute of the game the ref awarded Everton a free kick at the Gwladys Street end of the ground and Tony stepped forward. Pienaar touched the ball to Baines, Baines teed it up for Tony who smashed the ball through the six-man wall and beyond the Greek keeper – cue the long-awaited riot and scenes that will stay long in the memory of Tony, his family and the 17,508 fans present.

Following Moyes' departure and the arrival of his replacement Roberto Martinez from Wigan Athletic, Everton and Tony's fortunes dipped. After a bright start, the club slipped into mid-table obscurity and during four further seasons with the Toffees Hibbo managed just 16 appearances. This was largely due to a number of injuries, including a recurring groin problem and the emergence of young fullback Seamus Coleman who took his opportunity to fill in superbly. On 30 April 2016 Tony's appearance in a 2-1 home victory over Bournemouth proved to be his last game for the Blues. After his brilliant 26-year connection to Everton ended, Tony was linked with other clubs, most strongly Bolton Wanderers. However, he already had his plans mapped out. Three years earlier, Tony had purchased a 33-acre carp fishery, Lac De Premiere. It was a dream come true that can be traced back to the hours he had spent as a kid at the pond in Carr Lane.

Nowadays, if Tony is not at his Formby home with his wife Samantha, Halle or their other daughter Penelope, he is at his happiest when sitting on the banks of his lake in Northern France with a cup of coffee in one hand and a Pot Noodle in the other. During his excellent football career, Tony would pit his wits against some of the best wingers in the game and he was rarely found wanting. The challenge is now presented by carp of up to 70lbs in weight and whilst he may have had great difficulty making the net bulge as a player, he has no such problems as an angler.

PAUL FITZPATRICK

Paul Fitzpatrick's career as a professional footballer spanned 15 years during which time he played for eight English Football League clubs, one Scottish side, a Chinese outfit and eight non-league teams. He also dipped his toe in the water of management alongside a former European Cup winner and was there at the start of a top Premiership managers' journey.

Paul entered the world on 5 October 1965 in Oxford Street Hospital and grew up living in Steerscroft on the Cantril Farm estate. It was in the thriving Cantril Farm Junior Football League that he first cut his teeth playing for Steerscroft JFC under the watchful eye of Manager Tommy Fisher. Although Paul would later shoot up to be a strapping 6ft 4" centre half, he was a late developer. His early physique was more suited to him being a midfielder with a great turn of pace, good engine and a keen eye for goal. He won numerous trophies and medals whilst playing for Steerscroft, followed by Roby JFC in the West Derby U-14s League and enjoyed great success with his St Dominics School team. Paul is extremely grateful to taxi driver Jack Whittaker who was Manager of the Woodfarm Hey team. Every Tuesday and Thursday, he would give 16-year old Paul and Dave Higgins from Old Swan a lift in his cab over the water to Bebington Oval for training with the Tranmere youth and reserves teams.

Whilst Dave went on to enjoy an excellent career with Rovers, Paul's contract offer did not materialise so he began turning out for St Dominics and the Boundary pub team. However, when Liverpool Scout Jimmy Aspinall attended a Doms' game to check out centre-forward Kevin Harrison, Paul's overlapping, high-energy fullback play caught his eye. Jim wasted no time in seeking Mrs Fitzpatrick's permission to invite her son to a monthlong trial with the Reds. Paul loved getting picked up by the club's coach at Anfield and the journey to Melwood sitting alongside some of his heroes who were amongst the best players in Europe. During his trial he played in three victorious reserve team games and gave a good account of himself. However, this was Liverpool and 'good' wasn't 'good enough' so Chief Scout Geoff Twentyman broke the news that Manager Joe Fagan felt he was unlikely to break into the first team. This was hardly surprising considering that in one of the reserve games Liverpool had fielded nine full internationals!

It was not all doom and gloom though as Twentyman informed Paul that Bolton Wanderers Manager Charlie Wright wanted to take him to Burnden Park. On 1 March 1985, Paul put pen to paper on a two-year deal at Wanderers and made his debut a few weeks later. With 7,202 people present at The Den, Paul put in a Man of the Match performance but the Trotters were no match for promotion-bound Millwall who ran out 5-2 winners. He stayed in the team for the final three games of the season and made a further 11 appearances in the 85/86 campaign. However, following a terrible run of results in November, Wright left the club signalling the end of Paul's Bolton experience. Liverpool legend Phil Neal was appointed as the new boss, immediately installed himself at fullback making it time for Fitz to move on. As one door closed, another opened and former Leeds Utd and England player Terry Cooper who was Manager of Bristol City did not hesitate to snap him up and take him to Ashton Gate.

In an eventful couple of seasons with the Robins, Paul made 45 appearances and featured in a number of important games. On 24 May 1987, City faced Mansfield Town in the Freight Rover Trophy Final at Wembley. After the tightly-fought contest finished 1-1 after extra-time, the destination of the Trophy was determined by a penalty shoot-out. Paul had started the game on the bench but Cooper sent him on to join the

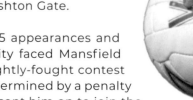

©Neville Chadwick Photography

action in the 115th minute. He was lined up to take a penalty if necessary but City's Gordon Owen and David Moyes failed with their attempts handing Mansfield the first major title in their lengthy history. The club narrowly missed a play-off place in his debut season but finished fifth following a solid 1987/88 campaign to win the right to pit their wits against Walsall to secure promotion. Sadly, the Saddlers defeated City in a replayed Final to join the ranks of Division Two. The club, and in particular Paul, fared better in the annual Gloucestershire Cup match which pitched together Bristol's two League clubs to compete for the Cup and local bragging rights. During his time at the club, Paul's side enjoyed the upper hand over Rovers in these games. He found the back of the net three times in these contests much to the delight of the City faithful with whom he always enjoyed a great rapport. Towards the end of the 87/88 season, Cooper left the club and Joe Jordan replaced him. Paul would also leave the southwest shortly after but not before he had helped one of his teammates to climb the first rungs of the managerial ladder.

Many of Paul's games for Bristol City were played alongside club captain David Moyes. They also shared a house together enabling a close bond to develop between the two which still exists. When Moyes invited Paul to give him a hand leading training sessions for local side Brunel Glazing he was more than happy to oblige. This may only have been in the fifth division of the Bristol Sunday League but it was the beginning of a journey which took Moyes to the top job at Preston, Everton, Man Utd, Real Sociedad, Sunderland and West Ham Utd.

The next stop on Paul's travels was Carlisle United, managed by former Bristol City Assistant Manager Clive Middlemass. The fee was £50,000 and over the next three seasons Paul ensured that it was money well spent by the Cumbrians. After a rocky start, which saw him spend a brief, two-game loan spell at PNE, he knuckled down to help drag the club up from the Football League's basement. Paul believes the visit of Liverpool in the third round of the FA Cup was a major turning point in the club's fortunes. On 7 January 1989, with 18,556 fans inside Brunton Park, Carlisle held their own against the Reds until John Barnes broke the deadlock in the 33rd minute of the game. Midfielder Steve McMahon added a brace in the latter stages of the game to seal a 3-0 victory but Paul's side gave a good account of themselves and were inspired by the experience. Carlisle subsequently enjoyed a great run of results and finished the season in a respectable 12th position. In addition, Paul scooped the club's Player of the Year award to bring the season to a satisfactory conclusion. Both the team and Paul carried this momentum into the following campaign. As the lynchpin of a resolute defence, he made 44 appearances to help propel the team to an 8th place finish. Again, Paul's performances over the season were acknowledged when he was proud to be included by his peers in the PFA Division Four Team of the Year. Unfortunately, the club failed to kick on from this and after three hugely enjoyable years Paul felt it was time to move on and turned down the offer of a new contract.

As a free agent there was a great deal of interest from clubs keen to secure Paul's services. Darlington Boss Brian Little sounded him out but although the former Aston Villa and England man impressed him, the trek to the North East did not. Paul also spent a week training with Leicester City but Manager David Pleat did not pursue his initial interest. Then, when Pleat was sacked by the Foxes and Little took over, everything stacked up nicely for Paul to belatedly join the club. In June 1991 he became Brian Little's first signing and played his first game alongside three other debutants in an opening day of the season Swindon Town stalemate. Paul got off to a flying start, finding the net in consecutive matches versus Grimsby Town and his old club Bristol City. Having only narrowly avoided relegation the previous year, Little's new-look side enjoyed a tremendous season and missed automatic promotion by just three points. They brushed aside Cambridge Utd 6-1 in the resultant play-off semi-final and Wembley, Blackburn Rovers and promotion to the top-flight beckoned. Although he had made 29 appearances and contributed a great deal along the way, Paul disappointingly was not included in the 13-man squad for the Final which Kenny Dalglish's Rovers won 1-0 courtesy of a Mike Newell penalty. As Little attempted to follow in Kenny's footsteps, he turned to the transfer market to bolster their playing staff. This further reduced Paul's playing opportunities and on 29 August 1992 he donned a Leicester kit for the last time in a 1-0 victory over Plymouth Argyle.

So began a turbulent period in Paul's career during which he played for four different clubs in less than a year. He was briefly reunited with former Boss Terry Cooper when he turned out on seven occasions for Birmingham City before joining Bury until the end of the season. Paul's nine appearances helped the Shakers reach the play-offs where they lost to York City who went on to beat Crewe and gain promotion to Division Two. At this time, Paul's former teammate David Moyes was nearing the end of his playing days and had progressed from coaching Brunel Glazing to occupying the Assistant Manager's position at Scottish First

Division club Hamilton Academicals. A telephone call from Moyes brought the central defensive partnership back together and Paul opened his Scottish experience with a defeat at the hands of Clyde. This was short-lived however, as Preston North End gave Moyes the player-coach opportunity he longed for in English Football and after just 18 games for the Accies, Paul followed him south of the border for a brief two-game dalliance with Northampton Town.

His time with the Cobblers was cut short by an exciting opportunity to travel to Hong Kong to take part in the newly formed Chinese League. Each participating club was allowed to recruit two foreign players to give the League a kick-start and, via the English PFA, Shenzhen FC had identified Paul as one of their targets. He jumped at the chance and was soon on the next available long haul flight to be acquainted with his new team. Paul settled in quickly and they romped to promotion and the China League Two title losing just one of their 14 games. Although it was a fantastic experience and one Paul is happy he accepted, he decided not to stay at the club when offered an extension to his contract. The following season Shenzhen again won the title to secure a place in the Chinese Jia-A League but homesick Paul had already returned to Leicestershire to be with his wife Yvonne and their young son James.

Paul's days of plying his trade in the Football League may have been behind him but still aged only 30, he had much more to offer the game. Brief spells with Rushden & Diamonds, Oadby Town and Leicester Utd preceded two promotion-winning seasons at Forest Green Rovers. He then accepted the difficult task of replacing Liverpool legend and TV pundit Mark Lawrenson as player-manager of Corby Town and coped admirably. After eight enjoyable months with the club, he joined Gresley Rovers where he was assistant to former Man Utd and England striker Gary Birtles. This was Birtles' first taste of management following a glittering playing career which had included winning the European Cup with Nottingham Forest. Paul combined his managerial responsibilities with making 42 appearances but after a bright start results went downhill and the duo left the club by mutual consent. Before calling it a day in 2001, Paul also had short spells with Kings Lynn and Workington Town where he played alongside former Liverpool and Spurs player Paul Stewart and ex-Everton and Aston Villa centre-half Derek Mountfield. Nowadays, having returned to live in Stockbridge Village, Paul has been known to pass on his knowledge by coaching some of the area's youngsters and has done a bit of scouting for Forest Green Rovers. He earns a living as a bus driver and the majority of his passengers are unaware that the man dropping them off at Huyton bus station has played hundreds of football matches with and against some of the best players the country has ever produced!

TERRY GORNELL

Accrington Stanley Manager John Coleman was a prolific non-League striker for a host of teams including Southport, Burscough and England. Having registered more than 500 career goals the former St Aloysius teacher knows a good player, particularly a centre forward, when he sees one. The fact that he recruited Terry Gornell on no fewer than five occasions speaks volumes about his opinion of the Huytonian.

Born on 16 December 1989, Terry initially grew up living in Huyton's Lyme Grove before the family moved a mile down Liverpool Road to live at 5 Cuper Crescent. As a boy, the dazzling floodlights at nearby Alt Park fascinated Terry. He could see them from his bedroom window and the first of his many personal goals was to play at the home of Knowsley United. He did not fulfil that particular ambition but did hit many other targets and achieved a great deal in a 316-game, five-club and 57-goal professional career which spanned nine seasons. His first taste of organised football came at the age of seven when he turned out for the St Aloysius U-10s team. In addition to being two or three years younger than his teammates and opponents, Terry was small for his age which could have been a problem. However, Manager Tony Higgins wisely employed him on the wing where he excelled and helped the team lift trophy after trophy. Aged eight, Terry attended training sessions at Prescot Leisure Centre conducted by Everton's Joe Doyle. Terry is extremely grateful to Joe for arranging his trial at Bellefield which resulted in a one-year contract with the Blues. Although a staunch Liverpudlian, Terry loved Tuesday and Thursday night training sessions and matches every weekend. He juggled this with playing for both the Allys School and U-10s teams and proudly captaining the Huyton Schoolboys side. When Everton coach Neil Dewsnip informed Terry that the club were letting him go, he was devastated. However, his dismay was short-lived.

He clearly recalls a week later an unexpected and initially unwelcome telephone call disturbing the Gornell household's Sunday morning tranquillity. Terry Jnr overheard from an adjoining room his dad sharply enquire who was on the other end of the call. The tone of Terry Snr's voice mellowed as the conversation unfolded. The caller was Tranmere Rovers Youth Coach Glyn Salmon who, having got wind of Terry's Bellefield departure, was inviting the youngster along to a trial at the club. The following weekend Terry's feeling of rejection was still raw as he nervously took to the field – he need not have worried as a couple of hours later he was a Rovers player with a two-year contract! Almost immediately after signing, Terry was converted into a centre-forward and he didn't look back. His game was developing brilliantly and in 2002 the highlight of Tranmere's appearance at the 'Ian Rush' tournament in Aberystwyth was when 13-year old Terry broke the competition's goal scoring record previously held by Michael Owen. His displays were catching the eye of a number of clubs including Man City, prompting Rovers to extend his contract by four years.

Unlike other League clubs, Tranmere did not stop their youngsters from playing for school or junior teams. Consequently, Terry found success with Recs Roby, Whiston Juniors and his Cardinal Heenan Secondary School side which took part in the ESFA U-14s Schools Cup in 2004. They safely negotiated their way through

nine rounds, scoring 36 goals, conceding only 10 and defeating teams from Runcorn, Warrington, Litherland, Blackpool, Oldham, Stockport, Nottingham, Doncaster and Birkenhead. On 28 April 2004, they faced Roding Valley HS from Essex in the Final at Northampton Town's Sixfields Stadium. A goal from Huyton youngster Joe Holt negated the opposition's strike and with the sides level after extra-time they shared the prestigious trophy and title. A month later, they were defeated by Woodchurch HS in the Liverpool Echo Cup Final at Prenton Park but had enjoyed a tremendous season with Terry spearheading their attack.

Former Liverpool striker Howard Gayle and fellow Huytonian Dave Bleasdale were in charge of Tranmere's U-16s and helped Terry immeasurably. In his autobiography '61 Minutes in Munich' Gayle states "Terry was a striker who lacked pace but was very good with the ball at his feet. He went through a period where he lost his confidence because he was frustrated that his pace was inhibiting his development. I took Terry to one side and told him that rather than being an Ian Rush going in behind defences, which he did not have the pace to do, I asked him to adapt his game and become more of a Dennis Bergkamp type of player who would drop deeper for the ball. To be fair to Terry he took this on board and it transformed his game." Terry does not dispute this analysis and attributes Howie's influence as being instrumental in him securing a crucial, precious two-year YTS deal at the age of 16. With the YTS in the bag, Terry made a pro contract and a place in the first team his next priorities. At the end of the 2007/08 campaign, he put pen to paper at Prenton Park to reach his first target. Whilst he had been on the bench for a few games, the breakthrough continued to elude him. This continued until 12 August 2008 when Boss Ronnie Moore introduced him to the action at Grimsby's Blundell Park in the 82nd minute of a Carling Cup 1st round 2-0 defeat. Terry was delighted to have been involved but was hungry for more and felt he was too far down the Rovers' pecking order to get the regular start he craved. A chance meeting with Accrington Manager John Coleman at a Prescot Cables game presented a solution. A couple of days after their brief conversation had alerted him to Terry's frustration, Coleman contacted Moore and a loan deal was swiftly arranged. Two days later, on 20 September 2008, Terry was a second-half substitute in a 3-0 reversal at the hands of Darlington.

Without the move, he would at best have been warming the Tranmere bench. He had now made his English Football League debut and eight days later he was handed his first start in the oldest league in the world with Rochdale providing the opposition. On 11 October Terry ticked another box in his list of ambitions when, in the 50th minute of a home game versus Bradford City, he netted his first goal to add to an earlier Jimmy

©Kipax Sports Photography

Ryan strike. Three Bantams goals in the last 10 minutes of the game handed them the points and took the shine off this milestone but did signify the start of a 'three goals in three games' purple patch for him. Terry made eleven Accy appearances and registered four goals before heading back to Wirral. The experience had enabled Terry to leapfrog some of his Tranmere rivals to a first team jersey and two days after returning to his parent club Moore pitched him into the starting line up in a 2-0 victory over Scunthorpe. Terry featured in eleven further Rovers games to take his seasons tally to 23 appearances. This increased to 32 games the following campaign but the season presented a host of problems for Terry which ultimately led to him leaving the club.

In the close season, Ronnie Moore had surprisingly been replaced by football legend John Barnes which theoretically could have been an exciting proposition for the Rovers faithful. In practise, it was a recipe for failure and his tenure lasted just three months. His successor was club physio Les Parry who fared little better. Tranmere Chairman Peter Johnson eventually saw the error of his ways and reinstated Moore but Terry had long since departed Prenton Park after being frustrated by the sequence of events. On 27 August 2010, John Coleman snapped him up on a permanent deal. After the turmoil at Tranmere this was the perfect antidote. He loved training and playing with his mates in a relaxed environment and in his fourth game he bagged a brace in a 3-0 demolition of Lincoln City. Terry became an important member of the team and his 13 goals helped the club to secure a Division Two play-off place, although they were defeated 3-0 by Stevenage Borough in the semis.

Terry loved his time at Stanley but, when Shrewsbury Town Boss Graham Turner came in for him, he believed that his ambitions could be realised at New Meadow and joined the club on 5 July 2011. An ankle injury picked up in training meant that Turner had to ease him into the season from the bench. He got a couple of minutes under his belt in each of their first two games but in their third match, versus Burton, Turner introduced him into the fray in the 67th minute trailing 1-0 to a Calvin Zola goal. Sixteen minutes later Terry opened his Shrews account with a brilliant header to snuff out Albion's lead and immediately endear himself to the club's fan base. On 28 April 2012, Terry's decision to join Shrewsbury was emphatically justified when, in front of 9,441 ecstatic fans, they secured a 1-0 win over Dagenham & Redbridge to guarantee the Salops their first promotion for nearly 20 years. The rest of the weekend is a bit of a blur for Terry with a civic reception and an open-top bus tour of the town attracting tens of thousands of fans lining the streets to salute their heroes. The 2012/13 season was initially a struggle for the club and Terry endured 13 games without a goal. Once again, John Coleman who was now occupying the manager's office at Rochdale stepped in with a proposal designed to benefit both his club and Terry. It paid off a treat.

Terry joined Dale for an initial loan period of two months. He made eight appearances, notched five goals and rediscovered his form and confidence. With these features back in his armour, it could be argued that Terry should then have returned to Shrewsbury to fight for his place. Instead, on 10 January 2013, the persuasive tongue of Coleman secured his signature on a permanent contract with Rochdale. Unfortunately, less than a fortnight later Coley had been shown the door and Terry didn't really see eye-to-eye with his replacement Keith Hill. Before the 2013/14 season had commenced, Terry had followed Coleman out of the Spotland exit to become a Cheltenham Town player. A goal in his second appearance (a 4-3 Capital One Cup defeat of Crawley Town) got him off to a good start but overall it was a poor season for the Gloucestershire club who finished a lowly 17th in League Two. The following campaign ultimately ended in huge disappointment for the Robins with relegation to the Vanarama National League. However, before their fate was sealed, Terry had departed to be reacquainted for the fifth and final time with John Coleman who had returned to Accrington Stanley.

Again, he hit the ground running with his first week back at the Crown Ground consisting of three games, two wins and two goals for Terry including a spectacular 90th minute overhead kick to grab a 1-0 win over Oxford Utd. The 2015/16 season saw Accy and Terry play some great football yet end in heartache. When, in the 92nd minute of their last game of the season, Lee Brown scored the winner for Bristol Rovers against Dagenham & Redbridge, they snatched automatic promotion to League One at the expense of Accrington who finished fourth. Even though they still had the opportunity to get promoted via the play-offs, Coleman's team were still reeling from the drama of the season's cruel conclusion and lost to Wimbledon in the semi-finals. Terry spent an additional season in League football before calling it a day. His final game was a 3-0 victory over Stevenage on 6 May 2017. He had a further year remaining on his contract but nine seasons of pro football had taken its toll on his body and he was struggling with a series of niggling injuries. It was not in Terry's nature to continue to pick up his wages and effectively cheat the fans who had been so supportive of him, so he made the decision to focus upon the next phase of his professional life.

Terry Gornell has a good head on his shoulders which he used to good effect to get on the end of crosses and find the back of the net but he also used it to make some wise decisions. During his playing days he had invested some of his earnings in property development which had given him an insight into the workings of various aspects of the financial services industry. After hanging up his boots, he gained the necessary qualifications to help him in his current employment of providing sound financial advice to former and current footballers and the wider public. Whilst he claims he doesn't miss playing the game, Terry is an avid Liverpool supporter, holds an Anfield season ticket and follows the Reds home and away.

LEE MOLYNEUX

Huyton's Mosscroft estate has produced many fine footballers, some of whom have graduated to the English Football League. On 10 January 2009, fullback Lee Molyneux added his name to that prestigious group when, aged 19, he took his place in the Southampton team which defeated Barnsley 1-0 at Oakwell.

Lee started his football journey at the tender age of seven with Wrexham. Two years later he was spotted playing in schoolboy football and invited to join Everton. He spent ten years with the Blues during which time he represented England in various age groups on 17 occasions. When Leighton Baines arrived at Goodison Park from Wigan Athletic and made the first team's left-back position his own, Lee decided, perhaps prematurely, his future lay elsewhere.

On 1 January 2009, he joined Championship side Southampton and Manager Jan Poortvliet threw him into action just nine days later. On his fourth appearance for the Saints with Swansea providing the opposition, he received his marching orders in what proved to be his final game for the club. Poortvliet had been axed a couple of days earlier and Lee subsequently moved down the pecking order signalling the end to his brief stay at St Mary's. A monthlong loan without a game at Port Vale was followed by the intervention of Mosscroft old boy Peter Reid who secured Lee's services until the end of the season as one of his first signings as Manager of Plymouth Argyle.

Ironically, his Pilgrim's debut was against Southampton and Lee repaid his new boss' faith in him by helping the team to a 1-0 win, Reidy's first victory since his appointment. However, the success was short-lived and Argyle ended the season in the relegation zone and after 12 appearances Lee left Home Park.

He bounced back from an enforced absence from the game with a successful trial at Accrington Stanley and in 2012/13 season he enjoyed his most sustained campaign with 43 appearances. At the turn of the year, Lee underwent a positional transformation which resulted in him getting amongst the goals and being dubbed the 'League Two Gareth Bale' - high praise indeed! He had always possessed the ability to get past a man so when he was pushed up into a wide midfield role he thrived. Add into the mix his power and precision from free kicks and it wasn't long before the plaudits came Lee's way. From his first 34 games as a pro, he had registered just a single goal - a superb 20-yarder versus Oxford in a thrilling 3-3 FA Cup draw played on the opening day of December 2012. Although he had to wait another three months and 13 matches before again finding the back of the net, Lee's brace against Rochdale in a 3-0 win on 26 February 2013 opened the floodgates. Eight goals from the final 13 games of the season represented a tremendous return for Lee and included a fantastic first-half hat trick as Accy overcame Barnet who at the time were managed by former

Dutch international Edgar Davids. Lee's performances earned him the club's Player of the Year award and the opportunity to play at a higher level with Crewe - he duly put pen to paper at Gresty Road on 1 July 2013.

During the opening weeks of the 2013/14 campaign, Lee pulled on a Crewe jersey nine times but didn't really get an extended chance to show what he could offer. In each of the matches he played, Manager Steve Davis used him as a late sub or, in each of his four starts, replaced him before the 90 minutes were up.

A change was required and following three winless games on loan at Rochdale, Lee returned to Accrington on 23 January 2014. He slotted back into the side immediately and found the net in just his third game on familiar turf. Remarkably, almost 12 months to the day since Lee scored his first-half hat trick versus Barnet, he repeated the feat when Stanley overcame Chesterfield by a 3-1 scoreline on 8 March 2014. His six goals from 17 appearances helped Accy to a solid mid-table finish to bring his loan spell to a successful conclusion.

Lee started the 2014/15 season back at Crewe but after just four games for the Railwaymen he returned to the Wham Stadium for his third spell as a Stanley player. He added another 14 appearances to his Accrington record before joining Tranmere Rovers on 13 January 2015 for an ill-fated conclusion to their season. Although the impact of Lee and other additions to the squad started well with a couple of wins and a draw, the rot set in as Rovers failed to win any of their final eight games consigning the club to relegation to the National League.

Lee had endured a couple of turbulent nomadic seasons so was delighted when Morecambe Boss Jim Bentley outlined his promotion plans for the club and offered him the stability of a two-year contract. Therefore, finishing in the lower echelons of League Two in each of Lee's seasons at Morecambe proved disappointing. However, with 88 appearances and eight goals Lee served the club well and pushed his league and cup tally beyond the 200-games mark before he turned his attention to non-league football. Guiseley, Chorley and Barrow welcomed him to their fold until, in the summer of 2019, he joined League of Wales outfit Bala Town as a part-time player. The outbreak of the COVID-19 pandemic put this development on hold and also temporarily affected his long-term plans.

Lee's father, also called Lee, had been a professional boxer and instilled in his son the importance of physical and mental conditioning in order to maximise performance. These traits, coupled with the knowledge and experience he had gained during a decade in the game, put Lee in an excellent position to help train young footballers, boxers and athletes to excel in their chosen field. In 2019 Lee opened his own gym and is excited to face any future challenges as he moves into the next phase of his life after full-time football.

©Kipax Sports Photography

CARL BAKER

Whiston Juniors were established in 1985 by Harry 'Skip' Warburton. His involvement in the club spanned four decades until he sadly passed away in 2018, aged 81. During this time, along with a brilliantly dedicated coaching team and supportive parents, he was actively involved in helping to give thousands of youngsters the opportunity to play and develop their game. The Windy Arbour club's alumni includes many players who graduated to make a living from football. Steven Gerrard, Joey Barton, Mark Ward, David Nugent and Lee Trundle are just a handful of those who are grateful to Skip and co.

Prescotian Carl Baker followed in the footsteps of his uncle Mark Ward and joined the club as a five-year-old. Five years later he was picked up by Liverpool where he loved the Melwood training sessions under the direction of Steve Heighway. It was, therefore, a huge disappointment when, six years later, the Reds former flying winger broke the news that the club were letting him go. Although this was a huge setback, Carl didn't give up on his dream of becoming a professional and combined working for Knowsley Borough Council with turning out for Tommy Lawton's Prescot Cables side. The Hope Street crowd were enthralled by his wide midfield play as was Southport Manager Liam Watson who raided his club's coffers to shell out "the best £2,000 I ever spent" to take Carl to Haigh Avenue. Carl enjoyed four seasons with the Sandgrounders and is hugely indebted to Watson for educating him in the expectations and demands put upon a professional footballer. Putting his advice into action, Carl flourished and played a massive part in helping the club win the Conference North at the conclusion of the 2004/05 campaign. He continued to develop and although he picked up the Player of the Year award, he was powerless to prevent the club from being relegated after a couple of seasons in the National Conference.

Whilst at Southport, Carl received international recognition when he was selected for the England C team on two occasions. The first, on 15 February 2006, was staged at Cambridge United's Abbey stadium as 3,025 spectators watched a fine 3-1 victory over Italy. He picked up his second cap in June 2007 when the 3 Lions put Finland to the sword by a single goal to nil. Carl's impressive progress was not lost on Morecambe Boss Sammy McIlroy and a couple of months after his second England appearance he sealed a move to the Shrimps with Southport receiving a record transfer sum for a departing player.

Carl made his Football League debut on 11 August 2007 (his son Louis' birthday!) in a 0-0 drawn game versus Barnet and, just three games later, a 3-1 victory over Mansfield included the first of his season's tally of eleven goals. Considering this was the club's first ever season in the Football League, an eleventh place finish represented a great achievement. Carl's 48 appearances attracted the attention of newly-promoted Stockport County and their £175,000 transfer bid was sufficient to persuade Morecambe to cash in. Unfortunately, unbeknownst to Carl, County were in financial dire straits and when the club entered administration they were docked ten points by the FA. Despite this, at the end of 2008/09 they managed to avoid relegation to League Two by the smallest of margins. Unfortunately, the writing was on the wall and the club could not avoid the drop to League Two at the end of 2009/10.

When, aged 16, Carl was released by Liverpool, he resolved that he would have to "pick myself up and be a big character." This was never more evident, on and off the park, than during this campaign which contained a record-breaking high and a heartbreaking low. His Hatters goal tally of 13 (a Bakers dozen!), was registered before leaving the club in January 2010 to join Coventry City. This figure contained a 22-day purple patch when he scored nine goals in five appearances. Carl kicked off with a hat trick versus Brighton on 22 August 2009 and followed that up a week later with a last-gasp equaliser opposing Southampton. He then became the first County player to ever score back to back hat tricks in an away fixture when they knocked Crewe out of the JP Trophy with a 4-1 win on 1 September.

However, ten days later tragedy struck when Carl's older brother Michael passed away after a battle with leukaemia. Knowing that it would have been his sibling's wish and showing tremendous fortitude, Carl pulled on a County shirt and took to Yeovil's Huish Park pitch just a couple of days later. The strength of character he had resolved to nurture as a teenager was prevalent as he rattled home an inspired brace in a 2-2 draw. After his opening goal, Carl ran to the dugout and grabbed a t-shirt displaying the poignant message 'For U Mike'. In addition, at full time he was presented with a condolence card signed by each of the 159 travelling Hatters fans - a lovely gesture greatly appreciated by all members of the Baker family.

Carl has always enjoyed a great relationship with the fans of the clubs he has proudly represented and this was certainly the case at Coventry. He made the first of 182 Sky Blues appearances on 9 January 2010 by entering the fray in the 76th minute of a 3-1 defeat of Barnsley. To this point in his career Carl had registered almost a half century of goals but it wasn't until his 31st Cov game that he found the back of the net. As the club struggled at the wrong end of the Championship table, goals were hard to come by but Carl was working his socks off for the cause and this was recognised with the Community Player of the Season award for 2010/11. In October 2011, Carl signed a contract extension but, in a repeat of his experience at Stockport, off the field the club was in turmoil with disquiet in the boardroom and aborted takeover bids. The season had started badly for Carl when he was sent off in the campaign's opening match, a 1-0 defeat opposing Leicester City, and a difficult season ended in huge disappointment as they suffered relegation to League One. This added to the club's financial woes which culminated in Coventry going into administration and, with a 10 points penalty imposed upon them, they finished in 15th place at the conclusion of the 2012/13 season.

In better news, Carl picked up the club's Player of the Season award after rediscovered his scoring touch by finding the net 15 times from 55 appearances. Another ten-point penalty the following campaign again damaged the club's ambitions as they dropped further down the table to finish in 18th place. This was a difficult period in the Sky Blues long history and on 26 September 2014 Carl parted company with the club after 182 appearances (many as captain) and 28 goals. Out of contract and the wrong side of 30, Carl needed to convince a club that he still had plenty to offer. Following a successful trial, he signed on the dotted line to join MK Dons of League One. In addition to being attracted to the way they played, Carl was a big fan of Manager and former Prescot Cables player Karl Robinson.

He made his Dons debut on 4 October 2014 in a 2-0 victory over Yeovil. It was the first of 35 outings in a hugely successful campaign. They were in contention for an automatic promotion place throughout the season and their hopes were alive as the battle went down to the wire. A fantastic run-in witnessed the Dons picking up 25 from a possible 27 points meaning that going into the last match of the campaign they trailed 2nd-placed Preston by a single point. They needed to account for Yeovil and hope that the Lilywhites slipped up - which is exactly what happened. Carl's seventh minute opener, his tenth goal since signing, put them on course for a 5-1 demolition of the Glovers whilst simultaneously Colchester were doing a number on Preston. An 82nd minute winner for The U's sent MK into the Championship and confined PNE to the playoffs where they redeemed themselves to secure the final promotion place. The leap into the second tier of English football for the first time in the club's relatively brief history (formed in 2004) proved to be a step too far. Despite the best efforts of Carl and his teammates, they dropped straight back down from whence they came.

Carl actually dropped two divisions as he began the 2016/17 campaign with League Two's Portsmouth. On 6 August 2016, Manager Paul Cook named his new signing in the starting eleven for their match facing Carlisle. Fratton Park's crowd of 17,570 consisted largely of Pompey fans who were ecstatic when, in the 42nd minute, Carl opened his account to level the game and give those supporters optimism for the rest of the season. He added a further eight goals to help Portsmouth accumulate 87 points to secure promotion as champions. However, after just four appearances at the start of the following season, the 34-year old left the club by mutual consent.

Injuries prevented Carl from fulfilling an exciting opportunity in the Indian Super League and a return to Coventry City suffered a similar fate. Although Carl didn't add any additional Football League and Cup appearances to his impressive tally of 403, he has been able to increase his non-league record with spells at Brackley Town and Nuneaton Borough. He combines playing with running a successful football academy. Just as Skip and the Whiston Juniors coaches helped Carl in his formative years, Carl and his qualified staff give local youngsters the benefit of the knowledge and experience he has accumulated during his excellent career. Carl's son Louis is a graduate of the academy and it was a tremendously proud moment for the Baker family when, in August 2021, Carl and Louis lined up alongside eachother in Nuneaton's first team. A couple of weeks later, with BBC's tv cameras present to cover their FA Cup first round tie versus Litchfield, Louis unleashed a tremendous shot from distance which beat the keeper much to the delight of the home crowd and his dad. It's unclear how long Carl will continue playing but when he does hang up his boots to concentrate on coaching, he can do so confident that in Louis and his two brothers Jaden and Keegan, the Baker legacy is in good hands.

©www.mphotographic.co.uk

JOEY BARTON

Joey Barton is, by his own admission, a complex character whose life on and off the pitch has contained a catalogue of highs and lows. The warts and all details can be found eloquently and honestly revealed in his autobiography 'No Nonsense'. However, this book is predominantly a celebration of our area's football narrative and only concerned with Joe's positive offerings - he has contributed a great deal, so read on.

Footballers come in all shapes and sizes and possess different attributes. For example, Joey Barton did not display the same silky skills and trickery as Lee Trundle. He wasn't gifted with the lightning pace of Callum Macmanaman or Mickey Quinn's lethal goal scoring ability. However, Joey once said "I took the ball off better players than me and gave it to better players than me and made a career out of it" and there lies the rub. Unless Trunds, Macca or Quinny had the ball at their disposal, their contribution to the cause was stifled. That said, you do not represent your country, pull on the shirts of four Premier League clubs and become one of the few Englishmen to ply their trade in both Scotland and France unless you do more than stop the opposition in their tracks.

Born on 2 September 1982, Joe hails from Huyton's St Johns estate. As kids, he and his mates played at every opportunity on makeshift pitches with temporary goals. His first taste of organised football was provided by his school, St Agnes (with whom he twice won the Hanson Cup) and St Annes Rovers playing in the Rainhill Junior League. It was Rovers' legend Harry Tyrell who arranged for young Joe to attend training with Everton - a dream come true for the Blues-mad 9-year old. Schoolboy forms were duly signed, however the dream was shattered when, after six years at Bellefield, Academy boss Neil Dewsnip brutally informed his dad that the club were releasing Joe. He was understandably heartbroken but that decision sparked a determined reaction in him to prove people wrong and a desire to be the best he could be. He got the chance to put this to the test almost immediately as the house phone rang off the hook with clubs wanting to get Joey on board. He joined Manchester City, seized the opportunity and three years later was rewarded for his efforts with a professional contract.

After advancing through the ranks he was desperate to make his first team debut but patience was required after he missed his first opportunity to do so. At the Riverside Stadium on 23 November 2002 and with City trailing 3-1 to Middlesborough, Manager Kevin Keegan gave Joe the nod to join the action. To his dismay, he discovered that his jersey, which he had left underneath the bench at half time, had been swiped, presumably by an opportunist Boro fan! With no replacement shirt to hand, Joe had to wait until 5 April 2003 for his next chance. Keegan named him in the starting line-up versus Bolton Wanderers and although they went down 2-0, Joey did enough to stay in the team for the remaining six games of the season. In his third game, at Spurs' White Hart Lane, he registered both his first goal and his first booking - it's fair to say that he picked up more cards (118 yellow, 9 red) in his career than goals, although finding the net on 37 occasions is not a bad record for someone whose job was to win the ball and give it to his teammates!

City finished 9th in the table, securing the final UEFA Cup slot for the following campaign. Their stay in the competition was brief - knocked out in the third round by Polish side Groclin Grodzisk - and finished a disappointing 16th in the League. However, with 39 appearances in all competitions, Joey established himself in the side and, over the following couple of seasons, became one of the first names on Keegan's and his successor Stuart Pearce's teamsheet.

In the 78th minute of an England friendly opposing Spain on 7 February 2007, Joe's growing reputation in the game was acknowledged when Steve McLaren sent him onto the Old Trafford pitch to replace Frank Lampard. The 1-0 defeat proved to be Joe's only cap as, with Lampard and Steven Gerrard occupying England's central midfield positions for a combined total of 220 matches, opportunities were limited. On the domestic front, City had succumbed to mid-table mediocrity with Joe being one of the few bright lights in an otherwise dim outfit. With seven goals, he was the club's top scorer in the 2006/07 campaign - a telling statistic. Off the pitch, a maelstrom of controversial events (not all of his making) ultimately resulted in Joey calling time on his relationship with the club.

©Andy Ford Photography

©Andy Ford Photography

On 14 June 2007, Newcastle United shelled out £5.8 million to take him to St James Park but an injury-hampered start to his Magpies career delayed his debut until 22 October when he joined the action as a 71st minute substitute in a 3-1 defeat of Spurs. It was the first of 84 games he played for the club during a turbulent four seasons which involved no fewer than seven managers at the helm. Injuries and a well-publicised spell in prison prevented Joe's appearance tally being higher. He managed just nine appearances in the ill-fated 2008/09 campaign which saw the club desperately attempt, unsuccessfully, to cling on to their Premiership status. To their credit, they bounced straight back to the top flight and although Joe missed the majority of the season due to a troublesome foot problem, he was back as the bounding pulse of the team for the final nine games to help them get over the line and to gain promotion as champions.

The Geordies cheered their heroes to a twelfth place finish in the Premier League but the 2010/11 season was not without its problems. The circumstances which led to the removal of Chris Hughton from the manager's office created a clash between the players and club's owners and the writing was on the wall for Joe and his teammates who fronted a mini revolt. He loved his time on Tyneside and would have been happy to wear the black and white for many seasons more than the four he spent there. Instead, on 26 August 2011, he found himself joining QPR on a free transfer. During two spells at Loftus Road, Joe made one game short of a century of appearances. The last match of his first stint provided the most memorable finale to a Premier League season ever and, for the first 55 minutes of the game, Joe was in the thick of the action.

On 'Super Sunday', 13 May 2012 at the Etihad Stadium, Man City played hosts to the Hoops with a great deal at stake for both clubs. Topping the table, the home side were tied on points with Man Utd but had a superior goal difference, whilst Rangers were embroiled in a relegation dogfight with Bolton Wanderers. A Wayne Rooney goal against Sunderland wrapped up the points for the Red Devils so anything less than a City victory would hand the title to their closest rivals. As the game entered injury time, ten-man QPR held a 2-1 lead. Their number had been earlier reduced when Joey waged a one-man war against the champions-elect leaving referee Mike Dean with little option but to send him off. A 92nd minute Edin Dzeko equaliser not only gave City a glimmer of hope, it also potentially put a nail in Rangers' coffin, depending upon the outcome of Bolton's game with Stoke. Then, just as the red side of Manchester prepared to celebrate, Sergio Aguero conjured up a neat one-two and rifled the ball into the back of the net to send City's fans delirious. The title was City's for the first time since 1968 and, to QPR's relief, their defeat didn't send them down as Bolton were unable to secure the three points necessary to save them.

The club may have avoided relegation but the whole final day experience left a bitter taste in Joe's mouth and he initially fell out of love with football. A dramatic change was required and he found it across the English Channel. The Stade Velodrome is home to Olympique de Marseille and became Joey Barton's home for the 2012/13 season. He and the fans enjoyed a fantastic relationship which, combined with a refreshing approach by the French media, allowed him to breathe and, in turn, reassess his career and renew his appetite for playing. Joey may have only been there on a seasonlong loan but the fans took him to their heart and the feeling was mutual. The Europa League provided the arena for Joe's first five games. A 2-2 draw versus Fenerbahce on 20 September 2012 handed him his debut and four games later he registered his only goal for the club in a clash with Moenchengladbach which also ended 2-2. His 25 appearances for the Phocaeans helped the club to the French Ligue runners-up spot and Champions League football. Despite the French wanting to retain Joey's services for the following campaign, which would have fulfilled his dream of playing in the continent's biggest competition, he returned to Loftus Road as a deal could not be struck between the two clubs.

Initially, Joe didn't want to be there and some fans and playing colleagues shared this sentiment. Even QPR Manager Harry Redknapp shunned him until clear the air talks enabled Joe to get back to pulling on his boots and winning people over. In Joe's absence, they had suffered relegation to the Championship but success is a great healer and his commitment to the cause during the 2013/14 campaign aided this process. His 39th appearance of the season took place on 24 May 2014 in the Wembley play-off Final in front of 87,348 fans. Not only would the winning team be promoted, the victory was reported to be worth up to £120 million. The game was a tight affair but swung in Derby's favour on the hour when QPR's Gary O'Neil received his marching orders from referee Lee Mason. However, the match remained goalless until the dying seconds when Rangers' substitute Bobby Zamora curled an unstoppable shot past the Derby County keeper to score the most precious of goals. Although the club had returned to the level they had been at before Joe had left for France, they were unable to stay there and suffered relegation at the end of 2014/15.

Burnley also dropped out of the country's top division and their Turf Moor home would be Joe's place of work for the majority of the following two seasons. His debut campaign for the Clarets consisted of 40 appearances which earned him a place in the PFA Team of the Year and the club promotion back to the Prem. A short acrimonious 8-match spell with Glasgow Rangers was followed by a return to Turf Moor where he helped the club avoid relegation before he brought the curtain down on his 432-game playing career.

Throughout his time as a player, Joe had never been shy when it came to discussing his managers' decisions, signings and tactics. It was, therefore, no surprise when he put his head above the parapet to become the new Fleetwood Town Manager in June 2018. He inherited a side which had finished 14th in League One the previous season and wasted little time recruiting players and staff he felt could improve upon that. Some of these had strong links to Huyton including coaches Andy Mangan and Clint Hill plus forwards Chris Long and Mark Duffy. His first season in charge resulted in an improved 11th place which, in a campaign curtailed due the Covid pandemic, was followed by the team finishing 6th and booking a place in the play-offs. Unfortunately, Wycombe Wanderers came out 6-3 on top in the semis and when the team started sluggishly at the start of the 2020/21 season Joe was relieved of his duties. Just a month later, he was installed as Manager of struggling Bristol Rovers. They had only won one of their previous 12 matches and were bereft of confidence. Despite Joe's best efforts, he was unable to stop the rot and the Pirates were relegated.

Love him or loath him (and that often depended upon whether he played for or against your club), Joey Barton is undoubtedly one of the most interesting characters to have been involved in football's recent history. Few of his peers have shown a greater desire to win at all costs whilst also being able to transfer their attention to non-football matters. He has impressed during appearances on Question Time, Newsnight, numerous other tv and radio shows as well as being a guest of the debating society the Oxford Union. Conversely, there are some big blots on his copybook and only time will tell if he will be perceived as Joey the hero or Joey the villain - let's hope it's the former!

Footynote:

Joey managed to steer his team back to League One at the first time of asking but only by the skin of their teeth. Anything less than the remarkable 7-0 victory they achieved on the last day of the season would have resulted in another season in League Two.

ANDY MANGAN

On 24 April 2004, 17-year old Andy Mangan boarded the Blackpool youth team coach bound for an away fixture versus Shrewsbury Town. Little did the ex-Thomas Becket pupil know that a few hours later he would be making his Football League debut!

When Mike Sheron pulled out of the first team squad a couple of hours before the kick-off of their away game against Chesterfield, Boss Steve McMahon hurriedly contacted the Youth Team Manager and instructed him to get Andy to Charnock Richards service station as soon as possible. A detour for the coach and a swift taxi ride ensured Andy met up with the first teamers with just minutes to spare. Because he had never been involved in McMahon's group before he did not have a shirt number so the Club Secretary hastily contacted the relevant authorities and Andy was allocated the number 30 shirt at the eleventh hour. The match at Saltergate was played in front of 4,117 supporters and in the 75th minute McMahon called Andy from the bench to replace Mathew Blinkhorn making him one of the youngest players to ever play for the Tangerines.

He made just one more appearance for the club before joining Northern Premier League side Hyde United on loan where his two goals in the last seven games of the season helped the club secure the League title. Accrington Stanley Manager John Coleman signed 'Mangy' in August 2005 and he opened his goal account for the Conference Premier side in a 3-1 defeat at the hands of Cambridge United in just his third game. Although many of his 45 appearances in his first season were as a substitute, he still managed to bag ten goals to make a significant contribution to the club gaining promotion to the Football League for the first time in half a century. He continued to warm the bench at the Interlink Express Stadium for another season before opting to join Chris Casper's Bury FC in the hope of starting more games. Andy hit the ground running and scored six goals before Christmas before a groin injury required surgery and he struggled to regain full fitness.

After a brief loan spell back at Accrington, in 2008 Andy signed for Forest Green Rovers of the Blue Square Conference League where he really began to make his mark as a prolific goal scorer and maker. In his first season he scored 30 goals from 49 games in all competitions which included three hat tricks and amazingly 16 goals from the last 14 games of the season. His contribution was acknowledged when he was presented with the club's Player of the Year award and the Golden Boot as the highest scorer in the League. However, in 2009 Andy was caught up in a betting scandal relating to a match between Accrington and Bury (although he wasn't playing for either club at the time of the alleged offence). The upshot of an investigation was that he was banned from football for five months. He returned to action on 23 January 2009 when he appeared for Wrexham in a 1-0 victory over Wimbledon. Dragons Manager Dean Saunders recognised a bit of himself in Andy with his pace and eye for a goal and he was top scorer for the club in his first season and followed that up with 16 in the next campaign.

Whilst at Wrexham, Andy represented England U-23s in the International Challenge Trophy, playing in the semi-final victory over Belgium and the Final defeat at the hands of Portugal. Domestically, Fleetwood Town manager Micky Mellon signed Andy in 2011 where he forged a fantastic strike partnership with future Leicester City and England forward Jamie Vardy. The pair terrorised defences and scored nearly 60 goals between them which played a massive part in the club winning the Conference title to secure a place in the Third Division of the Football League. A brief spell back at Forest Green was followed by a short stint with Luton Town before he was reacquainted with Mellon when he signed for Shrewsbury Town on 24 July 2014. His 12 months with the Shrews included some memorable moments for Andy. Just a few weeks after joining the club, his 38th minute converted free kick at Leicester City's King Power Stadium was enough to knock the Foxes

©Kipax Sports Photography

out of the Capital One Cup. Two months later in the fourth round of the same competition versus Chelsea, he came off the bench in the 75th minute and just 85 seconds later scored to equalise a Didier Drogba goal - real Roy of the Rovers stuff.

Andy's goals and assists helped Shrewsbury gain promotion to League One but financial fare play rules meant that the club were unable to retain him and in July 2015 he signed for Tranmere Rovers. However, after just six months, 22 games and 7 goals he returned to Shrewsbury's New Meadow ground and just three days later scored the winning goal to knock Cardiff City out of the FA Cup. When Mellon took over the managerial reigns at Tranmere Rovers Andy was on his way back to Prenton Park when his Manager signed him for the fourth time.

Footynote:

An additional 41 appearances for Rovers were followed by brief stints at Fylde and Bala before concluding his playing career with half a dozen games for Accrington Stanley. Andy always intended to stay in the game after hanging up his boots and, when Joey Barton offered him the chance to join his coaching staff at Fleetwood Town, he didn't hesitate to accept. Following a largely successful period in the dugout at Highbury, Joey parted company with Fleetwood and took charge of Bristol Rovers and Andy accompanied him.

DAVID NUGENT

The expression "if at first you don't succeed, try try again" originates from a proverb made popular in this country by educational writer William Edward Hickson. It was created to discourage school pupils from throwing in the towel or giving up on their dreams. The phrase could also have been the family motto of the Nugent clan.

Born in Mill Road Hospital on 25 May 1985, David Nugent grew up living in Salerno Drive on Huyton's Bluebell estate. He attended Park View Primary School and his mum Sandra recalls his Nursery teacher was the first person to acknowledge his sporting prowess. At the tender age of four, David got his first taste of organised football on a small, grass area adjacent to the St Aloysius club car park in Crosswood Crescent. Soon after, he graduated to play every Sunday morning for the Ally's on the bigger pitches at nearby Jubilee Park whilst Saturdays were dedicated to leading the Whiston Juniors forward line.

David's family are all staunch Evertonians and he clearly remembers his dad David snr taking him to watch the Toffees versus Manchester United on 9 September 1995. With chances aplenty, five goals, eight bookings and a sending off, the game had everything apart from the right result. United won 3-2 but David had seen enough to make him a Blue for life. David's overwhelming desire to become a professional footballer took the first of many knocks when, aged just six, Everton showed little interest in him after a trial at their Bellefield training ground. This resulted in him temporarily putting his allegiance to the Blues to one side to join Liverpool's Academy. Twice-weekly training sessions helped David develop his all-round game although he had reservations about his enforced conversion from centre-forward to playing on the wing. After six years with the Reds, David was released and on coach Hugh McAuley's recommendation, he joined top Kirkby team Keyways who had future Premiership players Leighton Baines and Ryan Taylor in their ranks.

He was still with Whiston Juniors and whilst playing in a tournament in Blackpool fate played its hand in shaping David's future. Sheffield United Scout Howard Revans was present to check out a prospect but his attention was drawn to David's Whiston teammates repeatedly mobbing him as he scored goal after goal. On the strength of what he had witnessed, Howard recommended Nuge to Sheffield United. The Blades trial didn't lead to anything but such was Howard's faith in David's potential that he arranged further trials with Sheffield Wednesday, Bolton Wanderers, Chester City, Tranmere Rovers and Crewe Alexandra. It was largely due to the efforts of David's mum (who regularly borrowed a car from a family friend) that he was able to travel up and down the country to attend each unsuccessful trial. Although the rejections hurt, they heightened his resolve to succeed. However, unbeknownst to him and those around him, David had an underlying problem which had been affecting his performances. A 300 - mile round trip to Northampton Town had resulted in another disappointment and significantly, David being told he was unfit. Tests by his doctor worryingly revealed that David had viral meningitis and after being hospitalised and successfully treated, mum Sandra played a big part in helping his return to fitness. Every day for three months they both painstakingly swam length after length at Huyton Leisure Centre until David was ready for his next trial which Howard had arranged for him at Bury's training ground. Sandra, filled with trepidation and fearing another thumbs down, had to be coaxed out of the car by Dave snr to watch the game. She needn't have worried as their son played a blinder, scored four goals and received a two-year YTS contract straight after the final whistle. David had finally been given his chance and he was not going to blow it. Following a hat trick on his youth team debut, he was reinstated as a central striker and he has been banging in goals from that position ever since.

Bury player-manager Andy Preece wasted no time in handing him his first team debut. On 23 March 2002, the 16-year old came off the bench to replace Paul Reid in the 84th minute of a 1-1 home draw versus Port Vale. He made three further substitute appearances in the last few weeks of the 2001/02 season and, in the final game of the campaign, he made his full Football League debut when Bury were defeated 2-1 by Peterborough United. The following season he notched his first goal against Darlington on 12 October 2002 to help the Shakers draw 2-2 with the Quakers. David scored an additional four goals from his 14 starts and 25 appearances from the bench to help the club to a seventh

©Martin Ogden Photography

©Martin Ogden Photography

place finish. This entitled them to compete in the play-offs where they faced Bournemouth. The Cherries beat Bury heralding the start of an amazing few seasons which took them all the way to the Premiership. David established himself in the team during the following campaign and was in scintillating form at the start of the 2004/05 season which made many clubs sit up and take notice of him. An opening day brace was followed by 10 further strikes to make him the club's top scorer, although he had left Bury long before the season had reached its conclusion. The Bury faithful were aware of the rumours linking Nuge with a move away from Gigg Lane. They had seen it before with Terry McDermott, Neville Southall, Lee Dixon and many others who had left the club to move onto a bigger stage. So it came as no surprise when, on 11 January 2005, he put pen to paper on a £100,000 transfer deal with Championship outfit Preston North End.

Manager Billy Davies opted to ease his new man into the side by giving him four successive starts from the bench. In the last of these on 12 February 2005 at Loftus Road in front of 15,620 spectators, he replaced Patrick Agyemang in the 57th minute of their contest with QPR. Rangers held a 1-0 lead but ten minutes later David levelled the score and the Preston fans had a new hero. Chris Lucketti added to David's strike and the points were secured, as was David's place in the starting line up until the end of the season. When added to his Bury tally, Nuge returned 21 goals from 45 starts and five substitute appearances and his contribution played a big part in the Lilywhites reaching the play-offs. David scored one of Preston's two semi-final goals against Derby County to secure safe passage to the Wembley Final. On 30 May 2005 and with 70,275 fans present, the scene was set for the Invincibles to live up to their old nickname and return to the top flight for the first time since the 1960/61 season. They had already twice accounted for their opponents West Ham United in the regular fixtures and were many people's favourites to win. However, when Bobby Zamora poked the ball home just before the hour mark the Hammers fans were blowing bubbles all the way back to the Boleyn Ground and the Premiership whilst the Preston fans returned home crestfallen. The following season also ended in disappointment when Leeds United defeated them in the play-off semis after they had finished fourth and just a single point short of automatic promotion.

Personally, David enjoyed a tremendous campaign - he established himself as an England U-21s regular, was the club's top scorer and his Championship peers voted for him as their PFA Young Player of the Year. Although promotion again eluded the club when they finished seventh in 2006/07, David continued to progress and from his 47 domestic appearances he found the net 17 times. Much to his delight, this prompted England Manager Steve McLaren to call him up to the full international squad for the Euro 2008 qualifying games. David loves scoring and although he offers much more than just goals to the team, goals are his currency. This was never more evident than on 28 March 2007 when he etched his name in the record books. In the 79th minute of England's match against European minnows Andorra at Espanyol's stadium in Barcelona, McLaren gave Andy Johnson the hook and sent David into the action. It was the first time that a Preston player had appeared for England since the great Tom Finney had done so 50 years earlier. It had also been eight years since Sunderland's Michael Gray had become the last player from outside of the Premiership to wear the three lions on his chest. David was keen to add to those impressive historical facts and three minutes into added time, he did. When Jermaine Defoe's shot crept under the Andorra keeper and was goal bound

David's predatory instincts kicked in. Without giving Defoe a second thought (he would have done the same) he rifled the ball home from inches out to become only the third player in England international history to have made one substitute appearance and scored one goal - Francis Jeffers and Paul Goddard being the others. David's goal sealed a 3-0 victory and with Steven Gerrard accounting for the other two goals, it made a unique Huyton hat trick.

By the start of the 2007/08 season, David's stock had understandably risen and Portsmouth Manager Harry Redknapp paid £6 million to take him to Fratton Park and the Premier League. He spent four years at Pompey and enjoyed mixed fortunes. Redknapp had assembled a large and expensive squad and competition for places was fierce. After starting the opening two games of the campaign, David was relegated to the bench. Although he only started five League games and made ten substitute appearances, it was not all doom and gloom. Whilst Premiership goals eluded him, he found joy in the cup competitions. He scored his first goal for the club in the closing minutes of a League Cup second round 3-0 victory over Leeds United on 28 August 2007. He followed this up with the only goal of the game in the next round of the same competition to account for Burnley. His only other goal that season came in the third round of the FA Cup. Having been brought on to replace Pedro Mendes at the start of the second half at Ipswich Town's Portman Road, Nuge found the back of the net just five minutes later to secure victory. This sent the club on a journey which went all the way to Wembley Stadium on 17 May 2008. With 89,874 people present and Cardiff City providing the opposition, David again found himself warming the bench. In the 69th minute and with Pompey leading 1-0 courtesy of a Nwankwo Kanu goal, Redknapp sent him into the action. Similar to every young football fan, David had always dreamt of playing in the FA Cup Final - the greatest cup competition in the world. He almost put the icing on the cake when a fierce rising drive forced the Cardiff keeper to make a fine near post save but Pompey saw the game out to lift the trophy for the first time in 69 years. Immediately after David had climbed the famous Wembley steps to receive his winners' medal, in a selfless gesture he gave the historic keepsake to his proud father as a timely birthday present.

Although the victory had represented a great achievement for the club, football has a short memory and after a poor start to the 2008/09 campaign Redknapp was shown the door. It is fair to say that David had not always seen eye to eye with him and he got more opportunities under his replacement Tony Adams. Goals were still hard to come by but he took great satisfaction when, on 18 January 2009, he scored his first Premiership goal at White Hart Lane against Tottenham Hotspur and their recently- appointed Boss - Harry Redknapp! After four substitute appearances at the start of the 2009/10 season, David joined Owen Coyle's Burnley side on a four-month loan. He made his debut on 12

©Martin Ogden Photography

September 1990 in a 4-0 thrashing at the hands of Liverpool but his home debut versus Sunderland a week later was a much more enjoyable contest. With 20,196 present and with the score standing at 1-1, Nuge came off the bench in the 57th minute of the game. Less than 20 minutes later he had endeared himself to the Turf Moor fans by netting two goals to secure the points for the Clarets. David's loan was extended with a view to a permanent move but despite scoring five goals and the club wanting him, personal terms couldn't be agreed so he returned to Portsmouth.

In David's absence, the club had been through a turbulent time which had resulted in player departures, financial difficulties and relegation to the Championship. He scored 13 goals as they finished a disappointing 16th in a season with few highlights. However, David always seemed to do well and score against clubs who would later sign him and this was the case when Leicester City were battered 6-1 at Fratton Park. His goal and overall performance impressed Foxes Boss Sven Goran Erikson sufficiently for the former England Manager to sign David before the start of the 2011/12 season. He made his debut in a 1-0 defeat at the hands of Coventry City on 6 August 2011 and eleven days later versus Bristol City, he scored the first of 16 goals which made him the club's top scorer. The following campaign also resulted in David leading their goal-scoring chart with a tally of 14 which included his first hat trick in a 3-1 win against Hull City. The team reached the play-offs with a sixth place finish and their semi-final tie opposing Watford will long stay in David's memory. He scored in both legs of the encounter and with the aggregate score standing at 2-2 and extra-time looming, Leicester were awarded an injury time penalty. Anthony Knockaert stepped up and not only was his strike saved by the Hornet's keeper but just 20 seconds later Troy Deeney blasted the ball into the Foxes' net to seal Watford's place in the Final.

Leicester's heartbreak of 2012/13 was matched by their elation the following season as, with Nigel Pearson now at the helm, they romped to the Championship title and automatic promotion to the Premier League. With 20 League goals, David was the club's leading scorer for the third successive season and his strike partnership with future England man Jamie Vardy struck fear into defences week after week. By Christmas 2014, it looked as if Leicester's stay in the top Division was going to be short-lived. Their 2-1 defeat at home to Tottenham on Boxing Day meant that they hadn't won a League fixture since 21 September when they turned Man Utd over 5-3 at Old Trafford and David had scored a 62nd minute penalty. They had not won in 13 matches and were rooted at the bottom of the table. Miraculously, they only lost one of their last nine games to haul themselves to safety and finish in a respectable 14th place. The Foxes carried that form into the following season to cause one of the biggest surprises in football history by winning the Premier League! Whilst David was delighted for Vardy and co, he was no longer a Leicester player having signed for Middlesborough on 14 August 2015 for a transfer fee of £4,000,000.

Championship side Boro lacked Leicester's flair but not their work ethic. Manager Aitor Karanka employed David in a lone striker's role, he worked his socks off for the team's cause and it paid dividends. They lost only two of their opening 11 fixtures and although he 'only' scored eight goals all season he was still the club's main source of League goals. The fact that 15 other members of the squad also found the back of the net gives some indication of the team's shared responsibility in this aspect of their approach to games. Moreover, it worked and in a nail-biting last game of the season they drew 1-1 with main rivals Brighton to guarantee the runners-up spot behind champions Burnley to secure automatic promotion. Although Karanka did his best to keep the Teessiders in the top flight, the style of play he had utilised successfully in 2015/16 failed miserably against the big boys. He was sacked a couple of months before the season ended with the club being relegated. Prior to this, David had also left after spending the majority of the season watching from the sidelines. On 9 January 2017, he joined Derby County for a fee of £2.5 million.

Footynote:

David's 17 goals from his 94 Rams appearances helped the club reach consecutive play-offs, both of which ended disappointingly. In 2019, twelve years after departing, he returned to PNE before joining Tranmere Rovers on loan.

CALLUM MACMANAMAN

Like all football-obsessed youngsters, Callum Macmanaman dreamt of playing in the FA Cup Final. Whether he was turning out for his first proper team Rainhill Utd or just kicking a ball around outside the family home in Sandhurst Road, just a long throw-in away from Whiston Hospital, thoughts of the oldest national football competition in the world would often occupy his thoughts. Unlike the vast majority of those youngsters, Callum's dream became a reality - and how!

Born on 25 April 1991, Everton fan Callum joined his beloved Toffees when he was just six years of age. He is extremely grateful to former Youth Academy coach Tosh Farrell who, along with his dad, he cites as the biggest influence on his career. As a young Gwladys Street ball boy, Callum loved watching his hero Duncan Ferguson at close quarters but that was the nearest he got to the action on the hallowed Goodison Park turf. Callum was devastated when, at the age of 15, he was released by the club and consequently did not kick a ball for months. Eventually, when he did put his boots back on, Wigan Athletic showed interest in him and his love of the game was rekindled.

Callum wasted little time making a positive impression in Wigan's youth sides and made his reserve team debut towards the latter stages of the 2007/08 season. The following campaign he consolidated his place in the second string when he was a regular on the team sheet and amongst the goals. His efforts were rewarded on 24 May 2009 when, in the 78th minute of the first team's clash with Portsmouth, Manager Roberto Martinez introduced him to the action as replacement for Charles N'Zogbia. Wigan registered a 1-0 victory and Callum entered the record books as the youngest player to represent the club in the Premier League. He spent the majority of the next two seasons in the reserves but got his first start in Wigan colours in a competition that proved to be very kind to him. On 8 January 2011 at Hull City's KC stadium 10,433 gathered to watch the FA Cup third round tie between the Tigers and the Latics. Callum seized his opportunity brilliantly and, in addition to creating the game's opening goal, his thumping strike from 20 yards found the back of the net and helped the club to a 3-2 victory. In October of the same year, in order to get more game time, Martinez sent Callum on a 14-game loan period to Blackpool. On his return, he continued to make the occasional appearance as a substitute but in the 2012/13 FA Cup competition, he came to the fore in great style. After less than convincing early round victories over Bournemouth and Macclesfield Town, Wigan's campaign gained momentum. They made short shrift of Huddersfield Town with a 4-1 victory as Callum netted his first FA Cup goal. His Man-of-the-Match performance prompted a revealing insight into the youngster's character from his Boss who stated, "Callum is a tremendous talent, but he gets a bit nervous before games. We had to tell him yesterday that he wasn't playing so he could get a good night's sleep. When we told him this morning that he was playing he was delighted, and you saw the result."

©Bernard Platt

©Bernard Platt

It is unclear if the same managerial tactic was employed in the quarter-final encounter with Everton but Callum was instrumental in the club reaching the semis for the first time in their history with a 3-0 victory over his boyhood club. The Latics scored their goals in a whirlwind five-minute spell with Callum grabbing the second goal on "the best day of my life." Remarkably, Callum was yet to start a Premier League game, but Martinez rectified this at the next available opportunity – a home game versus Newcastle United on 17 March 2013. An over-exuberant, mistimed tackle by Callum on the Magpies Massadio Haidara attracted a great deal of unwanted, negative media attention. To his credit, he was able to put this behind him and a week later he notched his first Premiership goal in a 2-2 draw with Spurs. The young winger carried this form into the semi-final fixture with Championship outfit Millwall and in the 78th minute he coolly rounded the keeper to slot home. This followed an earlier Shaun Maloney strike and made Callum's FA Cup Final dream a reality. On 11 May 2013, the 132nd FA Cup Final took place between Wigan Athletic and Manchester City at Wembley Stadium before a crowd of 86,254. With a later than usual kick-off time of 5.15pm, the match was expected to attract a worldwide television audience of more than half a billion people – a far cry from one man and his dog watching Rainhill United – and Callum revelled in it. Turning defenders inside out at the heart of the action, Callum was a constant thorn in City's side. In the 91st minute with extra-time and penalties looming, Ben Watson rose like a salmon to head home from a corner to seal one

©Bernard Platt

of the biggest FA Cup Final upsets of all time. Callum's outstanding performance earned him the Man of the Match award yet, although he was delighted, his celebrations were somewhat muted.

Unusually for the FA Cup Winners, Wigan were involved in a relegation dogfight and with two vital games to come, he and his teammates had to show tremendous restraint. The best Callum could manage was to dash to the Holt pub for a couple of pints before retiring to his bedroom in Sandhurst Road to reflect on the events of the day. Callum's meteoric rise to prominence was not lost on England U-21 Boss Stuart Pearce who named him in the squad for the UEFA Championships in Israel. On the same day, he picked up a nasty injury in a defeat to Arsenal denying him the opportunity to add to his four caps at U-20s level. The Arsenal result sent Wigan down to the Championship proving how fickle the game of football can be. Callum initially stayed loyal to the Latics but in January 2015 he made the difficult decision to leave the DW Stadium. His stock was high and he had plenty of potential suitors. In retrospect, opting to join West Bromwich Albion in a £4.75 million deal was probably a mistake. A player of Callum's ability should have been scaling new heights but at the Hawthorns his career stagnated. In a two-year spell, he spent more time warming the bench than on the field of play and was effectively frozen out by Manager Tony Pulis.

After spending half of the 2016/17 season on loan at Sheffield Wednesday and the following campaign in a West Midlands footballing wilderness, Sunderland Boss Simon Grayson paid an undisclosed fee to take Callum to the Stadium of Light. He made 26 appearances for the Black Cats and displayed the magic he had been unable to show in recent years. Callum became a fans' favourite and was happy but when he became aware of Wigan's interest in taking him 'home', the memories came flooding back and the lure proved too great to resist. On 20 July 2018, there was optimism in the Wigan air as Callum re-joined the Latics and supporters' thoughts drifted to when he was the best player on the pitch on the best day in their club's history. Unfortunately, the adage about not returning to your successful stomping ground were borne out when things didn't go as planned and Callum left the club less than a year later. After making just three starts and a further 21 appearances from the bench, he joined Luton Town on 4 June 2019.

Footynote:

Callum's 26 games in a Hatters jersey returned four goals before, in November 2020, he joined Australian club Melbourne Victory on a two-year deal. He scored the A-League goal of the season on his debut and found the net on three more occasions. In July 2021 Callum returned home to join Tranmere Rovers.

CONOR MACALANEY

Much-travelled striker Conor McAlaney had already plied his trade at no fewer than eight clubs before reaching his 26th birthday. Born on 12 August 1992, he grew up on Huyton's St Johns estate and attended Knowsley Hey School. He joined Everton as an 11-year old and stayed at the club for eight years, progressing swiftly through the ranks. Before later adopting a 'number 10' role, Conor was a prolific goal scorer and registered 49 times for the Blues under 18s, 21s and 23s to put himself in the first team frame. After being on the bench for a few games, he got the nod from David Moyes to join the action in the 76th minute of a League match versus Arsenal on 10 December 2011, replacing Phil Neville. With 60,062 in attendance, Robin Van Persie had just set the Emirates alight with a stunning left foot strike to give the Gunners the lead. Within minutes of entering the fray, Conor came within a whisker of levelling the game with a precocious half-volley but it wasn't to be and his debut ended in a 1-0 defeat. He followed this up a week later with a substitute appearance in a 1-1 home draw versus Norwich City.

Conor had to wait three years before again tasting first team action but in the interim he experienced a couple of curtailed loan deals. He came off Scunthorpe's bench in a League One stalemate before making his full League debut on 31 March 2012 when the Iron trounced Chesterfield with a resounding 4-1 victory. He got one more game under his belt before injury forced a return to Finch Farm where, the following season, he registered ten goals for the U-21s. Then, just four games into a seasonlong loan with Brentford, Conor suffered a broken leg which put paid to his involvement in the first few months of the 2013/14 campaign. He worked his socks off to regain fitness and on 11 December 2014, with qualification to the next phase of the Europa League secured, new Everton Boss Roberto Martinez handed Conor a first team shirt opposing Krasnodar. The game finished a disappointing 1-0 in the Russians' favour and it proved to be Conor's only start for the Toffees.

The remainder of his time at Everton was largely spent away from Goodison on a succession of loans. On 2 February 2015 he joined Cardiff City for whom he made eight appearances and scored two goals - including his debut League strike against Rotherham United a month after joining the Championship outfit. He began the 2015/16 season at Charlton Athletic's Valley Parade and made nine appearances for the Addicks before moving closer to home to join Wigan Athletic. A debut away goal in a 2-0 defeat of Sheffield United got Conor's four-month spell playing under Gary Caldwell off to a flying start and three more goals before the 2015/16 season came to a close helped the Latics gain promotion as League One champions.

Before Wigan's participation in the Championship was under way, Conor briefly returned to Everton then joined Oxford United on deadline day of the January 2017 transfer window. The loan spell involved 14 starts and five substitute appearances and returned an impressive ten goals. Conor twice walked away with the match ball after registering hat tricks against Chesterfield and Bury. When Everton decided not to renew Connor's contract at the end of the season, unsurprisingly there were a host of potential suitors wanting to snap him up. He opted to join Joey Barton's Huyton-driven revolution at Fleetwood Town and put pen to paper on a three-year deal at Highbury.

Despite getting 2017/18 off to a flying start with a debut brace versus Rotherham, Conor struggled to repeat his Oxford goal scoring exploits but still managed five League One goals from his 34 Trawlermen appearances. The following campaign started in a similar vein and although Conor's game is not just about hitting the back of the net, one goal from 19 outings was disappointing. Joey sent young Conor (he was still only 24) out on loan to Kilmarnock of the Scottish Premier and he announced himself to the Killie faithful with another debut goal (opposing Dundee). Before returning to his parent club, Conor scored two additional goals including the opener in a 1-1 draw with Steven Gerrard's Rangers. He started the 2019/20 season back in the Fleetwood fold but ended it out on loan with five games for Shrewsbury Town.

©Edward Garvey Photographer

Just as the doubters were perhaps beginning to question whether Conor would ever fulfil his potential, former Leeds and Liverpool player Harry Kewell swooped to recruit him to Olgham Athletic on a free transfer. Sometimes forwards are unfairly judged on their goal scoring record and at first glance, Conor's record of 29 goals from 149 appearances is not too impressive. However, on closer inspection, Conor joined 62 of those games from the bench and often played for just a few minutes. In addition, most clubs he had played for to this point had been struggling at the wrong end of the table and generally found goals hard to come by. Also, Conor was often utilised in a deeper role than the out and out striker position he had filled as a youngster. Kewell obviously considered the bigger picture and was delighted with his acquisition. On 5 September 2020 in an EFL Cup match opposing Carlisle, Conor scored on his debut for the fourth time in his career.

©Edward Garvey Photographer

Footynote:

This provided the launchpad for Conor to enjoy the most impressive goal scoring tally of his career. From his 46 appearances across all competitions he rattled home 21 goals. This attracted the attention of a number of clubs and in July 2021 he put pen to paper on a two-year deal with Salford City.

JON TAYLOR

When Harry Taylor formed a new junior football club, Recs Roby, his intention was to give local youngsters an opportunity to enjoy and develop their football skills in a friendly and organised environment. Little did he know that he was also sending his son Jon on a journey which would take in dozens of Football League grounds and stop along the way at one of the most iconic and famous stadiums in the world. Initially, at the age of six, Jon who was born on 20 July 1992 was considered too young to play for his dad's U-9s team. He consoled himself by kicking a ball about and watching from the touchline as older brother Ben and his teammates played on Roby Field around the corner from their Beechburn Crescent home. However, when his dad gave him a runout as sub versus Mags JFC Jon found the back of the net twice and a regular place in the side.

Jon also enjoyed early success in schoolboy football and was instrumental in helping his Roby Park Primary School team win an unprecedented hat trick of trophies. He proudly represented Huyton Boys and later Knowsley Boys for whom he twice scored Cup Final winners versus their Liverpool counterparts. His performances for Roby Park, Huyton Boys and Recs Roby helped him to secure a six-week trial with Liverpool. Six weeks became twelve weeks and this became eighteen weeks as the Reds dragged their heels about offering the youngster a contract. Aware that Wigan Athletic Scout Paul Kelly was keen for Jon to join the Latics and frustrated at Liverpool's indecision, his dad took him along for a trial - Jon signed for Wigan the following day and stayed for seven years! He loved his time at the club and as he crouched on the perimeter of the pitch as a Premiership matchday ball boy, he dreamt of one day crossing the touchline to join the action. Although Jon progressed well through the junior ranks, much to his surprise and dismay, when the YTS places were dished out he was not offered one. Whilst his ability wasn't in doubt, the Wigan hierarchy felt that he was too small to make the grade. The same reason was cited when Jon was turned down by Tranmere Rovers and Port Vale. Not for the first time, Tony Kelly (who at the time was a Wigan coach) came to the aid of a fellow Huytonian by recommending Jon to one of his former clubs, Shrewsbury Town.

Stinging from rejection but determined to succeed, 15-year old Jon was on fire in his trial games and the Shrews coaches were keen to give him a scholarship. First team Boss Gary Peters was another who had reservations about his size but in youth coach and former Welsh international Nigel Vaughan, Jon found a kindred spirit who had faith in his ability and potential. At 5'5" tall, Vaughan had overcome similar negativity and proved the doubters wrong by enjoying a lengthy career and bagging eleven caps for his country. He feared that Jon was about to be shown the door by the boss but was aware that Peters' own future at the club was far from secure. He advised Jon to dodge the bullet by going on holiday. He confided in his ever-supportive parents that his dream may be coming to a premature end and he may have to start looking for another line of work on his return to England. However, midway through his Tenerife holiday Vaughan rang him with the news that Peters had been sacked and the scholarship he craved had been given the green light. New Manager Paul Simpson wasn't the tallest player to ever grace a pitch but Jon wasn't taking any chances and supplemented his diet with milk shakes to bulk up. Consequently, his height and physique were no longer an issue and he developed skills and techniques which made his lack of inches an attribute. With a scholarship secured and Jon loving life in Walford College digs with his fellow scholars, he concentrated on improving his game and progressing. He shone for the youth team, was handed the captaincy and during his second year as a scholar he stepped up to join the first team squad.

On 1 July 2009, Jon delightedly put pen to paper on his first pro contract. Six months later on 2 January 2010 at Chesterfield's Saltergate Stadium, with Shrewsbury leading 1-0 but down to ten men, Simpson brought 17-year old Jon off the bench to replace Lewis Neal. It was backs to the wall for the sixteen minutes of Jon's debut but they hung on to get his career off to a winning start. Apart from a further substitute appearance towards the end of the 2009/10 season, Jon had to wait almost twelve months before further involvement with the first team. Jon will always be grateful to Simpson for helping him to make the breakthrough but when he left the club it was under his replacement Graham Turner that Jon really made his mark. After playing the second half of a televised 1-0 defeat at the hands of Bury, so impressed was Jon's new gaffer that he rewarded him with a full debut on 1 February 2011 and he did not let him down. Understandably nervous, Jon had a poor first half and began to wonder if he was up to the challenge. In the 55th minute of the game his doubts were dispelled. Following a Shrews corner, Ian Sharps pulled the ball back to Tayls who, from the edge of the box, rifled it past the despairing keeper much to the delight of the 4,343 present. A good debut became a great debut fifteen minutes later when Jon added a second. The game ended 3-0 to the blue and ambers - only their third win of the season from thirteen attempts. Jon also found the net in each of their next two matches making it four goals from three games in seven days. This represented a change in the Shropshire club's fortunes and Jon was at the heart of the transformation. They lost only three of their remaining nineteen games to reach the play-offs but a 2-0 aggregate defeat by Torquay United confined them to another season in League Two.

©Heather King Photography

There was to be no such disappointment at the business end of the following campaign as they romped to automatic promotion by finishing second in the table behind champions Swindon Town. A 38th minute header was sufficient to account for Dagenham & Redbridge and secure the necessary points with a game to spare. This signalled a long weekend of celebrations for fans and players alike, which included an open top bus tour and Town Hall reception. The step up to the third tier of English football proved to be a struggle and cost Turner his job before they succumbed to relegation in May 2014. Despite this, Jon continued to flourish and he registered six goals in 2012/13 and was the club's top scorer with nine goals in the relegation campaign - a decent return for a wide player in a struggling side.

His stock was high and continued to rise after Darren Ferguson signed him for Peterborogh Utd on 4 July 2014. From his twenty-five Posh appearances in his debut season, he scored three goals as they finished in ninth spot in League One. The 2015/16 campaign saw Jon double the number of games he played and quadruple his goals tally. His impressive 13 goals from the wing included a brace against Millwall, an 86th minute FA Cup equaliser versus WBA, a goal in the replay and a 90th minute winner in a seven-goal thriller versus Shrewsbury - a goal he did not celebrate as a mark of respect for his former employers. However, he surpassed all of these achievements in blistering fashion. Peterborough faced Blackpool on the final day of the 2015/16 season. Jon was warming the bench until being introduced to the action with just eighteen minutes of the game remaining. With the score standing at 1-1, Jon took the game by storm and in a dozen stunning minutes, he rattled home a hat trick to walk away with his first match ball. The game ended 5-1 and proved to be Jon's final game in Posh colours. Lower league legend Barry Fry was the Director of Football at London Road and it was not unusual for him to part company with a player who was nearing the end of their contract. Jon fell into this category so it was no great surprise for him to be at a new club when the 2016/17 season kicked off. However, for neither Jon or his agent to be involved in the discussions or negotiations with his new club WAS unusual to say the least. In his own inimitable style, Fry rang Jon and said "Hi Jon, we've sold you!" The manner of the deal was unconventional but there was no ill feeling from Jon as it was a 'win, win' for all concerned. Rotherham Utd were happy to break their record transfer fee and stump up £500,000 to get their man, Jon was delighted to be joining a Championship club and the fee represented good business for Posh.

On 6 August 2016, Jon made his Millers debut in a 2-2 home draw with Wolves in front of a crowd of 11,291. He registered four goals from forty-three appearances but points were hard to come by and a poor campaign ended in relegation. This was a huge disappointment for Jon and everyone associated with the club but these emotions were negated twelve months later. Following a fourth place finish, Rotherham overcame Scunthorpe Utd 4-2 on aggregate in the play-off semis with Jon breaking the deadlock in the first leg. On 27 May 2018 at a sun-soaked, world-famous Wembley Stadium and seemingly a million miles away from Roby Field, Jon took his place in the Rotherham line-up to compete against the Shrews for the final promotion place to the Championship. Sitting nervously but immensely proud amongst the crowd of 26,218 were Jon's girlfriend, his mum Yvonne and dad Harry who had set the ball rolling twenty years earlier. His parents had travelled all over the country to watch their boy throughout his career, usually alone. On this occasion, they were joined by dozens of Jon's family and friends who had made the journey from Huyton to wish him well. Similar to many players involved in big games, probably due to a combination of nerves and excitement, Jon has few recollections of the match. However, a quick glance at the record books will confirm that Rotherham defeated Shrewsbury by a scoreline of 2-1 after extra-time to return to the Championship at the first time of asking.

Once again, the division proved to be too tough a test for the Millers and the 2018/19 campaign ended in relegation. The season did contain some memorable moments including goals for Jon in each of the South Yorkshire derbies against Sheffield Wednesday and United. He also enjoyed facing Manchester City in the FA Cup at the Etihad stadium in front of 52,708 spectators - although he did not enjoy the 7-0 thumping they received! Another meeting with Premiership opposition ended in bitter disappointment for Jon and played no small part in his departure from the club. On 29 August 2018, they faced Everton at Goodson Park in the second round of the Caraboa Cup. As a lifelong Liverpool fan, Jon relished the chance to oppose their rivals from across Stanley Park but boss Paul Warne named him amongst the substitutes. Tayls did get a piece of the action when he left the bench in the 72nd minute of the 3-1 defeat but he was so incensed that he uncharacteristically went to see the manager the following day informing him that he wanted to leave the club. Warne had always told his players that if anybody wanted to leave the club he would grant their wish but on this occasion he refused. Warne reinstated Jon to the starting eleven for the weekend's fixture with Wigan but the damage was done. When Jon received the offer of a new contract at the end of the campaign, due to this and other factors, he turned it down. He signed for League One outfit Doncaster Rovers on 9 August 2019.

©Heather King Photography

LEE NICHOLLS

©john@thelightmonkey.com

There is plenty of evidence provided by eminent football statisticians supporting the argument that a goalkeeper's career is, on average, lengthier than that of an outfield player. In addition, keepers tend to hit their peak a few years later than their teammates. With this in mind, it is reasonable to assume that Huytonian Lee Nicholls who is in his late-twenties (and has already totted up in excess of 200 appearances) may still have his best years ahead of him and could go on to amass a huge tally of games played.

From an early age Lee, who was born on 5 October 1992, was impressing scouts with his agility, safe handling and immense potential. When he left Liverpool at 14 years of age, there were a host of clubs eager to recruit him and he opted to join Wigan Athletic. At this time, as a member of the Cardinal Heenan and Liverpool Boys U-15s sides he was helping them challenge for numerous trophies. In May 2008 he appeared in three finals at three Football League grounds in just five days. On Friday 16th Liverpool Boys defeated Brighton & Hove at Goodison Park 4-2 to lift the English Schools Trophy. Three days later at Prenton Park, the Merseyside and District title was secured when the same team swept Wirral aside by a scoreline of 3-0. The following day the last game of the triumvirate ended in a narrow 2-1 defeat for Cardinal Heenan. Harefield Academy from Middlesex were the victors at Watford's Vicarage Road and walked away with the ESFA Individual Schools Trophy. Whilst disappointing, to get so close to winning a competition which involved nine rounds and more than 1,000 teams nationwide cannot be deemed as failure, especially at the end of such a busy week for Lee.

In the summer of 2009 Lee signed scholarship forms with the Latics and his first pro contract followed in January the following year. On 8 February 2011, he proudly picked up his first international cap when he was between the sticks in a 1-0 reversal imposed upon England's U-19s by Germany at Chesterfield's ground in front of a 9,141-strong crowd.

Wigan Boss Roberto Martinez sent him out on loan to Hartlepool, Sheffield Wednesday and Shrewsbury Town but the Football League debut he craved failed to materialise. However, when Accrington Stanley Manager John Coleman welcomed him into the fold in a three-month deal on 24 February 2012, he threw the teenager in at the deep-end the next day. A 2-0 away defeat inflicted by top of the table Swindon Town was the first of nine appearances Lee made before returning to his parent club. The only victory during this spell accounted for Northampton Town and it was the Cobblers who presented Lee with his next taste of League action. A seasonlong loan with the East Midlands outfit kicked off with a goalless contest versus Rochdale. It was the first of 51 games he played in a season where he really announced himself to English football. Under the stewardship of Aidy Boothroyd, Northampton secured a 2012/13 play-off place after finishing sixth in Division

Two. They overcame Cheltenham Town 2-0 on aggregate in the semis and Lee was in impeccable form making numerous saves including keeping out a penalty attempt. A Wembley Final date in front of a crowd of 47,127 was secured but there was to be no fairytale ending for Northampton as they succumbed to three first half Bradford City goals. The Bantams were promoted whilst the Cobblers had to pick themselves up and try again the following season. Their task became more difficult when Lee returned to Wigan and, perhaps consequently, Northampton finished a disappointing 21st just three points above the relegation zone.

On 24 September 2013, Martinez' replacement Owen Coyle handed Lee his long-awaited Wigan debut in a League Cup third round tie. With Manchester City providing the opposition at the Etihad Stadium this was never going to be an easy introduction and so it proved. Lee was able to keep the Premiership millionaires at bay until the 33rd minute of the game but a late flurry of goals resulted in a 5-0 victory for the Citizens. It was a different story a month later when he made his Latics League debut. With regular keeper Scott Carson injured in the warm-up, the 21-year old was unexpectedly thrust into the fray versus Charlton Athletic. In a Man-of-the-Match performance, Lee pulled off a string of fine saves to deny the Addicks and help his side to a creditable scoreless draw. Before the turn of the year, he made a further seven appearances but was packing his bags for his sixth loan spell in September 2015. His destination was Bristol Rovers and he made the first of eighteen Pirates appearances in a 1-0 defeat to one of his previous loan clubs, Accrington Stanley. After spending three months at the Memorial Stadium he returned to Wigan but it became apparent that he needed to find a new permanent home to secure regular first team football.

When MK Dons Boss and former Prescot Cables player Karl Robinson invited him to Milton Keynes, he jumped at the chance. Initially, he was understudy to David Martin, son of former West Ham and England centre-half Alvin, and was only called upon for cup contests. His first game took place on 9 August 2016 in a thrilling League Cup tussle with Newport County. Losing 2-0, the Dons registered twice before snatching a last-minute victory courtesy of a Dean Bowditch strike. When, towards the run-in of the 2016/17 campaign, Lee was handed a prolonged spell in the team he seized his opportunity with both gloves and was the regular custodian of the keeper's jersey for the following three seasons. During this period, the club suffered relegation at the end of 2017/18 but bounced straight back to League One a year later.

In July 2021, after making 157 appearances for MK, Lee signed for Championship side Huddersfield Town. On 1 August, a clean sheet on his debut versus Sheffield Wednesday helped him settle in to the second tier of English football and he quickly made the goalkeeping position his own.

If the statisticians are to be believed, Lee Nicholls should have many more seasons and his best form ahead of him. The Terriers faithful will be hoping that this will be spent serving their club but such is Lee's talent he has regularly been linked with a move to one of the bigger clubs, most notably Liverpool and Man Utd. Wherever he plies his trade, it is guaranteed that he will give his all for his club and rattle up a host of appearances and clean sheets before the Huyton shot-stopper hangs up his cap and gloves.

©john@thelightmonkey.com

CHRIS LONG

Chris Long is an extremely talented and ambitious young footballer. He has always possessed the precious, uncanny knack of finding the back of the net with great regularity which has made him a much sought-after player. He was just five years of age when his mum and aunt took him and his cousin to play for Woolton side Springwood and rarely a game went by when Longy did not register his name amongst the scorers. Scouts were soon clamouring to take him under their wing with Manchester City, Liverpool and Everton amongst the forerunners to court him.

Following spells at City and Liverpool, he opted to join the Blues which was a bit of a coup for Everton as Chris was a massive Reds fan who idolised Michael Owen. However, the staff at Bellefield and in particular coaches Tony Farrell and Eddie Murray, made him feel so welcome that the choice was a no-brainer. Chris coupled training and playing for Everton with continuing to turn out for Springwood before joining Netherley Legion for whom he recalls scoring twelve goals in one game. As his reputation continued to grow, the goals also came thick and fast for Chris on enjoyable Everton tours of London, France and Germany. He signed for Everton when he was eight-years of age and steadily developed his game under the club's coaching staff. Football dominated his young life and when he wasn't playing for the Toffees, he would travel to Kirkby and Manchester to score goal after goal for Birkbeck JFC and Brendon Bees JFC respectively. Chris also made a massive impact for his St Margaret Mary's Primary School teams and once scored five goals at Anfield to help them win a year six Final. A place in the Huyton Boys team was a formality and it was playing for them that he got his first opportunity to play at Goodison Park following a 2-0 semi-final defeat of their Wirral counterparts with Chris grabbing both goals. He rose to the challenge by scoring the winner at the 'Street End' in a 2-1 victory over Liverpool Boys to secure the Everton Cup.

When Chris moved to Cardinal Heenan Senior School, Everton were unhappy about him representing the school but he reasoned that taking part in a competitive match was preferable to training and "there's nothing better than playing with your mates." Longy's efforts were being recognised on all fronts and he made his England U-16s debut on 15 October 2010 in a 4-0 defeat versus Wales. Then, on 30 March of the following year, he won his second cap as the nation's youngsters defeated Scotland 2-1 to lift the Victory Shield. Sandwiched between these games, the young striker made his debut for Everton's youth team when coming off the bench to face Bolton Wanderers.

Upon leaving school, Chris secured a two-year full time scholarship and made rapid progress under the guidance of Duncan Ferguson and Kevin Sheedy. In the 2011/12 season, he registered nine goals from 19 youth team games, scored a brace versus the Faroe Islands on his England U-17s debut and broke into the Everton reserves side for whom he made seven appearances and scored one goal. The following campaign proved significant for Chris. In addition to proudly picking up the Everton Academy Player of the Year award, he represented his country for the U-18s, U-19s and U-20s for whom he scored against Holland and Uruguay. In the close season, he took part in the U-20s World Cup Finals in Turkey.

Following his return from the tournament in July 2013 (where he had figured in matches against Iraq and Egypt), Everton handed him a two-year professional contract. Still only 18 years of age, it was felt that Chris would benefit from experiencing first team football and a week into 2014 he joined MK Dons on loan. Four days later on 11th January, he made his Football League debut when Dons' Manager Karl Robinson named him in the starting 11 in a League One match at home to Shrewsbury Town. Prior to kick off he "felt like a boy in a man's changing room" but those feelings soon disappeared. With the game 20 minutes old and the score standing at 1-1, Chris reacted quickly to a save by the keeper to force home his first Football League goal much to the delight of the majority of the 7,408 present. He enjoyed an additional three loan games before injury ended his season and he returned to his parent club. After his

MK experience, Chris turned his attention to breaking into the Everton team. He started and scored in a pre-season friendly against German side Paderborn and just before Christmas in 2014, he made the breakthrough when Everton faced Russian side FC Krasnodar in a Europa League group game. With qualification to the knockout phase already secured, Manager Roberto Martinez was afforded the luxury of being able to select a relatively inexperienced squad and team. In the 80th minute of the game, Chris was summoned from the bench to replace fellow Huytonian Conor McAleny. Although he obviously did not know it at the time, this proved to be his only first team appearance for the Toffees.

In January 2015, Brentford Manager Mark Warburton offered Chris the chance of first team football in the Championship. He jumped at the opportunity and describes this as his most enjoyable loan period. During five months at Griffin Park he turned out on eleven occasions for the Bees, winning seven games, drawing one with just three defeats. He scored four goals including a brace against Huddersfield on his full debut and a 44th minute screamer versus Blackburn Rovers. In addition to endearing himself to the Brentford faithful, his performances and goals helped the club to secure a semi-final play-off place. Chris came off the bench in the 71st minute of the semi-final second leg clash with Middlesborough but the tie was already beyond them. Boro ran out 5-1 winners on aggregate but lost to Norwich City in the Wembley Final.

The day after the semis Chris returned to Finch Farm - but not for long. His spell in the Championship had raised his profile in the game and confirmed his belief that his days at Everton were numbered. After turning down a contract offer from the Blues and ending his fifteen-year relationship with them, he considered various offers before putting pen to paper on a three-year deal with Burnley. Having been at Everton from such an early age, Chris would have loved things to have worked out differently. He is extremely grateful for everything the Everton staff did for him and is immensely proud to have worn the royal blue. Chris made his Turf Moor debut on 12 September 2015 in the dying minutes of a 3-1 victory over Sheffield Wednesday in front of 17,277 spectators. The Clarets' fans were desperate to see their boys return to the top-flight following their relegation the previous season and the team did not disappoint. Chris featured in eleven games for Manager Sean Dyche's side as they romped to the Championship title. However, at the start of the 2016/17 campaign Dyche sent Chris out on loan to Fleetwood Town - an unpopular decision with Longy. Hankering to be alongside his club mates and experiencing life in the Premier League, by his own admission Chris did not approach the move with the right attitude. He made 23 appearances in all competitions for the Cod Army and scored four goals. In retrospect, he acknowledges that the experience was another part of his learning curve but was delighted when, in January 2017, he left Highbury to join Bolton Wanderers until the end of the season. Fleetwood were in fourth place when Chris moved to the Macron Stadium and stayed there to reach the play-offs where they lost to Bradford City. Bolton however, managed to secure automatic promotion to the Championship by finishing runners-up to Sheffield United. Chris got ten games under his belt to take his season's tally to 33 and in only his second game for the Trotters, he found the back of the net in a 4-1 defeat of Walsall.

After returning briefly to Turf Moor, Chris was on the move again, this time to the East Midlands to join Northampton Town for the entirety of the 2017/18 season. It was an extremely difficult campaign for the Cobblers and ended in relegation to Division Two. Although Chris was 'only' a loanee, he was as upset by this as any other member of the squad. However, from Burnley's point of view, the purpose of Longy spending the season at Sixfields Stadium was to ensure he gained valuable game time and got amongst the goals - he did both. His 42 appearances returned nine of the team's 43 goals making him the club's top scorer. Whilst Chris has already played for seven different League clubs, made in excess of 100 appearances, scored goals aplenty, played in Europe and experienced the highs of promotion and the lows of relegation, it is important to remember that he is still in his early twenties. It is highly likely that with the degree of ambition and ability he possesses, his best years are still ahead of him. He certainly has the ingredients to become a top player at the highest level and maybe add full international honours to the junior caps he has already secured. As Chris puts it himself, "My career has only just begun. Watch this space!"

Footynote:

Since leaving Northampton, Chris has added Blackpool, Motherwell, a return to Fleetwood and his current club Crewe Alexandra to his cv, which boasts in excess of 200 career appearances and approaching 50 goals.

LIAM WALSH

©George Herringshaw

Born on 15 September 1997, Liam Walsh hails from Huyton's Western Avenue and joined Everton at the age of five. He attended Cardinal Heenan School and in 2012 gained the distinction of captaining the side which won the Premier League Under-14s Schools Cup. By defeating Bishop Challoner Sports College from London 1-0 at Sunderland's Stadium of Light they became only the second team in the history of the English Schools FA to successfully defend a national schools title. They followed this by finishing runners-up to St Eunan's College of Ireland in the British Isles Cup, losing in a penalty shootout. Shortly after, as part of Everton's youth education policy, Liam moved to Wade Deacon School in Widnes and combined his studies with impressively rising through the Blues Academy ranks.

With England U-16 and U-18 caps under his belt, Liam secured a full-time Toffees contract and loved learning from and training with the first teamers. A scorer of spectacular goals, Liam received the Premier League Youth Goal of the Season award for his outrageous halfway line strike versus Derby County in November 2015. A couple of months later he joined Yeovil Town on a one-month loan and made his debut in an FA Cup third-round tie versus Carlisle United on 10 January 2016.

Due to Storm Desmond, Cumbria fell victim to some of the worst flooding the country had ever seen and, with Carlisle's Brunton Park under water, the game took place at Blackpool's Bloomfield Road ground. Yeovil twice came from behind to secure a creditable 2-2 draw in front of 3,357 spectators. Liam gave a good account of himself and Boss Darren Way didn't hesitate to hand him his first Football League start against Morecambe a few days later.

Liam's ever-supportive family and friends would regularly make the lengthy trip from Huyton to Huish Park to cheer him on and continued to do so when the loan period was repeatedly extended. In all, Liam made 17 appearances for the Glovers and scored one goal (against Luton Town on 2 February 2016) before returning to Finch Farm.

The following season he chipped in with six goals as David Unsworth's side won the Premier League 2 title. However, as much as he loved playing for the Blues, having tasted first team football Liam felt he needed to be getting more of the same. A disappointing loan spell at Birmingham City resulted in just three appearances and an early recall to his parent club. Then, on 5 January 2018, Liam made the difficult but understandable decision to leave his boyhood club after 16 years on their books. Bristol City Boss Lee Johnson had tracked the Huytonian's development for a number of years and was delighted to acquire his services for an undisclosed fee. If Liam needed any confirmation that his decision was the right one, he got it four days later when, in the 72nd minute of the first leg of the Carabao Cup semi-final match opposing mighty Manchester City, he came off the bench to join the action in front of a crowd numbering 43,426. With the score locked at 1–1, the eight thousand Bristol fans at the Etihad nearly witnessed a dream start for

Liam when his half-volley almost found the back of the net before Sergio Aguero scored in the 92nd minute to give the Premiership outfit an advantage. The Citizens ran out 3-2 winners (5-3 on aggregate) in the return fixture to defeat the Robins and progress to the Final. However, this was a far cry from Finch Farm and Liam also made six Championship appearances before the season drew to a close with the Robins narrowly missing out on a play-off place.

Liam added another 11 Bristol appearances before joining Coventry City on loan at the start of the 2019/20 campaign. He hit the ground running with a 3-2 debut victory over Blackpool followed by a goalless draw with Burton. In the eighth minute of his third Coventry appearance he conceded a penalty from which Wimbledon took the lead. Jordy Hiwula restored parity before Liam made amends for his faux pas with an injury time winner to snatch the three points and endear him to the Coventry faithful. This was the first of four goals Liam netted for the Sky Blues from his 34 appearances for the club. One of these, versus Rochdale, warrants a special mention as it was a special goal - dubbed 'BEST SOLO GOAL EVER' by one Youtuber! In the 72nd minute with the score standing at one apiece, the young midfielder was in his own half when he gained possession before embarking upon a mazy run, skipping past five opponents and drilling the ball past the hapless keeper. Such was the quality of the goal and the form he displayed in his 34 appearances, that his teammates labelled him 'Messi' and voted him Coventry's Players Player of the Year.

Liam wasn't the only squad member to enjoy a great campaign and, with just three defeats all season, Cov topped the table at the conclusion of the 2019/20 campaign. Manager Mark Robbins would have loved to have retained Liam's services for their return to the Championship but recently-appointed Bristol Boss Dean Holden was having none of it and he returned to Ashton Gate. Unfortunately, injury seriously hampered Liam's involvement in the 2020/21 season but there should be little doubt that, when he returns to fitness, Liam Walsh should enjoy a very big future in the game.

Footynote:

In May 2021 Liam was one of eleven players released by The Robins when his contract expired. A couple of months later he found a new home at Swansea City's Liberty Stadium before joining fellow Championship side Hull City on loan until the end of the season.

MARK DUFFY

©Mike Williamson Morecambe FC

Mark Duffy's journey to join the ranks of professional footballers involved rejection, disappointment and a great deal of grit and determination. On more than one occasion he had doubts about making the grade and consequently he now fully appreciates how privileged he is to be doing a job he loves. Mark also believes that his route to the Football League has made him a better player and that today's youngsters would benefit from being exposed to what he experienced in order to succeed. His dismay at being released by Liverpool at the age of 17 after spending nine years at the club he loved knocked him for six and he didn't kick a ball for eight months. It was only after a few words of advice and encouragement from friend Lee Trundle that Mark began to believe in himself again. They grew up in adjacent streets in the Princess Drive area of Page Moss and Lee was well aware of Duff's potential. Trunds had trodden an unconventional path to becoming a pro footballer but when he joined Wrexham he changed his laissez-faire attitude and began reaping the benefits of his fresh approach. He knew that one disappointment did not necessarily signify the end for Mark and he arranged a trial for him at Wrexham. Mark did himself and Lee proud putting his career back on track. However, his dreams were again derailed when he left the Robins after two years as an apprentice and spent a season with Vauxhall Motors in the Conference North.

Worried that he may never fulfil his footballing ambitions, Mark got 'proper' jobs working as a scaffolder and then as a sports coach for Knowsley Council, which he loved. He combined this with playing with his mates for Prescot Cables and, under Manager Tommy Lawson, he excelled. The club's Player of the Year award was followed by interest from Southport Boss Peter Davenport who took Mark to Haigh Avenue on 31 January 2007. He had no problem stepping up to the Conference Premier level and took the progression comfortably in his stride. When fellow Sandgrounders Craig Noone and Carl Baker graduated to the Football League with Plymouth Argyle and Morecambe respectively, Mark was inspired. After getting another Player of the Year trophy under his belt it wasn't long before the rumour mill was working overtime and claiming that Mark would be following Carl to Christie Park. He responded by saying, "I've heard all the speculation and it would be a dream come true to play full-time in the Football League, it is a burning ambition of mine."

On 23 February 2009, Shrimps Manager Sammy McIlroy gave Mark an opportunity to make his dream a reality although initially for just three months. With Southport and Morecambe unable to agree a fee but both parties keen to do business, Duff joined the League Two club on loan with a view to a permanent deal being struck. The pressure was on Mark to deliver and he rose to the challenge. A day later he took his place on the Morecambe bench at Blundell Park hoping to get a taste of the action against Grimsby Town. On 57 minutes, the Mariners' Adam Forbes scored his and Grimsby's second goal of the game prompting McIlroy to withdraw defender Adam Yates and unleash Mark who was chomping at the bit to get on the pitch. Just over half an hour later the referee brought the game to a close with the score standing at 3-2 in Morecambe's favour with Mark playing no small part in the turnaround. During the remaining games of his loan, Mark helped the club secure fourth place in the table and a play-off tie versus Dagenham and Redbridge. Unfortunately, the Daggers battered the Shrimps 6-0 in the first leg of the contest giving them a mountain to climb. The task proved too great for Morecambe but they did win the return leg 2-1 with Mark netting in the last match ever played at Christie Park.

When the new season kicked off in their new stadium, the Globe Arena, the holders of Morecambe's purse strings had released the £20,000 necessary to make a delighted Duff their player on a permanent basis. All told, Mark made 76 appearances for the coastal town club, found the back of the net on seven occasions and presented the strikers with numerous assists. He was happy but curious to see how far he could progress. When Championship club

Scunthorpe United tabled a bid to take him to Glanford Park, a deal was sorted on 20 January 2011. This was not a good period in Scunnie's long history and during Mark's time wearing an Irons jersey they suffered relegation twice. However, Mark made in excess of 100 appearances for the club and maintained a high level of performance. This was evident at the 2012/13 End of Season awards ceremony when Mark scooped five accolades including another Player of the Year gong. When he joined Doncaster Rovers at the start of the 2013/14 campaign, Mark was hoping that the club would match his aspirations. After promotion to the Championship at the conclusion of the previous season, Rovers Manager Paul Dickov shared Duff's optimism and they got off to a bright start. Yet despite their best efforts, a disastrous run of results at the business end of the season saw them finish in 22nd place and Mark suffered the indignation of his third relegation in four seasons.

Although his clubs may not have been faring well, Mark was still held in high esteem by managers up and down the country and on 1 July 2014 he joined Birmingham City. Boss Lee Clarke had signed a raft of players in the close season adding to an already large squad. Mark hardly got a look in and spent the majority of his two seasons as a Blue on loan at Chesterfield and then Burton Albion. He squeezed in three games for the Spireites before Jimmy Floyd Hasselbaink took Mark to Burton. Duff was aiming to move his career back in the right direction and he did so brilliantly. He appeared 45 times for the Brewers and chipped in with eight goals and 11 assists as they clinched the League One title. Recognition of Mark's resurgence was provided by his peers whose votes handed him a place in the PFA League One Team of the Year. When Mark's loan spell concluded, many people believed the move would become permanent but Sheffield Utd's newly-appointed Manager Chris Wilder had other plans. Mark returned to Birmingham to weigh up his options and whilst there were more lucrative contracts on offer, hugely ambitious Wilder sold his vision for the Blades to Mark.

On 1 June 2016, Duff joined the Bramall Lane club to become the first signing made by his new boss and from the off it was apparent that Mark and the club were a good fit. The fans really appreciated his high-tempo, never-say-die approach to the game and the previous disappointments of relegation made the success of his debut season in South Yorkshire even sweeter. They romped away with the League One title by accumulating 100 points, a massive 14 points ahead of their nearest rivals Bolton Wanderers. For the second season on the bounce, Mark tasted the success of promotion coupled with the personal distinction of inclusion in the PFA's League One Team. After a six-year absence from the second tier of English football, the Blades gave a solid account of themselves by finishing tenth in the Championship table. Mark contributed with 39 appearances and three goals, the first of which was an absolute cracker. The Steel City Derby on 24 September 2017 was a passionate affair with United and Wednesday providing the 32,839 crowd with a thrilling encounter. The game was delicately poised at 2-1 to the Blades when, in the 65th minute, Owls substitute Lucas Joao levelled the score to the obvious delight of the home fans. Not to be outdone, Duff who had entered the field of play a few minutes earlier, picked up the ball on the edge of

©Mike Williamson Morecambe FC

Wednesday's box, twisted and turned before unleashing an unstoppable shot from an acute angle past the keeper. The net bulged just one minute and forty-seven seconds after the Wednesday goal to curtail their celebrations, send the United supporters delirious and write Mark's name in local football folklore. With a further Blades goal added ten minutes later, the game finished 4-2 in their favour.

Whilst Wilder's team enjoyed a solid first Championship season, their second was fantastic. When Leeds United and Aston Villa shared the spoils on 28 April 2019, the result handed the Blades promotion to the Premier League prompting Wilder to exclaim, "What a day to be a Blade. Next season will be a fabulous experience for everyone involved." Unfortunately for Mark, despite playing a major part in their success with his 38 appearances and six goals, 'everyone' did not include him. In the close season, Wilder prepared for their first campaign with the big boys since 2007 by drafting in a number of loanees. Consequently, although Duff would dearly have loved to pit his wits against the best in the business, he took a pragmatic view that his Bramall Lane game-time would be limited. When, on 8 August 2019, Championship club Stoke City expressed an interest in taking him on loan, he accepted the challenge of attempting to emulate the Blades' success.

Disappointingly, Mark's five-month stay at the Bet365 Stadium involved just two starts and seven appearances from the bench. A change was vital and it came in the shape of another loan. On 11 February 2020, Mark made his Den Haag debut in a 4-2 Dutch Eredevisie defeat versus Sparta Rotterdam. This was the first of five games he played for the club before the Corona virus pandemic signalled a premature end to his time in Holland.

Having made more than 500 career appearances and registered in excess of 50 goals and countless assists, Mark has proved himself to be a player of tremendous calibre. Whilst he still has a great deal to offer on the pitch, he is laying the foundations for when his playing days are over by taking his coaching badges. It is irrefutable that the knowledge and experience he has picked up on his footballing journey make him an ideal candidate to stay involved in the game to help future generations of aspiring young players.

©Mike Williamson Morecambe FC

Footynote:

In September 2020 Mark joined Fleetwood Town. His 31 appearances for The Trawlermen included a goal-scoring encounter with Everton in the EFL Cup. Although defeated 5-2, finding the net three minutes after coming off the bench was a satisfying moment for the lifelong Liverpool fan. On 31 August 2021 Mark joined Tranmere Rovers.

BILLY MERCER

If the measure of a good coach is the progress his 'pupils' make coupled with the level of their performance, Billy Mercer is one of the best. Since joining Burnley FC as the club's goalkeeping coach in January 2000, his dedication and commitment to improving his shot stoppers has resulted in Tom Heaton, Nick Pope and most recently Bailey Peacock-Farrell receiving international recognition (although Farrell had already been capped by Northern Ireland prior to his August 2019 arrival at Turf Moor). In addition, he has worked tirelessly with seasoned internationals such as Joe Hart, Paul Robinson, Matt Gilks, Diego Penny and Anders Lindegard to become one of the country's most respected coaches in his area of expertise.

Born on 22 May 1969, Billy became a keeper at the age of 14 when he volunteered after none of his Steerscroft JFC teammates fancied going between the sticks. Although a late starter, he made up for lost time and his agility, bravery and safe hands soon attracted attention in the Cantril Farm Junior League. He joined Liverpool as a youngster and turned pro in August 1987. With Bruce Grobbelaar and Mike Hooper ahead of him in the pecking order, Billy joined Rotherham United on loan and made the move permanent on 16 February 1989. Patience was required as future PNE Manager Kelham O'Hanlon wasn't prepared to relinquish his position easily. Billy had no complaints as his rival to the keeper's jersey put in some stunning performances as the Millers gained promotion as Fourth Division champions at the end of the 1988/89 campaign. The following season Manager Billy McEwan presented Merce with a couple of opportunities to show the club's fans what he could offer. On 1 January 1990 Bristol Rovers were the visitors to Millmoor with the majority of the crowd of 7,750 hoping to kick off the New Year with a win - a three goals to two scoreline in their favour didn't disappoint. Five days later he followed up his Football League debut with an away trip to Brentford which resulted in a disappointing 4-2 reversal. The club endured a poor 1990/91 campaign which cost the manager his job mid-season and the club it's Third Division status. In an effort to improve their fortunes, McEwan and new Boss Phil Henson both made changes to the team, handing Billy 13 League and five Cup appearances.

At the conclusion of the 1991/92 campaign, the club made an immediate return to Division Three as they finished runners-up to Burnley. Billy had become an integral part of the meanest defence in the division with just 37 goals conceded during their 42 League games. Next, a solid season and 11th place finish in the newly-formed Barclays League Division Two saw Billy make 48 appearances in all competitions. However, a bright start to the following campaign was brought to an abrupt and premature end when he picked up a season-ending injury during a 2-1 away defeat at the hands of Huddersfield Town on 11 December 1993. In Billy's absence, young keeper Matt Clarke seized his chance with both gloves and consequently Billy only added three more Millers appearances to the 135 he had already totted up before he left for pastures new.

On 12 October 1994 Billy made the short journey from Millmoor to Bramall Lane to join Sheffield United after impressing Manager Dave Bassett a few months earlier on the club's pre-season tour of Australia. However, during fourteen months with the Blades he made just four appearances and spent a frustrating two-month loan spell warming the Nottingham Forest bench. Billy needed a stable environment and regular football - he found both at Chesterfield via another loan deal. He joined the Spireites in September 1995 when their first choice keeper Andy Beasley picked up an injury. So impressed was Manager John Duncan by Billy's 12-game contribution that when Beasley suffered a relapse he snapped him up on a permanent basis for a fee just shy of £100,000. The club finished seventh and missed the play-offs by a single point in Billy's debut campaign at Saltergate. Over the next three campaigns he registered 135 appearances in all competitions as Chesterfield finished 10th, 10th and 9th in Division Two. On the face of it, this trio of seasons appear solid but unspectacular. However, hidden within those statistics lies a truly amazing FA Cup story.

Their mid-table League performances were dramatically overshadowed in the 1996/97 season when the club reached the semi-final of the world's oldest cup competition. Victories over Bury (1-0), Scarborough (2-0), Bristol City (2-0), Bolton (3-2), Notts Forest (1-0) and Wrexham (1-0) put the club just one game away from a

©Andy Ford Photographer

Wembley Final. On 13 April 1997, an Old Trafford crowd of 49,640 witnessed one of the most dramatic and controversial contests in the history of this magnificent competition. Their opponents Middlesbrough, managed by former Utd and England skipper Bryan Robson, contained a host of international players including the world class Juninho and Ravanelli and were overwhelming favourites to dispose of their rivals. Billy later recalled "One of my memories of the day of the game was looking at the newspapers and all the pundits were predicting 3-0, 4-0 or 5-0 for Boro. It gave us a bit of a push. The team spirit was incredible."

The game started as expected with Robson's men applying all the pressure but Billy and his defence stood firm. Then, in the 37th minute, the tie swung slightly in the Spireites favour when Boro defender Vladimir Kinder received his marching orders after picking up his second yellow card. Most people still expected the Teesside club to have too much for the Derbyshire outfit but in the 54th minute Chesterfield's Andy Morris opened the scoring with a neat finish. Six minutes later, club captain and current Burnley Boss Sean Dyche extended their lead from the penalty spot to send their fans delirious. However, in the 64th minute, Italian centre forward Fabrizio Ravanelli bundled the ball into the back of the net to reduce the deficit to a single goal. Five minutes later, with the game hanging in the balance came the moment of controversy that will haunt Chesterfield fans for evermore. With the ball pinging around the Boro box, forward Jon Howard unleashed a shot which struck the underside of the crossbar and bounced down onto the pitch. If goal line technology had existed at the time, referee David Ellery's watch would have alerted him to the fact that the ball had crossed the line and a goal would have been awarded. Despite television replays showing that the ball had clearly crossed the whitewash and the linesman running back towards the halfway line satisfied that a goal had been scored, Ellery waved play on. To add insult to injury, less than a minute later, the official awarded a dubious penalty to Middlesbrough. Huytonian Craig Hignett stepped up and from the spot he placed a firm shot under the body of his hometown mate Mercer and parity was restored. When Boro took the lead in the first half of extra-time, it looked like the Premiership side had broken the Spireites hearts but with 119 minutes on the clock fullback Jamie Hewitt sent a looping header over the keeper to silence the Boro fans who were celebrating victory.

The game was a classic and Billy Mercer made a host of saves but, despite again performing heroics in the replay, he was unable to prevent Middlesbrough's sealing a 3-0 win and a place in the Wembley showpiece. By virtue of poor refereeing, Chesterfield were denied the chance to write their names in the record books by becoming the first club from the third tier to reach the FA Cup Final. There are fans and pundits who claim that when an official makes a costly mistake, these things even themselves out over time. You would have to go a long way to find a Chesterfield supporter who would subscribe to that opinion.

All told, Billy made 176 appearances at Saltergate before leaving on 26 October 1999 when he signed for Tony Pulis at Bristol City for a £300,000 fee. Due to a serious groin injury, he managed just one full season, during which he appeared 32 times. Although previously denied a Wembley FA Cup Final appearance, he did play at the famous stadium shortly before its demolition. On 16 April 2000 with 75,057 supporters cheering on Bristol City and Stoke City, the clubs competed for the Auto Windscreens Shield. The Potters ran out 2-1 winners in a game which proved to be one of Billy's last in professional football. After his enforced retirement, Billy was invited to stay on at Ashton Gate as the Robins goalkeeping coach heralding a new chapter in his career. He quickly earned a reputation as a fine coach and in 2004 was recruited to Sheffield Wednesday's staff by Boss and fellow member of the goalkeepers union, Chris Turner. When Turner and his replacement Paul Sturrock parted company with the Owls, Billy was installed as Assistant Manager by the South Yorkshire club until Brian Laws took over. After four years at Hillsborough, Laws left to become the new Boss of Premier League Burnley and Billy joined the Clarets soon after. With over a decade of service under his belt at Turf Moor, Billy is currently the longest-serving member of the club's backroom team. He is held in the highest esteem by goalkeepers up and down the country, especially those he has coached and helped during the 30-odd years he has been involved in the game.

Footynote:

When, on 15 April 2022, Burnley Manager Sean Dyche was given his marching orders by the club, his backroom staff, including Billy, were also casualties of the questionable decision. It won't however, be long before Billy Mercer is back on a training pitch providing goalkeeping coaching of the very highest calibre.

CHRIS PILE

It could be argued that because Chris Pile has never appeared in an English Football League fixture, he should not be included within these pages. However, his inclusion is totally merited. Born on 4 April 1967 at Whiston Hospital, Chris lived at 37 Wallace Drive on Huyton's Mosscroft estate. His first school was St Aidan's Primary and at the tender age of seven he would pester older brother Simon to let him join in as he and his friends played footy on nearby King George V Playing Fields. Simon eventually succumbed to the badgering - on the condition that Chris went in goal, an unpopular position with most youngsters. However, Chris was a natural and was soon diving full-length at players' feet not only on the field but also in the street and playground - irrelevantly picking up numerous cuts and bruises in the process.

Chris has clear recollections of his first organised game for the school team in a 1-1 draw with Malvern School. St Aidan's did not have a particularly strong team which kept Chris busy between the sticks and gave him a chance to display his goalkeeping prowess. Despite his best efforts, a clean sheet was a rarity and something he craved as much as a centre forward yearns to score. His performances for the school earned him a place in the Huyton Boys side, managed by St Joseph's Headteacher Mr Welsh. Chris continued to develop his game and word of his performances began to spread. Local junior football legend Harry Tyrell invited Chris and his mum to the annual St Annes away fixture versus Romford Royals. Based in Essex, the Royals were run by a fellow footy fanatic Harry had met years before on holiday in Devon. Chris had recently had his tonsils removed and was too ill to participate but he went along for the ride. When regular keeper Mark Rabone broke a finger shortly before kick-off, Chris' tonsils were forgotten as he put in a Man of the Match debut performance. This signalled the start of a successful and enjoyable trophy-laden couple of seasons for Chris and St Annes U-11s. When Chris progressed to St Augustine's Senior School, he remembers playing for Mr Roderick's team and the open-age side Littlewoods Sports. He was obsessed with goalkeeping and modelled himself on Liverpool keeper Ray Clemence who, like Chris, was right-handed and left-footed, a definite plus in the eyes of goalkeeping aficionados.

Possibly helped by his experience of playing in open-age football, Chris was selected for the District U-15s team when he was a year younger than his teammates. He recalls the high of winning the Welsh Shield versus Pontypridd and the low of losing 10-1 to Telford Boys. Despite that tonking, Chris was obviously doing a great deal right because it was around this time that Football League clubs started to take an interest in him. Offers to spend the summer holidays training with Birmingham City and Aston Villa were rejected, but when Liverpool invited him to Melwood on Tuesday and Thursday nights he accepted immediately. Chris trained hard, absorbed and acted upon the coaching staff's advice and secured an YTS apprenticeship, which he started five days after leaving school. On his 17th birthday he became a full-time pro and was fifth in the Anfield goalkeeping pecking order.

This was a fantastic period in the history of Liverpool FC and Chris lays claim to playing a small part in the continuation of the success story. With a place in the 1984 European Cup Final in the bag, the last training session before the match ended with a penalty shoot-out. The apprentices took on the first teamers selected to take Liverpool's pens should the outcome of the game be decided in this way. Young Chris adopted an unconventional yet effective approach to facing the penalties by moving his body around on his goal line but keeping his feet on the line. Slightly worryingly, the youngsters defeated the first teamers with ease and when keeper Bruce Grobbelaar walked back to the changing rooms with Chris he asked him about his antics. Chris explained he was just trying to get into the head of the pen taker in order to put him off. Bruce's legendary 'spaghetti legs' routine a couple of days later in the Final's decisive penalty shoot-out, helped the Reds lift 'Old Big Ears' - did young Chris sow the seed in his mind? Whilst this may be open to debate, there is little doubt about his involvement 12 months later - it made the record books of European football and ensured Chris a place amongst Huyton's Titans!

On 29 May 1985 Liverpool were again in the European Cup Final. In a Central League fixture a couple of weeks earlier, reserve goalie Bob Bolder had broken his ankle, presenting Chris with an amazing opportunity. At the Heysel Stadium and sporting the number 17 jersey, Chris took his place on the bench alongside Liverpool legends Jan Molby, Sammy Lee, Craig Johnstone and Gary Gillespie to become the youngest player to ever be involved in a European Cup Final. Unfortunately but understandably, this fact rarely gets a mention due to the tragic pre-match terrace trouble which resulted in the deaths of 37 Juventus fans.

The following season Bolder moved to Charlton Athletic elevating Chris to reserve team keeper but Grob was an ever-present thus denying him the chance to make his first team debut. Ironically, the following season when Chris slipped a disc in training, the club bought Mike Hooper as cover for Bruce. Soon afterwards, Grobbelaar was injured and Hooper slotted in and played 73 games for the club before moving to Newcastle Utd. Tranmere Rovers Manager Frank Worthington signed Chris for the 1987/88 season after his contract was not renewed at Anfield. Once again, Billy O'Rourke the custodian of the keepers' shirt never missed a game and Chris was consigned to the reserves. Bury Boss Martin Dobson offered Chris a monthlong trial and he impressed sufficiently to be offered a contract with the Shakers. On the day he was due to sign he broke a bone in his hand scuppering his chances.

Chris was still only a young man and was philosophical and optimistic about still having a future in the game. Out of the blue, he received a phone call from an agent offering him the chance to play in New Zealand during our close season. Chris accepted, believing that it would be a good opportunity to keep fit and weigh up his options for the following season back home. A couple of months later Celtic were rumoured to be lining up an offer to take Chris to Parkhead. Even though he had only been playing for Waterside Karori in Wellington for a short time, he had fallen in love with the club, city and country. He decided that his future lay in New Zealand. Apart from a brief spell back in England (when he played 11 games for Southport in the Northern Premier League in the 1991/92 season), Chris has lived in New Zealand ever since. He enjoyed great success as a player and has built a fantastic reputation as a first class goalkeeping coach. In addition to setting up his own coaching schools, he has been involved with the New Zealand international youth squad. Chris returns to England regularly to catch up with family and friends but no trip is complete unless a game at Anfield is included in his itinerary.

LAURENCE WILSON

Yellow and red cards are an occupational hazard for professional footballers, particularly combative defenders like Laurence Wilson. Yet, although he racked up 45 yellows and 5 reds during his English Football League career, that statistic perhaps gives an inaccurate impression of his ability. Laurence was a cultured player who possessed a great left foot and vicious shot which he put to great use during his 353 games in English football.

Born in Huyton on 10 October 1986, he joined Everton at the age of eleven. Whilst at the Academy, he represented England at all youth levels and was a member of the 2005 squad which finished runners-up in the Eufa U-19s tournament, defeated by France 3-1 in the Final at Belfast's Windsor Park. However, with Everton, the closest he got to a taste of first team action was occupying a place on the bench for a Champions League qualifier versus Villarreal. Laurence spent the last three months of the 2005/06 season on loan at Mansfield Town and made his Football League debut on 11 February 2006 as a 63rd minute substitute in a 2-2 draw with Wycombe. Three days later he made his first start as the Stags overcame Grimsby at Field Mill in front of a crowd of 3,053. All told, Laurence made 15 appearances and the experience helped him to make the decision to leave Goodison Park to play regular League football. Mansfield were keen for him to stay with them but on 31 May 2006 Laurence became a Chester City player. With a good pre-season behind them, they got off to a flyer with a 2-0 home victory over League newcomers Accrington Stanley. Laurence started the match and his performances throughout the campaign made him immovable from Mark Wright's starting eleven. His 49 appearances included a purple patch when, from 10 games over a two-month period, he scored five goals from open play. During Laurence's trio of seasons with Chester, the club endured a constant struggle at the wrong end of the League Two table and battled to retain their League status. On 2 May 2009 they finally succumbed when a 2-1 defeat to Darlington on the last game of the season resulted in relegation to the Conference National. Before the following season was under way, Morecambe provided a new residence for Laurence and he got the first of two spells with the Shrimps underway with a 2-2 draw with Hereford. Although they enjoyed an excellent season, it ultimately ended in disappointment. A fourth place finish secured a play-off place but in the first leg of their semi-final versus Dagenham and Redbridge the wheels came off with a 6-0 defeat. A 2-1 victory in the return encounter was too little too late. Sandwiched between Laurence's initial 123 games for Morecambe and his return to their Mazuma stadium in July 2014, he made seven appearances for Rotherham before spending a largely uneventful season and a half at Accrington Stanley. He added a further 58 Morecambe games to his tally then crossed the Welsh border for spells at Bangor City and Connah's Quay before bringing the curtain down on a career which had spanned 13 seasons.

©Matt Rushton Morecambe FC

GREG TANSEY

Very few aspiring young footballers turn down the opportunity to join Liverpool Football Club but in 2006 18-year old Greg Tansey did just that.

Born on 21 November 1988, the Mosscroft youngster had already crucially made the breakthrough to Stockport County's first team when the Reds enquired about taking him and teammate Ryan Crowther on a tour of Milan with a view to signing them upon their return. Greg was understandably tempted but decided that his dream of enjoying a career in the game would be best served by initially staying with the Hatters. Whilst there will always be a question of "what if ...?", 13 years and almost 400 games as a pro proved that Greg's decision was a wise one. Unfortunately for Crowther, he accepted Liverpool's offer, failed to make an impression and ended his career without making a single Football League appearance.

Greg had joined County's youth set up after spending time with Whiston Juniors, Everton and Manchester City. He became a full-time professional on 26 September 2006 and made his first team debut the following month in a 1-0 Johnstone's Paint Trophy victory over Macclesfield. Boss Jim Gannon handed him an additional four appearances in his debut campaign as County narrowly missed out on the play-offs. A year later, not only did the club reach the play-offs, but a 3-2 Wembley defeat of Rochdale in the Final secured promotion to League One. However, although Greg featured in 16 County matches, he wasn't involved in the teams' run-in. Instead, he joined Blue Square Premier League outfit Altrincham on loan to help their battle to stave off relegation, which they managed by the skin of their teeth.

The following three seasons were probably the worst in Stockport's long history. County entered into administration in 2008/09 and were in free fall. An 18th place finish was followed by relegation to League Two and then, in the club's 100th season in the Football League, they suffered the ignominy of dropping to the Conference when they again finished bottom of their division.

One of the few bright spots of this period was the emergence of Greg as a force to be reckoned with. His fruitful midfield partnership with Carl Baker ended when the Prescotian joined Coventry City in the 2010 January transfer window. Greg stepped up to the plate and replaced Carl as the club's top scorer when he notched ten goals during their ill-fated 2010/11 campaign. This included a purple patch of four goals from three appearances which resulted in Greg receiving the December League Two Player of the Month award. At the conclusion of the campaign it was time for Greg to seek pastures new and he found them north of the border with Inverness Caledonian Thistle who he joined on 30 June 2011. Since forming in August 1994, Caley had risen rapidly through the ranks to ply their trade in the Scottish Premier League. Greg settled in quickly and scored a brace in just his third game for the club, a 3-3 draw with Dunfermline. In what proved to be the first of two stints at the Caledonian Stadium, his 39 appearances and five goals helped the club secure another season in the Premiership with a tenth place finish. However, by the time the 2012/13 campaign had started Greg was back in England after joining Stevenage Borough on 25 May 2012. His contribution of finding the net on nine occasions during his 66 games for the Boro is impressive considering almost a third of his appearances came from the bench. It was as a substitute when, on 28 August 2013, Greg fulfilled a football dream as Stevenage travelled to Goodison Park to face

©www.mphotographic.co.uk

Everton in a Capital One Cup tie. The game's significance to Greg was not lost on the Liverpool Echo's Phil Kirkbride who put the paper's readership in the picture. In a two-page spread he reported that in the mid-1950s Greg's grandfather Jim Tansey had made 142 appearances as a Toffee and the Stevenage midfielder grew up listening to tales of his time as a Royal Blue. Consequently, Greg was and still is a fanatical supporter of the L4 club. As a youngster he held a Bullens Road season ticket and only stopped going to the game when his own career began to take off. Boro Manager Graham Westley wasn't swayed by sentiment and named Greg amongst the substitutes. However, in the 53rd minute of the game, with the score standing at one apiece, Greg joined the action to fulfil a lifelong dream of sharing the hallowed turf with the Blues. A win and a goal from Greg would have provided the storyline for him to regale to his own future offspring and he almost got both. As the ref checked his watch with full-time approaching, Greg unleashed a trademark shot from fully 40 yards but Toffees keeper Joel Robles produced a flying save to deny him and send the game into extra-time. A Marouane Fellaini goal in the dying embers of the match handed Everton the victory.

Less than five months later on 17 January 2014, Greg returned to Inverness to embark upon the most settled and successful period of his career. He added a further 151 games to his previous Caley tally, registered 25 additional goals and created many memorable moments to share with the family. The day after returning to the club he joined the action from the bench to help Thistle to a 1-0 victory over Aberdeen. Then, a fortnight later, he started in one of the season's most enthralling games. On 2 February 2014 Inverness faced Hearts in a League Cup semi-final and in the 54th minute Greg rifled home from 25yards to put his side in front. However, when Gary Warren received his marching orders following a foul and Hearts scored from the resultant free kick, the game swung in their favour. Four minutes later, Hearts unsurprisingly took the lead and when another Caley player was sent for an early bath to reduce them to nine men, the game looked done and dusted. But the Highlanders hadn't read the script and in the 95th minute centre forward Nick Ross pounced to remarkably restore parity and send the game into extra-time. No further goals were added, taking the tie to penalties, which Inverness won 4-2 securing the club's first visit to a major Final.

If the semi had everything, the Final was a bit 'after the Lord Mayor's Show'. Caley and their opponents Aberdeen failed to light up Celtic Park and again the outcome was determined by ten attempts from 12 yards. Unfortunately, it was the Dons who lifted the trophy by winning the shootout 4-2, proving to the Inverness faithful that it can be great to win a game on penalties but it's a terrible way to lose.

Teams often claim that they will learn from huge disappointment and return stronger only for their words to disappear into the ether. This was not the case with Inverness who in 2014/15 finished third in the League, won the FA Cup and qualified for the Europa League - their best season ever. On 30 May 2015, Falkirk provided the Cup Final opposition at Hampden Park. The game finished 2-1 in Caley's favour with James Vincent snatching a late winner to land their first major trophy. In the process, Greg became the first Huytonian to win the cup which had first been competed for 150 years earlier.

The following campaign kicked off with a short-lived Europa League experience when Romanian side Astra Giurgiu accounted for Inverness by an aggregate score of 1-0, a disappointing yet interesting experience. Although Greg registered an impressive nine goals, it was in the main a disappointing season as the club finished 7th in the Premiership. Worse was to come the following season when just seven wins from their 38 games left the club bottom of the pile and relegated to the Championship. Aberdeen had shown interest in Greg for a couple of years and on 9 June 2017 he joined the club from the Granite City. Sadly, after just nine first team appearances, which were either side of a three-match loan spell at Ross County, Greg left Pittodrie. During his 18 months there he had spent the majority of the time on the treatment table, attempting to overcome complications following a botched hernia operation.

Unfortunately, he reluctantly called it a day after a painful eight-game comeback with St Mirren. Perhaps ironically, one of his last matches as a professional player took place at Ibrox Stadium where Rangers, managed by Steven Gerrard, inflicted a 4-0 thumping on the Saints. Twenty years earlier, Steven had been a massive inspiration to Greg when he returned to present the end of season trophies at the club where it began for both of them, Whiston Juniors.

Since retiring from playing, Greg has secured his coaching badges and embarked upon an exciting venture which will involve coaching youngsters in both a one to one environment and in full team set ups. He is hoping to give something back to the game which he thoroughly enjoyed participating in for many years.

MORE GAMES THAN ME!

This book features players who have made a record number of appearances for their clubs; players who have stayed at one club long enough to be rewarded with a Testimonial match (and in one case, two Testimonial matches!) and players who have totted up hundreds of League appearances by playing dozens of games for a variety of clubs. On the other hand, there are a number of players who have played just a handful of games and some who have made just a single Football League appearance. However, the magnitude of playing ANY Football League games should not be underestimated. Millions of young hopefuls have attempted to achieve this over the years and, for various reasons, failed. Therefore, every player within these pages is included on merit and should be applauded.

One such player was Huytonian midfielder **Brian Johnson** who on 21 April 1968 was called from the bench by Manager Dave Russell to make his one and only Football League appearance for Tranmere Rovers. The game, played at Stockport's County ground in front of 2,569 supporters, resulted in a 1-0 victory for the home side. Brian left Prenton Park shortly after to join Northwich Victoria but could quite rightly be proud of his achievement.

Prescot Grammar School pupil **Derek McClatchey** was a member of the all-conquering 1971 Huyton Boys team that won the English Schools Trophy. The programme for the Final stated, "Most of Huyton's goals come from the quicksilver Lancashire Boys striker Derek McClatchey." Derek signed for Liverpool as an apprentice in May 1973 but, due to the sheer quality of his competitors for a place in the starting line-up, he was unable to make the breakthrough to the first team. However, in 1976 he joined Southport on loan and made his Football League debut on 13th February of the same year. A 4-0 defeat inflicted on the Sandgrounders by Crewe Alexandra at Gresty Road with 1,966 looking on was followed by losses to Northampton Town (1-0) and Rochdale (2-0).

When Liverpool released him, Derek responded to the disappointment by carving out an excellent career in non-League football. In addition to playing for Barrow, Fleetwood and Maghull, he spent ten seasons with Marine, mainly in the Northern Premier League. Between 1977 and 1987 he scored in excess of 200 goals and was the club's leading marksman for six consecutive campaigns. His contribution to Marine was acknowledged with a Testimonial match versus Everton in May 1988 before Derek returned to Southport. His career concluded with spells at Warrington Town and St Helens Town.

Winger **John Foy** and forward **Terry Nolan** are two players who have made it to these pages by virtue of a single League game for Southport. Born on 28 May 1950, Foy enjoyed an illustrious amateur career which spanned many years and clubs including Burscough, Kirkby Town, Skelmersdale Utd, Ormskirk and Bangor City. He joined Southport on amateur terms on 1 August 1974 and 16 days later was in the team defeated 2-1 by Mansfield Town.

Nolan's career kicked off at Prescot Town whose Chairman at the time was George Glover. Glover was acquainted with former Liverpool player Alan A'Court who was Assistant Manager at Stoke City. He tipped him off about Terry and, impressed with what he saw, A'Court recruited Terry to Stoke City in 1977. He played regularly in the reserve side but left to join Southport the same year. He appeared once for Port as a substitute when he came off the bench to replace George Jones in a 1-1 draw with Huddersfield Town on 22 April 1978 in what proved to be Southport's last home game in the Football League. Terry played for two additional seasons at Haigh Avenue making 51 Northern Premier League appearances and registered 14 goals. His final game before emigrating to Australia took place on 16 February 1980 with Oswestry Town providing the opposition. Terry played for St Helens Town and Macclesfield Town during a brief return to these shores before venturing back to Oz where he had a lengthy career playing for Broadmeadows City, Eltham Diamond Valley and Rosanna.

One player whose name constantly crops up in conversation as "one who should have made it" is **Joey Duncan**. In 1965, he played for Huyton Boys and lit up the Woodhead Cup Final in which Huyton defeated Stretford boys. Three years later on 1 December 1968, 18-yearold Joey signed for Wrexham. He made his one and only League appearance when the gaffer gave him the nod versus Workington Town (1-0). Although Joey did not grace the Football League again he gained legendary status with his performances for Blaenau Festiniog in the Welsh League and closer to home for South Liverpool, Longview Labour and the Eagle during their National Cup glory years.

Midfielder **Gordon Byron** who was born in Prescot on 4 September 1953, was on Sheffield Wednesday's books in the early 1970s but had to wait until he joined Lincoln City to make his Football League debut in 1974. It proved to be the first of six games he played for the Imps before he moved to non-League Clifton Town and later Alfreton Town. **Dave Bleasdale**, originally from Fairfield Close in Huyton, was a highly promising Liverpool midfield apprentice in the early 1980s. He was a regular in the reserve team but, like many other understudies at the club, the success and consistency of Liverpool's record-breaking team meant that he had to visit pastures new in order to graduate to first team football. Preston North End Manager Gordon Lee took Dave to Deepdale where he played the first of seven games for the club on 3 September 1983 in a 3-3 Division Three draw at home to Brentford before a crowd of 3,799. He later signed for League of Ireland club Cork City where he enjoyed a couple of season playing under Chelsea legend Bobby Tambling. His Irish connection continued when Wigan Athletic Boss and former Northern Ireland international Bryan Hamilton took him to Springfield Park. Unfortunately, with just five games under his belt, Dave sustained a serious hamstring injury putting an end to his pro career. He enjoyed spells at Barrow, Altrincham and St Dominics before passing his coaching badges and joining Tranmere Rovers' Centre of Excellence and then Dave Ridler's management team at Prescot Cables.

Goalkeeper **Steven Farrelly** began his playing career with Chester City in 1983 in the old Division Four. After spending time outside of the League at Macclesfield Town, he returned when signing for Rotherham Utd on 7 January 1995. He played seven games for the club but was powerless to prevent them finishing 23rd in Division Two and suffer relegation. The following season Steve signed for Scunthorpe Utd and the club finished mid-table in Division Three. Upon leaving Scunny, he carved out a non-League career with Barrow, Kingstonian, Farnborough Town and Woking.

There cannot be many ex-players from the lower divisions of the Football League who have been honoured by the Queen but **Michael 'Tosh' Fielding** can make that particular claim. Central defender Tosh from the Cantril Farm estate was a member of Everton's 1984 FA Youth Cup-winning team. When Blues Boss Howard Kendall told him he was releasing him, Tosh was distraught. He joined Southport determined to prove the Blues wrong and got an early chance to do so. His first game for the Sandgrounders was a friendly versus the club who had just released him and from the first minute to the final whistle Tosh ran the show. He did not put a foot wrong and reckons that consequently the Everton Manager put his entire youth team on the transfer list the following day! On 8 January 1984, he signed for Second Division Barnsley but was immediately sent on loan to Rochdale. After six games for the Spotland club a disillusioned Tosh quit the game and returned home. However, he was always determined to make a further impression on life and achieved this years later. He committed himself to helping unemployed youngsters from Cantril Farm to return to the job market. In 2010 he was invited to Buckingham Palace to receive an MBE in recognition of his sterling efforts. More recently, Tosh was seen working in the corner or at ringside watching his boxer son Rocky as he progressed to become WBA Super Middleweight Champion.

Prescotian centre-half **Garry Lowe** also played briefly in the Football League when, after failing to break into the first team at Crewe, he joined Bury. On 2 November 1985 Garry replaced Terry Pashley from the bench to debut in a 1-0 defeat versus Swansea City. He then added a single Freight Rover Trophy and three more League appearances to his tally before leaving the Shakers. **Stephen Hill's** Rochdale career got off to a flying start with two unexpected victories. Player-Manager Paul Simpson introduced the young left back into the action as an 82nd minute replacement for Simon Grand against table-toppers Hartlepool on 14 December 2002. Prior to kick-off, Dale sat a lowly 15th in the Third Division but swept aside the team from County Durham by four goals to nil. A month later, the 20-year old from Prescot lined up in an FA Cup fourth round tie opposing Coventry City. A home crowd of 9,156 roared the side on to a 2-0 victory over the Sky Blues to upset the formbook. However, apart from finding the back of the net in a 3-2 reversal to Macclesfield Town, there were few high points in Stephen's additional eleven Dale appearances. After spending a month on loan at Morecambe, new Boss Steve Parkin released him. Three seasons with Radcliffe Borough were followed by a spell at Leigh RMI before he returned to Borough to bring the curtain down on his career.

The name **Ian Callaghan** is famous throughout the world of football. The Liverpool & England player made nearly one thousand appearances in a glittering career. However, he is not the only person of that name to have graced the pitch of an English Football League match. Born on 5 August 1969, our Ian Callaghan made a couple of appearances in Bolton Wanderers 1987/88 promotion-winning team. After leaving Burnden Park in June 1988, he joined Northwich Victoria who were managed by former Manchester United midfielder Sammy McIlroy. His lengthy non-League career involved various teams including his hometown club Prescot Cables.

Huytonian **Danny Vaughan** played seven games for Crewe Alexander in 1992 before Wigan Athletic Manager Kenny Swain took him to Springfield Park. He was in impressive form in the pre-season friendlies before picking up a nasty injury. On 21 August 1993 Danny took to the field at Torquay United's Plainmoor ground to make his debut. The game finished 1-1 but before the referee's final whistle had been blown, Danny was back on the treatment table. He made just three more appearances for the Latics before the injury called time on his promising career.

Another player who fell victim to a serious injury was Whiston-born **Kevin Hannon**. Formerly a pupil at Prescot

C of E and Whiston Higherside Schools, he was a member of numerous trophy-winning Whiston Juniors sides. Extremely grateful to the "dedicated band of local people who have run the Juniors for such a long time" he stated in a Wrexham matchday programme feature in 2000, "They have a genuine passion for the game and they are all totally committed to the club's development and its on-going success." He picked out the now sadly-departed Harry 'Skip' Warburton for special praise when he said, "Skip deserves a mention...I owe him an awful lot as do a good number of other lads – because his advice and encouragement were extremely beneficial to me as I was learning the ropes." Not for the first time, Wrexham striker Karl Connolly gave a player a foot up when he arranged for the young left fullback to attend a Robins trial. Kevin rose to the challenge and for the following three years he applied himself superbly to rise through the ranks. His first taste of League football came on 25 September 1999 when Stoke City were the visitors to the Racecourse ground. In the 66th minute of the game, Manager Brian Flynn introduced Kevin to the action as a replacement for Mike Ryan. Wrexham lost the game 3-2 but having made the breakthrough, Kevin was hoping this would be the start of a long and successful career. Little did he know, that single substitute appearance would prove to be his first and last. In May 2001 on the advice of a specialist, 21-year old Kevin announced his retirement from the game he loved. A rash tackle in a heated friendly against Icelandic side Throttur Reykjavik resulted in a broken fibula and a dislocated ankle. Treatments and operations proved fruitless and although Kevin later played non-League football for, amongst others, Atherton Laburnum Rovers, Prescot Cables and Knowsley South, his experience is proof that football can be a cruel sport.

Midfielder **Danny Carson** was still part of the youth set up when he first appeared for Chester City. Manager Kevin Ratcliffe pitched the young Huytonian into battle with 77 minutes on the clock of a 2-1 defeat away from home versus Brentford on 28 November 1998. His first Seals start took place on 23 March 1999 when Shrewsbury Town scored two with no reply in front of a crowd of 2,903. Danny's only other appearance in Chester's colours came in a 5-0 Worthington Cup mauling at the hands of Aston Villa with 22,613 present at Villa Park on 21st September of the same year. His 86th minute replacement of Neil Fisher proved to be his final appearance before he left to join Winsford United.

Paul Boardman became one of former England goalkeeper Peter Shilton's first signings when he took over the Plymouth Argyle Manager's job in March 1992. After scoring on his debut in a 2-1 defeat of Bournemouth on 28 November 1992, Boardie picked up a nasty knee injury which restricted him to just two further appearances before he had to call it a day. Paul then followed in his father Stan's footsteps and became a stand-up comedian working extensively on the after-dinner circuit before carving out a successful career as a presenter on numerous television programmes.

Footynote:

The players contained in this section of Huyton's Titans may not have broken any appearance records or been rewarded for extended service with a testimonial match but it can not be overemphasised how playing ANY games in the English Football League is a tremendous achievement. They may not have played many games but they have played MORE GAMES THAN ME ! !

EXTRA TIME

A True Blue

On Saturday, 14 May 1966 at Wembley Stadium, Huytonian **Eddie Cavanagh** became an Everton legend. Trailing 2-0 to Sheffield Wednesday in the FA Cup Final, Toffee Mike Trebilcock reduced the deficit in the 59th minute and made it all square five minutes later. Almost instantly, Eddie sprang into action and ran onto the field of play. He later described his actions thus, "When it came back to 2-2 that was something else, wasn't it? As soon as that ball hit the net I was on me bike…" Smartly dressed in a suit, shirt, tie and braces, he bounded onto the hallowed turf and, in an act of unbridled passion, hugged and kissed members of the team many of whom knew him from his days as a Blues Central League player. As the world watched on, Eddie realised he was being chased by a policeman, "I'd seen this bizzie coming after me and he caught up with me and got me by the coat. But I just took it off!" Encouraged by the 100,000 crowd, Eddie continued to evade his pursuers. The copper who had liberated Eddie's jacket lay prostrate on the pitch as his colleagues took up the chase which ended in spectacular fashion as one of London's finest rugby-tackled Eddie to the ground. "He got me down. I just put my hands back and I think about six of them had me pinned down like I was one of the train robbers." Initially ejected, irrepressible Eddie was back amongst the crowd to witness Everton's Derek Temple score the winner. Eddie Cavanagh had written his name in Everton folklore and became almost as famous as the players he adored. He sadly passed away on 9 December 1999.

A Real Red

Dressed from tip to toe in red and white, **Lenny (Dr Fun) Campbell** and his little hand-puppet accomplice **Charlie**, were instantly recognisable and known all over the world. As a young man, Lenny worked as a Butlins Red Coat before becoming a lifeguard at Huyton leisure centre. He was a regular at St Aloysius Social Club where, with a permanent beaming smile, he performed MC duties. These often included belting out his favourite Beatles songs and, reflecting his love of The Fab Four, the wrought iron front gate at his Rupert Road home was adorned with the words 'Strawberry Fields'. Throughout the Eighties and Nineties, Dr Fun's enthusiasm lit up Anfield and he continued to bring a smile to the faces of many fellow Kopites until he passed away in early 2007. Nowadays, visitors on a tour of Anfield can see Charlie and Lenny's matchday outfit proudly displayed in LFC's Museum in recognition of his unique contribution to the club's history.

©www.welloffside.com

The Men in The Middle

Love them or loathe them, referees are an essential piece of the football jigsaw. Without them it would obviously be impossible to enjoy the sport that we, and they, love.

Those officiating at the first ever Prescot & District League matches on 2 September 1939 were **L Murphy, A Stott, C Williams, F Brownbill, J R Winn, G A Lawrenson, J Staunton** and **W Doran**. Seven years later the Prescot Referee's Association was created. One of the area's finest referees at this time was **Bill Evans** who, on 23 March 1946, took charge of the FA Cup semi-final match between Derby County and Birmingham City. Staged at Hillsborough with 65,013 present, the tie required a replay after finishing 1-1. Derby were the victors and went on to win the first post-war Final. Mr Evans lived at 29 The Rooley, Huyton and had been a League ref for just seven years. He is probably the most successful of our officials although Huytonian **James Tattan** can rightly boast that he ran the line at more than 50 Premier League matches during the late 90s and early 2000s - an amazing achievement. Unlike James, **Bob Mallet** may not have been the linesman at Old Trafford in front of 67,844 spectators (Man Utd v Fulham, 4/2/2006) but he did become a hugely respected figure via the thousands of games he took control of during his 48 years in the role.

Unfortunately, but unsurprisingly, a shortage of officials has always been a problem locally and nationally making Bob's contribution to football even more remarkable. We should be grateful to those who, for little financial reward, stand in the middle of the pitch, whistle in hand, often taking flak from all directions.

Therefore, a well overdue pat on the back is afforded to our refereeing fraternity which has over the years included **A Abbott, J Aspinall, Dean Ball, Dennis Batley, R Bibby, Alan Butler, H Boardman, Tony Brennan, J Brumfitt, W Burgess, R Burns, J Burton, J Connolly, Peter Crabb, D Daniels, Gary Dinsmore, Ken Dixon, T Doherty, Alan Doolan, Paul Doolan, A Einig, E Fitzpatrick, T Fitzpatrick, J Flynn, Mike Forrest, Peter Forrest, K Gibson, John Goodwin, Chris Hale, Steve Halligan, Paul Healey, J Hinton, B Holmes, Brian Hughes, Tom Jackson, D Johnson, Martin Jones, W Jones, Len Kelly, Jim Kennedy, J Lacey, Ron Langley, Les North, D McCarthy, R McLintock Tony Magee, E Murray, T Moss, R Norton, Gerry O'Brian, R Pickavance, John Porter, P Povey, Keith Radcliffe, Harry Rimmer, Terry Roscoe, G Simpson, S Stevenson, Tommy Swift, Ronnie Taylor, R Thompson, Ste Turton, W Wilkinson, Alan Willoughby, Jon Worrall** and his sons **Joel and Sam Worral** and last but by no means least, young female referee **Izzy O'Connor**.

The Huyton Baddies and Fatties

Throughout the Seventies and Eighties, the '**Huyton Baddies**' banner was present at every Liverpool home and away game. The Baddies were a notorious group of Reds fans who operated out of the Huyton Park pub on the St Johns estate. There are countless tales of the gang's antics at home and abroad, although the one about the circus strongman throwing one of their number through a pub window surely has to be taken with a pinch of salt. The story goes that by way of retribution for the attack, the Baddies made a late night visit to the touring circus which was located on King George V Playing Fields. After wiping the floor wi h the circus personnel, they proceeded to open the animal cages resulting in a host of beasts, including a lion, roaming the streets of Huyton! True? Who cares, it's a great story! What is undoubtedly true is that the Huyton Baddies banner was seen throughout the world as the lads followed their heroes around the globe.

In more recent years, the **Huyton Fatties** have picked up the baton in supporting the Reds far and wide. The group, the brainchild of **John Joynt**, may adopt a more comedic approach than that of the Baddies but their support of LFC is no less passionate. During their pomp, the Baddies allegedly wiped a few smiles off the faces of rival fans. The Fatties, via their banners, badges and terrace chants aim to bring a smile to the faces of all and sundry.

THE NEXT GENERATION

It could be argued that Junior Football is all about enjoyment and fitness and that graduating to play the game for a living is for the vast majority an unrealistic pipedream - and there is nothing wrong with that. However, if the past century is anything to go by, for some the dream may become a reality.

Former Liverpool and Merseyside Schoolboys Captain, Prescotian midfielder **Regan Griffiths** is a member of Crewe Alexandra's first team squad. Spotted playing for Whiston Juniors, for whom he bagged a hatful of goals, he joined the Railwaymen's academy and signed his first professional contract on 1 July 2018. He made his first team debut in a Football League Trophy game versus Shrewsbury Town on 10 Nov 2020 and followed this up with his full league debut when he started against Portsmouth eleven days later. A loan spell with Notts County gave Regan valuable experience which he has taken onboard to become a regular member of manager Dave Artell's squad.

Aged 16, **Sonny Hilton** joined Fulham from Tranmere Rovers on 1 July 2017 . The attacking midfielder had been with the Wirral club from the age of six and represented Huyton Boys before moving from St Margaret Mary's to Cardinal Heenan school where he qualified to represent Liverpool Boys. A black belt in Tae Kwon-Do, after moving through the Fulham ranks and picking up U-17 international caps, Sonny enjoyed a three month loan spell with TPS Turku of Finland. On his return he was handed the captaincy of the U-23s and is currently aiming to make the breakthrough to the first team.

Huytonian **Bobby Duncan** comes from good footballing stock. Numerous members of his extended family, which includes Steven Gerrard amongst its number, have appeared in the English Football League. A natural goalscorer, he joined Manchester City's youth ranks before moving down the East Lancs to sign for Liverpool. He made great progress wearing the Liver bird on his chest and even appeared for the first team in a pre-season friendly opposing Tranmere. However, after a fantastic debut season as a Red when he scored 30 goals from 43 academy appearances, the last thing Bobby needed was a bit of controversy and negative publicity - but that's exactly what he got. Just as Liverpool fans were taking him to their hearts, he upped sticks and signed for Italian club Fiorentina in a reported £1.8 million deal. Twelve months later he was back on British soil when he signed for Derby County. Still only in his early twenties, Bobby has plenty of time on his side to make the most of his undoubted ability.

Born on 2 May 2000, **Callum Wright** is currently on loan at Cheltenham Town. He made a goal scoring debut for the Robins on 16 February 2021 in a 2-1 defeat of Walsall and made a massive contribution from his 17 appearances to the club's promotion to League One. His parent club Leicester City are delighted with his progress as he has taken the step up in class comfortably in his stride and found the back of the net at a rate of one goal every three games. It will be extremely interesting to observe how his career unfolds.
It remains to be seen if these lads can fulfil their potential but they are all well placed to do so.

All of the above started their careers with local junior outfits. There is every chance that one or more of the youngsters contained in the following pages will follow in their footsteps.

City of Liverpool JFC

AFC Knowsley JFC

St Annes JFC

Whiston Jr FC

DEADLINE DAY

There were a few last-minute additions to the Titans squad who, should there ever be an updated version of this book, will receive more extensive coverage.

COLE STOCKTON

Cole Stockton has in excess of 300 games and almost 100 goals under his belt in a career which has seen him turn out for six different clubs. The strapping, goal-hungry, old-fashioned centre forward has enjoyed spells at Tranmere, Southport, Hearts, Carlisle, Wrexham and is currently banging them in for Morecambe who he joined for the third time on 1 July 2019.

IAN MCKINLAY

Ian McKinlay from Huyton's St John estate, made his Southport debut on 8 October 1966 in a 4-1 demolition of Luton Town in front of 4,485 Fourth Division fans. He found the net in his second appearance for the Sandgrounders when defeating Barrow by the same score line two days later. Managed by former Everton player and future Everton Manager Billy Bingham, Port finished second in the table behind Stockport County to gain the club's first ever promotion. Ian made nine additional appearances before a knee injury, picked up in an FA Cup tie facing Barnsley, ultimately resulted in him calling time on his career. He made a few Northern Prem appearances for Wigan Athletic and would later turn out for local outfit McGoldrick FC.

PAIGE WILLIAMS

Left-footed defender Paige Williams attended St Margaret Mary's school in Pilch Lane and started her football career playing for Liverpool Feds before joining Everton. Between the ages of 15 and 23 she represented England at every level and made her Everton debut in 2013. She spent two years with the Toffees before moving to Italy as a professional for Brescia, with whom she won the league and cup double. In 2017, after making seven appearances for Hellas Verona, she returned home and spent three seasons with Birmingham City. In August 2020, Paige completed her Merseyside Fire and Rescue Service training and became a full-time Firefighter.

LAYTON STEWART

Huytonian Layton Stewart is a prolific goal scorer who has rapidly propelled himself through Liverpool's youth team ranks. If the former Rainhill High School pupil is able to fulfill his promise, the Reds will have a tremendous player on their hands.

JON NOLAN

Jon Nolan joined Everton at the age of seven but was released after eleven years at the club. After initially losing interest in the game, a trial with non-league Stockport County rekindled his enthusiasm - Jon made 62 appearances for the club and hasn't looked back. The midfielder is currently on the books at Bristol Rovers under the management of fellow Huytonian Joey Barton. In addition to a couple of seasons with County, his decade long journey to the Memorial Stadium has included spells in non-league with Lincoln City, Wrexham and Grimsby and in the Football League with Chesterfield, Shrewsbury Town and Ipswich Town.